Creating Adobe® Acrobat® Forms

Creating Adobe® Acrobat® Forms

Ted Padova

WILEY

Wiley Publishing, Inc.

Creating Adobe® Acrobat® Forms

Published by
Wiley Publishing, Inc.
111 River Street
Hoboken, NJ 07030
www.wiley.com

Copyright © 2002 Wiley Publishing, Inc., Indianapolis, Indiana

Published simultaneously in Canada

For general information on our other products and services or to obtain technical support, please contact our Customer Care Department within the U.S. at 800-762-2974, outside the U.S. at 317-572-3993, or fax 317-572-4002.

Wiley also publishes its books in a variety of electronic formats. Some content that appears in print may not be available in electronic books.

Library of Congress Cataloging-in-Publication Data:

Library of Congress Control Number: 2002106034

ISBN: 0-7645-3690-7

Manufactured in the United States of America

10 9 8 7 6 5 4 3 2

3B/RV/RQ/QT/IN

About the Author

Ted Padova is the author of the top selling *Acrobat PDF Bible* (Hungry Minds) that's currently in its second edition. Additionally, he has written *Teach Yourself Visually Acrobat 5* (Hungry Minds, May 2002). He has authored and coauthored several books on Adobe Acrobat, Adobe Photoshop, and digital imaging. He has owned and operated a digital imaging service bureau and photo finishing laboratory since 1990; teaches classes on Acrobat, Photoshop, and digital imaging at the University of California; participated as a member of the alpha and beta teams on Adobe Acrobat for Adobe Systems; and has served as a national and international conference speaker on Adobe Acrobat and PDF Forms.

Credits

Acquisitions Editor
Michael Roney

Project Editors
Kenyon Brown
Rev Mengle

Technical Editor
Lori DeFurio

Copy Editor
Kenyon Brown

Project Coordinator
Dale White

Cover Image
Michael Trent

Graphics and Production Specialists
Beth Brooks
Sean Decker
Melanie DesJardins
Gabriele McCann
Kristin McMullan
Barry Offringa
Betty Schulte
Julie Trippetti
Jeremy Unger

Quality Control Technicians
Laura Albert
John Greenough
Andy Hollandbeck

Proofreading and Indexing
TECHBOOKS Production Services

Посвящается Милочке

Preface

Over the past several years, readers of my *Acrobat PDF Bible* have written to me regarding a variety of questions related to Adobe Acrobat. Of the questions asked, inquires concerning some aspect of PDF forms have outnumbered all other Acrobat features more than ten to one. In addition, people in many different market sectors have approached me with the question, "Why don't you write a book on Acrobat PDF forms?" From government to business and education, people have asked for something specific to address the complexity of creating PDF forms.

When I first approached my publisher (Hungry Minds, Inc., a division of John Wiley & Sons) with the idea of writing a book on Acrobat PDF forms, my proposal went to committee and was promptly rejected by the assortment of personnel approving new book proposals. The belief of the committee members was that there wasn't enough general interest in addressing a subset of Acrobat functionality like PDF forms.

Fortunately, my acquisition editor, Mike Roney, with his continuing support and confidence suggested I try to accumulate some data supporting the idea that PDF forms are of interest to a much larger group of people than the handful HMI thought existed. With Mike's words of encouragement and willingness to take it back to committee, I went forward and sent emails to people whom I thought could help support my argument.

In a short time letters arrived from people like Paul Showalter of the U.S. Internal Revenue Service; Christine Yarrow, Publisher of Adobe Press; and Kurt Foss and Karl DeAbrew of Planet PDF who sent letters and a mountain of data to support my claim. And with more letters and growing support from colleagues and users, the battle was soon over. The HMI team took only a few minutes to look over the arguments and the *Creating Adobe Acrobat Forms* book was born.

The result of the support from many PDF experts and interested users is what lies ahead in the pages of this book. Over the past three years I have saved letters from readers, reviewed all the letters, and answered EVERY question any reader has asked me regarding PDF forms. If you have any curiosity related to designing, creating, or using Acrobat forms, this publication is for you.

How This Book is Organized

This book is an effort to deliver a *real-world* publication for getting the novice, intermediate, or advanced user up to speed in creating PDF forms in Adobe Acrobat. Each chapter details specifics related to Acrobat forms from initially designing a form in an authoring application to using all of Acrobat's features related to authoring and using PDF forms. Exercises in each chapter provide a tutorial approach while supporting text offers you an explanation for the background of each concept being addressed.

From the novice to the advanced user, sophisticated examples of using the Acrobat implementation of JavaScript walk you through steps to produce code necessary for creating smart forms and user interactivity. Regardless of the kind of work you do, you can find some utilitarian purpose from the examples of forms ranging from personal use, business, education, law, government, and finance.

Part I: PDF Form Basics

In the first part of the book we take a look at the forms industry and begin to understand the importance for producing electronic forms in business, education, and government. The initial chapters deal with forms design and how to convert application documents to the PDF format. Chapters follow describing fundamental tools to create form fields in Acrobat. By the end of Part I you should have a clear understanding for why PDF forms are growing in popularity and knowing the basics for constructing forms in Adobe Acrobat.

Part II: Working with JavaScript

The second part deals with JavaScript and how scripts are used in forms for any kind of work you do. This part begins with explaining JavaScript for the non-programmer. If you haven't written any programming code, don't be intimidated by the chapter titles. All effort has been focused at starting with a presumption of not knowing a programming language. For more advanced users, subsequent chapters offer more sophistication for using JavaScript in Acrobat forms. Real-world examples are used with forms for adding interactivity, animation, data routing, and more.

Part III: Distributing Forms

The third part of the book handles PDF forms distribution. Using forms in local work environments with network servers, uploading PDFs to Web servers and submitting data, and distributing PDF forms on CD-ROMs are included in Part III. Preparing files for document Accessibility, tagging PDFs, and securing forms are all included in this section to add the polish before forms are distributed.

Part IV: Working with Real-World Forms

The last part of the book begins with coverage of special design assistant tools and Acrobat plug-ins. At the end of the book, we amplify our view of creating real-world forms with plenty of JavaScript to add interactivity and sophistication using the example forms that you'll find on the CD-ROM.

CD-ROM

The CD-ROM accompanying the book offers a collection of forms that are related to the examples in each chapter. If you have never created a PDF form or written a line of JavaScript code, you can rework the sample forms and copy/paste fields and JavaScript into your own designs with little modification. All the forms on the CD-ROM are completely open so you can easily see how each form field was constructed. For a complete description of the CD-ROM contents, turn to the "What's on the CD-ROM" appendix.

Bonus material

As an extra bonus, my two top-selling eBooks are included on the CD-ROM. These eBooks are completely open and accessible for examining form fields and discovering more JavaScript code. The books are currently sold as online publications and are only made available free to the owners of this publication.

I've also included a bonus Chapter 17, "Organizing Real-World Workflows." This chapter discusses creating workflow solutions for office workers and examines many things that you'll want to consider before distributing your forms.

Prerequisites for Creating PDF Forms

Whether you have used Acrobat is not important to learn from the chapters that are contained in this book. A basic introduction is offered to explain how documents are converted to the Portable Document Format. Once in PDF form, you can begin to use the tools and methods described in this book. Therefore, you don't need to begin studying other sources to produce forms in Adobe Acrobat.

In regard to programming in JavaScript, you don't need a foundation in any programming language to make use of the techniques described in Part II. I cover the basics of adding a JavaScript to a form and explain how scripts can be copied and pasted between forms. Most of the scripts denoted in text in the book are available for copying from the tutorial files on the CD-ROM and pasting them into your own forms designs with little modification.

Platform Audience

The screen shots in the book have a Windows bias. As I wrote the book, I used Microsoft Word on the Macintosh and used Acrobat on my Windows machine. The forms designs were created on a Macintosh and copied across my network to my PC. In some cases, fields and JavaScript routines were developed on the Macintosh, and in other cases the fields and JavaScript were added in Windows. Therefore, all the forms were developed in part on both platforms.

The text in the book references both Macintosh and Windows use of Acrobat and delineates distinctions when applicable. For Macintosh users, note that the screen shots equally apply to you unless the text states differently or a screen shot from the Macintosh is used to clarify an example.

Staying Connected

Use of Acrobat forms is growing at impressive proportions. Changes in how forms are designed and created can be expected, and there will always be more to learn about Acrobat, forms, and industries supporting their use. To keep abreast of current trends, you'll want to obtain information as it becomes available. You can find PDF forms related essays, articles, and news at many different Web sites. For starters, look at

✦ **Adobe Systems.** Visiting Adobe Systems (`http://www.adobe.com`) is your first stop in searching for information regarding Adobe Acrobat, forms, ePaper solutions, and new release information. Stay connected to Adobe by visiting their Web site regularly. Be certain to make periodic stops at the Acrobat Web page to look for any maintenance upgrades to Acrobat Reader, Acrobat Approval, and Adobe Acrobat.

✦ **Planet PDF.** One of the best sources of Acrobat-related information and tips, tricks, and techniques for using both Acrobat and creating Acrobat PDF forms can be found at the Planet PDF Web site (`http://planetpdf.com`). If you have a question, post it on the user forum. If you need a solution, search through the articles at Planet PDF. If you need a third-party software plug-in, search the Planet PDF Store.

You can also

✦ **Search the Internet**. Many different users in the PDF community host Web sites where PDF forms can be found, and tips associated with creating PDF forms are routinely published as free downloads. Search for PDF forms in your Web browser and look around the thousands of search results you find.

✦ **Attend a conference.** National and international seminars and conferences are held just about every week somewhere on the planet. Among popular conference programs offering PDF related seminars and talks are Seybold Seminars (http://www.seyboldseminars.com), Open Publish (http://www.open-publish.com), and DigiPub Corporation's PDF Conference (http://www.pdfconference.com). The DigiPub bi-annual PDF Conference is entirely devoted to Acrobat and PDF. It is held in the eastern and western United States twice a year. Be certain to check any of the above conference programs by visiting the Web sites. One conference can equip you with information that might otherwise take many months of dedicated study.

✦ **Send an email.** If you have a question about this book or want to suggest something for a future volume, send me an email at ted@west.net. This book includes a response in one way or another to every question related to forms I've collected from readers over the past few years. If I missed something relative to your work that you think should be shared, by all means send me a message.

What's a Computer Book Without Icons?

Several icons have been used throughout this book, which may make reading it a little more enjoyable and helpful.

 These icons indicate some sort of power-user secrets that offer you shortcuts and alternative methods to create great forms.

 These icons identify interesting tidbits. Just some things I thought you might want to know.

 These icons indicate warnings to caution you against potential problems when working in Acrobat or creating Acrobat PDF forms.

 The CD-ROM contains support files to help you step through the exercises. When you see these icons, the filenames and locations for the respective support files are denoted in the text adjacent to the icons.

 These icons point you to other places in the book in which you can find more information on a given topic. If you need to gain more information about a topic that's being discussed, jump to the cross-references for additional descriptions.

Acknowledgments

Producing a 650 page book on any computer software program is not the result of the efforts of a single individual; but rather, it is a collaboration of many people who collectively contribute time, effort, and have some degree of dedication to the project. This book is the culmination of a team effort, in one way or another, from the following individuals and I wish to thank them all for their participation, comments, and generosity.

First and foremost this book would not have been published if it hadn't been supported by my Senior Acquisitions editor Mike Roney who stood fast in his deliberation of the project concept against many skeptics. Thanks Mike for your continual support and advocacy on my behalf.

The people at Adobe Systems who helped me develop an argument for why a book on Acrobat Forms needed to be published. Thanks goes to Bruce Chizen, CEO of Adobe Systems; Christine Yarrow, Publisher of Adobe Press; Scott Lehrbaum, Senior Product Manager of Adobe ePaper Solutions Group; and Marcus Chang and Teresa Buono for always being available to answer questions.

I could ask for no more in a Technical Editor than Acrobat Developer Evangelist of Adobe Systems, Lori DeFurio. Lori carried her laptop throughout Asia, the Pacific Rim, and North America spending late nights examining every detail of this book and providing me suggestions and comments that added the polish to the work. This publication is that much better because of Lori's contributions and I could not have accomplished the job without her. Thanks Lori for doing such a superb job.

A special thank you to my Project Editor who doubled also as a Copy Editor, Kenyon Brown. Ken went beyond editorial review of this work and equally contributed to the design and layout. Thanks Ken for all your hard work on this project.

I also want to acknowledge Media Coordinator, Travis Silvers; Laura Moss, Senior Permissions Editor; Rev Mengle, Editorial Manager; and Dale White, Production Coordinator, and all the production staff at Hungry Minds, Inc.

People in the background who supported the project with letters and continual support for moving forward include my Planet PDF friends Karl DeAbrew, Kurt Foss, and Richard Crocker; Carl Young of the bi-annual PDF Conference; Paul Showalter of the U.S. Internal Revenue Service; and Carol Cini of the U.S. Federal Government Printing Office.

If you find some of the JavaScript routines to be a challenge, you need a wizard in your corner whom you can always count on as a friend, mentor, and generous colleague. Fortunately I had such a person in Kas Thomas. Thanks Kas. Without you I'd still be working on a few routines.

All the product vendors who contributed demo software and shared their thoughts, some of whom include: Vicki Blake of Enfocus Software; Ayca Katun of BCL Technologies; Peter Thorsen of experTelligence; Tim Sullivan and Gina O'Reilly of activePDF; Viginia Gavin of Appligent; Srikant Rajan and Sabu Francis of Tangent Software; and Gary Armstrong of Lantana.

My PDF conference speaker pals whom I see about three to four times a year at conferences and who always provide me with valuable input: Max Wyss, Thomas Merz, Michael Patrick, Shlomo Perets, Leonard Rosenthol, and many others who speak at the annual PDF and Seybold conferences.

People who contributed designs and artwork: Stephen Schafer of Shaf Photo; Sherry Schafer of Schafer Design; and my life long best friend Dr. Lisle Gates who permitted me to use photos of his patent pending golf swing.

A special thank you to my favorite whining companion Barbara Obermeier who stopped writing her Photoshop books twice a week to remind me to purchase lotto tickets and win enough money to take us both out of book Hell.

And finally the most important contributors: the many readers of my *Acrobat PDF Bible* who wrote letters asking for solutions related to Acrobat PDF forms. For all of you, this book was inspired from your comments and suggestions.

Contents at a Glance

Contents

Part II: Working with JavaScript   191

Chapter 7: Getting Started with JavaScript 193

Chapter 8: Writing JavaScript Routines 215

Part III: Distributing Forms 317

Chapter 11: Using Acrobat Security 319

Chapter 12: Working with Accessible and Tagged PDFs 353

PDF Form Basics

Getting Started with Acrobat Forms

Before we jump into forms design and use Adobe Acrobat software, let's first take a look at the forms industry and try to develop an understanding for why electronic forms, in particular Acrobat forms, are a viable resource for any business.

This chapter covers a short overview of the forms industry in the United States, and looks at the use and delivery costs that are associated with analog forms compared to electronic forms. In terms of Acrobat forms, we'll look at the tools used for creating PDF documents and the tools used to view, fill in, and print Acrobat forms.

Understanding the Forms Industry

Over the past three decades, people have commented about the "paperless office" with some degree of notion that we may eventually experience this phenomenon. What is much more common among office workers is the belief that we are producing more paper in businesses than before the advent of the computer revolution. Today, people in the business and government sectors believe we have grown quantum leaps in paper production to sustain office operations.

According to the U.S. Department of Commerce Census of Manufacturers Report of 1992, American manufacturing of business forms has actually declined as compared to the prior report in 1982. In both domestic production and import/ export markets, office forms have declined in total sales and the labor force has been reduced over 10 percent. The manufacturing, shipping, and related costs of distributing business forms were estimated by the U.S. Department of Commerce at $7.4 billion annually almost a decade ago.

Determining an accurate figure as to how much money is spent in the United States on production of business forms is difficult to determine. Different societies and professional groups report many different figures. Employment profiling by the HR Chally Group, for example, reports that aggregate sales from the top three forms' producers, Reynolds & Reynolds Company, Moore Business Forms, and Standard Register Company, report higher figures than the U.S. Commerce Census reports.

Production of printed forms is yet only one segment of the entire distribution of business office forms. Offices with computers and laser printers generate in-house forms to suit individual administration and market needs. Human resources departments, production lines, finance departments, legal and contracts divisions, and all other corporate offices typically generate custom forms that are designed to be used internally in companies and via eCommerce Web sites.

Regardless of which extreme you believe, the costs of producing business forms—added to the costs of all the forms that are generated internally, and the costs of producing, completing, and routing the forms to keep businesses on the move—is staggering. At the least we can conclude that the forms industry, with the costs of managing forms for both domestic and foreign business, is a multi-billion dollar enterprise.

Comparing costs

Let me offer but one small example of how analog forms' routing and distribution costs can impact a company's bottom line. As an example, let's take a look at the world of computer book publishing. Authors writing books like the one you're reading receive monthly reports on their individual sales figures. Many of these figures are related to royalty payments to be distributed to authors. A given monthly report is generated by an office worker who prints a copy of the report for an author, keeps a copy for an internal file, and routes another copy to the publisher's accounting office.

Costs associated with producing the form are a few cents to print each copy, the cost of a printed envelope, and the cost of a stamp to mail the author's copy. Each report runs about $.64 including printing and mailing. If 5,000 titles are in print from a large publishing firm, the total monthly cost results in $3,200. In a year, the amount would be $38,400. In a decade, the total amount would cost the publisher just under one third ($320,000) of a million dollars.

As a comparison, examine the costs of distributing electronic forms. As in the above example, all computer book authors are required to submit manuscripts and images via the Internet. Therefore, all authors have access to e-mail. The cost of distributing a PDF form from the publisher, notwithstanding labor costs, is $0.00. That's Zero with a capital Z. Since anyone can obtain the free Adobe Acrobat Reader software to view a PDF file, there is no hidden cost to the recipient of the form.

Let's take another look at a real-world cost analysis. Assume you work in a large corporation with more than 1,000 employees. On any given day, 50 employees are away from the office buildings. Some may be on sick leave, some on vacation, some on business trips, and so on. If every employee needs to complete a Request for Leave form, then 50 forms a day could conceivably be produced.

Assume a form is duplicated at a copy machine, the employee contacts a supervisor, the supervisor signs the form and routes it to accounting, and an accounting clerk enters the data in a computer. Further assume it costs a few cents for the photocopy and about 10 minutes for all employee time for routing the form and keying the data.

The cost for copying and labor at a fixed labor rate of $12.00/hour would be $2.02 per request. The daily cost would be $101 and an annual cost would be $26,260. For 10 forms related to various company procedures, distribution costs would be over $260,000 per year.

Assuming you can cut the labor by 70 percent through electronic routing and elimination of a need for keying in data, the $260,000 figure would be reduced to $78,000. The end result is $182,000 in annual savings. That's a savings for only 10 forms in a company of 1,000 employees. Imagine what kind of savings can be experienced in the U.S. Federal Government, large educational institutions, and industry-wide enterprises.

Obviously it is difficult to factor in all variables to isolate costs for routing individual forms. But as a broad generalization, it is safe to assume that many different forms used in organizations routed through analog means are often much more costly than electronic forms' usage. Especially if form data input is redundant between workgroups.

Why are Acrobat forms cost effective?

Assuming we agree on the fact that electronic forms' usage is more cost effective than using analog forms, the other cost consideration is the tool that produces, views, and/or prints the form. With regard to Adobe Acrobat as a tool, Adobe Systems offers employers several solutions.

The freely downloadable Adobe Acrobat Reader software can be installed on any computer system without cost to the user. Acrobat Reader has the capability to view, fill in, and print any Acrobat form. However, the data entered on a form cannot be saved with the Reader software.

For people who need to save form field data in an electronic file and need to digitally sign a document, Adobe offers a low-cost solution with the Acrobat Approval software. At a retail price of $39.00 per user, and many aggressive pricing structures for site licenses, Approval can cut software costs significantly for the population of people who need to save populated PDF forms and digitally sign them.

Users who author forms and edit PDF files need the full version of Adobe Acrobat. In corporations where the administration and art departments develop forms, the relatively few users of the full version of Acrobat results in a nominal cost compared to the potential savings resulting in electronic forms distribution.

Compare the costs of the Acrobat solutions to site license costs for other business software and you find extraordinary differences—especially in large companies where non-office workers are using the free Acrobat Reader software. If the costs of managing electronic forms and purchasing the tool to handle the forms are saving money over alternative means, it makes sense to develop an electronic workflow. And, it makes sense to use Adobe Acrobat for as much forms' handling as is economically feasible.

What Are Acrobat PDF Forms?

The definition of an Acrobat PDF form varies greatly among many users. The universal common ingredient is that all documents are in fact Portable Document Format (PDF) files. If you explore the World Wide Web and seek out PDF forms, you find documents in one of three categories. Analog forms are sometimes scanned and saved in PDF format as a scanned image. These forms are static and intended for the end user to print the file, fill it in, and fax it back to the forms provider or route it through an organization. The second type of PDF form is a document authored in some application, then converted to PDF. The appearance of the form is often better than a scanned document, but the means of completion and routing is the same as above. The third kind of form is much more dynamic. An authoring application document is converted to PDF; the form's content, such as field boxes, menus, signature fields, and more, is created from within Adobe Acrobat. These forms enable users to fill in and route data electronically.

Of the three types of forms described above, the dynamic form edited in Acrobat is much more efficient and more purposeful for any organization. Creating smart forms eases the burden of forms completion for users and optimizes electronic data workflows for any company using forms for almost any purpose. It is the creation of these forms that will be the subject of all the following chapters.

Scanned paper forms

Oddly, some companies often print an electronic file to an office printer, then scan the printed document back into digital form, and save the file as a PDF document. The PDF may then be distributed electronically via e-mail, hosted on a network server, or hosted on a Web server.

Among the three kinds of forms described above, the scanned document (an example is shown in Figure 1-1) is the least efficient. If a file already resides on a computer, there is no need to print and scan it. Any file of any type can be converted to a PDF file. If scanned documents are used, the appearance of the form will always be much more degraded than the original and the file size will always be much larger.

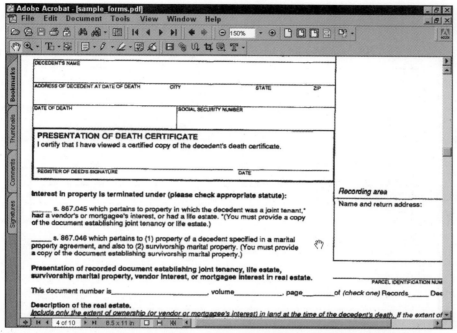

Figure 1-1: A form printed and then scanned on a flatbed scanner. The text in the document is obviously jagged and less attractive than the original authored document.

Static forms

From an authoring application, a form is designed and then converted to a PDF document such as in the example that is shown in Figure 1-2. The form appearance is much better than the scanned form and the file size is much smaller, however the end user must print the form and manually fill in the form fields.

Redundancy and extra labor costs are evident with static forms. When a user completes an analog form, the data are supplied on the form. When the provider receives the form, the data then need to be keyed into a computer by a technician or office worker. If the end user has an opportunity to key in the data electronically, the redundancy and extra labor costs are eliminated.

Static forms are perhaps the largest collection of PDF forms found on Web sites. Users are quick to convert authored documents to PDFs, but sometimes little effort is used to make the forms more efficient.

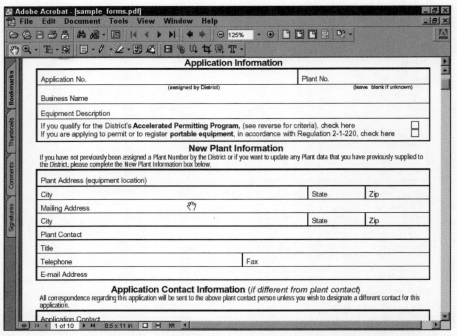

Figure 1-2: A form is converted to a PDF document from the authoring application. Although the form appearance and file size are improved over the scanned form, the end user needs to fill in the form manually and the office worker needs to key in the data.

Dynamic forms

Dynamic forms are one step above static forms. These forms contain form fields where a user can complete the form electronically. Dynamic forms require some extra effort for the forms provider. The workflow consists of first converting the form to a PDF document and then opening it in the full version of Adobe Acrobat. In Acrobat, form fields and design elements are created as shown in Figure 1-3.

Dynamic forms can also be created as *smart forms*. A smart form can include fields where automatic calculations and field completion help prevent user entry errors. Calculations, such as total amounts, sales tax, and item costs, can be programmed on a form. Taking unnecessary tabulations away from the end user can often help eliminate errors and more efficiently process sales orders.

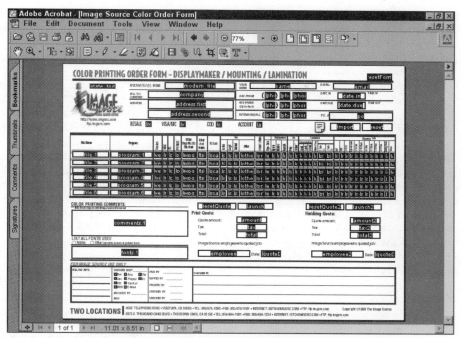

Figure 1-3: Dynamic forms include form fields where data can be entered electronically by the end user. When the Form tool is selected, all the form fields appear as shown in the figure.

Converting Files to PDF

A workflow for forms design begins with an authoring application. Authoring applications can include almost any kind of program that can integrate text, images, and elements such as lines and boxes. Microsoft Office programs, desktop publishing programs, illustration programs, dedicated forms design programs, and similar software can be used to create a form design. Once a design is created, the document then needs to be converted to a PDF file. Conversion from authoring applications to PDF can occur through several means.

Converting to PDF from Acrobat

The full version of Adobe Acrobat is required to create, modify, and edit an Acrobat form. From within Acrobat, a command is available to convert many different file types to PDF. Choose File ➪ Open as Adobe PDF to display the Open dialog box.

In the Open dialog box, click on the down arrow to open the pull-down menu for Objects of Type (Windows) or Show (Macintosh). At a glance you can see the file formats supported by the Open as Adobe PDF command as shown in Figure 1-4. Only the file types listed in the menu can be converted to PDF with this command.

For most form creation tasks, using the Open as Adobe PDF command cannot be used. Text files need to be ASCII text and only unformatted text is converted to PDF with this option. If you use Microsoft Word or another word processor for creating a form design, the document cannot be converted with the Open as Adobe PDF command.

The primary use for Open as Adobe PDF is when form elements need to be integrated in a form. For example, you may have an employee data form that includes a photo of an employee. When the form is designed, you can create a box where a photo image can be imported into the form. If using a digital camera or flatbed scanner, image files saved as JPEG, TIFF, or other similar image formats can be opened in Acrobat. When using the Open as Adobe PDF command, any one of these file formats opens the image and instantly converts it to PDF.

As a general rule, realize that using the Open as Adobe PDF command is typically a secondary operation and not the main source of converting forms designs to a PDF document.

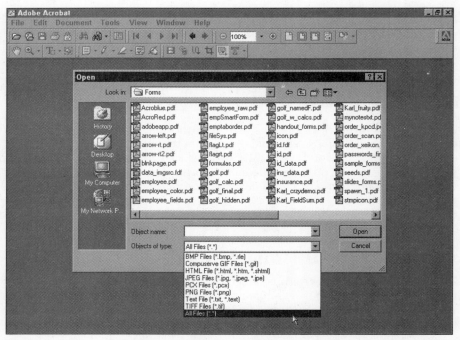

Figure 1-4: The pull-down menu in the Open dialog box displays all acceptable file types available for converting to PDF with the Open as Adobe PDF command.

Exporting to PDF

The Portable Document Format has become a widespread standard among users for file sharing and exchanges. Not only used for forms, PDF is well integrated in almost every industry. As a result, many software manufacturers have supported PDF file conversion from within their application programs.

There are a few different means for exporting to PDF depending on the program used. In some programs you can choose File ⇨ Save As and choose PDF as the format. When the file is saved, the document is converted to PDF. And, once in PDF form, it can be opened in an Acrobat viewer. Some other applications may use File ⇨ Export as a command to create a PDF file. Yet other applications may use tools or other types of menu commands generally found under the File menu.

To understand further the support for PDF file conversion, Table 1-1 lists many popular office and design programs that are capable of converting the host document to a PDF document.

Table 1-1 Programs That Convert Host Documents to PDFs		
Program	**Method for PDF Conversion**	**Special Requirements**
MS Word	PDFMaker	Installed with Acrobat
MS PowerPoint	PDFMaker	Installed with Acrobat
MS Excel	PDFMaker	Installed with Acrobat
Adobe PageMaker 7	File ⇨ Export to PDF	Supported by program
Adobe PageMaker 6.x	File ⇨ Export to PDF	Plug-in downloaded from Adobe's Web site
Adobe InDesign 1.x, 2.x	File ⇨ Save As	Supported by program
Adobe FrameMaker*	File ⇨ Save As	Supported by program
Adobe Illustrator 8, 9, 10	File ⇨ Save As	Supported by program
Adobe Photoshop** 4, 5, 6, 7	File ⇨ Save As	Supported by program
CorelDraw 8, 9, 10	Publish to PDF	Supported by program
QuarkXPress 4.x	Utilities ⇨ Export as PDF	XTension downloaded from Quark, Inc.
Macromedia FreeHand 7, 8, 9, 10	File ⇨ Export	Supported by program

* FrameMaker Version 6 and below at times produce unreliable PDFs. Often a better option is to print to disk and distill the PostScript file in Acrobat Distiller.

** Photoshop files are like scanned images. As a forms producer, Photoshop would be undesirable. For image elements to be integrated in forms, Photoshop PDFs can be used effectively.

Using Acrobat Distiller

All the programs that are listed in Table 1-1, and almost any other program residing on Windows and Macintosh computers, can have the authoring application document converted with the Acrobat Distiller software.

Acrobat Distiller is used as either a background or foreground application. While running in the background, Acrobat Distiller launches automatically (which is transparent to the user) when a file is printed to the Acrobat Distiller printer (Windows) or Create Adobe PDF (Mac OS). When using these printer drivers, Acrobat Distiller actually produces the PDF document whereas the conversion occurs with a single step by printing to the respective printer according to your platform.

As a foreground application, Acrobat Distiller is used to convert files to PDFs in a two-step process. First, a file needs to be *printed* to disk. When you print a file to disk it is saved as a PostScript file. Once in PostScript, the document can be converted to PDF with the Acrobat Distiller program.

Note Because Acrobat offers you a one-step operation for PDF conversion, you may wonder why the details of using the two-step operation are explained here. Printing files to PostScript can be advantageous when the same document needs to serve multiple purposes. If you print a PostScript file to disk and distill the file with one set of Job Options, you can repurpose the document by distilling again with another set of Job Options. Such a task might be used when creating the same PDFs for office use, Web use, and prepress use. In some workflows, it may be more efficient to first produce a PostScript file, then distill the same PostScript file several times with different Distiller Job Options.

Acrobat Distiller is an executable application that ships with the full version of Adobe Acrobat. Distiller is launched from within Acrobat by choosing Tools ⇨ Distiller. The Distiller program opens in the foreground while Acrobat remains open in the background. You can also open Distiller independent of Acrobat by opening the Acrobat folder, then opening the Distillr (Windows) or Distiller (Macintosh) folder and double-clicking on the Distiller application icon.

Once Distiller is launched, choose File ⇨ Open and open a PostScript or EPS file. Distiller processes the PostScript file and converts the file to PDF.

Acrobat Distiller has many different settings that can be customized for defining attributes for how the PDF file is created. These options appear as Job Options, and some presets are installed when you install Adobe Acrobat. As a general setting, when you open Acrobat Distiller and wish to convert PostScript or EPS documents to PDF, use the eBook Job Options settings as shown in Figure 1-5.

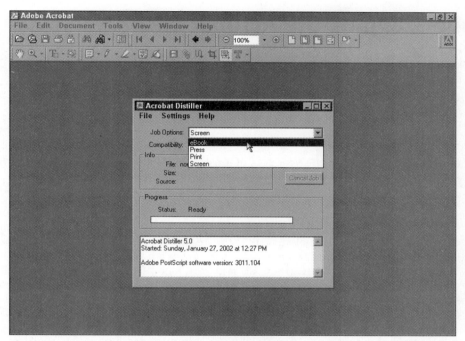

Figure 1-5: From the pull-down menu for Job Options, select eBook. Use these settings for forms used in your office and designed to be printed on local office printers.

Acrobat Distiller Job Options are complex and extensive. A complete explanation for using the Distiller application is beyond the scope of this book. For help and more understanding on how to use the Distiller program, choose Help ➪ Acrobat Help in Acrobat. Online help guides are installed with the program. You can browse the chapter for Acrobat Distiller to gain more understanding on how to use the program and how to prepare PostScript files to be converted to PDF. For the designs covered in this book, you can generally use eBook Job Options for forms designed to be printed on desktop printers and when distributing forms on CD-ROMs.

Cross-Reference

For more information on Job Options, see Chapter 2, "Using Authoring Applications."

Note

A separate Windows installer for the Acrobat PDFWriter is included on the installer CD-ROM. PDFWriter was designed as a simple tool to convert office documents to PDF. For forms design and almost any other kind of document intended for distribution, avoid using the PDFWriter software.

Understanding the Acrobat Viewers

The line of Acrobat products represents almost an entire division within Adobe Systems, Inc. There are products designed as stand-alone applications, enterprise solutions, online hosting services, and add-ons in the form of Acrobat plug-ins. You can use all of these products with files that have been converted to PDF.

Acrobat viewers

For the forms designer, the products of most interest are the Acrobat viewer products. There are three Acrobat viewers you should become familiar with to help guide users for viewing, printing, and completing your forms.

Acrobat Reader

At the low end of the Acrobat viewers is the Adobe Acrobat Reader software. Reader is a freely distributed application intended for users who need to view and print PDF files. Reader users can fill in form fields and print a populated PDF form. Reader, however, cannot save data once entered on a PDF form. A tool and menu command exist for saving a copy of a PDF form within Acrobat Reader, however, the saved copy is only an exact duplicate of the original file before any form fields were completed.

Adobe estimates that more than 300 million computer users have the Acrobat Reader program installed. The number of copies of Reader installed by users makes it one of the most popular computer programs (including operating systems) in existence today.

Among viewing and printing uses, Reader (shown in Figure 1-6) is capable of performing searches to find text strings in PDF documents that have been indexed with the Acrobat Catalog software. If a company has a repository of forms that have been indexed with Acrobat Catalog, invoking a search helps the user find a form quickly throughout multiple servers. Acrobat Search, however, does not work on Web-hosted servers.

Cross-Reference For more on searching PDFs and using Acrobat Catalog, see Chapter 17, "Organizing Real-World Workflows," which you'll find on the book's CD-ROM.

Reader can also be used to submit data to a Web server. With the right programming in the Acrobat form and proper programming by a Web administrator, forms can be designed with buttons to submit data to a server. Once on the server, server-side routines can collect and route data.

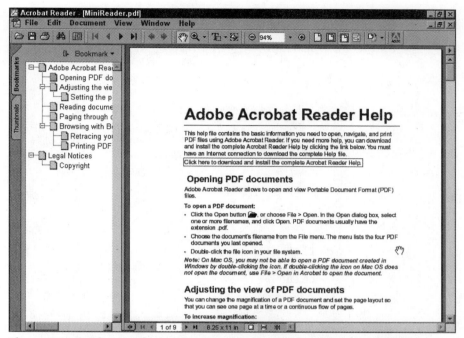

Figure 1-6: Acrobat Reader has fewer tools and menu options than the other Acrobat viewers.

Acrobat Approval

In earlier releases of Acrobat software prior to version 5, Acrobat Business Tools was a medium-strength application with features more limiting than Acrobat, but more enhanced than Acrobat Reader. When version 5 of Acrobat was released, Adobe Systems discontinued Business Tools. Shortly after the release of Acrobat 5.0, the Acrobat Approval software was announced with the intent of replacing the Business Tools program.

Acrobat Approval (shown in Figure 1-7) is an Acrobat viewer that can only be purchased online from Adobe's Web site at www.adobe.com/store. The product sells for $30.00 for a single-user copy; site licenses are priced very aggressively and drop the per-user price significantly.

As an intermediary viewer, Approval is capable of saving populated forms while maintaining complete data integrity. Additionally, Approval allows digital signing of PDFs and verification of digital signatures. All the capabilities for performing searches and submitting data to servers are handled the same in Approval as found in Acrobat or Acrobat Reader.

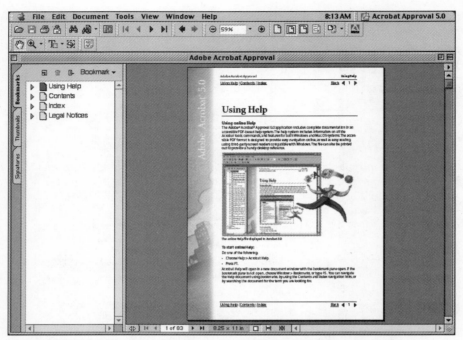

Figure 1-7: Acrobat Approval appears very similar to Acrobat Reader. However, Approval users can save form data and digitally sign documents.

Cross-Reference   For more on digital signatures and verifying signatures, see Chapter 11, "Using Acrobat Security."

Adobe Acrobat

When users purchase the Adobe Acrobat software, it is commonly referred to as the *full version* of Acrobat. The central core of the Acrobat suite of applications is referred to as Acrobat. Hence, all future references in this book will be to Acrobat as the main authoring application.

Acrobat takes off from where Reader and Approval leave you hopelessly wanting more. With Acrobat you can edit, modify, and alter PDF documents as well as completely create a smart form. With various choices for form field types and the ability to script actions with the Acrobat implementation of JavaScript, Acrobat reigns as the superior contender among document delivery programs.

In addition to Acrobat, companion programs mentioned above ship with the Acrobat software. Acrobat Catalog and Acrobat Distiller, respectively, perform their own functions for creating search indexes and converting PostScript to PDF.

Acrobat supports a plug-in architecture whereby third-party software manufacturers can develop tools and add-ons designed for special editing purposes. If Acrobat cannot perform a given task, chances are you can find a third-party plug-in to support your needs.

 Cross-Reference For more on third-party plug-ins that are helpful in creating PDF forms, see Chapter 14, "Using Form Design Assistants."

Web viewing PDFs

One of several plug-ins offered by Adobe with all the Acrobat viewers includes Web browser plug-ins for Netscape Navigator and Microsoft Internet Explorer. When you visit a URL where a PDF file is hosted, the PDF file is displayed inside the browser window. In addition to the Web browser tools, you have access to many of the Acrobat viewer tools (see Figure 1-8).

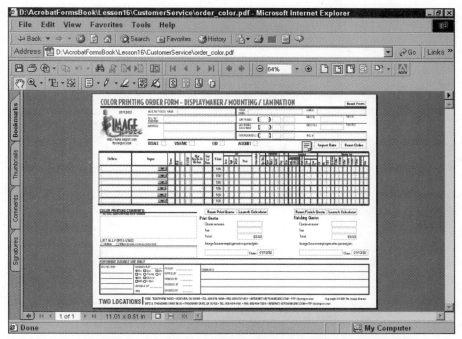

Figure 1-8: A PDF file is viewed inside Microsoft Internet Explorer. Both the Explorer tools and the Acrobat tools are visible in the document window.

Forms that are hosted on Web sites can be opened inside a Web browser window and the forms can be completed and submitted without leaving the Web browser application. Among other benefits, PDF forms completion does not require an uninterrupted Internet connection. Once the PDF is downloaded, the file can be saved from any Acrobat viewer. Forms completion can be handled offline or online. If offline completion is used, the Acrobat or Acrobat Approval software is needed. When the form is completed online, a button designed to submit the data reconnects the user to the respective URL where the data are submitted with any of the Acrobat viewers.

Summary

✦ The United States forms industry is a multi-billion-dollar business. Through electronic distribution and use of electronic forms, many entities can reduce significant costs that are associated with circulating analog documents.

✦ PDF forms are electronic files that are saved in the PDF format and designed with form fields to be completed electronically. Some forms appear in PDF format as static documents without fields and electronic fill-in capabilities.

✦ PDF documents originate in authoring applications and are then converted to the Portable Document Format. Many programs offer direct export to PDF while others require using Acrobat menus and tools to convert files.

✦ Acrobat viewers include the free Acrobat Reader software, Acrobat Approval, (which is offered as a direct download from Adobe's Web site), and the complete Adobe Acrobat software that you must purchase through software resellers or order online from Adobe Systems.

✦　　✦　　✦

Using Authoring Applications

Creating an Acrobat form involves the use of two computer programs. An authoring application is used to design the form and Acrobat is used to add the form elements. In terms of creating a form design, almost any program capable of creating the appearance you desire can be used.

The preference for what application to use for the initial design is a personal choice. If you are a competent PowerPoint or Excel user and either of these programs can handle your forms design tasks, by all means use the program that you prefer.

If you are open to learning new programs and you wish to use the most efficient application for forms designs, then there are better choices than using Microsoft Office applications as design tools. What's important is to realize that not every program may handle all your design needs. At some point you may need to use some application other than your preferred program to effectively design a form. Therefore, a little understanding of the tools at your disposal is helpful when needing to expand your forms designer tool chest.

In this chapter we'll look at several different authoring applications for designing a form and look at using Acrobat for making changes in the design and modifying the content.

Using Microsoft Word

Certainly the most popular among the Microsoft Office applications is Microsoft Word. Memos, letters, manuals, and forms can be created in Microsoft Word. As an authoring application,

Word is used in offices to print in standard sizes to desktop printers. When creating forms from standard-size pages, conversion to PDF documents is a relatively easy task.

When you install Adobe Acrobat after your installation of Microsoft Office, Acrobat installs a macro accessible through tools added to the Microsoft Office toolbars. Click on the PDF Maker macro appearing in the Office applications toolbars and the document is converted to PDF.

However, forms designed for use on computer monitors may be created for non-standard sizes. If a non-standard size is to be used in creating a form from MS Word, there are a series of steps you must follow before producing the PDF document. Let's look at an example of a step-by-step process for creating a form design of a non-standard size from Microsoft Word and converting the file to PDF with the PDF Maker macro.

Defining the paper size for the printer (Windows only)

The first of the series of steps involves creating a custom paper size recognizable by the PDF Maker used in Microsoft Word.

1. Open the Printers folder by choosing Start ⇨ Settings ⇨ Printers from the Status Bar.

2. Click on the Acrobat Distiller printer icon.

 Note   By default, the Acrobat Distiller printer is installed with Acrobat.

3. Choose File ⇨ Server Properties in the Printers folder as shown in Figure 2-1.

4. In the Print Server Properties dialog box, click in the Create a New Form check box.

5. Enter a name for your form in the Form Description box. (I used 6 x 8.) Enter a value for the Width and Height for the new page size. In this example use a width of 6 inches and a height of 8 inches as shown in Figure 2-2.

6. Click the Save Form button then click OK in the Print Server Properties dialog box.

The new page size is now available as an option when you set up page sizes in Microsoft Word.

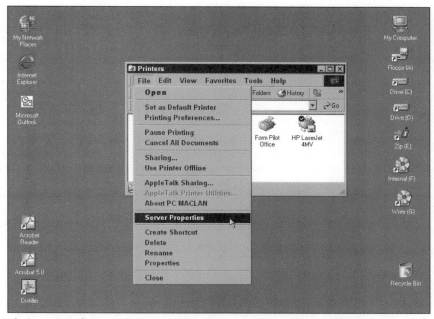

Figure 2-1: Choose File ➪ Server Properties in the Printers folder to open the Print Server Properties dialog box.

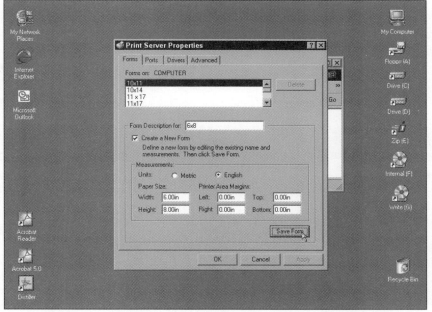

Figure 2-2: Click in the Create a New Form check box. Enter a name for the Form (6 x 8). Enter values for Width and Height for the new page size.

Adjusting printing defaults

Before you can create a PDF file from Word or any other Office application, you need to set some attributes for the printer defaults. Follow these steps to change your printer's default settings:

1. Right click the mouse button on the Acrobat Distiller printer icon in the Printers folder to open a context menu.

2. Select Properties from the menu options as shown in Figure 2-3.

3. The Acrobat Distiller Properties dialog box opens. Click on Printing Preferences button on the General tab.

4. The Acrobat Distiller Printing Preferences dialog box opens. Click on the Adobe PDF Settings tab in this dialog box.

5. Deselect the item for "Do not send fonts to Distiller" as shown in Figure 2-4. In some circumstances, your PDF creation may be more successful by disabling this item.

6. Click OK.

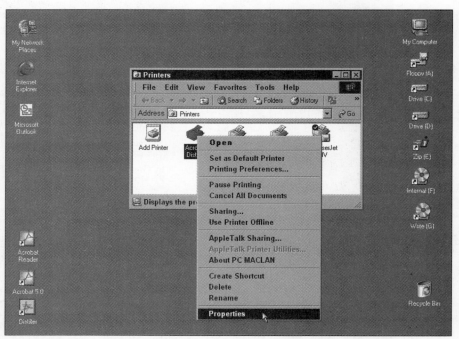

Figure 2-3: Right click the mouse button on the Acrobat Distiller printer icon to open a context menu. Select Properties from the menu options.

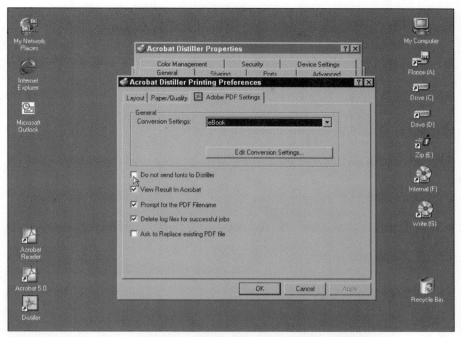

Figure 2-4: Disable the check box for "Do not send fonts to Distiller".

Creating a PDF file from Microsoft Word

When Acrobat 5 is installed after Microsoft Office, the PDF Maker macro utility is installed in the Office folder. Excel, PowerPoint, and Word recognize the PDF Maker macro and display two tools and a new Acrobat menu in each of the office products. This feature is available for both the Mac OS and Windows users. On Windows, be certain to use Microsoft Office 98 or greater. On the Mac OS, be certain to use Microsoft Office 2000 or greater.

Note

The PDF Maker macro is not available for Microsoft Publisher. If you use Publisher, you can convert documents with the Acrobat Distiller program explained later in this chapter.

1. Create a design in Microsoft Word. You can use image elements imported in Word and use any of the formatting capabilities used for any other kind of document. Be certain to set margins to accommodate the size of the document without allowing too much margin space. If using a smaller size page, the default margins will likely be too much. In this example, a form is created using the new page size that was added earlier when the custom page sizes were discussed.

2. Choose File ⇨ Page Setup. In the Page Setup dialog box, as shown in Figure 2-5, select a page size from the Paper Size pull-down menu. If you added custom pages in the Print Server Properties dialog box, they also appear among the menu choices.

Note   In this example, the server properties are assigned to the Acrobat Distiller printer. If you wish to have the properties assigned globally as a default for all printers, don't select any printer when changing the properties as explained previously. The new settings will be applied as a default for all printers.

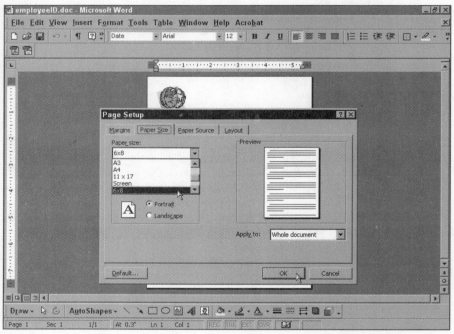

Figure 2-5: In the Page Setup dialog box, all the custom pages that you may have defined in the Print Server Properties dialog box appear also in the pull-down menu for Paper Size.

3. The PDF Maker macro is accessible as a tool from the Word toolbar or from the Acrobat menu. Choose Acrobat ⇨ Convert to PDF or click on the Convert to PDF tool on the toolbar. (See Figure 2-6.)

Tip

Acrobat installs two tools in the Windows toolbar. The Convert to Adobe PDF and the Convert to Adobe PDF and Email tools are shown in Figure 2-6. If you select the Convert to Adobe PDF and Email tool, the PDF is produced and your e-mail program is launched with the resultant PDF attached to a new e-mail message. To distinguish the difference between the tools and prevent you from inadvertently launching your e-mail program, place the mouse cursor over one of the tools. Pause a moment and wait for a tool tip to appear. The tool tip informs you what tool lies beneath the mouse cursor. Move the cursor to the desired tool, wait for the message, and click when the proper tool is reported in the tool tip.

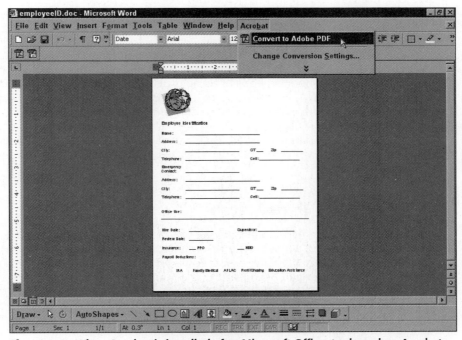

Figure 2-6: When Acrobat is installed after Microsoft Office, tools and an Acrobat menu appear in the Office applications. Click on Convert to PDF to convert the open document to a PDF file.

4. Word prompts you for a filename and location for the Adobe PDF document. Word exports the file as PostScript and launches the Distiller application in the background. Your Word document remains in view in the foreground while the Distiller program converts your file to PDF. When finished, the resultant PDF document opens in Adobe Acrobat.

Tip   By default, the PDF document opens in Acrobat after conversion. If the resulting PDF document does not open in Acrobat, choose Acrobat (from the menu in your Office application) and choose View Results in Acrobat. When the menu option is enabled, the PDF document is opened in Acrobat immediately after conversion.

Using Layout Programs

Desktop publishers and graphic designers use page layout programs for anything ranging from a one-page advertisement to a complete book or manual. Among the more popular layout programs are Adobe PageMaker, QuarkXPress, Adobe InDesign, Adobe FrameMaker (a common choice among technical writers), and Microsoft Publisher. All these programs, with the exception of Microsoft Publisher, have capabilities for producing PDFs via an export command. Whereas programs like QuarkXPress, Adobe InDesign, and Adobe PageMaker are choices for professional graphic designers, any one of these programs are well suited for a forms designer. Once again, it comes down to a personal choice. Pick any application in the group and you are well equipped to design a form for any purpose.

As an example, compare a program that is capable of exporting directly to PDF and another program in which exporting to PDF is not provided. In both examples, a PDF can be produced.

Using Adobe PageMaker

Because Adobe PageMaker ranks among one of the top-selling programs for page layout software when considering cross platform usage, look at how PageMaker handles forms design. If you use another layout program, much of what is accomplished in PageMaker can be applied to the application of your choice.

1. Create a form in a layout program. For this example, a form is created in Adobe PageMaker 7.0 as shown in Figure 2-7.

2. Save the file. Most programs require that the design you create must first be saved to disk before you can export to PDF.

3. Choose the Export command to produce the PDF. Depending on the program you use, the menu option for creating a PDF varies from one program to another. In regard to PageMaker, PDFs are created by choosing File ⇨ Export ⇨ Adobe PDF.

4. The export dialog box from your authoring application can vary between programs offering different attribute choices for producing PDFs. However, almost all programs offer a choice for Job Options. If the option for selecting eBook Job Options exists, make the choice from the pull-down menu selections. In PageMaker, the eBook Job Options are available on the General tab, as shown in Figure 2-8.

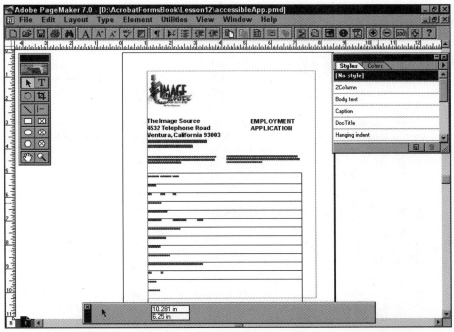

Figure 2-7: Adobe PageMaker is one of several layout applications well suited for forms design.

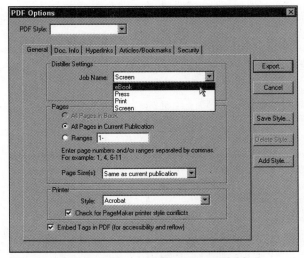

Figure 2-8: Job Options choices are available for selection on the General tab in the PDF Options dialog box. Job Options choices are made from a pull-down menu.

Note   The Job Options settings available to you appear in a pull-down menu. More information about the Job Options settings can be found in the Acrobat online help guides that are explained in Chapter 1. In simple terms, you can use the Screen Job Options for Web hosted documents. Use the eBook settings for office forms that need to be printed on desktop printers. Use the Press Job Options for files that need to be sent to commercial print shops. Selecting one of these three options satisfy almost all of your forms needs.

5. Another dialog box opens prompting you for a filename and destination. Provide a name for the resultant PDF and open the folder where the file is to be saved.

6. Click on Save and the file is converted to PDF.

Using Microsoft Publisher

Among the layout applications, Microsoft Publisher is the only commercial-level layout program that doesn't use a direct export to PDF. Therefore, Publisher can be used to demonstrate how any application document can be converted to PDF. In regard to Publisher and similar applications where an Export to PDF feature is not included in the program, the document can be printed to a file and the resultant PostScript file can be distilled in Acrobat Distiller. These steps can be performed in a one-step operation depending on what options you choose in the Print dialog box and what operating system you use.

On the Mac OS, you can use the Create Adobe PDF option from the printer dialog box. If using an older printer driver not supporting Create Adobe PDF, open the Chooser and select the AdobePS printer driver. For LaserWriter Printer drivers 8.5 and above, choose the LaserWriter printer driver. From the pull-down menu for Printer, select Create Adobe PDF. You have a choice for Job Options in the Print dialog box and can make the selection for the Job Options from the respective pull-down menu, as shown in Figure 2-9.

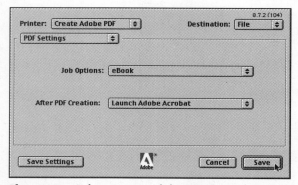

Figure 2-9: Select Create Adobe PDF from the Printer pull-down menu. Job Options are selected from the Job Options pull-down menu.

Note   Always select a PostScript printer driver when converting to PDF. If you use a non-PostScript desktop printer as the printer selected in the Chooser (Mac OS) or Print dialog box (Windows), you can experience problems when creating PDF files.

In Windows, you can access the Acrobat Distiller printer described earlier in this chapter. Print to the Acrobat Distiller printer and the PDF is created on-the-fly. To illustrate using Microsoft Publisher and printing to the Acrobat Distiller printer, follow these steps:

1. Create a form in Microsoft Publisher. If you have another application used for designing your forms, you can follow the same steps.

2. Choose File ➪ Print.

3. In the Print dialog box, select Acrobat Distiller from the pull-down menu choices as shown in Figure 2-10.

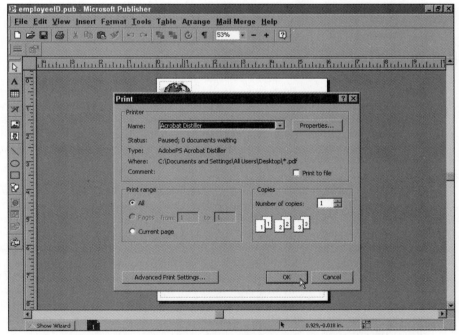

Figure 2-10: In the Print dialog box, the Acrobat Distiller printer is selected for the Printer Name.

On the Mac OS, select Create Adobe PDF from the Printer pull-down menu as shown previously in Figure 2-9.

Note   You can use any authoring application to create PDFs in this manner.

4. Click OK (Windows) or Save (Mac OS).

5. The Save dialog box opens. Supply a filename and choose a destination folder for the resultant PDF.

6. The final file opens in Adobe Acrobat and appears the same as files converted previously from Microsoft Word and Adobe PageMaker.

 Tip   If you wish to postpone distillation of the PostScript files when accessing the Acrobat Distiller printer on Windows or the Create Adobe PDF option on the Mac OS, you can print the files to disk as PostScript without accessing the Distiller application. On the Mac OS, use any PostScript printer driver and choose File as the Destination. On Windows, select the box for Print to File. You can print a collection of files to PostScript to speed up your workflow. When you are ready to distill the files, select all files from a common folder and drag them on top of the Distiller window. Distiller converts the PostScript to separate PDFs.

Using Illustration Programs

Many forms are single page designs. If the body copy on a form is not too extensive and the tools for sophisticated paragraph formatting are not needed, then you may find an illustration program to be your ideal design tool. In the commercial arena for illustration programs there are three major contenders. Adobe Illustrator, CorelDraw, and Macromedia FreeHand collectively consume almost the entire market for dedicated illustration programs.

Use of these tools is also a matter of personal choice. Each application can serve as an outstanding design program for forms. Personally, I would give an edge to Adobe Illustrator. Because the same software company manufactures both Illustrator and Acrobat, the two products have evolved to work in concert with each other. Adobe Illustrator is written with core PDF technology and supports many new features such as transparency when saved as a PDF file. Acrobat can open Illustrator native files without conversion. If you need to go back and edit an Illustrator PDF file, you can easily save the Illustrator editing capabilities in the PDFs that you save from Illustrator. In essence, you can easily go back and forth between Illustrator and Acrobat without loss of data or integrity. The same is not true of any other illustration program.

To gain more understanding for the ease of converting Adobe Illustrator files to PDF, follow these steps:

1. Create a forms design in Adobe Illustrator. For this example Adobe Illustrator 10 is used. However, several earlier versions of Illustrator work equally as well. If you use another illustration program, follow the steps and use the method for exporting to PDF specific to your program.

2. Choose File ➪ Save As.

3. The Save As dialog box opens. Provide a filename and select a destination folder for the saved file.

4. Click Save. The Illustrator Native Format Options dialog box opens as shown in Figure 2-11.

5. Be certain the check box for Create PDF Compatible File is enabled.

6. Click OK.

7. Open Adobe Acrobat.

8. Choose File ➪ Open.

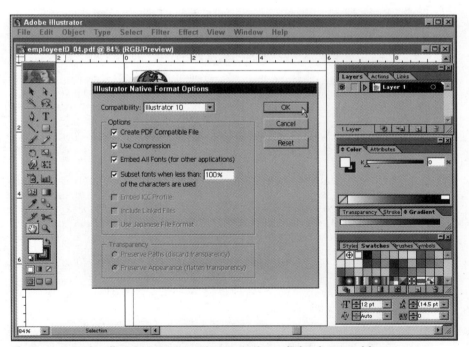

Figure 2-11: The Illustrator Native Format Options dialog box enables you to preserve Illustrator editing features and create a compatible PDF file.

9. Select All Files (*.*) from the Files of type pull-down menu in Windows, as shown in Figure 2-12. On the Mac OS, select All Files from the Show pull-down menu.

10. Select the file to open and click Open. The Illustrator document is opened in Acrobat without a file conversion.

Note   Adobe Illustrator offers you an option to save directly in PDF format. You can follow the steps above and save with the PDF format selected in the Save dialog box. There are circumstances where you may wish to save as a PDF as opposed to a native Illustrator document. If you import images in Illustrator and find the images disappear when opened in Acrobat, return to Illustrator and save as a PDF file.

For converting CorelDraw and Macromedia Freehand files, there are export options In Freehand, choose File ➪ Export and choose PDF as the export format. In CorelDraw, choose File ➪ Publish to PDF. Both programs export to a PDF file.

Figure 2-12: In order for Acrobat to recognize native Illustrator (.ai) files, select All Files (*.*) from the Files of type pull-down menu (Windows) or All Files from the Show pull-down menu (Mac OS).

Working with Scanned Forms

Given the fact that virtually any document capable of being printed can be converted to PDF via the Acrobat Distiller printer (Windows) or the Create Adobe PDF (Mac OS), there would never be a need to print a form and scan it back into a digital file. Where scanned documents may be needed is when you have a paper form without the digital file. If you want to design a form equal to the appearance of the original paper document, then you may wish to use the scanned image as a template.

Creating a form template

Using one of the layout or illustration programs mentioned earlier, you can import a scanned image file in one of the programs discussed and position text and objects over the template. When the form design is complete, delete the imported image and convert the document to PDF.

To begin, you first need to start with a scan. Scan a form to be used as a template on a desktop scanner. The quality of the image needs to be sufficient enough to clearly read all the text on the form and see the form elements such as lines, boxes, margins, and so on. For image items such as logos and illustrations, don't attempt to trace complex drawings. You can easily return to the scanner and scan these items at higher resolutions and import the scans into your design.

The ideal application for recreating forms from scanned paper documents would be an authoring application providing layers where individual layers can be locked and hidden temporarily from view.

All the illustration programs mentioned earlier offer layers with all the options you need to display, hide, and lock layers. Figure 2-13 shows a scanned image imported into Adobe Illustrator. There are two layers in the illustrator file. The background layer is the Scan, and the Artwork resides on top of the scan. In order to fix the scanned image into a stationary position, the layer is locked. All the text and image elements are added on the artwork layer.

Periodically, you will want to hide the template so the artwork can be viewed for detail and completion. With programs supporting layers, you can hide a layer temporarily from view, examine the artwork, then bring the layer back in view to continue. Figure 2-14 shows a partially completed form with the template hidden from view.

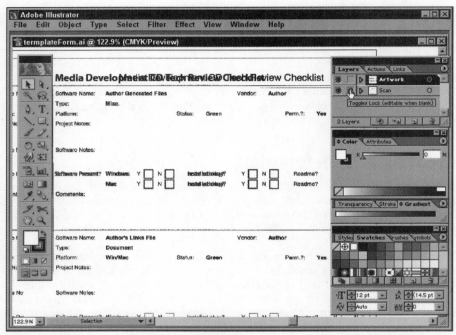

Figure 2-13: A scan is used as a template in Adobe Illustrator. The Scan is locked to prevent moving around the document page. The Artwork layer contains text and elements added to recreate the form.

When you finish designing a form, it is important to delete the template. Not only is the template a distraction from the new design, but also the scanned image significantly adds to the file size.

Note   Be certain to avoid scanning any copyrighted forms. If a form has a trademark or copyright symbol, do not use the form as a template even if you create a slight modification on the design. There are many commercial forms carrying copyrights. So be careful not to endanger yourself or your company with a copyright violation.

Converting scans to text

Acrobat is capable of scanning directly from within the program. In addition to Acrobat Scan, an Optical Character Recognition (OCR) feature is also available via a command called Paper Capture. Following the first release of Acrobat on Windows, Paper Capture became available from Adobe's Web site as a free downloadable plug-in. As of this writing, a Mac OS version has not yet been released for Acrobat 5. If you use a Mac OS computer, be certain to check the Adobe Web site periodically for the Paper Capture plug-in that should also become a free download for Mac OS users.

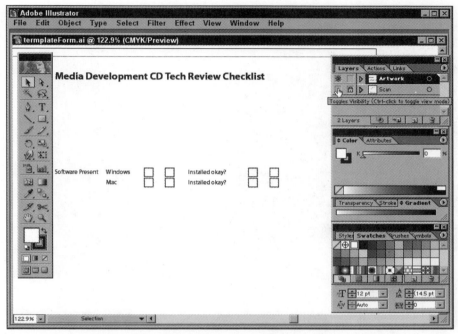

Figure 2-14: When the template is hidden, the artwork is displayed to clearly view all the new items added to the form.

Using Paper Capture (Windows only)

Whether using scans created from within Acrobat with Acrobat Scan or scans imported from image file formats with the Open as Adobe PDF command, once converted to PDF, you can instruct Acrobat to search through the image file and convert all recognizable text. The essential ingredient for using Acrobat Paper Capture is that you have sufficient resolution in the image for Paper Capture to perform the task. Image resolutions between 200 ppi (pixels per inch) and 300 ppi work well with Paper Capture.

When the scanned document appears in the Acrobat Document Pane, choose Tools ➪ Paper Capture. Acrobat pauses momentarily and then begins reading the image to find recognizable text. When the conversion is complete, you need to determine if Acrobat accurately interpreted the text. Paper Capture marks words as *suspects* if what it interprets as text does not match its dictionary. To survey the document and review all the suspects, choose Tools ➪ TouchUp Text ➪ Find First Suspect, as shown in Figure 2-15.

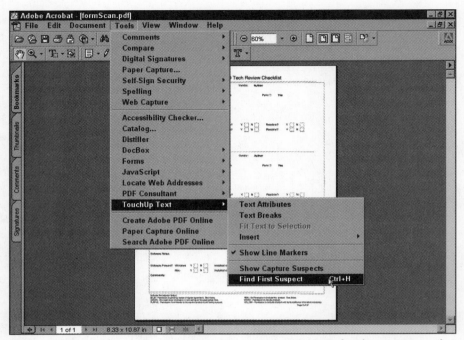

Figure 2-15: After Paper Capture completes text recognition, the document needs to be searched for suspects that may be incorrectly interpreted by Acrobat.

A dialog box opens and Acrobat stops at the first suspected word. In order to see the text on the page, be certain to zoom in on the document. All the Acrobat tools are available while the Capture Suspect dialog box is open.

If the highlighted suspect is correctly spelled, press the Tab key on your keyboard. Pressing the Tab key instructs Acrobat to accept the suspect and move to the next suspected word, as shown in Figure 2-16. If the highlighted text is inaccurate, type the correct spelling to replace the highlighted text, then press the Tab key.

When Paper Capture completes its search, the Capture Suspects dialog box disappears. All the recognizable text is now accessible and can be searched.

Note   The above discussion related to scanning forms is intended to describe a workflow where occasional documents need to be scanned and used as templates or recognized for text. For industrial strength solutions, you may wish to use a program such as OmniForm, which is covered in Chapter 14, "Using Form Design Assistants," or Adobe Acrobat Capture. More information on Acrobat Capture can be found on Adobe's Web site at www.adobe.com/acrocapture.

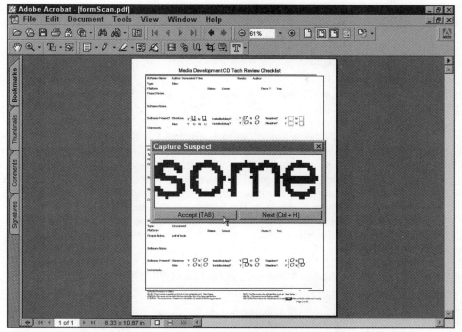

Figure 2-16: When the suspect is correct press the Tab key. If incorrect, type the correct spelling and then press the Tab key.

Exporting text from Acrobat

When large bodies of text appear on a form, you may find Paper Capture a time saver over keying in the text on a new form. If you use Paper Capture to convert an image file to recognizable text, you have two elements on the page. The background data is the image file and the text appears over the background. At this point you need to eliminate the image. Because Acrobat doesn't treat layers like the illustration programs mentioned earlier, the task is to extract the text from the PDF and get it into an authoring application.

There are several ways you can move text to an authoring application. Choices available for exporting text include saving the text to a separate file or copying and pasting text.

To save text from a PDF file, choose File ➪ Save As. From the Save As Type pull-down menu, select Rich Text Format (*rtf). Click Save and the file is saved as RTF. Any of the authoring programs described earlier are capable of importing RTF files.

If you have a passage that you want to quickly move to another program, you can elect to copy and paste text. Click on the Text Select tool on the Acrobat Command Bar and drag through the text to be copied. When the text is selected it appears highlighted. Right click (Windows) or Control click (Mac OS) and select Copy from a context menu as shown in Figure 2-17.

Open the authoring application to be used to design the form and select Paste from the Edit menu.

Tip   If copying all text after a Paper Capture, choose Edit ⇨ Select All or press Ctrl+A (Windows) or ⌘+A (Mac OS). If you have more than one page of text to copy and wish to copy a few pages among many pages of text, choose View ⇨ Continuous. Zoom out so more than one page appears in the Document Pane. Select the Text Select tool and drag from the top of the first page down through all pages. If you hold the mouse button down at the bottom of the screen, pages scroll enabling you to select text on more pages. After selecting the text, copy it as described above and paste the text into a word processor or text editor.

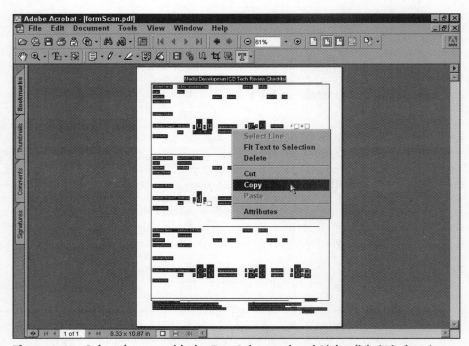

Figure 2-17: Select the text with the Text Select tool and Right click (Windows) or Control click (Mac OS) to open a context menu. Select Copy from the menu choices.

Converting HTML Forms

There may be situations where you have forms already designed for Web sites in HTML and need to have the same form as a PDF. Rather than recreate the form in an authoring program, you can convert the HTML and often maintain the form integrity when converted to PDF. Acrobat can convert all form fields and combo and list boxes, and preserve some scripting. To convert an HTML form to PDF, do the following:

1. Open Acrobat and click on the Open Web Page tool (or choose File ⇨ Open Web Page) on the Acrobat Command Bar. (Or just drag the HTML file into Acrobat.)

2. Enter the URL where the form is located in the Open Web Page dialog box. Be certain to enter 1 for the number of Levels to be downloaded in the Open Web Page dialog box.

3. Click the Download button. Acrobat converts the HTML file to PDF.

4. Click on the Form tool on the Acrobat Command Bar. All the form fields on the page are highlighted, as shown in Figure 2-18.

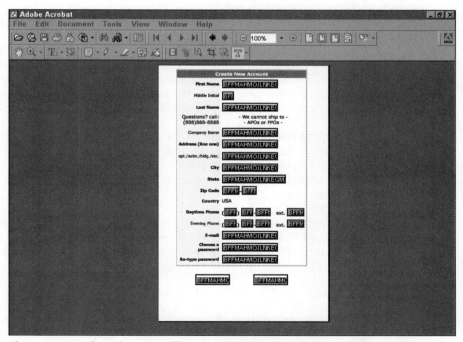

Figure 2-18: When the HTML file is converted to PDF, the form fields are live and useable.

If you need to edit the form, you can make minor edits or completely redesign the background. The form fields can be copied and pasted into a new design if so desired. With complex forms, having the ability to preserve the form fields saves much time compared to starting a new design.

Cross-Reference   For more on copying and pasting fields, see Chapter 5, "Creating Form Fields."

Using Layout Grids and Guides

All the layout and illustration software mentioned earlier in this chapter makes use of rulers, grids, and guides. When designing forms, a grid can help determine where form fields are located and ease the placement of the field boxes. When grids and guides are used in the authoring application, the same grid with major and minor gridlines can be used in Acrobat.

Designing with grids in authoring programs

To begin a design in an authoring application where gridlines are used, the first step is to establish the major and minor gridlines. It is also important to set the zero point fixed at a specific location. Typically, the zero point is set to the top left or bottom left corner of the page.

In an authoring application, you need to access a grids and guides dialog box to define the number of major and minor guides. Access to the dialog box may be through a preference setting or a menu command. In a program like Adobe Illustrator, all grids and guides settings are handled in a preference dialog box.

Tip   Authoring applications provide options for grids appearing on top of the design elements or behind them. If the grid is distracting when designing a form, set the grid lines behind the design elements. When you complete the design and want to view the grid on top of the design, return to the grids and guides settings and set the guides to the front.

When you return to the document page, be certain to set the zero point to a corner on the page. In Figure 2-19, the zero point is set to the top left corner. The major gridlines begin at the zero point and it is easy to determine where the major guidelines are set when the PDF is opened in Acrobat.

After the zero point is set, be certain to instruct your authoring program to snap all elements to the grid. This feature is typically found in a menu command, but can also appear in preferences settings. In Illustrator, choose View ⇨ Snap to Grid. When the grid has been set and the snap to feature enabled, you're ready to start the design. Complete the design and export to PDF.

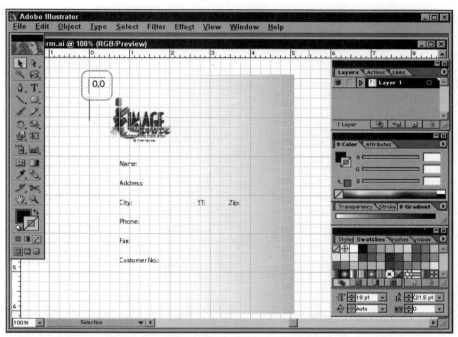

Figure 2-19: In Adobe Illustrator, the zero point is set to the top left corner of the page. After choosing the Snap to Grid command, the design is completed.

Working with grids and guides in Acrobat

When you open a design in Acrobat where the gridlines need to match between the authoring program and Acrobat, the same major and minor definitions need to be used. In Acrobat, choose Edit ➪ Preferences ➪ General (Ctrl+K for Windows or ⌘+K for Mac OS). In the Preferences dialog box, click on Layout Grid in the left panel. On the right side of the dialog box, set the Width Between Lines and Height Between Lines to the same major guideline settings used in your authoring program. For minor guidelines, set the value in the Preferences dialog box for Subdivisions equal to your authoring program.

In this example the width and height are set to 1 inch and the subdivisions at 4 to match the grid in Adobe Illustrator. Figure 2-20 shows the settings that match the Illustrator Guides and Grids Preferences settings.

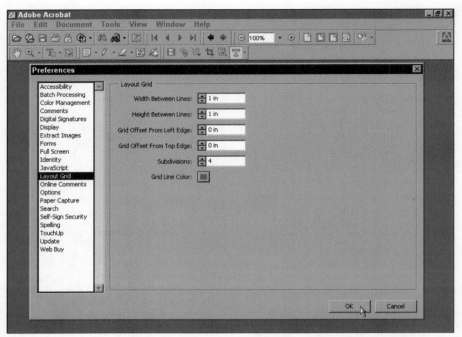

Figure 2-20: In the Acrobat Preferences dialog box, the grids and guides are set to match the settings used in the authoring application.

After entering the values for the Layout Grid in the Preferences dialog box, be certain to use the snap-to guides feature in Acrobat before adding field boxes. Choose View ➪ Snap To Grid. When the check mark is visible in the menu, all fields snap to the subdivisions. In this example, the field boxes snap to ¼-inch gridlines.

Tip

By default, Acrobat does not need a zero point definition. The page zero point is automatically set at the lower left corner of the page. In addition, Acrobat provides no rulers. If you need to use rulers for accurate placement of form fields in addition to the grid, you can acquire a plug-in that provides vertical and horizontal rulers. Visit www.aroundtablesolution.com and find ARTS Toolbox or ARTS Rulers (formerly known as Ari's Toolbox or Ari's Rulers). The ARTS Rulers plug-in is free.

When form fields are drawn on a page where the Snap To Grid command has been enabled, all field boxes snap to both major and minor gridlines. If you nudge field boxes with the arrow keys on the keyboard, each time an arrow key is struck, the field box jumps to the next gridline. In Figure 2-21, the first field box that is drawn snaps to the grid beside the text where the name field appears.

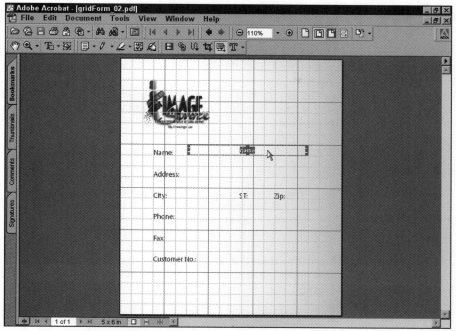

Figure 2-21: When field boxes are drawn, they snap to the grid making it easy to precisely position the form fields.

Working with grid templates

When you design a form in a layout or illustration program, you use a WYSIWYG (What You See Is What You Get) style of drawing objects and placing text on a page. The same WYSIWYG style is extended in Acrobat when field boxes are drawn. Creating a form with tools from the layout application and in Acrobat is relatively easy because you can see the position of objects and text when they are drawn. However, when you use advanced features in Acrobat, such as programming statements in JavaScript, you have no visual reference for where objects fall on a page. In JavaScript, as explained in Chapter 8, "Writing JavaScript Routines," you can execute routines to add fields and comments on a form. In the JavaScript code, you need to specify x and y coordinates for which field or comment rectangles are drawn. A programming reference to an object might be something like: [0,0, 100,200]. In this example, a field or comment rectangle is drawn from the lower left corner of the page (0,0) where the lower left corner of the rectangle begins. The width is 100 points and the height is 200 points (100,200). Thus x = 0 and x = 100, and y = 0 and y = 200 or [x,y,x,y].

Refer to Chapter 8, "Writing JavaScript Routines," for more information about executing routines.

When you program the coordinates in a JavaScript routine, finding the exact position for where a field box or comment begins and ends somewhere other than the lower left corner can often be a challenge. If you use the layout grid described earlier, you need to physically count the gridlines to determine the coordinate values to be coded in a script. Finding a location in the top right quadrant can take some time to count all those gridlines to find the coordinates needed for a programming routine.

Creating a grid

As a tool to assist your forms design and programming steps, you can create a grid template with coordinate values specified every 10 or 20 points apart and use the template each time you need to use coordinate values in a JavaScript routine. Usually all pages in Acrobat begin with 0,0 in the lower left corner. I say usually because some pages may be rotated due to the way the PDF was created and the PDF producer used to create the document. In a few cases you may find exceptions, however, most often the lower left corner at 0,0 is the default. On a standard U.S. Letter page (8.5 x 11 inches), the top right corner is 612,792 points. Therefore, the width is 612 points or 8.5 inches and the height is 792 points or 11 inches.

To create a template, you are best served by using an illustration program. Draw a line at the bottom of the page and another at the top of the page. The top line might best be drawn at 790 points. Use a blend tool or fountain steps in the illustration program to create lines every 10 points apart. For the height, the number of blended steps would be 78, resulting in lines every 10 points from 0 to 790. Do the same for the horizontal lines, creating 60 steps for a range between 0 and 610 points.

After the grid has been created, add text to indicate the coordinates about every 50 points apart. Save the file as a PDF file and then open it in Acrobat. The grid in a Fit in Window view would look something like Figure 2-22. When you zoom in on the grid, the coordinates spaced every 50 points apart should look like Figure 2-23.

Using a grid template

After the template has been created, you'll want to use it for determining coordinates on a page in a PDF file and transferring the coordinate values from the template to the PDF form. The gridTemplate.pdf file in the Chapter 2 folder on the book's CD-ROM is a template that was created in Adobe Illustrator. To understand how to use the template when determining coordinates on a form, use the tutorial file and follow these steps:

Both the empSmartForm.pdf file and the gridTemplate.pdf file are located in the Chapter 2 folder on the book's CD-ROM.

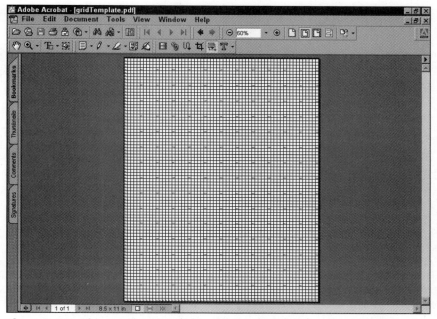

Figure 2-22: After creating the grid template, open it in Acrobat. The Fit in Window view shows the grid without much detail due to the number of lines in the document.

1. Open a PDF form in Acrobat. For this exercise, use the empSmartForm.pdf file in the Chapter 2 folder on the book's CD-ROM. Open the grid template (gridTemplate.pdf) so that both files are open in Acrobat.

2. On the form where the coordinates need to be assessed, select the Square tool positioned under the Note Comment tool on the Acrobat Command Bar.

3. Draw a rectangle where you wish to determine the coordinates. The rectangle drawn should be in a position where you wish to supply coordinate values in a JavaScript routine to draw a comment rectangle or a field rectangle. Use a 4 point stroke on the rectangle or a size that you can comfortably see in a Fit in Window view as shown in Figure 2-24.

4. Select the Hand tool and click on the rectangle to select it. Choose Edit ➪ Copy to copy the rectangle to the clipboard.

5. Select Window and select the grid template file appearing at the bottom of the Window menu. Because both files are open in Acrobat, the filenames appear at the bottom of the Window menu.

6. Choose Edit ➪ Paste. The pasted rectangle is positioned at the same precise location on the grid template as where it was copied from on the form. In a Fit in Window view, you cannot see the coordinate values.

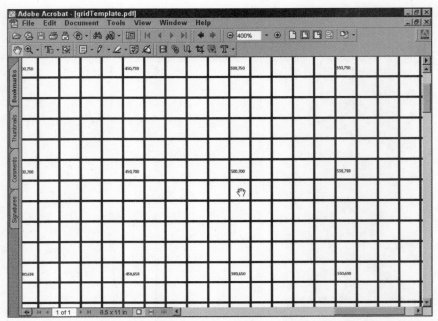

Figure 2-23: When you zoom in on the grid, the coordinate values are easily visible.

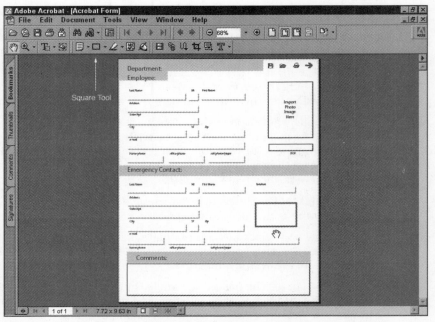

Figure 2-24: Draw a rectangle with the Square tool in the area where the coordinates need to be determined.

7. Zoom in to the rectangle until you can see the coordinate references on all sides, as shown in Figure 2-25. In this example, the approximate coordinate values are [373,207, 490,292]. The first value on the template is the x value that reads left to right horizontally. The second value is y value that reads bottom to top vertically. Thus, a value of 350,200 is 350 points from the left side and 200 points from the bottom of the page.

8. Record the values and you're ready to add them to a routine where the coordinates are needed. If the added element is not precisely positioned, you can return to the code and tweak the location by adjusting the coordinate values.

For an understanding on how to use these values in a JavaScript routine, see Chapter 8, "Writing JavaScript Routines."

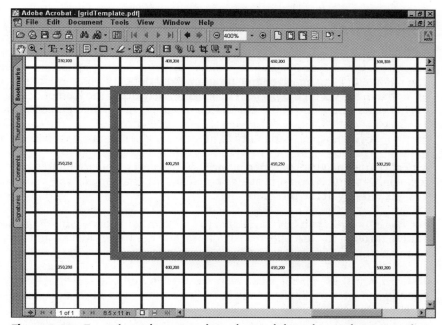

Figure 2-25: Zoom in to the rectangle and record the values. When you write the statement for adding elements with JavaScript, you'll know what values to add to the routine without any guesswork.

Modifying Forms

Many of the forms you design very often require modification to the design. If you have legacy files without the original authored document file, you may need to make changes to update the form. Perhaps a minor edit needs to be made and you don't have the native document immediately accessible. Or, perhaps you may wish to design a form with temporary boxes where fields are to be precisely positioned and then later wish to remove the temporary items.

Regardless of the situation, modifying forms can be a constant exercise. How you approach the modifications is important and needs to be handled appropriately in order to economize your efforts. In this section, examine changing individual image elements and later in this chapter look at changing page designs.

Editing images

To begin, you need to understand the differences between images and objects. Images are raster-type images like scanned artwork, photographs, and other artwork you might edit in an image-editing program like Adobe Photoshop. Objects, on the other hand, are vector shapes and text. Vector artwork is the kind of design you might create in any one of the illustration programs mentioned earlier in this chapter.

In Acrobat you have no capability to modify image or vector data without the use of a third-party plug-in. Images need to be exported to an image editor to change any aspect of the image appearance or size. With objects, you are limited to very basic text changes, and Acrobat provides no means for changing artwork shapes or designs directly in the program.

For raster images, you have available to you another avenue with dynamic image editing through the use of external editors. Furthermore, you can add image data to an existing PDF document without returning to the authoring program.

To learn how these changes can be performed in Acrobat, let's first start with image editing, and later we'll take a look at adding an image to a PDF document.

Editing a raster image

Raster images like photos, scans, and similar items can be edited in programs like Adobe Photoshop, Adobe Photoshop Elements, and Corel PhotoPaint. The editor used with Acrobat is determined in the General Preferences dialog box. By default, Adobe Photoshop is used if Photoshop is installed on your computer. To change the image editor to another application, choose Edit ➪ Preferences ➪ General. In the Preferences dialog box, select TouchUp in the left panel. On the right side of the dialog box, select the Choose Image Editor button. The Choose Image Editor dialog box opens, as shown in Figure 2-26. Navigate to the editor of choice in the Choose Image Editor dialog box and select the application. Click Open in the dialog box and the program selected is used for editing raster image artwork.

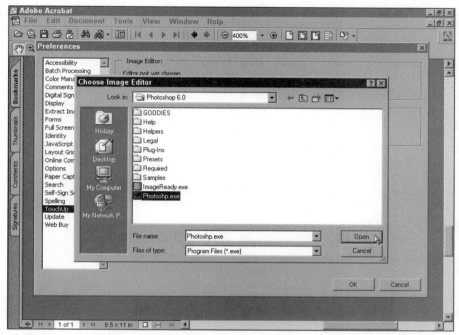

Figure 2-26: In the Preferences dialog box select TouchUp, then select the button for Change Image Editor. Locate the editor to use and click Open in the Choose Image Editor dialog box.

Note   If you have Adobe Photoshop installed on your computer, Acrobat automatically chooses Photoshop as the default image editor. If you wish to use Photoshop, you do not need to visit the General Preferences dialog box.

When the image editor has been selected, you can launch your editor from within Acrobat and make changes to images in the editor. After changes are made, you can save the edits and the edited image is updated in the Acrobat PDF document. This dynamic updating of edited images requires you to follow a precise sequence of steps:

On the CD-ROM   The `gridForm.pdf` file is located in the Chapter 2 folder on the CD-ROM.

1. Open a PDF file with an image to be edited. In this example use the `gridForm.pdf` file located on the CD-ROM in the Chapter 2 folder.

2. Click on the TouchUp Object tool on the Acrobat Command Bar.

3. Select the image to be edited.

4. Right click (Windows) or Control click (Mac OS) to open a context menu as shown in Figure 2-27 (Ctrl+double-click for Windows or Option+double-click for Mac OS).

5. Select Edit Image from the menu options.

Tip   You can also click on the image with the TouchUp Object tool to select it, then right-click (Windows) or Control+click (Mac OS) the selected image to access the Edit Image command.

6. Acrobat launches your image editor and opens the selected image from the PDF file. In the image editor, you can resample the image, change color modes, change brightness values, and so on. In this example, downsample the image and size it down to a smaller size, then change the color mode from RGB color to Grayscale. All these edits result in a smaller file size.

7. Choose File ➪ Save in your image editor. Be certain to choose Save. If you choose Save As, the file won't be updated in Acrobat.

8. Quit the image editor and return to Acrobat.

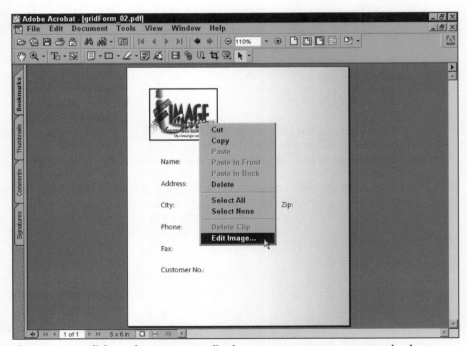

Figure 2-27: Click on the Image to edit, then open a context menu and select Edit Image.

When you view the Acrobat PDF file, the image is updated reflecting changes made in the image editor. If you save the PDF file, the edits are preserved. If you don't like the result, close the file without saving or choose File ➪ Revert to restore the original PDF appearance.

Pasting image data

There may be times when a last-minute change needs to be made on a PDF form. Perhaps the company logo was not included or an image element needs to be added to the design. As a quick fix, you can copy and paste image data.

The important thing to remember when pasting data on a PDF form is that no data from an authoring application can be copied and pasted on the PDF document. The only way you can use copy and paste is when copying data from a PDF document to a PDF document. To illustrate, the following steps are used to paste an image on a PDF document:

1. Open a file in Acrobat where the image element needs to be added. In this case, use `gridFormNoImage.pdf`.

On the CD-ROM

You'll find the `gridFormNoImage.pdf` file in the Chapter 2 folder on the book's CD-ROM.

2. Choose File ➪ Open as Adobe PDF.

3. In the Open dialog box, select the file type to open. In this example, select a TIFF file, as shown in Figure 2-28.

4. If a file is open in Acrobat, a dialog box opens to prompt you to make a choice for appending the image to the current document or creating a new PDF file. Select Create New Document and then click OK to convert the image to a separate PDF.

5. Select the TouchUp Object tool from the Acrobat Command Bar and click on the image.

6. Right click (Windows) or Control click (Mac OS) to open a context menu.

7. Select Copy from the menu options.

8. Choose Window ➪ *<filename>*. In this case the filename is `gridFormNoImage.pdf`. All open files appear at the bottom of the Window menu. Select the filename of the document you wish to add to the image.

9. Be certain the TouchUp Object tool is still selected on the Acrobat Command Bar and open a context menu.

10. Select Paste from the menu options as shown in Figure 2-29.

Figure 2-28: Image files can be converted to PDF when using the Open as Adobe PDF command. From the Objects of Type (Windows) or Show (Mac OS) pull-down menu, the compatible file types are displayed.

11. Click the image with the TouchUp Object tool and drag it around the Document Pane to the desired location. In Figure 2-30, the image was moved to a position similar to the original design.

Tip

If you copy and paste images between documents with different page sizes, the pasted image may not appear on the document page. If the image is not visible after pasting, zoom out to see a smaller view of the PDF page. Click the area above the page on the top left side. If you see a rectangle appear when clicking the mouse button, drag the rectangle on top of the page. The image is moved from outside the page to the page area.

Editing objects

Acrobat interprets any design element that is not of a raster type as an object. Both type and vector art work are considered objects. Object editors work the same way as image editors, and deciding which editor to use is also handled in the Preferences dialog box. Object editors can be any of the illustration programs discussed earlier in this chapter. Adobe Illustrator, if installed on your computer, is the default object editor. To make a change in editors, select a different editor in the Preferences dialog box described earlier when changing image editors.

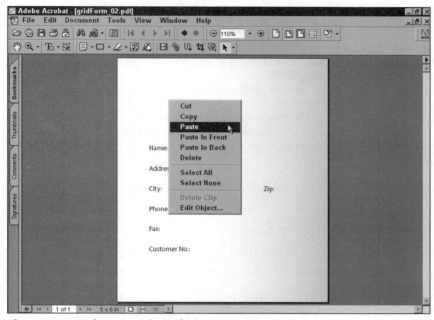

Figure 2-29: Select Paste from the context menu options.

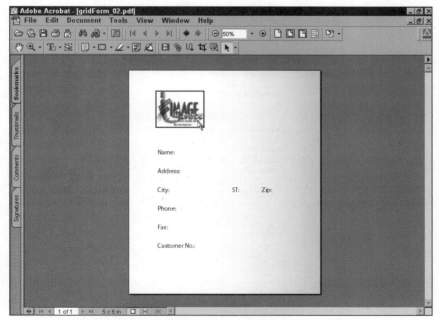

Figure 2-30: The pasted image can be moved around the page with the TouchUp Object tool.

Editing text

Text editing in Acrobat is limited to single lines of text. If you need to make a change where paragraph editing is needed, then you must either return to the authoring application or open a body of text in an object editor.

As a caveat, not all object editors perform the task of text editing very well. The best source for an editor is Adobe Illustrator. However, depending on the font used and the type of fonts, you can experience some limitations even when using Illustrator. The only way to determine whether an editor works with modifying text blocks in PDFs is to try. If it doesn't work, then your only option is to return to the authoring application.

To make a quick fix on a form without returning to the authoring application, follow these steps:

1. Open a file to be edited in Acrobat.

2. Click on the TouchUp Object tool on the Acrobat Command Bar.

3. Select the body of text to be edited and open a context menu as shown in Figure 2-31.

4. Select Edit Object from the menu options.

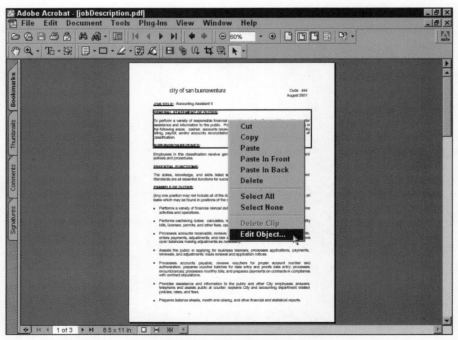

Figure 2-31: Click on an object with the TouchUp Object tool and open a context menu. Select Edit Object to launch the default object editor.

Note When selecting items with the TouchUp Object tool, you can immediately recognize whether the item is an image or an object by opening a context menu. Images display Edit Image as a menu choice and objects display Edit Object as a menu choice.

5. In your object editor, select all the text. Notice how the paragraph is broken up. Each tiny square in the text block represents a break in the text. In Figure 2-32, the text breaks are outlined with a key line. In order to edit the text block, it needs to be reformed so all paragraph editing features, such as word wrap, can be preserved.

6. Bring guidelines from the rulers to the edges of the body of text. In Illustrator, I drew two horizontal and two vertical guidelines to frame the text block. Notice the handles on each corner of the object in Figure 2-32.

7. Select all the text.

8. Choose Edit ⇨ Cut.

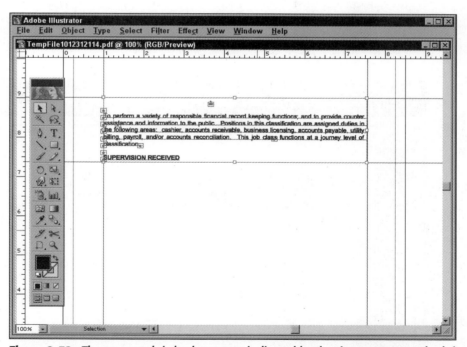

Figure 2-32: The paragraph is broken up as indicated by the tiny squares on the left side of each line and in the center of the body of text. Guidelines have been drawn around the body of text.

9. Drag open a rectangle with the Type Tool beginning at the top left corner of the guideline intersection and drag to the lower right corner intersection. The text cursor appears blinking in the top left corner after releasing the mouse button.

10. Choose Edit ⇨ Paste.

11. The text is reformed into one contiguous block of text. All the paragraph editing attributes, such as word wrap, are preserved when the text is edited. In this example, a few lines of text were edited in the paragraph as shown in Figure 2-33.

12. Save the file and quit Illustrator (or your object editor).

When you return to Acrobat, the edits are dynamically updated just like the images edited earlier in this chapter.

Editing vector objects

Vector objects are illustrations created in vector art programs like those mentioned at the beginning of the chapter. Common designs created in vector art illustration programs might be illustrations for logos, logotypes, freehand drawings, or lines and box elements that are commonly used in forms.

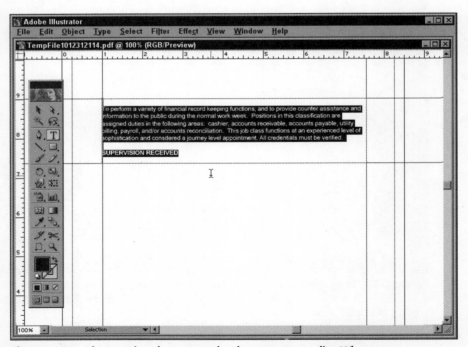

Figure 2-33: After pasting the text, make the necessary edits. When you select all the text, notice how the copy is one contiguous text block.

Acrobat interprets each object in an illustration program as a separate element. If you have a design where a pen or geometric tool has been used to create different elements, then all the elements need to be selected in Acrobat in order to edit the entire illustration.

To understand more clearly how to edit objects in your object editor, follow these steps:

1. Open a PDF file with the object to be edited.

2. Select the TouchUp Object tool from the Acrobat Command Bar.

3. Drag the TouchUp Object tool around an object to select all the individual elements, as shown in Figure 2-34.

4. Open a context menu and select Edit Objects.

5. In Adobe Illustrator, I changed several items for color and transparency. A line of text was also added to the design, as shown in Figure 2-35. After finishing the edits, choose File ➪ Save.

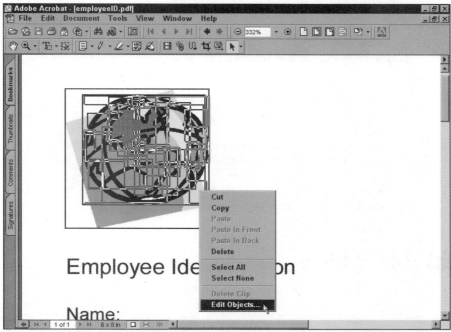

Figure 2-34: Select all elements in the artwork and select Edit Objects from a context menu to open the object editor.

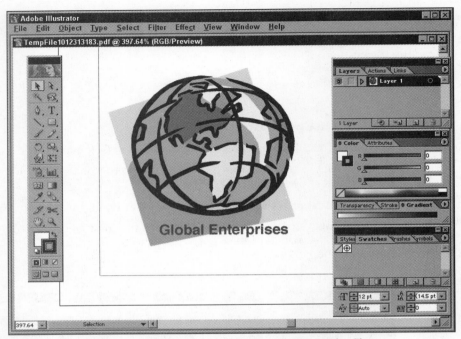

Figure 2-35: Edit the artwork in the object editor, then save the file.

6. Quit the object editor.

7. View the results in Acrobat. Notice, again, the PDF file is dynamically updated.

Tip　Some objects you attempt to edit may be rotated in the PDF file after editing due to the way the image was created or the page orientation of the PDF file produced. If your artwork appears rotated after editing, revert to the previous version of the PDF file. Select the object again and open it in the object editor. Select all the elements and rotate the image before editing the elements.

Editing Pages

At times, a complete redesign of the form or changes in a multiple page document may be needed. Creating Acrobat forms involves two steps. The design of the form performed in the authoring application and the form fields added in Acrobat. If a form has been completed and then needs to have one or the other of these tasks reconstructed, you can preserve one step while reworking the other. For example, suppose a form has been completed and the background design needs to be changed. In this case, you can change the design while preserving the fields in the form.

To understand this a little more, realize that Acrobat treats the page elements similar to programs supporting multiple layers. In Acrobat terms, the background data (or page design) resides on one layer, while all the form fields, comments, bookmarks, links, and destinations reside on a separate layer. Therefore, you can change the background and replace the original version of the background data with a new edited background.

Changing background designs

If you design forms with temporary items used for reference points where fields are later created in Acrobat, you may wish to initially design a form with these elements that will eventually be deleted. You might add some dummy type to determine what font sizes appear best, rectangles where you want field boxes to be drawn, or other guidelines to facilitate placement of field boxes. After the form fields are created in Acrobat, you'll want to delete the temporary elements to finish the form.

You may also need a complete redesign of the background after form fields have been added on a form. In this regard, you will want to preserve the fields while changing the background. To help understand how changes are made to backgrounds while preserving form fields, follow these steps:

On the CD-ROM

The `emplyeeRaw.pdf` file is located in the Chapter 2 folder on the book's CD-ROM.

1. Create a form in an authoring program. In this example, a form was created and converted to PDF. I used dummy fields on the `emplyeeRaw.pdf` form that is located in the Chapter 2 folder on the book's CD-ROM to determine form field placement and point sizes for text, as shown in Figure 2-36.

2. Create the fields in Acrobat. In this example, all the fields were added in Acrobat and rectangular boxes were used to determine the size and location of the fields.

3. Save the file after completing all the fields by choosing File ⇨ Save.

4. Return to the authoring program and delete the temporary items. Any changes for image elements, color, text, and so on can be made on the new design. Convert the file to PDF after editing. Be certain to save the PDF file with a different filename than the name used for the original file.

5. Open the old design with the form fields in Acrobat.

6. Choose Document ⇨ Replace Pages. The Document menu contains several options for page editing. It is important to use the Replace Pages command in order to preserve all the form fields.

7. The Select File With New Pages dialog box opens.

8. Select the new edited file in the dialog box and click Select.

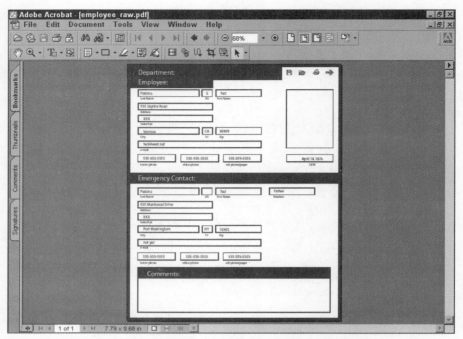

Figure 2-36: The original design is opened in Acrobat. From here, form fields are added.

9. The Replace Pages dialog box opens, as shown in Figure 2-37. If you have only one page, then click OK. If more than one page is to be replaced, then the Replace Pages dialog box can accommodate multiple-page replacement. Choose the page range and the page(s) to be replaced in the dialog box.

Figure 2-37: Select the page range and click OK. If only one page exists in the open file, then click OK without making any changes in the dialog box.

10. A confirmation dialog box opens. Click OK to replace the page(s).

11. If any form field needs to be moved, you can select fields with the Form tool and press the arrow keys on the keyboard to nudge the fields into position. The final PDF file, as shown in Figure 2-38, displays the new background while all the form fields have been preserved.

Repurposing forms

Legacy files and documents designed for different output needs may periodically need to be repurposed. If you have form fields, links, bookmarks, or similar items in a PDF document, you can change the PDF creation attributes by using the Replace Pages command. For example, assume an employee manual with bookmarks and forms was originally created for print. The image resolution of raster images may have been sampled at a high resolution for commercial printing output. If the same manual is to be used on an intranet or downloaded from a Web site, the image resolution for the images would be better sampled at a lower resolution resulting in faster download times.

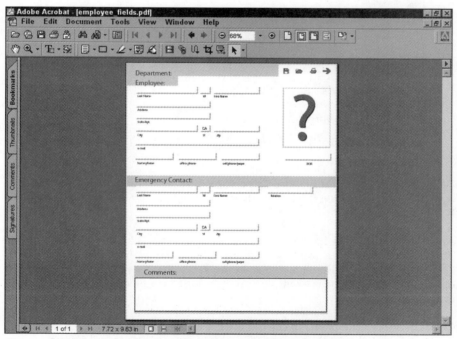

Figure 2-38: The final PDF file contains the new background design, while the form fields have been preserved.

Furthermore, global editing of multiple pages back in an authoring application may need to be performed. For example, you may need to make a number of corrections after form fields, bookmarks, and link buttons have been added in Acrobat. You'll want to preserve these Acrobat additions when updating the file.

To repurpose a PDF document, open the PDF file and choose File ➪ Save As. In the Save As dialog box, select PostScript File (*.ps) (Windows) or PostScript File (Mac OS). Be certain to choose a different name for the file in the Save As dialog box to avoid overwriting the PDF file with the Acrobat elements.

A PostScript file is written to disk. Open Acrobat Distiller and select Screen for the Job Options, as shown in Figure 2-39. Screen Job Options downsample all images to 72 ppi (pixels per inch). If the file was originally designed for commercial printing, the downsampling will significantly reduce the file size.

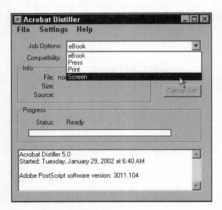

Figure 2-39: In Acrobat Distiller, select Screen from the Job Options pull-down menu choices.

To distill the PostScript file, drag it on top of the Distiller window. If Acrobat is open and you don't see the Desktop, choose File ➪ Open in Distiller and open the PostScript file.

After the new PDF file has been created, return to Acrobat and open the old file. This file contains all the structure including form fields, bookmarks, and so on. Choose Document ➪ Replace Pages. In the Replace Pages dialog box, enter the entire page range. In this example I created a file to replace all 17 pages in the old document. The page range was set from 1 to 17, as shown in Figure 2-40.

Click OK and all the pages in the old file are replaced with the pages in the new file. After replacing the pages, choose File ➪ Save As and save the PDF file to completely rewrite the file. Using the Save As command and rewriting the file to disk optimizes the file resulting in a smaller file size.

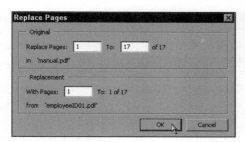

Figure 2-40: All the pages are targeted for replacement. In the top field boxes, 1 and 17 are entered to replace all 17 pages.

Tip

You can also use the same method for handling any font embedding problems. If you edit text in a PDF file, the embedded fonts are unembedded. If the fonts are installed on your computer and Distiller monitors the font folders, redistilling the file re-embeds the fonts. For a detailed description on monitoring folders with Acrobat Distiller, see the Help guide installed in your Acrobat folder. The file is opened by choosing Acrobat ➪ Help ➪ Acrobat Help.

Editing the Open Page view

When users open your PDF files, you'll want them to see your forms at the beginning of the first field where the user starts data entry. In some forms, you may want the entire page to be reduced to a Fit in Window view. On other forms, you may wish to zoom in on the page so all fields can be clearly viewed. Rather than rely on user preferences established by each individual user, you can override default views and embed them in your documents.

Controlling opening views is handled in the Open Options dialog box. To open the dialog box choose File ➪ Document Properties ➪ Open Options, as shown in Figure 2-41.

In the Open Options dialog box, select the down arrow for Magnification and choose a zoom view for the default view. For Page Layout, select Single Page. If you select the box for Display Document Title, then the title supplied in the Document Summary appears at the top of the Acrobat window. This option gives you an opportunity to supply any filename you want to organize your files while the users sees a more descriptive title when opening the document. As a final item, if you have bookmarks and want them to be displayed, select the Bookmarks and Page radio button. Figure 2-42 shows the Document Open Options dialog box with an actual size (100%) magnification and a Single Page layout.

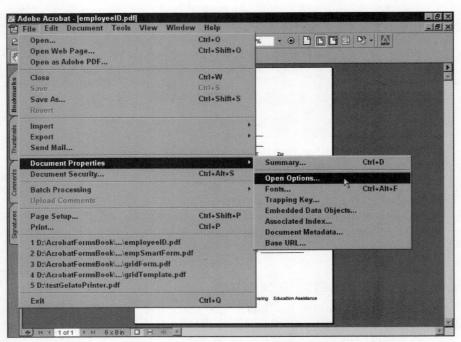

Figure 2-41: To open the open viewing options, choose File ➪ Document Properties ➪ Open Options.

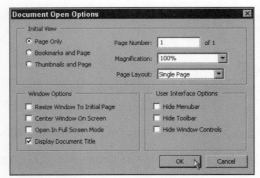

Figure 2-42: Determine the magnification and page viewing attributes in the Open Options dialog box.

Cropping Forms

If page sizes display too much margin area for comfortable viewing, you can trim the pages by cropping them in Acrobat. There may be times when page sizes need to be polished or you may have inadvertently missed a step in setting up the right page size before converting to PDF. Either way, Acrobat offers you a means of trimming the page.

Using the Crop tool

From the Acrobat Command Bar, select the Crop tool. Drag a marquee around the page area where the cropped boundary is needed. When you release the mouse button, four handles appear at each corner of the cropped rectangle. You can drag any one of the four handles to move the cropped rectangle and resize the crop region.

When the crop area is properly identified, double-click the mouse button or press the Num Pad (numeric keypad) Enter key on your keyboard. The Crop Pages dialog box opens, as shown in Figure 2-43.

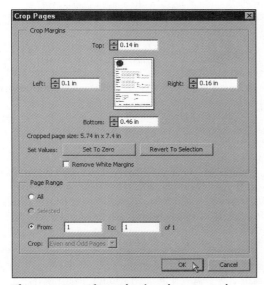

Figure 2-43: After selecting the area to be cropped with the Crop tool, double-click or press the Enter key on the numeric keypad to open the Crop Pages dialog box.

The edges can be nudged by clicking on the up and down arrowheads on each side of the thumbnail preview. When the red rectangle in the Crop Pages dialog box displays the area you want to crop, enter the range of pages to be cropped to size. If only one page exists on your form, the default reads From 1 to 1 of 1. Click OK and the page(s) is cropped.

Tip

Cropping pages in Acrobat does not eliminate any data. If you have background elements with images and you crop the page area, the file size remains the same after cropping. To honor the crop region and eliminate excess data, save the file as PostScript, distill the PostScript in Acrobat Distiller, and use the Replace Pages command as described earlier in this chapter.

If you have an image file that needs to be cropped with no text on the PDF page, save the PDF file after cropping as a TIFF file. Use the Open as Adobe PDF command and the new PDF file opens with the excess data eliminated.

Cropping from a menu command

You can also open the Crop Pages dialog box by choosing a menu command. To open the Crop Pages, choose Document ⇨ Crop Pages. The Crop Pages dialog box opens. In the Crop Pages dialog box, edit the Crop Margins field boxes for Top, Bottom, Left, and Right sides. You can enter values in the field boxes or click on the up or down arrows to change the unit values.

Choosing the Crop Pages command can be a benefit when you have a form comprised of several different pages created in different authoring applications and the page sizes are not the same size. To trim all pages in a document to a size matching a given page, do the following:

1. Open the page that represents the fixed size you want all pages.

2. Choose Document ⇨ Crop Pages.

3. In the Crop Pages dialog box, assess the page size in the Cropped page size display, as shown in Figure 2-44. If you need to crop this page, nudge the sides by clicking on the arrows. Assess the final size measured in the dialog box and make note of the page size. In this example, the final page size is 8.5 x 7.25 inches.

Note

You can use the readout in the Status Bar if the page requires no trimming. You must navigate to the page, assess the page size, and make note of the final size to trim all pages. If the final page size is measured against a page that needs some trimming, follow the steps above.

4. Click OK in the Crop Pages dialog box.

5. Navigate to another page and choose Document ⇨ Crop Pages.

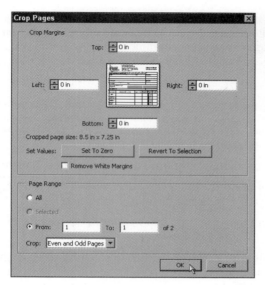

Figure 2-44: Open the Crop Pages dialog box on the page that represents the document trim size. Make any adjustments for trimming edges and note the page size. This size is to be used as the final trim size.

6. In the Crop Pages dialog box, adjust the page margins so the Cropped page size display reads the same size as noted above and shown in Figure 2-45. In this example, the page size reads 8.5 x 7.25 inches to match the page size that was noted in Figure 2-44, previously.

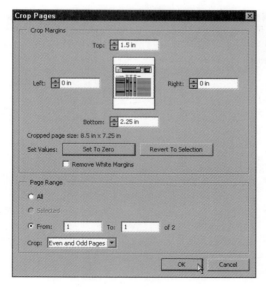

Figure 2-45: Adjust the margins to match the page size from the first page assessed in the Crop Pages dialog box and click OK.

If the margins on each page differ, you need to crop each page individually. If the data on the pages are in the same position with the same margins, you can select All for the page range and crop all pages to a common size.

Summary

✦ The PDF Maker macro installed by Acrobat eases the PDF creation process from Microsoft Office applications.

✦ Most page layout and illustration programs support direct exports to PDF.

✦ Any file capable of being printed can be converted to PDF via printing to PostScript and distilling the PostScript file in Acrobat Distiller.

✦ Acrobat Gelato is a standalone program and printer driver that is used for creating PDFs from any authoring program.

✦ You can convert Web pages to PDF from within Acrobat by using the Open As Adobe PDF command. In addition, other compatible formats with Open As Adobe PDF can also be converted to PDF from within Acrobat.

✦ You can edit images and artwork dynamically through the use of external editors. Adobe Photoshop and Adobe Illustrator are the default editors for images and artwork, respectively.

✦ Using the Replace Pages command is a powerful tool when you want to repurpose PDF documents or edit authored documents and subsequently change background designs after form fields have been added to a PDF file.

✦ You can crop PDF pages to custom sizes and crop to common page sizes through the use of the Crop tool.

✦   ✦   ✦

Understanding Field Types

After you have a design created and converted to PDF, it's time to populate your form with form fields. Acrobat offers you seven different field types. Each type of form field is used for a different purpose, and they have different properties, appearances, options, and actions that can be associated with the fields. In this chapter, you will learn how to create all the seven field types and some attributes specific to each one.

Understanding Form Field Basics

Before we start creating fields, there a few things to understand about some requirements for defining fields in Acrobat. The rules are few, so you don't need to remember too much with regard to what you can and can't do about creating fields. However, the few things noted here about field properties should be understood and strictly followed to save you editing time and frustration.

Using the Form tool and Field properties

All fields are created with the Form tool. You can access the Form tool by pressing the F key on your keyboard or selecting the Form tool from the Acrobat Command Bar. To create a field, select the tool and drag open a rectangle to the approximate size for the field. When the mouse button is released, the Field Properties dialog box opens. All assignments for field attributes are handled in the Field Properties dialog box.

Naming a field

Regardless of which field type you create, Acrobat requires you to provide a name for the field before you exit the Field Properties dialog box. Names are important and Acrobat keeps track of all fields according to name.

Under most circumstances, all field names must be unique. If you have a field you name as `total` and you create a second field you likewise call `total`, you cannot supply different data in the two fields. Acrobat sees both fields as the same and expects that you want the same data values to be used in both fields.

When creating fields, be certain all the field names you provide are unique. Under some special circumstances detailed in Chapter 5, there are some exceptions. However, under most conditions, each field must have a different name.

Cross-Reference For a better understanding of creating and naming fields, read Chapter 5, "Creating Form Fields."

Understanding name attributes

Field names can use alpha characters, numbers, or both to identify the field. All field names are case-sensitive. Case-sensitivity is important when merging data between forms. If the exact name doesn't appear the same on two separate forms, the data won't merge.

When choosing names, it is best to always be consistent. If you capitalize the first character in a name, then be certain to use the same case structure with all your field names. If you use lowercase letters, then be consistent and always use them. Additionally, avoid using spaces between characters. There is no substitute for consistent naming conventions and it will save you much time when creating calculations, merging data, or writing scripts.

Naming nomenclature

The type of name that you give to a field is often of equal consideration as providing unique names for each field. You can, for example, use names such as `firstTotal`, `secondTotal`, `thirdTotal`, and so on for a series of rows that are totaled in the last column. Another means of naming fields is to use a parent and child name. If you use names such as `total.1`, `total.2`, and `total.3`, Acrobat provides much more flexibility when it comes time to add calculations and duplicate fields.

The parent is the *total* item in the names above and the child is the number at the end of the name. The period (or decimal point) separates the parent from the child. As a matter of practice, use names with parent/child conventions when creating a series of fields in rows or columns.

Using appearance attributes

Fields can be displayed with a variety of different appearances including keylines, fills, and colors. If a field requires no special appearance to distinguish it from the background design, fields can be displayed without an appearance.

For learning more about field appearances, see Chapter 4, "Understanding Field Properties."

Setting the field tab order

A field tab order is determined in the same order in which the fields are created. Users can jump from field to field when filling in a form by pressing the Tab key. A field tab order can be changed with a menu command. Therefore, if fields have been created on a form and another field is later added, don't worry about the tab order until you complete the form design.

For learning more about setting tab orders, see Chapter 5, "Creating Form Fields."

Copying and pasting fields

Unlike links in Acrobat, form fields can be copied and pasted on a page, between pages, and between documents. When a field is copied and pasted, the field name and the field attributes are retained in all pasted copies.

For learning more about copying and pasting fields, see Chapter 5, "Creating Form Fields."

Understanding default field attributes

When a field type has been selected in the Field Properties dialog box, all subsequent fields added to your form assume the same field appearance unless you manually change the field type in the Field Properties dialog box for a new field. Fields of common types when assigned attributes assume new default attribute choices based on the last assignment of the attributes for the same field type.

Understanding Text Fields

The default field type when you first use the Form tool is the Text field. Text fields are a bit misleading because they handle both text and numeric data. If you want to create fields where numbers are used, you use the Text field type.

Text fields can be created for text data entered on a single line or for large passages of text. Text can be scrolled in a field and can be left justified, right justified, or centered. Numbers can assume different formats and symbols like currency, percentages, time formats, and date formats.

For all the field types created in this chapter, the classEnroll.pdf file located in the Chapter 3 folder on the book's CD-ROM will be used.

To understand more about creating text fields, follow these steps:

On the CD-ROM   For this exercise (and for all the other exercises in this chapter), you can use the `classEnroll.pdf` file that you'll find in the Chapter 3 folder on the book's CD-ROM.

1. To create a Text field, select the Form tool on the Acrobat Command Bar and drag open a rectangle. The Form tool can also be selected by pressing the F key on your keyboard.

2. Release the mouse button. Immediately after release of the mouse button the Field Properties dialog box opens, as shown in Figure 3-1.

3. Enter a name for the field in the Name box.

4. Click on the down arrow for Type and select Text from the menu list.

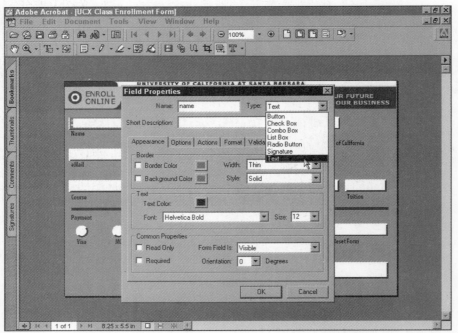

Figure 3-1: Immediately after releasing the mouse button, the Field Properties dialog box opens. To create a Text field, select Text from the pull-down menu for Type.

5. Deselect the boxes for Border Color and Background Color on the Appearance tab.

6. Click OK.

7. Select the Hand tool on the Acrobat Command Bar or press H on your keyboard.

8. Position the cursor over the new text field and click.

9. Type a name in the Name field.

Notice that when the Form tool is selected, the field in Figure 3-2 is displayed with the field name inside the field box. The field is also highlighted and displays handles along the left, center, and right sides of the field box. To resize the field, drag a handle outward or inward in the direction to be resized.

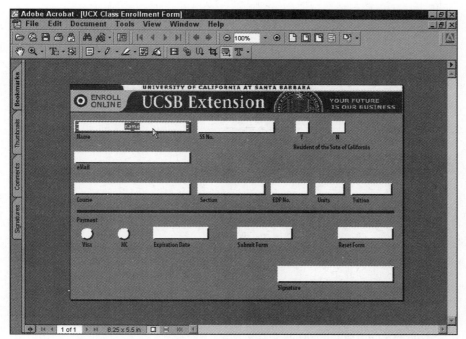

Figure 3-2: The field name appears inside the field box when the field is selected.

To deselect a field, click anywhere in the Document Pane with the Form tool or select another tool from the Command Bar. To edit form fields, always first select the Form tool. To reopen the Field Properties dialog box, double-click the field to change the properties. If a field is selected, you can also press the enter key on the Num Pad to open the Field Properties dialog box.

Note

Be certain to use the Enter key on the Numeric keypad to reopen the Field Properties dialog box and not the Enter (Return) key on the main keyboard. If you strike the Enter (Return) key, you may find Acrobat scrolling pages in multiple-page documents.

Understanding Check Boxes

Check box fields are used to check a single item or make choices from several options. When a Check box is clicked, by default a check mark is displayed in the box. Check boxes can be deselected by clicking on a check mark. This behavior offers you an on/off type of operation. When you need to provide users an option to select an item or decide later to deselect the same item, use a Check box.

To understand more about creating Check boxes, follow these steps:

1. Select the Form tool (press F on the keyboard).

2. Drag open a rectangle around the area where the Check box is to appear.

3. Provide a name for the Check box in the Field Properties dialog box.

4. Select Check box from the field types pull-down menu as shown in Figure 3-3.

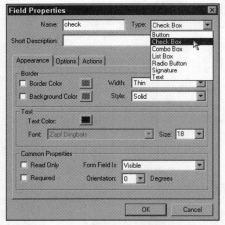

Figure 3-3: Select Check box for the field type from the pull-down menu for Type.

5. Select 18 Point for the text size from the pull-down menu for Size as shown in Figure 3-4. If the text size is too large, the field box may clip the check mark.

6. Click OK to return to the Document Pane.

7. Select the Hand tool on the Acrobat Command Bar or press H on the keyboard.

8. Click in the Check box.

Figure 3-4: Set the text size to 18 point to ensure the check mark is clearly visible but not too large.

Figure 3-5 displays the check mark inside the field box. Click again on the Check box and notice the check mark disappears.

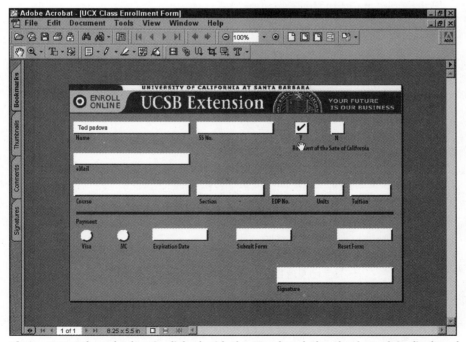

Figure 3-5: When the box is clicked with the Hand tool, the check mark is displayed inside the field box.

Tip

When field appearances contain no borders or fills, the Field boundaries are invisible to the user. If your designs appear enhanced when providing exaggerated check marks, open up the field Appearance properties and select a larger font size. For example, if you have a form with small point sizes and many different form fields, use a large exaggerated check mark about twice the point size of the text to make it obvious to anyone that a box is checked. Larger check marks are viewed easily when the form is seen in a Fit in Window view.

Understanding List Boxes

List boxes are used for selecting one or more options from a scrollable window. The window can appear as small as a single line of text or larger to display several choice options in the list. For any items in a list not visible in the field box, scroll bars and ↓ and ↑ arrows enable users to scroll the contents. To create a List box, follow these steps:

1. Select the Form tool (F).

2. Drag open a field box.

3. Provide a name in the Name field.

4. Select List box from the pull-down menu for Type as shown in Figure 3-6.

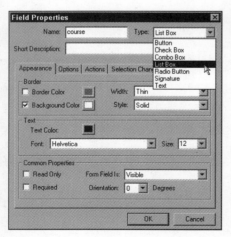

Figure 3-6: Select List box for the field type then click on the Options tab in the Field Properties dialog box.

5. If you click OK after selecting the field Type for a List box, there is no choice for the user to make a selection. Each item in a List box must be defined in the Field Properties Options tab. Click on the Options tab.

6. Enter an item in the Item field and click the Add button to move the item to the lower List box.

7. Continue adding new items until you have a list appearing similar to Figure 3-7.

8. Items are listed in the List box according to the order of entry. If you want to sort the items, click the Sort Items check box. In this example, items were sorted resulting in an alphabetical order as shown in Figure 3-7.

Figure 3-7: After selecting the Sort Items check box, the items in the lower list appear in alphabetical order.

9. Click OK in the Field Properties dialog box.

10. Select the Hand tool (H).

11. If the List box only displays a single line of text, you need to click on the up or down arrows to display more choices, as shown in Figure 3-8.

12. Select the Form tool (F).

13. Click on the List box field.

14. Drag the center bottom handle down to open the field box larger.

15. Select the hand tool (H).

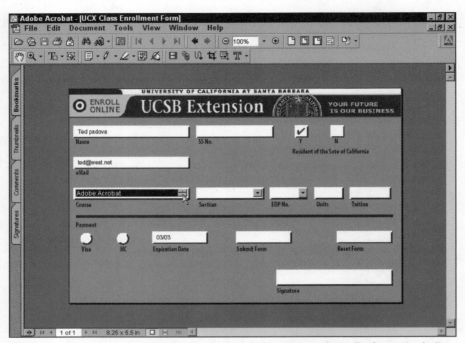

Figure 3-8: Because the List box height is only large enough to display a single line of text, clicking on the up and down arrows scrolls the box to reveal more choices.

Notice the field box reveals more choices without scrolling, as shown in Figure 3-9. Understanding the behavior of List boxes will be an important design consideration. If you want the boxes to open larger, the background elements and fields positioned below the box need to be taken into consideration for color and space, respectively.

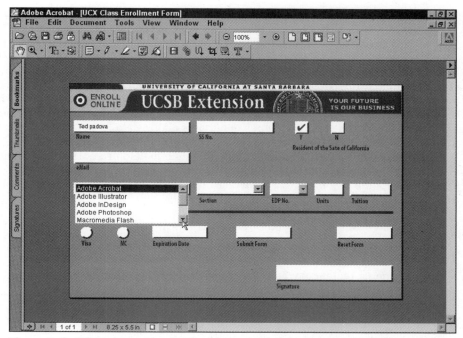

Figure 3-9: When the List box is sized larger, more choices from the list are visible without scrolling.

Understanding Combo Boxes

Combo boxes are similar to List boxes in that both field types offer you a list of items. However, there are a few distinctions between both types of boxes, such as:

✦ **Appearance.** List boxes display a scrollable list. Combo box items are selected from a pull-down menu.

Cross-Reference For a thorough explanation of setting field appearances, see Chapter 4, "Understanding Field Properties."

✦ **Editable.** List boxes are fixed and no user editing for changing a choice can be made. Combo boxes provide you a means of allowing users to supply a user-defined choice in addition to the listed items.

✦ **Multiple Selections.** List boxes enable you to determine whether the user can make multiple selections for the choices provided in the list. You can make multiple selections by Ctrl+clicking (Windows) or ⌘+clicking (Mac OS) for noncontiguous selections. Shift+clicking on both of these platforms selects items in a contiguous group. Combo boxes are restricted to single selections from the options in the list.

✦ **Spell Checking.** List boxes offer no spell checking for the list of items supplied in the Field Properties dialog box. With Combo boxes, you can spell check the list after completing the Field Properties dialog box.

It is important to understand the differences between the field types before you start assigning properties to them. If you decide to use a List box for creating a field for a user to make a choice for a state or country of residence, and then later wish to change the field type to a Combo box, all the list items are lost. Switching back and forth between the two field types eliminates all list data.

If attributes are of no distinct advantage for using one field or another in a design, using a Combo box can provide an advantage where space considerations are important. Combo box choices are made from a pull-down menu and require much less space than a List box.

To understand how to create Combo boxes, follow these steps:

1. Select the Form tool (F).

2. Drag open a rectangle where the Combo box will be located.

3. Enter a name for the field.

4. Select Combo box from the Type pull-down menu.

5. Click on the Options tab in the Field Properties dialog box.

6. Enter a name in the Item field and click on Add to move the item to the lower List box. Continue adding several items to the list like the example shown in Figure 3-10.

Figure 3-10: List items for Combo boxes are added in the same manner as those created with the List box.

7. Select the item for Editable. When the item is selected, any list item can be modified to create a different response. If you don't want the field to be checked for spelling, check the box for Do Not Spell Check.

8. Click OK to accept the choices and exit the Field Properties dialog box.

9. Select the Hand tool (H).

10. Click the down arrow on the Combo box to open the pull-down menu. Make your choice by selecting an item in the list shown in Figure 3-11.

Note You can make only one choice with Combo boxes.

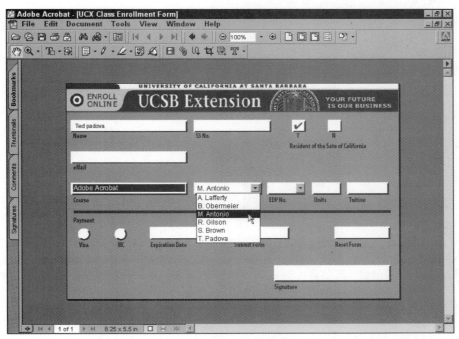

Figure 3-11: Choice selections are made by first clicking on the down arrow to open the pull-down menu, then clicking on a list item.

Creating list items defaults

Regardless of whether you create a List box or a Combo box, the default item appearing in either list is determined in the Field Properties dialog box. When you view the Options tab in the Field Properties dialog box and click on an item in the lower list window, the selected item becomes the default selection.

At times you may want to have no items appear as the default or perhaps a dummy item such as dashed lines or perhaps a line of text for a message. Use a blank as an example. On the Options tab, press the space bar on your keyboard in the Item field. Click on the Add button.

If the Sort Items check box is not selected, the new field appears at the bottom of the list. To reposition items in the list, click on any item and select the Up or Down buttons. If the blank you created in a list appears at the bottom of the list, select it and click the Up button until the blank field reaches the top of the list as shown in Figure 3-12.

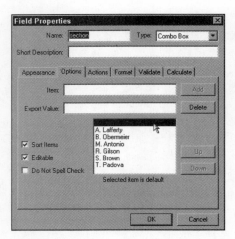

Figure 3-12: By striking the space bar once while in the Item field, the Add button becomes active. Click Add to add the blank field to the list. To move an item up or down, select the item in the lower window, and click on the buttons for Up or Down to move the item in the respective direction.

Before exiting the Field Properties dialog box, click on the field to fix the default appearance. In this case a blank field was created. Click on the blank in the lower List box and click OK in the Field Properties dialog box. When you return to the document and click on the Hand tool (H), the default appearance of the field is a blank, as shown in Figure 3-13. If you reset a form, all default items reappear for both List boxes and Combo boxes.

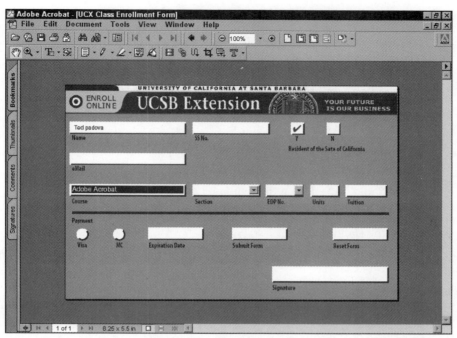

Figure 3-13: When the form is viewed in the Document Pane, the default appearance for the field shows the item last selected in the Field Properties dialog box. In this example the appearance is an empty field.

Understanding Radio Buttons

Radio buttons are similar to Check boxes. You should realize that both Check boxes and Radio buttons can be created with the same appearances and they can be designed to be used for identical purposes. Their intent however, is distinguished by a few factors that offer you a slight difference among the attributes you can assign to them. Radio button and Check box differences include:

✦ **Disabling.** When a Check box is created, the Check box can be deselected by clicking in the enabled Check box. When a Radio button is selected, it can only be disabled by selecting another Radio button that is designed to disable the companion button, or by resetting the PDF form.

✦ **Appearance.** The appearance for a Radio button differs from a Check box only when the Check Style is selected for Circle (see Chapter 4 for Appearance settings). When a border color is used, Radio buttons appear as circles and Check boxes appear as squares (or rectangles). All other Check Style appearances between the two are identical.

✦ **Intent.** Although you can design either button to suit identical purposes, the intent for a Check box is commonly used for making choices for an either/or condition or a series of multiple choices for a given question. The intent for using a Radio button is commonly used only for an either/or condition (for example, making a choice for gender, credit card, and so on).

To understand more about creating Radio buttons, follow these steps:

1. Select the Form tool (F).

2. Drag open a rectangle where the Radio button will be located.

3. Enter a name for the field.

4. Select Radio button from the Type pull-down menu.

5. Click OK to accept the choices and exit the Field Properties dialog box.

6. Select the Hand tool (H).

7. Select the Radio button. The field displays a solid circle (bullet), as shown in Figure 3-14.

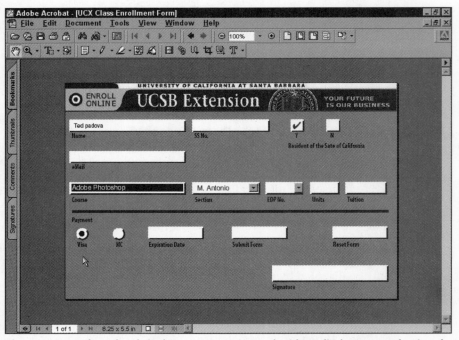

Figure 3-14: When the default appearance is used with Radio buttons, selecting the field with the Hand tool displays a circle.

8. Select the Radio button again. You'll notice the bullet does not disappear. Once the Radio button is selected, you cannot disable it. To offer the user a choice between two selections for either Check boxes or Radio buttons, a second button needs to be created.

Duplicating fields

The exception to the rule for using unique names in all your fields is when creating Check boxes and Radio buttons for alternative choices. When two or more fields have the same name, clicking in one box deselects the other box(es). Therefore, if you want to create two Radio buttons for the user to make a choice between two items, all you need to do is duplicate the field. The name and attributes are duplicated along with the field box.

Acrobat provides several means for duplicating fields. In this chapter, one of the ways to duplicate a field is discussed. The method used here is a common task you'll use many times when creating forms. Be certain to understand it well before moving on to the next chapter.

For more information on duplicating fields, see Chapter 5, "Creating Form Fields."

To duplicate a field, follow these steps:

1. Select the Form tool (F).

2. Select the Radio button created above, keeping the mouse button down when you select the field.

3. Press Control (Windows) or Option (Mac OS) and press the Shift key.

4. With both keys depressed on your keyboard, drag right to the position where the next Radio button is to appear.

5. Release the mouse button. The field is duplicated.

In the above series of steps, use of the Shift key constrains the direction you drag the mouse. To duplicate a field, the Shift key is not needed. When you want fields precisely aligned horizontally or vertically, use the Shift key along with the Control (Windows) or Option (Mac OS) key. If alignment is not necessary, simply use the modifier key and drag to any position on the form.

6. Repeat the same steps for the Check box created earlier.

7. Click back and forth between the Radio buttons and the Check boxes. Notice that when one box is selected, the other respective field box is deselected. This behavior is due to the fact that the names of the fields for the respective field types are identical. If the names were different, clicking in one box would not deselect the other.

Understanding Button Fields

Buttons behave similar to links in Acrobat. When you create a button, you typically associate an Action with the button very much like a Link action. You may wonder why Acrobat offers us Button fields when we can do the same things with Links. The advantage of using Button fields over Links include:

✦ **Copy/Paste.** Links cannot be copied and pasted. Form fields can be copied and pasted within a document or between documents.

✦ **Duplication.** Links cannot be duplicated in any manner. Form fields can be duplicated as described earlier and can further be duplicated across all pages in a document.

✦ **Icon Appearances.** Links can only have the Link rectangle appearance changed in terms of border color, border style, and border width of the rectangle drawn. Form fields have an additional advantage with the ability to import icons for displaying appearances.

✦ **Text Appearances.** Links are usually drawn around text on a page. If text is not available on the background design, the Link does not support text within the rectangle border. Form fields can have text created inside a field border.

✦ **Rollover Appearance Changes.** Because Links do not support icon appearances, no rollover effects can be created. Form field buttons can display rollover effects.

✦ **Sizing.** Links need to be manually sized individually. A group of form fields can be sized to the same width and height respective to a selected field.

✦ **Alignment.** A group of Links cannot be aligned to each other. Form fields can be aligned to each other.

✦ **Locking.** Links cannot be locked to position. Form fields can be locked.

✦ **Palette Management.** Links have no palette to help find and manage them. Form fields have a Fields palette where fields are easily found and managed.

✦ **Nudging.** Links cannot be moved or sized with keystrokes. Form fields can be nudged with arrow keys on the keyboard for positioning and sizing.

The one advantage a Link has over a Button field is the ability to link to a destination without any complex coding. In all other cases, form field buttons have a clear advantage. For almost all linking to views or invoking actions, you'll find using a Button form field much more advantageous than using Links.

To understand more about creating a Button form field, follow these steps:

1. Select the Form tool (F).

2. Drag open a rectangle where the button is to be located. In this example, a button is created that, when clicked, resets the form and clears all data entries.

3. In the Field Properties dialog box, select Button as the field Type.

4. Enter a name for the field. In this example, use the name `reset`. You'll find using *reset* a name you'll use many times for the same kind of button.

5. Click on the Options tab.

6. Select Text only from the Layout pull-down menu and type **Reset Form** in the Text field box, as shown in Figure 3-15.

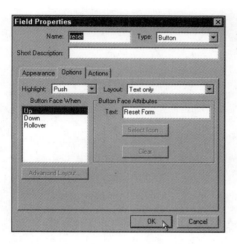

Figure 3-15: The Options tab enables you to enter text for the button description when a Button field type is used.

7. Click Actions to open the Actions tab.

8. Click Add to open the Edit an Action dialog box.

9. From the pull-down menu for Type, select Reset Form, as shown in Figure 3-16.

Figure 3-16: The Action Types are selected from the pull-down menu in the Edit an Action dialog box.

10. Click Set Action, then click OK in the Field Properties dialog box.

11. Select the Hand tool (H).

12. Click the button created to reset the form.

When the button is selected, all the field data are cleared and the defaults for all the fields are restored, as shown in Figure 3-17.

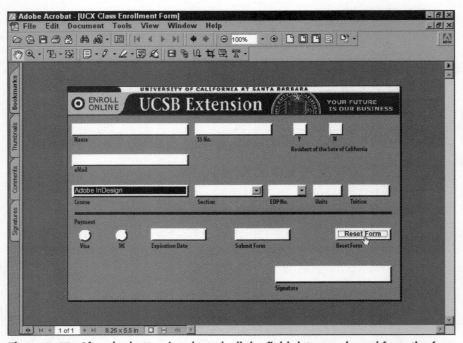

Figure 3-17: After the button is selected, all the field data are cleared from the form.

Understanding Signature Fields

Acrobat Self-Sign Security is one of the great features in working with Adobe Acrobat and Acrobat Approval. You can sign a document with a digital signature for authentication and you can secure the document against unauthorized viewing or changing a PDF.

Before you can create digital signatures, you need to first create a signature profile. For other users to verify your signature, they need to acquire a public certificate from you for the purposes of verifying your signature. You can likewise acquire public certificates from others to determine whom you may want to authorize viewing or changing a form. At this time, let's take a brief look at creating the signature field:

All the matters related to creating profiles and using them are addressed in Chapter 11, "Using Acrobat Security."

1. Select the Form tool (F).

2. Drag open a rectangle where you want to include a signature on the form.

3. Provide a name for the field and select Signature from the Type pull-down menu.

4. Click on the Signed tab.

5. Select the Mark As Read-Only Radio button.

6. From the pull-down menu select Just These Fields.

7. Click on the Pick button, as shown in Figure 3-19.

8. In the Select a Field dialog box, select a field and click Add, as shown in Figure 3-18. Repeat the process to select a few fields, then click on the Close button.

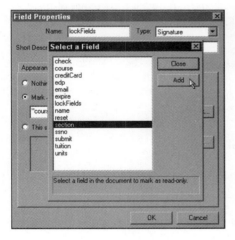

Figure 3-18: Select the fields to be locked with the digital signature by clicking on the field and selecting the Add button.

9. Examine the list in the Signed properties dialog box to be certain all fields to be locked are listed in the box below the pull-down menu, as shown in Figure 3-19.

10. Click OK in the Field Properties dialog box.

When you add Signature fields to a form, you sign the form by selecting the Hand tool (H) and clicking on the field. When you select a Signature field without logging in with your User Profile, Acrobat prompts you with a dialog box, as shown in Figure 3-20. At this point you can log in with your User Profile or create a profile by clicking on the New User Profile button.

Figure 3-19: All fields to be locked when the user signs the form are listed in the Field Properties dialog box.

Don't be concerned about some of these terms related to signatures, such as User Profile, certificate, logging on, and so on. A detailed coverage of digital signatures is covered in Chapter 11, "Using Acrobat Security."

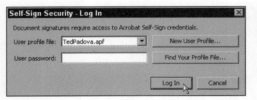

Figure 3-20: When clicking on a Signature field, Acrobat prompts you to log in with your User Profile.

Acrobat Field Types

The seven field types that are used with Acrobat forms can accommodate almost any user need for any kind of form desired. In this chapter, we examined the fields and created at least one field for each type for the most simplistic uses. There is much more available with form fields when associating actions and adding more dynamic interactivity for the end user. Before the bells and whistles are added to fields, it is important to understand what field types are available and when to use them. As an overall guide for understanding more about Acrobat form fields, mark Table 3-1 as a page to return to for a quick glance when comparing field attributes.

Table 3-1
Summary of Acrobat Form Field Types

Field Type	Use	Appearance
Text	Data Entry (text, numbers, dates, time, and so on). All user-supplied input is handled with this type.	Boxes created for user data entry. Boxes can be either single or multiple lines, and either scrollable or not scrollable.
Check boxes	On/off fields usually to accept a closed-ended question or a choice between two or more options. Also often used for making several selections among a group of options.	Single character marks when on. The default is a check mark.
Radio buttons	Choices for two or more options. Usually only one choice for a set of options are made with this field type.	Single character marks when on. The default is a bullet.
List boxes	Choices for single or multiple selections from a list. Each choice can be designed for user editing.	A scrollable window with up/down arrows.
Combo boxes	Choices for preset options. Only one choice per field can be made. No options available for user editing of listed options.	A pull-down menu with a down pointing arrow to display the options.
Buttons	Designed to invoke an action. When the cursor is positioned over a button field, the cursor appearance changes to a hand with the index finger pointing upward.	Icons and text can be used for the button appearances.
Signatures	Used as a container for a digital signature.	When a form is signed, the appearance changes to the User Profile display created for the signature appearance.

If you haven't created any forms in Acrobat prior to reviewing this chapter, you should now have enough information to explore form field authoring on your own. When the sample form used in this chapter is complete, it should look something like Figure 3-21 when the Form tool is selected. (See classEnrollPopulated.pdf to see my results.)

Use the classEnroll.pdf file (which is found on the book's CD-ROM) that was described at the beginning of the chapter and see if you can complete the form for the remaining fields.

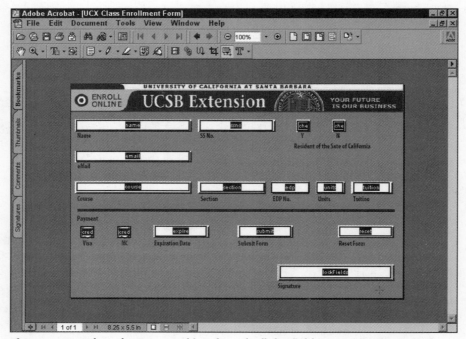

Figure 3-21: When the Form tool is selected, all the field types are represented with rectangular boxes. The field names appear inside each box.

Notice when the Form tool is selected, all the fields you created on a page appear as rectangular boxes. There is no way to distinguish at a glance what types of fields are used. For a more descriptive view of fields, you have another tool in the form of the Fields palette. If the palette is closed however, the fields appearing on the form all look like the same field types.

For more information regarding the use of the Fields palette, see Chapter 5, "Creating Form Fields."

Spend a little time playing with the field types and look at some of the different options for each field in terms of appearances and options in the Field Properties dialog box. Create a form and fill in the form fields. For example, when the classEnroll.pdf form is filled in, it appears the way that it is shown in Figure 3-22.

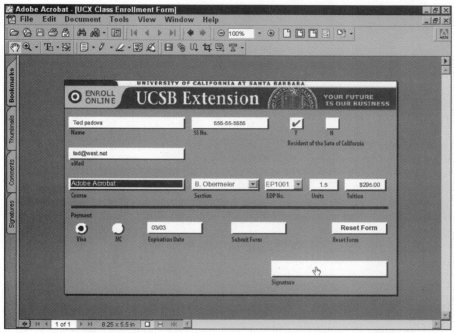

Figure 3-22: When the form fields are populated, the data appear as illustrated in the figure.

For a more detailed description of appearances and options, see Chapter 4, "Understanding Field Properties."

Saving Forms

After completing a form, it needs to be saved to disk. Acrobat can save the updates you make on a form by choosing the File ➪ Save menu command. Executing the command updates your edits. However, Acrobat keeps track of redundant information when you add, delete, modify, and create form fields. This tracking results in larger file sizes. If you host PDF forms on the Web or replicate CD-ROMs, you'll want to optimize the files and reduce the file size for each form in the most efficient manner. To do so involves completely rewriting the file.

Before rewriting a PDF document, it's a good idea to check a few preference settings to ensure Acrobat optimizes a file. Open the Preferences dialog box by choosing Edit ➪ Preferences ➪ General. In the Preferences dialog box, select Options in the left panel. Check the items for Allow Fast Web View and Save As Optimizes for Fast Web View, as shown in Figure 3-23.

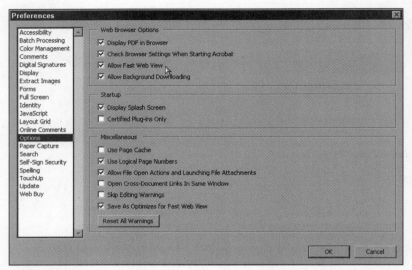

Figure 3-23: Check both check boxes in the Preferences dialog box before saving the final PDF form.

Click OK in the Preferences dialog box. Choose File ➪ Save As to open the Save As dialog box. The name that is supplied in the Object name field is the same filename as the PDF you began editing. If the location on your hard drive remains the same as where the file resides, clicking on the Save button opens a warning dialog box. Acrobat asks if you want to replace the old file with your new updated form. Click OK and Acrobat rewrites the entire file optimizing it as it is rewritten.

If you fill in a form, the same situation prevails. The longer the form, the bulkier the file size becomes. Whenever completing a form, use the Save As command to rewrite the file and optimize it.

Summary

✦ All form fields, with the exception of a few circumstances, require unique field names.

✦ You can use text fields for both text and numeric data.

✦ You can use Check boxes and Radio buttons for similar purposes. Radio buttons are frequently used for either/or conditions, while Check boxes are often used when multiple responses are permitted.

✦ Combo boxes and List boxes offer similar features. Combo boxes are limited to a single user response from a pull-down menu, while List boxes offer users an option for multiple choices from a scrollable box. List boxes also offer users an ability to edit the list items.

✦ You can use Signature fields for digitally signing a document with Acrobat's Digital Signature feature.

✦ After designing a form, use the Save As command to completely rewrite the file and optimize it for smaller file sizes.

✦   ✦   ✦

Understanding Field Properties

In Chapter 3, "Understanding Field Types," you were intro-duced to Field Properties for creating a single field for each field type. There are numerous choices available to you for setting appearance, options, and actions properties. When learning complex computer programs like Adobe Acrobat, we sometimes need to move back from the task-oriented experi-ences and pick up a little background information. Rather than walk through a series of exercises, this chapter offers you a basic description for some of the detail related to field properties. Read through this chapter and keep it bookmarked for future reference when you need a short description for assigning different form field properties.

Setting Field Appearances

Field appearances can be assigned to any field type. The same appearance settings are identical for all the field types dis-cussed in Chapter 3. These appearance settings relate to the display of the rectangle box drawn for a field and the different settings you can specify for each of the types.

Appearances are more of an extension of your form design. If you create a form on a blank white page, then appearance settings will be important to help the user find fields where data entry is needed. If your designs include displays where it is obvious to users where a field is located on a form, then the appearance settings are not as critical.

Field appearance settings offer several different attribute choices for fields. The first is the display of the field box. Other appearance settings have to do with text fonts and styles, field visibility, and appearances that may be assigned to buttons.

Creating borders and fills

The first of the appearance items in the Field Properties dialog box deals with the style of a border, its color, and a various assortment of fills that can be assigned to the field rectangle. Borders and fills are assigned to the field rectangles and therefore they can be used with any of the seven field types covered in Chapter 3. The options for borders and fills include:

✦ **Borders.** If a border or key line is to be used, select the Border Color check box on the Appearance tab.

✦ **Color.** The color swatch adjacent to Border Color on the Appearance tab defaults to black. To change a color, click on the swatch as shown in Figure 4-1.

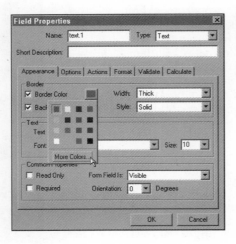

Figure 4-1: Click on any color swatch in the Field Properties dialog box and a pop-up menu opens. Select a preset color or click on More Colors (Windows) to open the system color palette.

On Windows, custom colors are selected by clicking on the More Colors button at the bottom of the palette shown in Figure 4-1. When you click on the color swatch on the Mac OS, colors are selected from the system color palette shown in Figure 4-2.

✦ **Background.** To fill the inside contents of the field rectangle, click in the Background Color check box. The same color options used for Border Color are available for background fills.

✦ **Width.** The size of the key line border can be made from three choices available in the pull-down menu, as shown in Figure 4-3.

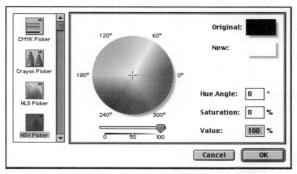

Figure 4-2: When you click on the color swatch in the Field Appearances dialog box on the Mac OS, the system color palette opens. Move the slider below the color wheel to change the value and click inside the wheel to change the hue and saturation.

Figure 4-3: Click on the down arrow to open the pull-down menu for Width. Key line borders can be set for one of the three menu options.

✦ **Style.** The appearance of the border and the background fill can assume any one of five different styles chosen from the menu choices for Style, as shown in Figure 4-4. Some of the choices apply to the border, such as Dashed, and some styles apply to the background fill, such as Beveled.

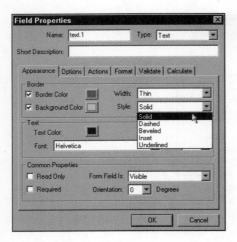

Figure 4-4: Different styles for border and fill appearances are made from the Style pull-down menu.

Creating text

Text appearances determine fonts, point sizes, and colors for text. When a user enters text in a text field, the appearance attributes for the text are visible when text is typed in the field boxes. The use of fonts is important for all your forms designs where PDFs are exchanged between computers, operating systems, and users with different versions of Acrobat. If you use fonts unique to your system, other users may not see text you type in field boxes. If you use system fonts such as Arial and Times New Roman, which are available to all Acrobat 5 users on Windows and Macintosh systems, users viewing PDFs in Acrobat 4 may not see text you type in the field boxes. Therefore, to be safe, always use the Base 14 fonts of Courier, Helvetica, Times, Symbol, and Zapf Dingbats.

When you open the Font pull-down menu, the Base 14 fonts appear above a dashed line in the menu, as shown in Figure 4-5. Stay above this line when specifying type and all users of any Acrobat viewer or version will see the text contained in field boxes.

✦ **Text Color.** The color swatch offers choices for text colors the same as the border and background fills described above.

✦ **Font.** Click on the down arrow to open the pull-down menu. All the fonts loaded in your system are available for font usage in fields. However, it cannot be overemphasized that you should always plan on using the Base 14 fonts.

✦ **Size.** The pull-down menu for Size determines point sizes for text. Among the point size options is Auto, as shown in Figure 4-6. When Auto is selected, Acrobat sizes the font automatically to fit the height of the field box. Point sizes not available from the preset choices in the menu are entered in the Size box by typing in the values. Acrobat accepts point sizes ranging from 2 points to 144 points.

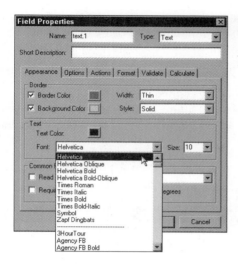

Figure 4-5: When choosing fonts for field boxes, always use the Base 14 fonts appearing above the dashed line in the Font pull-down menu.

Figure 4-6: Point sizes can be selected from preset options or by typing in a point size between 2 points and 144 points in the Size field box.

Using Common Properties

Several miscellaneous options are available at the bottom of the Appearance Properties dialog box. You can set these options for any of the seven field types. Common Properties include:

✦ **Read Only.** When the Read Only check box is selected, no data entry is permitted in the field box. Read Only fields can be helpful when you want to supply text boxes that offer hints or help information to guide a user in properly completing a form. Read Only fields may also be used to prevent users from changing calculated data for price, sales tax, shipping fees, and other similar fixed-cost units.

✦ **Required.** When the Required check box is selected, the field must contain data before it can be submitted. If you want a user to complete a form and then click on a button to submit the data to a Web server, you can define the essential fields that need to be filled in before the form can be sent to the URL where the data are collected.

✦ **Form Field Is.** There are four options for visibility for fields as shown in Figure 4-7. The default is Visible. You can hide a field, keep it visible but prevent it from being printed, or hide a field but print it. In terms of hidden fields, you may wish to have a field hidden until a user responds to a question with a specific response. If one question is, for example, answered yes, then the second field becomes visible. If the response is no, then the field remains hidden.

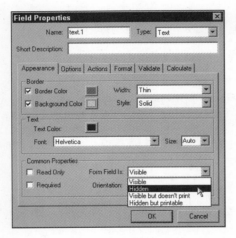

Figure 4-7: Four options are available for field visibility.

✦ **Orientation.** Fields can be rotated and result in four different appearances. The default is 0 (zero). Text can be set to 90 degree rotations by selecting the options from the pull-down menu. You may want to use a rotated field box to supply text on a page and use the Read Only option. In this case, you can offer information while economizing space on a form.

Creating Radio buttons and Check box options

Radio buttons and Check box field types by default use the Zapf Dingbats font. The font in the Appearance settings cannot be changed to another font. Special characters are used from the Zapf Dingbats font to represent the appearance for these fields. The choices for the text characters used are made on the Options tab. When you use either a Radio button or a Check box, click on the Options tab. For Check boxes, the pull-down menu for Check Style displays six style options, as shown in Figure 4-8. The same styles exist for Radio buttons, but the pull-down menu is referred to as Radio Style.

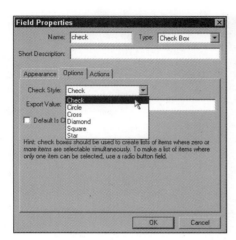

Figure 4-8: Six different characters can be used for either Check boxes or Radio buttons. These choices are made on the Options tab.

Creating Button field appearances

When a Button field type is created, you are provided with a different set of appearances from which to choose. Border and fill attributes are similar to the other field types; but in addition to these settings, you can import an icon to be displayed inside the field box. Icons can be selected from any PDF file or any file compatible with the Open as Adobe PDF command.

When creating Button fields, you typically associate an Action specified on the Actions tab. It would be useless to have a button that does nothing unless you want to add a design element to a form. Actions are discussed a little later in this chapter. For now, follow these steps to create a button with an icon appearance.

1. Select the Form tool (F).

2. Drag open a rectangle where the button is to appear on the form.

3. Supply a name and choose Button for the field type. You can set appearance settings for Border and Background or leave them unchecked. In this example, leave the items unchecked.

4. Click on the Options tab.

5. Select Icon Only from the Layout pull-down menu, as shown in Figure 4-9.

6. Click the Select Icon button.

7. The Select Appearance dialog box opens. Click on Browse and find the file to be used for an icon (a PDF file, or any file compatible with the Open as Adobe PDF supported formats).

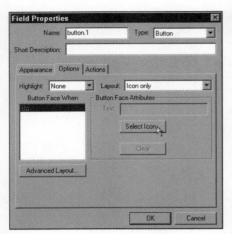

Figure 4-9: Click on the Options tab and select Icon Only from the Layout pull-down menu.

8. Click Select in the Open dialog box. The icon to be imported is displayed in the Select Appearance dialog box, as shown in Figure 4-10.

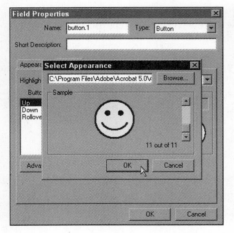

Figure 4-10: After selecting a file in the Open dialog box, the Select Appearance dialog box displays the icon that is used for the button appearance.

Tip   For easy access to a library of icons, use the Stamps files that are located in the Acrobat Folder inside Acrobat: Plug-Ins: Annotations: Stamps: Enu. The icon used in Figure 4-9 was taken from the Faces.pdf file that is located in the ENU folder.

9. Click OK in the Select Appearance dialog box. When you return to the Options tab, the dialog box shows the image to be used for the button appearance.

10. Click OK on the Options tab. The Button field reflects the new appearance on the PDF.

Button appearances can also include text or a combination of text and an icon. From the Layout pull-down menu on the Options tab, select one of seven different options. Use of text enables you to set type in the Text field box below the pull-down menu. Text can be used alone or positioned adjacent to an icon. The relative position for text and icons is self-described in the menu selections. For a clearer view of all the appearance properties, look at Figure 4-11.

On the CD-ROM   The file in Figure 4-11 is `howdyBlank.pdf`, which you'll find in the Chapter 4 folder on the book's CD-ROM.

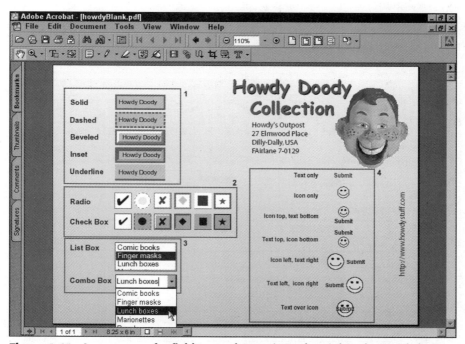

Figure 4-11: Appearances for field types shows 1) Border and Background choices for Text fields; 2) Radio and Check boxes with different borders and backgrounds and different radio and check styles; 3) List and Combo boxes with black borders and white fills; and 4) the seven different layout options for Button fields.

In mastering an understanding for appearance attributes for field types, there is no substitute for practice. Open the `howdyForm.pdf` file in the Chapter 4 tutorial folder on the book's CD-ROM and create different field types. Change the appearance properties back and forth to help gain an understanding of how these appearances are applied to the different field types.

You'll find the `howdyForm.pdf` file in the Chapter 4 tutorial folder on the book's CD-ROM.

Using Appearance Preferences

You may design a form where you don't want any of the appearance settings discussed above assigned to fields. You may have a form where a field is created in an open space and the user sees no indication that a field exists. As an example of a form designed without field appearances, compare Figures 4-12 and 4-13. Figure 4-12 shows a form with the Form tool selected and all the fields visible. However, when the user selects the Hand tool, the fields without appearance settings are not visible, as show in Figure 4-13.

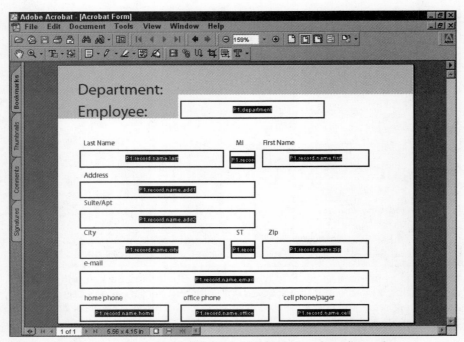

Figure 4-12: A form viewed with the fields visible during the edit mode.

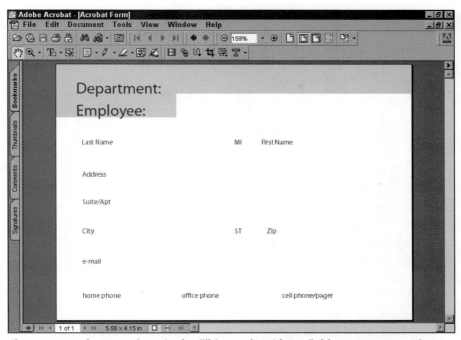

Figure 4-13: The same form in the fill-in mode without field appearance settings gives no indication to the user where the fields are located.

Setting field highlight preferences

Ideally you want to design forms that make it easy on the user to complete the form fill-in, so some indication that a field exists will be helpful to the user. If the design is better suited without any field appearances assigned to fields, Acrobat provides a means where a field boundary can be temporarily displayed as the user tabs to a field. Field highlight attributes are assigned in the Preferences dialog box. To adjust highlights, choose Edit ➪ Preferences ➪ General.

In the Preferences dialog box, select Forms from the list on the left side of the dialog box. The right side of the Preferences dialog box displays the Forms preference settings. Select the Highlight Form Fields check box to enable a field highlight when the user enters a field. If you want to change the default color of the highlight, click on the Highlight Color swatch, as shown in Figure 4-14. From the preset colors, click on the value you want or click on More Colors to open the System color palette and choose a custom color.

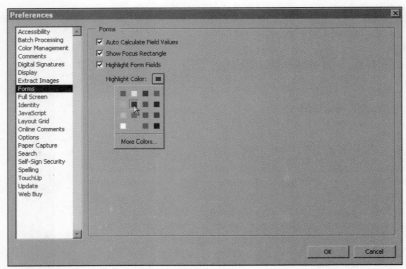

Figure 4-14: To adjust the forms preferences for field highlights, select the Highlight Form Fields check box and choose a highlight color.

Click OK in the Preferences dialog box. When you return to the form, press the Tab key. Acrobat takes you to the first field in the tab order and highlights the field. Fill in the form and the highlight stays active until you leave the field, as shown in Figure 4-15.

Press the Tab key on your keyboard. The previous field highlight disappears and the next highlight becomes active.

Caution   Preference settings are specific to the user's Acrobat viewer and not the form you design in Acrobat. If you adjust your preferences to display field highlights and save the PDF, the user who opens the form only sees field highlights if the preferences are adjusted on the computer viewing the file. If you want the user to enable field highlights, you may wish to add a note comment or help menu informing the user the steps needed to display the highlights as the user tabs through the form.

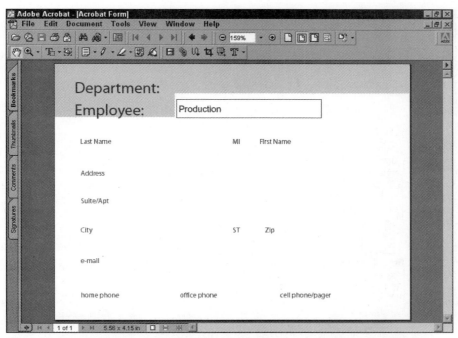

Figure 4-15: When you enter a field, the field rectangle is highlighted with the highlight color selected in the forms preferences.

Setting Focus Rectangle preferences

The other preference setting found in the Forms preferences is the Focus Rectangle. If you enable the Focus Rectangle in the Forms preferences, it has a similar effect as the Highlight when tabbing through all field types except Text fields and Combo boxes. If the preference setting is enabled, a dashed marquee within the field called the Focus Rectangle is displayed for the appearance, as shown in Figure 4-16. The Focus Rectangle appears after a Button field, Check box, Radio button, List box, or Signature field is tabbed to in the form or after one of these fields is selected.

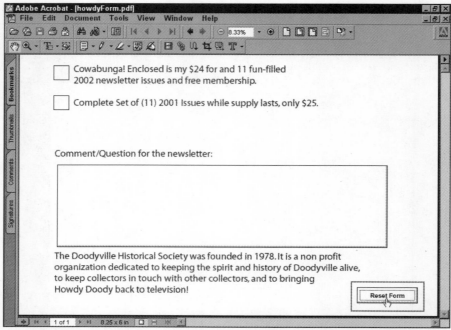

Figure 4-16: When Show Focus Rectangle is enabled in the Forms preferences, the appearance for Button field, Check boxes, Radio buttons, List boxes, or Signature fields displays a marquee when the user tabs to a field or after the field is selected.

Enabling the preference setting offers a benefit for users to find field types like buttons, List boxes, and Signature fields. When the Focus Rectangle appears, the user knows the field is active or contained on the form if no appearance settings have been assigned to a field.

Focus Rectangles are also user specified. If a user does not have the Focus Rectangle active in the Forms preferences, the rectangle doesn't appear on the form. Once again, you need to create a note or help menu to inform the user it would be best to enable the preference setting.

Setting Options

In the preceding section we looked at some of the Options settings for Radio and Check box fields. In Chapter 3 we looked at Options for List boxes and Combo boxes. With these field types, choices in the Options settings determine appearance and content of fields. With the remaining field types, the Options vary according to each field type. Choices made in the Options settings for any given field further describe attributes for specific field properties.

Using Text field options

Text fields are commonly used for open-ended data entry. Text fields can contain either numbers or text characters. The term *text* in this section refers to both. After creating a field and supplying a name and attributes for appearances, click on the Options tab. The various options for Text fields are shown in Figure 4-17.

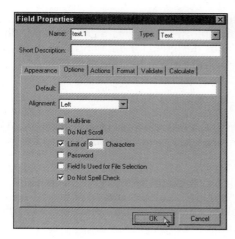

Figure 4-17: Options for Text fields are established on the Options tab.

Attribute settings for Text fields options include:

✦ **Default.** The text you add in the default field appears on the form as if a user typed the text in the field. Unless the field entry is changed, the default data contents are interpreted by Acrobat the same as if a user entered data. A situation where you might use a default value could be for supplying a state name or company headquarters address. If most users filling in the form use the default values, then the field(s) only needs to be edited by a few users to whom the default data doesn't apply.

✦ **Alignment.** Text typed in a field is aligned to one of the three choices made from the pull-down menu.

✦ **Multi-line.** If you create fields where the data requires more than a single line of text, click on Multi-line.

✦ **Do Not Scroll.** If the check box is selected, text can only be supplied to fit the field box. A warning beep sounds when no more text can fit in the field box regardless of whether the multi-line item is checked or not.

✦ **Limit of _____ Characters.** The user cannot enter more than the number of characters specified. Uses for limiting characters might be for phone numbers, social security numbers, zip codes, credit card numbers, and so on.

✦ **Password.** When enabled, the text typed in the field box displays a series of bullets (Mac OS) or asterisks (Windows). Anyone seeing the computer monitor will not know what characters are typed. The Password item does not password protect a field.

✦ **Field Is Used for File Selection.** When this item is enabled, all other check box options become unavailable. When a PDF form is submitted to a server, the path for an accompanying file is also submitted.

✦ **Do Not Spell Check.** Text entered in a field can be dynamically spell checked. If a misspelled word is typed, Acrobat informs you dynamically by underlining misspelled text in red. If you have fields designed for data entry, such as proper names, disable spell checking. By default, this box is checked.

Using Button field options

Setting appearances for buttons with text and icons was described earlier. In addition to the Options described so far, there are a few more Options settings for Button fields that can be set. These include:

✦ **Highlight.** Four appearance settings are available from a pull-down menu. The highlight appearances reflect the click on a button field. When the mouse button is depressed, the highlight determined from the menu choices is displayed before any associated action is invoked.

✦ **Button Face When.** If the Highlight is set to Push, options become available for this item. Among the choices is Rollover. If Rollover is selected, you can use two icon displays. One icon is used for the default display. When the mouse moves over the cursor, another icon is displayed much like a Web browser rollover effect. To create the Rollover appearance, click on Rollover, then click on Select Icon. Follow the steps described earlier to import the second icon.

✦ **Advanced Layout.** Clicking on the Advanced Layout button opens the Icon Placement dialog box, shown in Figure 4-18. In this dialog box you can position the icon within the field box by moving the horizontal and vertical sliders. Options for scaling and distortion are also made from pull-down menus.

✦ **Clear.** Once an icon has been selected for the button appearance, you can delete it without deleting the field by clicking on the Clear button.

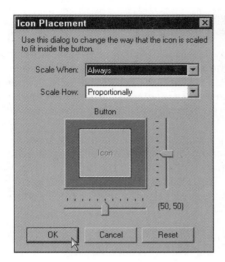

Figure 4-18: Icon placement and scaling are set in the Icon Placement dialog box.

Using Check box and Radio buttons options

In addition to the appearance settings for the symbol displayed inside the field rectangle when either of these fields is clicked, two other options are available. First, you can supply an export value for either field type. The export value may be used in a calculation. For example, if a condition is Yes, then do something, or else do nothing. The default for the export value is Yes. You can change the value to any other text or a number. The second item available to you in the Options dialog box for these field types is a check box for Default is Checked. When enabled, the default value prevails.

Cross-Reference

For an example of using different export values, see the Customer Service forms illustrated in Chapter 16, "Creating Forms for Real-World Uses." Take a look at `displayMakerCalculator.pdf` and `mountFinish.pdf` files that are located in the Customer Service folder.

Options for the remaining field types have been covered either in this chapter or in Chapter 3. For a Signature field, there is no Options tab. Rather than Options, the Signature fields use another tab called Signed.

Cross-Reference

For more on the Signed tab, see "Using Signed Properties," later in this chapter, and the discussion on digital signatures in Chapter 11, "Using Acrobat Security."

Defining Actions

An action can be associated with any field type and all field types use the same action choices. Action types for fields are the same as action types that can be associated with links. All action types are established in the Actions tab of the Field Properties dialog box. In addition to the type of action to be associated with a given field, you can employ an action based on various behaviors with the mouse movement.

Several Actions can be assigned to the same field and several mouse behaviors can be added to the same field, all with different actions. You may want to add a Mouse Enter action, a Mouse Up action, and a Mouse Exit action all to the same field. When the mouse enters the field, an action is invoked. When the mouse button is clicked, another action is invoked. When the mouse cursor exits the field, a third action is invoked.

Understanding mouse behavior

When you open the Actions tab, the first item to select is a choice under the When This Happens list. The default is a Mouse Up action, as shown in Figure 4-19. When the default mouse behavior is used, clicking in a field with an action assigned to it invokes the action when the mouse button is released—thus, Mouse Up. The other items from the list include:

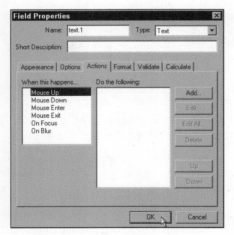

Figure 4-19: When assigning an action to a field, first make a selection in the When This Happens list.

✦ **Mouse Down.** The action is invoked when the mouse button is pressed down. As a rule, you may wish to use Mouse Up over a Mouse Down action. Users will expect your form actions to be consistent with other applications, such as Web browsing, when clicking on buttons where Mouse Up actions are the norm. This may not always be the case, but common protocol is to use the Mouse Up behavior to invoke an action.

✦ **Mouse Enter.** The action is invoked when the mouse cursor enters the field boundary. You might create a help field on your form. When the mouse cursor moves over a field, another field used as a help field opens and becomes visible to the user. When the mouse button is clicked, a different action might be executed.

✦ **Mouse Exit.** When the cursor leaves the field boundary, the action is invoked. Using the above example, when the mouse leaves the field, the help field might hide from view.

✦ **On Focus.** A user will usually tab through a form filling in the fields. If you want to associate an action when the user tabs to a field, use the On Focus behavior. Clicking the mouse in the field also executes the same action as tabbing to the field.

✦ **On Blur.** When the user tabs out of a field or uses a mouse action to move to another field, the action is invoked. This item is the opposite of the On Focus behavior.

Adding Actions

After deciding what mouse behavior is used to invoke an action, you need to add one or more actions to the field properties. Adding an action is handled by clicking on the Add button on the Actions tab. When you click on Add, the Add an Action dialog box opens. Actions are selected from the pull-down menu for Type, as shown in Figure 4-20.

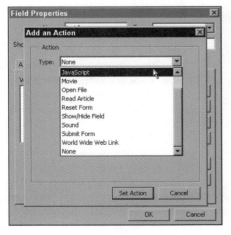

Figure 4-20: Click Add on the Actions tab to open the Add an Action dialog box. Click the down arrow to open the pull-down menu displaying the action types.

✦ **Execute Menu Item.** An action can execute any menu item as well as execute a number of options found in the Bookmarks, Thumbnails, Articles, Destinations, and Info palettes. To add an Execute Menu Item action type, open the pull-down menu for Type and select Execute Menu Item. The Edit Menu Item button appears in the dialog box, as shown in Figure 4-21.

Figure 4-21: Select Execute Menu Item from among the Type menu choices. The Edit Menu Item button appears in the Add an Action dialog box after the menu item is selected.

Click on the Edit Menu Item button in the Add an Action dialog box. On Windows, the Menu Item Selection dialog box opens. This dialog box is a mini representation of the menus found across the top of the Acrobat window. Additionally, there are palette names appearing in the dialog box. Click on an item to open the respective menu choice, as shown in Figure 4-22. Click OK and OK again in the Add an Action dialog box. The action is now set for the mouse behavior.

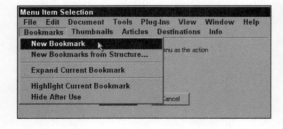

Figure 4-22: On Windows, the Menu Item Selection dialog box opens. Click on a menu name to open the menu and make a choice for the menu item to be executed.

On the Macintosh, menu item selections are made from the top-level menu bar. When you select Execute Menu Item, a dialog box opens instructing you to use the regular menu commands, as shown in Figure 4-23.

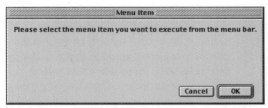

Figure 4-23: On the Macintosh, an alert dialog box informs you to use the top-level menu bar to make menu selections.

Note   When opening the Type pull-down menu in the Add an Action dialog box, not all options are immediately available. The above item for Execute Menu Item is hidden in a scrollable list. Use the arrow keys or scroll bar to move up and down the list and select the action type you wish to use.

✦ **Import Form Data.** When the action type is selected, a button appears in the Add an Action dialog box for Select File. Click on the button and select the data to be imported.

✦ **JavaScript.** JavaScripts are written in Acrobat or written in a text editor selected for use with Acrobat. On the Macintosh, you need to use the Acrobat editor. On Windows, you have an option to use the editor supplied by Acrobat or select an alternate text editor to write JavaScripts.

Cross-Reference   For more on JavaScript and how to use the editor, see Chapter 7, "Getting Started with JavaScript."

✦ **Movie.** The Select Movie button appears in the Add an Action dialog box. Click on Select Movie and open the movie to be acted on when the user clicks on the field. Note: You will have to add a Movie to the PDF document using the Movie Tool.

✦ **Open File.** The Select File button appears in the Add an Action dialog box. Find the file to be imported by clicking on Select File and find the file to open, much like you do for importing form data and movies.

✦ **Read Article.** When the user clicks on a field, the user is taken to the first paragraph of an article thread. In the Add an Action dialog box, clicking on the Select Article button enables you to select the article to be used. Article threads are not typically a feature used with forms and therefore are not addressed in this book. To learn more about Articles in Acrobat, see the Acrobat user documentation.

✦ **Reset Form.** Used for clearing form data, the Select Fields button appears in the Add an Action dialog box. Click on Select Fields and the Field Selection dialog box opens, as shown in Figure 4-24.

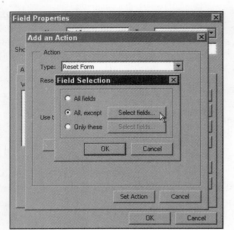

Figure 4-24: When you click on Select Fields, the Field Selection dialog box opens. If either the second or third radio button is selected, you can make individual field selections for which fields will be included or excluded when clearing the form data.

If all fields are to be cleared of data, select All Fields and click OK. If fields are to be selectively chosen for those that need to be cleared, click on one of the other two radio buttons and click OK. The second Field Selection dialog box opens, as shown in Figure 4-25. Click on a field and click Add or Remove to determine what fields will be cleared in the document. Click OK through the dialog boxes to return to the Field Properties dialog box.

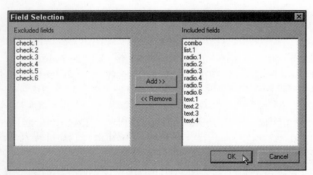

Figure 4-25: Click on a field name, then select either Add or Remove to add to or remove from the list of fields to be cleared.

Caution   If you use fields for help messages as suggested earlier in this chapter, resetting a form without quantifying fields for clearing data will clear all text data in your help fields. Be certain to study your form and review it thoroughly before creating a Reset button.

✦ **Show/Hide Field.** The Edit button appears in the Add an Action dialog box. Click on Edit and the Show/Hide Field dialog box opens, as shown in Figure 4-26. By default, all fields are visible. Select the fields to hide by clicking on the field name and selecting the Hide radio button. If a field is hidden, select the field to show and select the Show radio button.

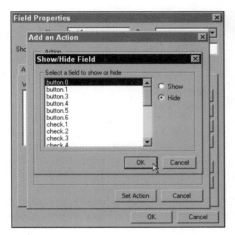

Figure 4-26: Click on a field name, then select the Show or Hide radio button.

✦ **Sound.** Sound files are added much like movies. Whereas movie files are linked to the PDF file, sound files are embedded in a PDF file. Click on Select Sound and find the file to add. When you open the sound file, it is converted and embedded in the PDF file. After embedding sounds, they can be played across platforms.

✦ **Submit Form.** Form data are submitted to URLs. Click on Select URL and the Submit Form Selections dialog box opens, as shown in Figure 4-27. The export format for the data type includes four different choices. You can choose to export FDF (Form Data Format) files native to Acrobat, HTML, or XML, or submit the populated PDF file. The Field Selection items are similar to those used in the Reset Form action type.

Cross-Reference

For more detail on submitting forms and the data types used to submit to Web servers, see Chapter 13, "Submitting and Distributing Forms."

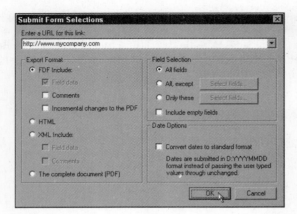

Figure 4-27: The Submit Form Selections dialog box offers four choices for the type of data to be submitted to a URL.

✦ **World Wide Web Link.** The Edit URL button appears in the Add an Action dialog box. Click on the button and the Edit URL dialog box opens, as shown in Figure 4-28. Be certain to enter a complete URL in the dialog box, including the `http://` if a Base URL has not been defined for the form. Base URLs can be established for a form by choosing the File ➪ Document Properties ➪ Base URL command. Setting up a Base URL is not necessary if you supply a complete URL address in the Edit URL dialog box.

Figure 4-28: Enter the URL in the Edit URL dialog box. If Base URL is not established in the preferences dialog box, be certain to add the complete URL address.

✦ **None.** When None is selected, no action is invoked when the field is selected. None may be used to import an image to add as a design element. Once the image is imported, you may want the button to do nothing, thus defining the action as None.

As you can see, there are many options that are available to you for associating actions with fields. When you add JavaScripts as field actions, the possibilities are infinite. In terms of action types related to Acrobat forms, the most frequent actions you will use include: Execute Menu Item, Import Form Data, JavaScript, Reset Form, Show/Hide Field, and Submit Form. Try to spend some time creating several of these field types to become more familiar with them.

Using Formats

After you determine field appearances, move through the options and work with actions, you'll notice that many of the remaining settings in the Field Properties dialog box contain options unique to specific field types. Whereas the previous settings apply to most of the field types, the Format tab is only available for Combo boxes and Text fields. Formatting is especially important for number data with number strings, dates, and times. When either a Combo box or Text field is chosen for the field type, the Format tab appears in the Field Properties dialog box. When other field types are selected, the Format tab is not available. Among the Format options are:

✦ **None.** When None is selected, no special formatting is used.

✦ **Number.** Number choices range from the number of decimal places to formatting styles such as currency symbols. To select different currency symbols, open the pull-down menu for Currency Symbol, as shown in Figure 4-29. Additional settings provide options for Separator Styles for different language expressions and negative number displays.

Figure 4-29: Click Number in the left pane of the Format tab to open choices in the right pane.

✦ **Percentage.** When a number is to be represented or calculated as a percentage, select Percentage from the Format properties. Percentages can be defined with user-specified decimal places and separator styles.

✦ **Date.** Date fields can be displayed in a variety of styles when Date is selected from the Format properties. Select an item in the scrollable list or type the data format in the box below the list.

✦ **Time.** Time units can be selected from choices for 12 or 24 hour time formats. AM/PM extensions are also available.

✦ **Special.** The default special options include zip code formats, phone numbers, and Social Security Numbers. Additional special options cannot be used for this choice. For additional special options definitions, see Custom, below.

✦ **Custom.** Formats not available from the presets can be made via a JavaScript routine. You can create a custom format by clicking on Custom and selecting the Custom Format Script Edit button, as shown in Figure 4-30. Also available are Custom Keystroke Scripts. Select the second Edit button to add a custom keystroke script and write a JavaScript routine. When clicking on either Edit button, the JavaScript editor opens where a script is coded. For more on custom JavaScripts, look at the chapters contained in Part II, "Working with JavaScript."

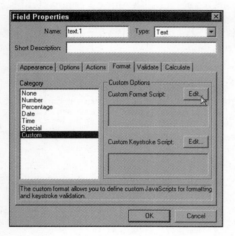

Figure 4-30: Custom formats and custom keystroke validation are handled in the Custom Format options.

Validating Data

Validating data ensures that the data entered by a user falls within a range defined by you or adheres to custom validation criteria you specify in JavaScript. If, for example, you create a survey form and ask for user responses for age where age ranges in separate fields are 21–30, 31–40, 41–50, and so on, then you want to validate the data supplied by the user; you can validate a user's response. If a user enters 32 in the field where you expect a response to be between 21 and 30, the field validation reports an error and asks the user to reenter the data.

The "Value must be greater than or equal to" field box, shown in Figure 4-31, is only active when a Number or Percentage is selected in the Format dialog box. Custom validation is handled with JavaScript. Click on the Radio button for Custom Validate Script, then select the Edit button to open the JavaScript editor. Any one of the choices on the Format tab, except None, enables you to create a JavaScript for custom validation.

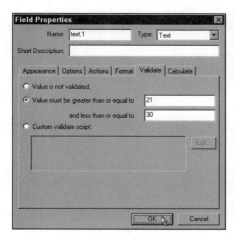

Figure 4-31: Validation for entering a range of data in the two field boxes can only be used when either Number or Percentage is selected from the Format properties.

When a user enters data that does not conform to the validation, a dialog box opens, as shown in Figure 4-32. The dialog box displays the criteria for the data to be entered.

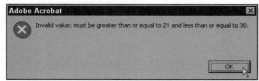

Figure 4-32: If a user enters data outside the range you use for the validation, a dialog box opens informing the user the data entered are outside the range. In this example, a number needs to be within 21 to 30.

Note

The actual scripts used to format data described earlier for validate data are covered in several chapters in Part II, "Working with JavaScript." The importance of the descriptions covered in this chapter is to understand that often there are relationships between the format attributes, the validate attributes, and other assignments made from other tab options. When you move on to calculating fields or writing scripts and find errors in your programming, there may be occasions where the routine you create requires a specific format for a field. Try to gain an understanding for the relationships in the Field Properties settings before moving on to calculating fields or writing JavaScripts.

Calculating Fields

Data calculations are available only for Combo boxes and Text fields. In the Field Properties dialog box, click on the Calculate tab to open the Calculate properties. Calculations can be made either from preset operations or by writing custom calculation scripts in JavaScript. In order to calculate data, be certain to inspect all the number formats specified in the Format properties. If you leave all your number fields set to None (the default), the Value Is the Radio button that appears in Figure 4-33 won't be active.

Figure 4-33: If numbers don't have proper format assignments, the Radio buttons for creating a calculation from either a preset formula or Custom calculation script won't be active. In this example, the numbers were properly formatted in the Format tab before addressing the Calculate tab.

To use a preset calculation formula, select the Value Is the Radio button and open the pull-down menu, as shown in Figure 4-34. Among the choices for preset calculation formulas, you can calculate the sum, product, average, minimum, and maximum values for a group of fields.

After selecting the preset formula to use, click on the Pick button. The Select a Field dialog box opens where all the fields in your form are listed in a scrollable box, as shown in Figure 4-35. Click on a field to add to the formula. Click on each field to be added, then click Close. When you return to the Calculate properties, all the fields are listed in the field box below the Value Is the Radio button.

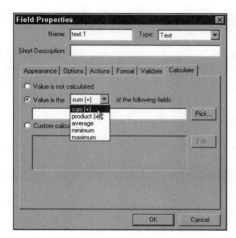

Figure 4-34: Click on the down arrow in the Field Properties dialog box to open the pull-down menu for preset calculation formulas.

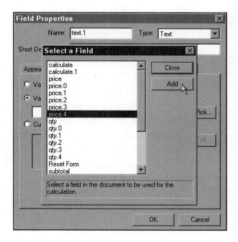

Figure 4-35: Click on each field to be added to the formula and click on the Add button in the Select a Field dialog box. Click Close after adding all the fields to be calculated.

If you need to use other math operations such as subtraction, division, or other formulas, you need to write a custom calculation script. Select the Custom calculation script Radio button and click on the Edit button. As with the Format and Validate properties, the default JavaScript editor opens where the code is written.

Cross-Reference A discussion of custom Calculation scripts begins in Chapter 7, "Getting Started with JavaScript."

Using Selection Changes

A tab for Selection Change appears when a List Box field type is used. Only the List box has this setting. Create a List box and click on Selection Change to open the dialog box shown in Figure 4-36.

Figure 4-36: The Selection Change properties only become available for List box fields.

The choices are either the default to do nothing when List box selections are changed or to execute a JavaScript when a List box item changes. Uses for this particular feature may be something like disabling a sales tax calculation and hiding the sales tax field when a change is made for the state where a product is shipped and no sales tax fees are needed for that particular state.

Using Signed Properties

A description for Signed properties was discussed in Chapter 3. The Signed tab only appears for Signature fields.

Cross-Reference

To review more on the properties, turn back to Chapter 3, "Understanding Field Types."

Cross-Reference

For a full review of working with Acrobat Self-Sign Security, see Chapter 11, "Using Acrobat Security."

The options for all the field types offer you some consistent properties choices and many that vary according to the field type selected. For a quick glance at all the properties that can be assigned to each field type, look over Table 4-1. You may wish to bookmark this page and refer to it often when developing your initial forms designs.

Table 4-1
Summary of Form Field Properties

Field Type	Appearance	Options	Actions	Format	Validate	Calculate	Selection Change	Signed
Text	X	X	X	X	X	X		
Button	X	X	X					
Check box	X	X	X					
Radio button	X	X	X					
Combo box	X	X	X	X	X	X		
List box	X	X	X				X	
Signature	X			X				X

Summary

✦ You can design all fields with different design appearances in the Appearances tab within the Field Properties dialog box.

✦ Options properties change according to field type. All fields, except for the Signature field, have unique options settings.

✦ You can assign actions to any field type. Among the actions settings are menu commands, JavaScript, resetting forms, and other actions specific to forms designs.

✦ The Format properties are often used to format numbers, especially when calculations are performed.

✦ The Validate properties offer you opportunities to verify correct data entries.

✦ Selection changes apply only to List boxes.

✦ The Signed properties offer you options for locking data fields when documents are digitally signed.

✦　　✦　　✦

Creating Form Fields

Now that you have a basic understanding for working
with field properties and understanding the difference
between all the form field types Acrobat provides you, we
can begin to create and manage fields on a form. How to use
the Form tool and how to create forms fields for real-world
designs is the central theme for this chapter.

Naming Fields

In Chapter 3, "Understanding Field Types," we took a brief
look at naming nomenclature for form fields. The importance
of using parent/child names was emphasized in Chapter 3.
This convention cannot be overly stated and it will be important for all your forms designs to make the best use of field
names. For a real-world view of understanding the importance
for why parent and child names are used, let's walk through a
few examples.

Duplicating fields

If you create fields that have appearances, sizes, and other
attributes identical for multiple fields on a form, then your
construction for fields will be much easier if you can duplicate
a field rather than drag open new field rectangles for each
common field type. Duplicating fields moves you through the
field construction stage much faster than creating each field

independently. As an example, assume you want three individual groups of fields for identifying information. One group may be for the information for the user who places an order, the shipping address for the recipient, and the vendor address. Each group needs a name, address, city, state, zip, and phone number. Rather than create individual fields for each group, you can create a single group, then duplicate it twice for the other two groups. To perform steps in this exercise, open the doodyvilleOrder.pdf form in the Chapter 5 folder on the book's CD-ROM. The blank form is shown in Figure 5-1. Notice the three areas on the form where identifying information fields need to be created.

On the CD-ROM   You'll find the doodyvilleOrder.pdf form in the Chapter 5 folder on the book's CD-ROM.

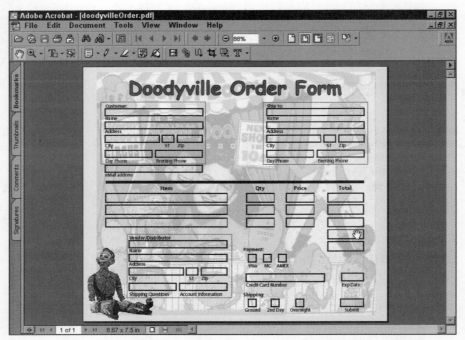

Figure 5-1: The doodyvilleOrder.pdf form requires three groups for identifying information.

1. Create a text field for the first line where the name appears. Name the field *name.1* in the Field Properties dialog box, as shown in Figure 5-2.

Tip

When you use the Form tool to create a field box and complete setting up the Field Properties dialog box, Acrobat assumes you wish to continue creating more fields and keeps the Form tool active. If you want to create a single field and return to the Hand tool after completing the Field Properties dialog box, press the Ctrl key (Windows) or Option key (Mac OS) before selecting the Form tool in the Acrobat Command Bar. After clicking OK in the Field Properties dialog box, Acrobat selects the Hand tool for you.

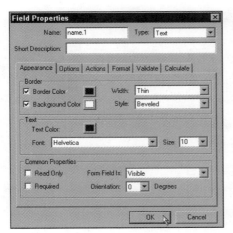

Figure 5-2: Create a Text field and name the field *name.1*.

2. Create text fields for each of the other fields naming each field with a parent/child name as shown in Figure 5-3.

Tip

To quickly create new fields, you can duplicate a field and edit the field name. After creating the first field in this exercise, click on the field and press the Ctrl key (Windows) or Option key (Mac OS) and drag down. To constrain movement, add the Shift key when dragging. When the field rests in proper position, press the Enter key on the Numeric Pad to open the Field Properties dialog box. Rename the field by selecting the name and editing the text. Click OK in the Field Properties dialog box.

3. After completing all fields in the first group, hold the Ctrl key (Windows) or Shift Key (Mac OS) and drag a marquee through the fields.

Tip When selecting multiple fields with a modifier key depressed, the marquee does not need to completely surround the fields but needs to pass through all the fields to be selected in the group. Drag the marquee through the fields and release the mouse button. All the fields are selected.

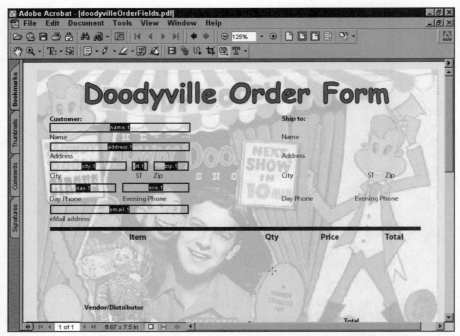

Figure 5-3: Each of the fields in the first group contains parent/child names.

4. Press the Ctrl key (Windows) or Option key (Mac OS), click on a field, and drag in the direction where the second group of fields is to be positioned. *Note:* In this example, the `email.1` field was not selected. The fields are duplicated, as shown in Figure 5-4.

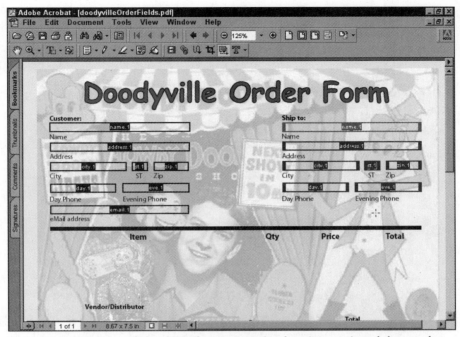

Figure 5-4: Hold the Ctrl key (Windows) or Option key (Mac OS) and drag to the area where the second group of fields is to be located.

5. The fields are exact duplicates of the first group. These new fields need to have unique names or the data entered in one field will appear the same in all fields with identical names. To rename all fields, keep them selected as a group and press the plus (+) key on your keyboard. All the fields are incremented from the child name. In this example, the names appear as `name.2`, `address.2`, `city.2`, and so on.

6. Repeat the process and duplicate the second group to complete the fields for the third group, as shown in Figure 5-5.

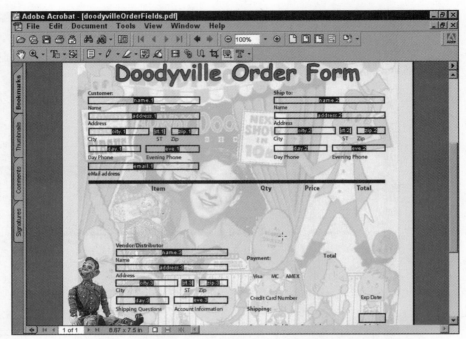

Figure 5-5: Select the second group of fields and drag with the modifier key depressed to the third group position. Press the plus (+) key to increment the child names again.

Duplication of fields can only be performed in this manner if the field names contain a child name expressed as a `.n` (dot-n) in which `n` is a number. If you name fields like `name`, `address`, `city`, and so on, you would have to rename all the fields individually.

Note   The method used for duplicating fields described here only works on individual pages in a PDF file. If you wish to duplicate fields from one page to another, you must use the copy/paste commands or Duplicate menu command described later in this chapter.

Calculating on names

Another reason for using parent/child names is when you want to easily create a calculation. In Figure 5-6, the form has three lines with amounts placed in fields named `total.1`, `total.2`, and `total.3`. A grand total needs to be calculated for the total.

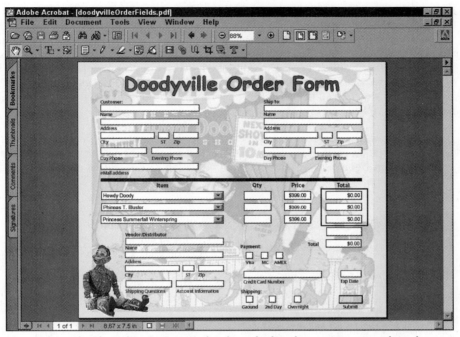

Figure 5-6: The three line items need to be calculated to create a grand total.

If you create a Text field (with Format properties of Number or Percentage) and click on the Calculate tab, then select the Pick button, the Select a Field dialog box opens. Summing data in a column is handled by scrolling the dialog box and clicking on a field, then clicking on the Add button, as shown in Figure 5-7. The steps need to be repeated for every field to be used in the calculation.

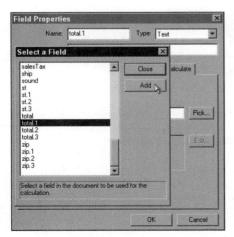

Figure 5-7: To sum data in a column, select the Pick button in the Calculate dialog box. Click on each item to be used in the calculation and click on the Add button.

If parent/child names are used, you can simplify the process by selecting sum (+) for the Value Is The pull-down menu and entering the parent name in the field box, as shown in Figure 5-8. Or, you can select the parent name in the Select a Field dialog box, shown in Figure 5-7. In this example, only three fields are used. If the form had a long list of fields, the task would take a little time to pick each individual field in a column. However, when using parent/child names, the process is simplified by adding a few keystrokes in the field box for the Calculate properties or selecting the parent name in the Select a Field dialog box.

Note   When you type a parent name in the field box, you enter the name with or without quotation marks. When you revisit a field by opening up the properties after a name has been added, Acrobat places quotation marks around each name in the field box automatically.

Figure 5-8: When parent/child names are used, you can simplify adding fields in a column with a common parent name by typing the parent name on the Appearance tab or selecting the parent name in the Field Properties dialog box.

Tip   When adding columns or rows among fields with parent/child names, it's a good idea to get in the habit of typing names in the field box rather than using the Pick method from the Field Properties dialog box. If you have a long list of fields, it can take a little more time to scroll the box to find each individual parent name. When summing multiple parent names, type each parent name in the field box and separate the names with commas.

Performing this kind of calculation only works when parent/child names are used and all the parent names are identical. The benefits of using parent/child names are much more obvious when writing JavaScripts that need to loop through a series of fields on a form to produce a result.

Cross-Reference   For more information on using parent/child names with JavaScripts, see the chapters in Part II, "Working with JavaScript," beginning in Chapter 7, "Getting Started with JavaScript."

Copying and Pasting Fields

Duplicating fields as described above works well when you have fields on a single page and need to duplicate the fields on the same page. If you have multiple pages where fields need to be duplicated between PDF documents, you need to use the copy and paste menu commands. Fields can be copied and pasted on the same page, to different pages in the same document, and between PDF documents.

As you know, fields must have unique names when data are to be entered in rows or columns and their results need to be unique. In some cases, you may wish to have identical field names to exchange data between PDF files. An example where unique names might be used is when you have identifying information that remains consistent between documents. For example, suppose you have a Human Resources department using PDF forms. All the employee identifying information, such as name, address, phone, emergency contact, and so on might be used in part or in total on performance evaluations, tax forms, pension plans, job descriptions, and so on. Rather than typing the information on each separate form, you can import data into a form. The main requirement for importing data is all form fields must be named *exactly* the same including case-sensitivity.

If you design forms independently, creating new form fields each time a form is designed, you run the risk of making mistakes with field names. A typo, forgotten letter case, forgotten nomenclature, and so on can cost you time when debugging the form. A much better method is to use the copy and paste commands. When a field is copied, the field names and attributes reflect a carbon copy of the original. When pasted into the destination form, you can be certain all fields match each other exactly.

In Figure 5-9, a file is used to store customer identification information. To copy fields, select the Form tool and press the Ctrl key (Windows) or Shift key (Mac OS) and drag through the fields to be copied. Right-click the mouse button (Windows) or Control+click (Mac OS) to open a context menu. Choose Edit ➪ Copy. The fields are now copied to the system clipboard.

You may wish to keep the file open from where the fields are copied in the event more fields need to be copied or a mistake was made by not selecting all fields to be pasted. In this regard, leave the file open and choose File ➪ Open. Open the file where the fields need to be pasted and choose Edit ➪ Paste.

Note   Pasting fields can be handled in a context menu only when a field exists in a document and a field is selected. If you try to open a context menu without a field selected, Acrobat won't know you want to handle menu commands respective to fields options. The menu options from context menus on document pages with nothing selected only support navigating and searching the document. When using menu commands for managing fields, always be certain to first select a field with the Form tool before you open a context menu.

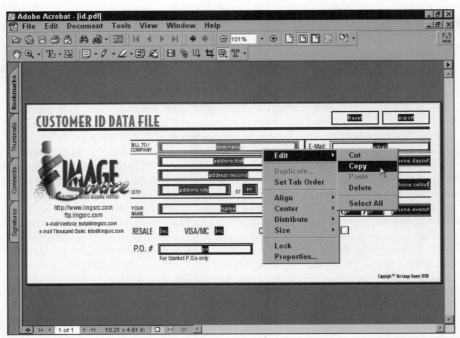

Figure 5-9: Select all fields you want to copy and open a context menu. Choose Edit ⇨ Copy to copy the fields to the system's clipboard.

When the fields are pasted, you may need to move them around the page. You can move fields by clicking on one of the selected fields in a group and dragging around the document page. You can nudge fields into place by striking the up, down, left, and right arrow keys. The fields move respective to the direction of the arrow keys

If you need to return to the original file, choose Window ⇨ *filename* where filename is the name of the file where the fields were copied. Select additional fields in the same manner and copy and paste them into the destination document. When the fields are positioned, they are ready to be filled in, as shown in Figure 5-10. Data can also be imported from forms where the field names have identical matches.

Cross-Reference   For more on importing and exporting data, see Chapter 13, "Submitting and Distributing Forms."

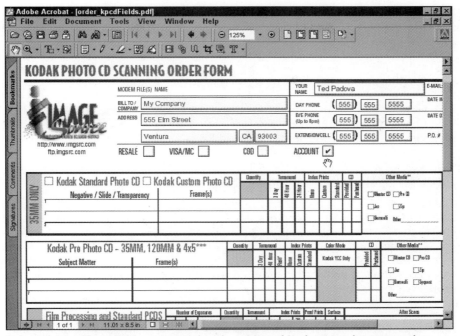

Figure 5-10: When fields are pasted and positioned in the new document, data can be imported into only those fields where field names match exactly to the fields from which the data are exported.

Organizing Fields

Duplicating fields is but one avenue for quickly populating a form with fields. To precisely size, align, and distribute fields, Acrobat offers menu commands to help speed up the process of designing a form. If you create forms with multiple columns and rows, using the menu commands help you complete your design much faster, and the appearance of the fields on the form will be much more attractive than manually moving fields into position.

Understanding the anchor field

Regardless of what operation you perform to organize a group of fields, it is critical to understand the priority of the field selection and to what field all other fields are aligned or sized. When you select a group of fields, all fields become highlighted with a blue selection. Among a group of selected fields, one field is highlighted in red. This field I refer to as the *anchor field*. When you use a context menu command to organize fields, they are aligned or sized in reference to the anchor field. When a group of fields is selected, you can change the anchor field by clicking on any field among the selected fields. There is no need to use a modifier key when changing the anchor field. Therefore, you don't need to use the Control/Shift key when changing the anchor field among a group of selected fields.

Deselecting fields occurs when you click outside any field box. If you click within a field box, it becomes the anchor field. Deselecting fields can also occur by clicking on another tool in the Acrobat Command Bar.

Aligning fields

Field alignment can be handled by menu commands for aligning fields along the left, right, top, bottom, vertical centers, and horizontal centers. These alignment options can all be selected from a context menu. To align fields in any direction, select a group of fields and open a context menu, as shown in Figure 5-11. From the context menu, choose Align ⇨ Left to align the fields on the left side. Note the anchor field selected is the top field in this example. To change the anchor field among a selected group, click on a different field.

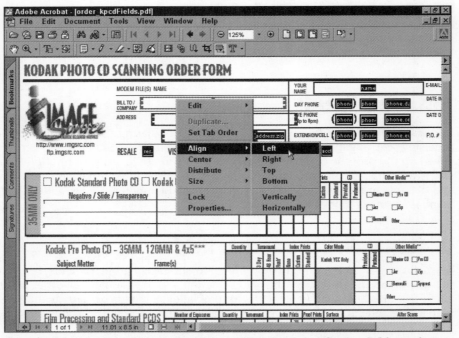

Figure 5-11: From a context menu, choose Align ⇨ Left for aligning fields on the left side of the anchor field form field rectangle.

Note By now you should be familiar with multiple-field selection and opening context menus. For a review, see the preceding pages. Future references to multiple selections of fields are cited as *select all fields in a group*. Opening a context menu by Right-clicking (Windows) or Control+clicking (Mac OS) is simply referred to as *open a context menu*.

The vertical and horizontal alignment commands are used when fields of different sizes are to be aligned. In the above example, all fields aligned were the same size. If you have field boxes of different widths down a column, choosing Align ➪ Vertical in the context menu aligns the centers of the field rectangles. The same holds true for the height of field boxes along a row of fields when using the Align ➪ Horizontal command.

Sizing fields

If fields are created independently without duplication, you may wish to uniformly size all field boxes in a column or row. Sizing fields are also adjusted in reference to the anchor field. To size fields to the same size as the anchor field, select all fields in a group to be sized. If the red highlight does not appear on the field to be used as the anchor field, click on the field with the fixed size. Open a context menu and choose Size ➪ Both, as shown in Figure 5-12.

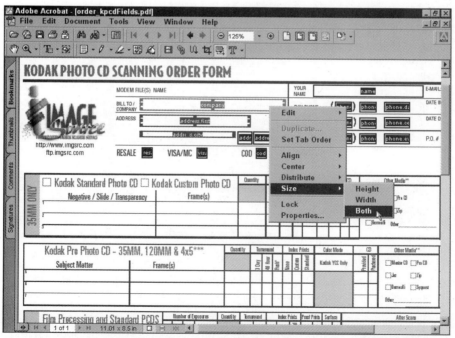

Figure 5-12: To size fields to a common field size, select all the fields to be sized, and click on the field to be used as the anchor field. Open a context menu and choose Size ➪ *option*. Where *option* is a choice for Height, Width, or Both.

If fields need only a Height or Width adjustment, make the respective choice in the context menu.

Distributing fields

Of the three options for organizing fields discussed here, the Distribute command is one you are likely to use quite often. If you duplicate fields and have no need for alignment or sizing, adjusting fields to be equidistant from each other is handled by the Distribute command. Rather than use an anchor field, Distribute assesses the top field position in a column (left in a row) and the bottom field position (right in a row) and adjusts the distance for all selected fields in the column (or row) to make them equidistant to each other.

To use the Distribute command, select a group of fields in a column and open a context menu. Choose Distribute ➪ Vertically (use Horizontally when distributing rows), as shown in Figure 5-13.

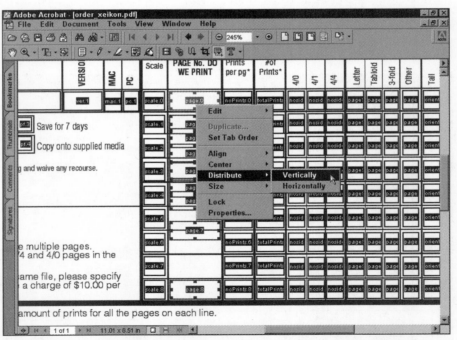

Figure 5-13: To set the fields in a column to be equidistant to each other, select the fields and open a context menu. Choose Distribute ➪ Vertically.

After selecting the menu command, the individual fields are positioned with a uniform distance between the field rectangles, as shown in Figure 5-14.

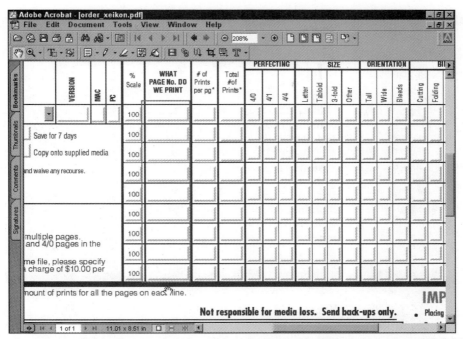

Figure 5-14: Select the Hand tool and view the fields after distributing them. All fields appear with equal distance between the field boxes.

Deleting fields

Deleting fields can be accomplished through several means. The field or fields to be deleted must first be selected before addressing any menu commands or keys on the keyboard. After selecting a field(s), press the Delete key (Windows) or Delete (Backspace) key (Mac OS). You can also choose Edit ➪ Delete to remove the selected field(s). If you select a field or group of fields and open a context menu, choose Edit ➪ Delete, as shown in Figure 5-15.

If duplicate fields with the same field names appear anywhere in the open PDF file and you attempt to delete one of the fields, Acrobat opens an alert dialog box, as shown in Figure 5-16. If you want to delete only one of the identical fields, click No. If all fields with the same name are to be deleted, click Yes.

Note When the alert dialog box opens and suggests more than one field will be deleted, all fields are deleted if you select Yes whether they are selected or deselected. Exercise care when deleting a field among a group of fields with identical names. If uncertain about what fields will be deleted, click No and check the fields on the form.

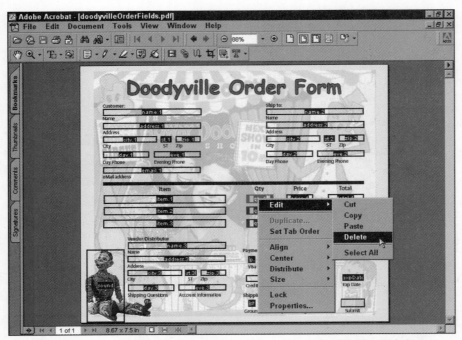

Figure 5-15: To delete fields with a context menu, select the field(s) and choose Edit ➪ Delete in the context menu.

Figure 5-16: If fields have the same name and you attempt to delete one of the fields, Acrobat opens an alert dialog box. Click No to delete only the selected field or Yes to delete all fields with the same name whether selected or not.

Creating Table Arrays

A nice new addition to Acrobat 5 is the ability to create tables. This feature can save you much time when creating long lists of columns and rows. A table in Acrobat represents all the fields across each row and all the fields down each column. To automatically create a table, you need to first create a single row or column of fields.

After the single row or column is created, you use a different modifier key to select the fields and drag the cursor in the direction to fill the table. To understand how to create tables in more detail, follow these steps:

On the CD-ROM To follow the steps in this exercise, use the `xeikon_order.pdf` file that you'll find in the Chapter 5 folder on the book's CD-ROM.

1. Create fields across a row for several columns. In this example do not use parent/child names.

2. Press the Shift key (Windows) or ⌘ key (Mac OS) and draw a marquee around the fields to select them. The selected fields appear with a dashed line around the selection. When the cursor is placed over the center handle, it changes to a vertical line with an arrowhead at either end, as shown in Figure 5-17.

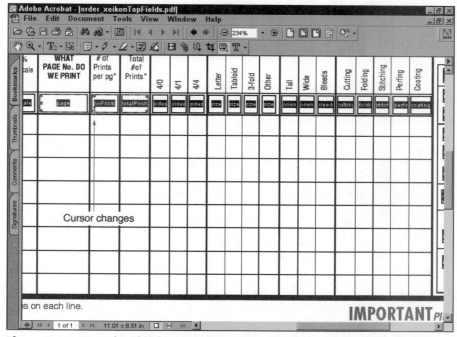

Figure 5-17: Press the Shift key (Windows) or ⌘ key (Mac OS) and marquee the fields to be used in the array. When the cursor is positioned over the center handle, the cursor appearance changes to a vertical line with arrowheads.

Note   If you have any fields with duplicate field names used for Radio buttons or Check boxes, do not include them in your selection. An array cannot be created when duplicate field names are used. Select all fields that do not have duplicate names to create the array, as shown in Figure 5-17. In this example, only selected fields with unique names are used.

3. Place the cursor over the center handle. Press the Ctrl key (Windows) or ⌘ key (Mac OS) and drag down (Figure 5-18).

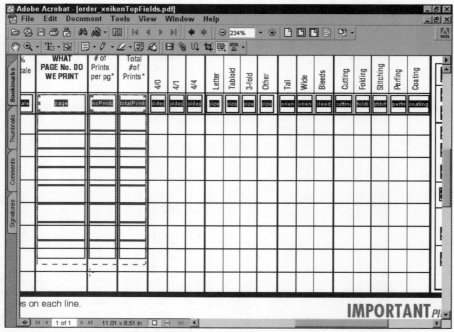

Figure 5-18: After dragging the center handle down, the fields to be duplicated appear within the marquee selection.

4. Strike the Numeric Pad Enter key or the Return/Enter key. The fields are duplicated. Acrobat likewise names all the fields with parent/child names beginning with *field*.0 where *field* is the name of the field provided in the top row.

5. The fields need to be distributed after they have been created. Acrobat cannot distribute multiple columns. Therefore, you need to distribute each column individually. Move the bottom row in the first column down to position, select the fields in the first column, and open a context menu. Select Distribute from the menu choices as described earlier in this chapter. Repeat the process for each column, as shown in Figure 5-19.

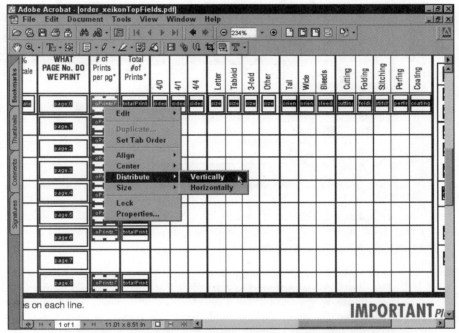

Figure 5-19: Move the last row down to position. Begin with the first column and select all fields in the column. Open a context menu and choose Distribute ➪ Vertically. Repeat the process for each column.

When fields have the same name, you need to duplicate the fields with the other method described earlier in this chapter. Each of the duplicate named fields need to have parent/child names in order to duplicate each row. Press the Ctrl key (Windows) or Shift key (Mac OS) and select the row that needs duplication. Ctrl+click (Windows) or Option+click (Mac OS) and drag down to position. Press the plus (+) key to increment the field name and repeat the process, as shown in Figure 5-20. Continue with the same steps until all rows have been populated.

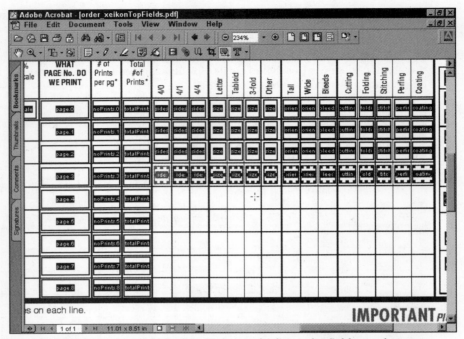

Figure 5-20: For fields with duplicate names, duplicate the fields one by one as described earlier in this chapter.

Note

In Chapter 3, "Understanding Field Types," it was made clear that Radio buttons and Check boxes designed to offer either/or choices should be named the same field name. When one button is selected, the other fields with the same name are deselected. For these kinds of fields you need to use the field duplication method described above. If a Radio button or Check box is not designed to be used for either/or responses, then be certain to provide unique names. When the field names are unique, they can also be included among selected fields for creating arrays.

After completing the form, be certain to test all your fields. Begin at the top row, as shown in Figure 5-21, and fill in the fields with dummy data to be certain all fields accept the data as you expect.

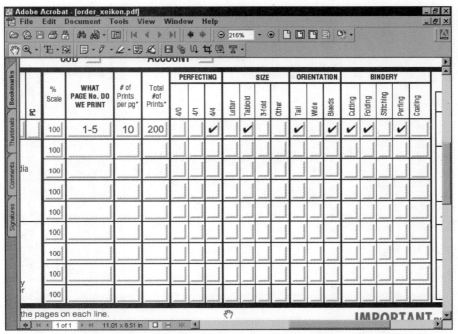

Figure 5-21: After completing your form, be certain to test the fields with dummy data to be certain all fields work properly.

Setting Tab Order

When a user fills in a form, pressing the Tab key sends the cursor to the next field in the established field order. The order is determined in the same order you add fields when you create the form. Typically there will always be adjustments, and fields will commonly be created out of a logical tab order. Before you distribute the final form, be certain to check the tab order to see if tabbing through the document has a logical flow.

To view the tab order at a glance, you must first select the Form tool, then choose Tools ➪ Forms ➪ Fields ➪ Set Tab Order, as shown in Figure 5-22.

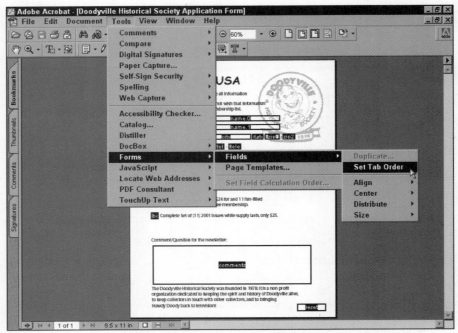

Figure 5-22: To set the Field Tab order, first select the Form tool then choose Tools ⇨ Forms ⇨ Fields ⇨ Set Tab Order.

To practice resetting the tab order, use the doodyvilleApplication.pdf file that you'll find in the Chapter 5 folder on the book's CD-ROM.

After executing the menu command, Acrobat displays all the fields on a page with a number indicating the tab order, as shown in Figure 5-23. When a user presses the Tab key, the first field is selected. If the field is a Text field, a blinking cursor appears inside field number 1 indicating that the field is ready to accept type. If a field other than a text field is the first field on the page, the field becomes high-lighted with a focus rectangle.

For setting Focus Rectangle preferences, see Chapter 4, "Understanding Field Properties."

In Figure 5-23, the first field is numbered 8 indicating it will be the 8th field selected when the user tabs through the fields. On this form, the tab order needs to be reset. To begin organizing the tab order, click on the first field where you expect the user to begin data entry. Clicking on field 8 in this example changes the number to 1. Click each successive field in logical order to renumber all the fields.

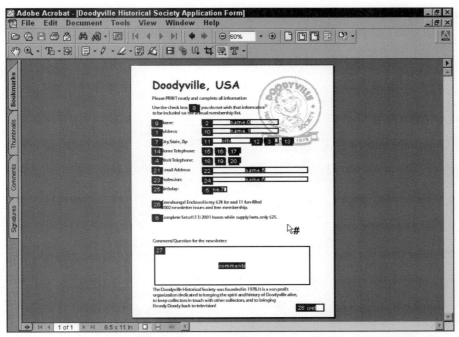

Figure 5-23: When you choose Tools ⇨ Forms ⇨ Fields ⇨ Set Tab Order, all the fields appear with numbers indicating the current tab order.

Often you will find that some fields in the middle of the document may need reordering. Rather than click through all the fields beginning with the first field, you can instruct Acrobat to begin your sequence anywhere in the document. Figure 5-24 shows fields 15 and 16 following field 12. In this example, fields 15 and 16 need to be changed to 13 and 14 following field number 12.

To reorder fields from any position other than the first field, press the Ctrl key (Windows) or Option key (Mac OS) and click on the field preceding the field to be changed. In this example, hold the Ctrl/Option key down and click on field 12. This action tells Acrobat you wish to begin on field 12 and the next field you click on becomes field 13. Move the cursor to the field numbered 15 and click. The field changes from 15 to 13 or the number following the field you selected with the modifier key. Continue clicking on subsequent fields to reorder all fields out of logical tab order. When you complete the reorder process, the form displays the new order.

Tip

If a large number of fields are added to a form and you have a group that needs to be at the end of the tab order, you can choose Edit ⇨ Cut. Return to the Edit menu and select Paste. When you cut fields and paste them back into the form, the pasted fields occupy the last tab order.

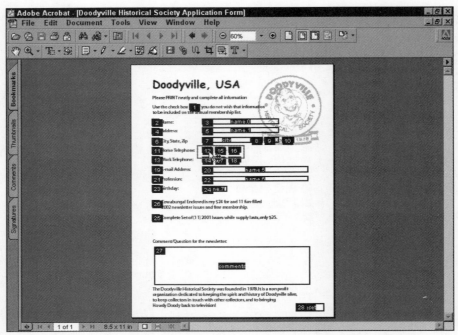

Figure 5-24: This document shows fields 15 and 16 following field number 12. The reordering of the fields needs to begin with 12 followed by 13 and 14.

Spell Checking Fields

Acrobat offers you dynamic spell checking for form field entries as you type. Much like word-processing programs, spelling errors are noted with a red underline for all suspect words. If Acrobat does not have a word in its dictionary, the word is flagged with a red underline. You can add words to the dictionary and customize it to suit your industry or individual needs. In addition, several dictionaries are available for foreign language usage and special industries.

Auto spell checking

When you assign field properties for either Combo boxes or Text fields, you can determine whether spell checking will occur when data are entered in the field. For both these field types, the Options settings in the Field Properties dialog box offer you the option for leaving spell checking on or turning it off. If you leave the check box unchecked for Do Not Spell Check, as shown in Figure 5-25, spell checking is performed automatically as the user enters data in a field.

Figure 5-25: When Combo box and Text fields are to be spell checked, leave the check box unchecked for Do Not Spell Check.

When you create fields for proper names, it may be a good idea to enable the check box. A client's name and a manufacturer's product you might list on a form are some examples of names not needing spell checking.

When text is entered in a field box with spell checking enabled, the suspect words appear with a red underline, as shown in Figure 5-26.

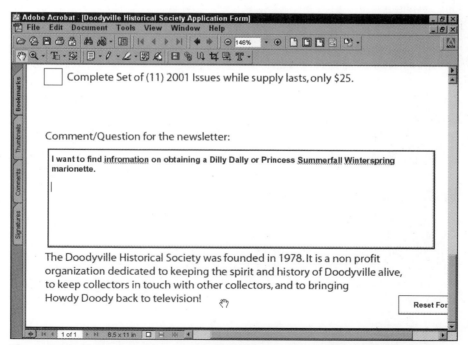

Figure 5-26: Suspect words are underlined in red when spell checking is enabled.

As one reviews the text, you can easily see the misspelled words. Move the cursor to the words to be corrected and either click and insert type or delete the necessary characters to edit the text. As you correct words, Acrobat continues the spell checking. If the word in question is found in the loaded dictionary, you can continue changing characters until the red underline disappears. In Figure 5-27, the spelling was corrected on the words found in Acrobat's dictionary, but the proper names are still flagged for misspellings.

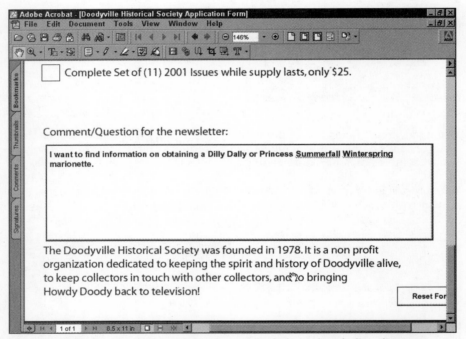

Figure 5-27: When the corrected words are typed, the red underline disappears from the previous suspects. Proper names not found in Acrobat's dictionary remain as suspects.

Manual spell checking

You can spell check Comments and Form fields by using the Spell Check Form Fields and Comments tool in the Acrobat Command Bar or by choosing Tools ➪ Spelling ➪ Spell Check Form Fields and Comments or by pressing the F7 key on your keyboard. Executing any of these actions opens the Check Spelling dialog box, as shown in Figure 5-28.

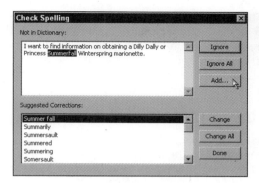

Figure 5-28: Click on the Spell Check Form Fields and Comments tool in the Acrobat Command Bar or press F7 to open the Check Spelling dialog box.

Acrobat checks the spelling on all comments and form fields. When a suspect is found, a list at the bottom of the dialog box offers suggestions for correctly spelled words with close matches. Click Ignore to move to the next word or you can select a word in the list and click the Change button to change the spelling to a match in the list or you can add a word if Acrobat does not offer a substitution.

Managing dictionaries

To use a dictionary for another language or load a dictionary for a specific industry such as legal, medical, or science/technical, choose Edit ⇨ Preferences ⇨ General to open the Preferences dialog box. In the left pane, select Spelling. The left pane displays the available dictionaries you can use, as shown in Figure 5-29.

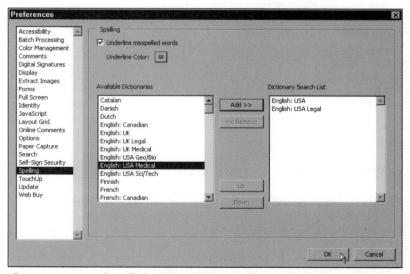

Figure 5-29: You handle loading additional dictionaries in the Preferences dialog box.

To load another dictionary, click on the name from the scrollable list and select the Add button. The dictionary is added to the Dictionary Search List. Click OK in the Preferences dialog box and run the spell checker. All words found in comments and form fields are checked against all dictionaries listed under the Dictionary Search List.

Adding words to a custom dictionary

You can create a custom dictionary and add words to it. Acrobat keeps track of your dictionary and lists all the words added to the dictionary in a list. At any time you can remove items from the list and delete them from your dictionary. To create a custom dictionary, choose Tools ⇨ Spelling ⇨ Edit Dictionary.

The Edit Dictionary dialog box opens. In the Word field, type the word that you want to add to your dictionary. Click on the Add button and the word appears in the list box below the Word field, as shown in Figure 5-30. To delete a word from the dictionary, click on the word in the lower list and select the Remove button.

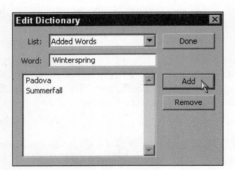

Figure 5-30: To add words to a custom dictionary, enter a word in the Word field and click on the Add button in the Edit Dictionary dialog box.

Click Done when finished. Regardless of the dictionary you select in the Preferences dialog box, your custom dictionary is always active. Check the spelling in a document and the words are matched against all loaded dictionaries and your custom dictionary.

Creating Tool Tips

As an added assistance to users completing forms, you can add tool tips much like those found in application software programs to describe tools in toolbars. A tool tip by default appears as a pop-up message inside a yellow rectangle. A tool tip opens when the cursor is placed over a form field. You can set the message that appears in the tool tip in the Field Properties dialog box.

Tool tips are available for all field types. To create a tool tip, open the Field Properties dialog box and select the Appearance tab. The item for Short Description is where you type the message that becomes the tool tip. In Figure 5-31, "Customer address" is added in the Short Description field.

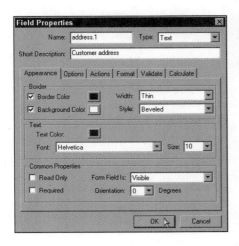

Figure 5-31: The message typed in the Short Description field in the Appearance properties determines what message appears in the tool tip.

Click OK in the Field Properties dialog box and select the Hand tool (H) when you return to the Document Pane. Place the cursor over the field where the Short Description was supplied. Notice in Figure 5-32, the message for *Customer address* appears as a tool tip.

Note   Short Descriptions serve dual purposes. When creating accessible forms, the Short Description field is used for instructions for users with screen readers.

Cross-Reference   For more on creating accessible forms and using the Short Description field, look over Chapter 12, "Working with Accessible and Tagged PDFs."

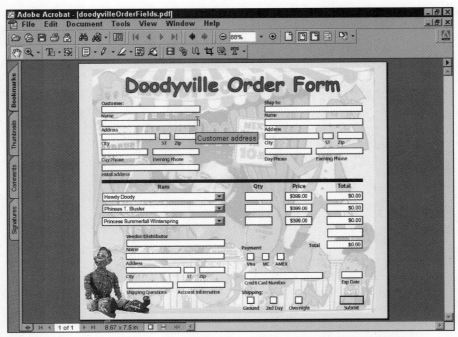

Figure 5-32: When the cursor is placed over a field with a Short Description message, the tool tip opens displaying the message.

Using the Fields Palette

As another item for managing fields, Acrobat 5 introduced a Fields palette. To open the palette, choose Window ➪ Fields. The palette opens in the Document Pane. All the fields created on a form are listed by name in the palette. When you use parent/child field names, a parent name is listed like a bookmark with all child fields listed in a nested hierarchy. In Windows, field names can be expanded by clicking on the plus (+) symbol in the palette, as shown in Figure 5-33.

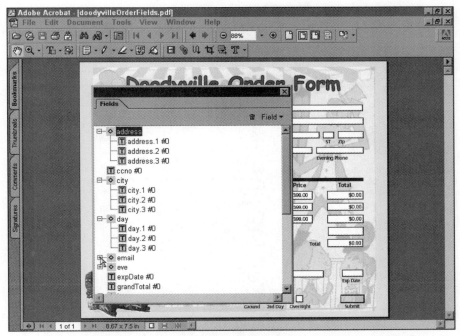

Figure 5-33: Nested lists can be expanded in Windows by clicking on the plus (+) symbol adjacent to a parent name.

On the Mac OS, you expand nested fields by clicking on the right-pointing arrow, as shown in Figure 5-34.

In addition to the lists of fields, you have menu commands available from a pull-down menu in the palette. The same commands explained earlier in this chapter for organizing fields are provided in the palette menu as well as other menu commands like creating page templates and setting the calculation order. To open the palette menu, click on the down-pointing arrow adjacent to the word *Field* at the top of the palette.

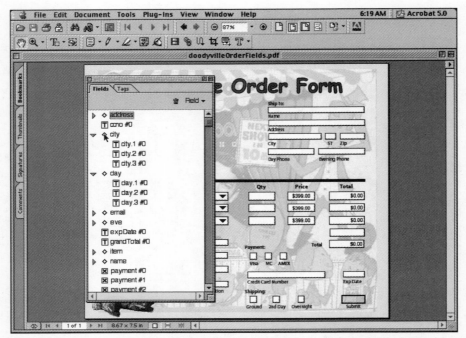

Figure 5-34: On the Mac OS, click on the right-pointing arrow to expand a nested list.

If you select a field in the palette and open a context menu, menu options are available with choices a little different than those found when opening a context menu in the Document Pane. Figure 5-35 shows the menu options available when opening a context menu in the Fields palette.

Among the context menu choices is the menu command Go To Field. This command can be very helpful when creating forms with extraordinary numbers of fields. You can find field names in the palette, select the field in the palette, then choose the command. Acrobat highlights the field on any page in the PDF document where the selected field is located. If you need to address a field's properties without locating the field in the document, you can click on the field name and choose Properties from the context menu options.

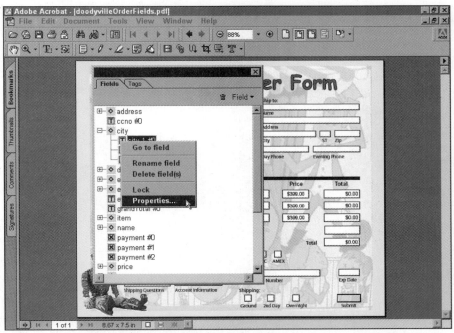

Figure 5-35: Select a field in the Fields palette and open a context menu. Among the menu choices is the Go To Field command that finds a selected field in a document.

Renaming fields

The Fields palette offers you an advantage when global renaming of fields is needed. You can edit a parent name at the root of the hierarchy in the Fields palette and all fields with child names change automatically. In the Fields palette, select a parent name and open a context menu. From the menu options, choose Rename Field, as shown in Figure 5-36.

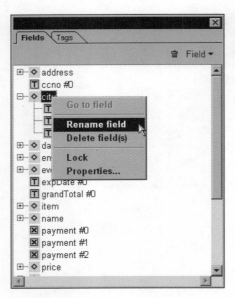

Figure 5-36: Select a field in the Fields palette and open a context menu. From the menu options, choose Rename Field.

The field name can be selected or the cursor can be inserted anywhere on the line of text representing the field name. Edit the text to rename the field, as shown in Figure 5-37.

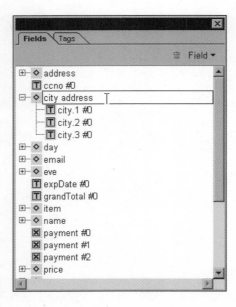

Figure 5-37: Edit the text for the field name in the Fields palette.

When the name has been changed, press the Numeric Pad Enter or Enter/Return key. The name is now changed for all parent names in the group, as shown in Figure 5-38. If you make a mistake, the operation is undoable. Choose Edit ➪ Undo Multiple Field Property Change or press Ctrl+Z (Windows) or ⌘+Z (Mac OS).

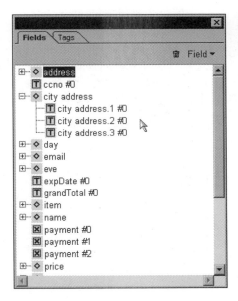

Figure 5-38: After editing the field name and pressing the Enter key, all field names in the parent list are changed.

Locking fields

Acrobat enables you to lock a field against inadvertently moving it around the document page. Locking fields can be made through context menu commands by selecting the field in the Document Pane or by opening a context menu in the Fields palette. When a field is locked, it's not totally protected. You can cut the field from the page and set the tab order on locked fields. If you attempt to edit the properties of a locked field, Acrobat opens a warning dialog box and asks if you want to unlock the field.

To unlock fields, return to a context menu and choose Unlock. When the context menus are opened from a selected field, either Lock or Unlock appears as a menu choice. If Lock is displayed as a menu option, the field is currently unlocked. The converse is true for locked fields.

Docking the Fields palette in the Navigation Pane

The Fields palette can be a handy tool when you create forms in Acrobat. To make the palette easily accessible, you can add it (dock it) to the Navigation Pane. Click on the Navigation tool on the Acrobat Command Bar or press the F5 key on your keyboard. When the Navigation Pane is in view, click on the Fields palette tab and drag it to the top of the Navigation Pane, as shown in Figure 5-39. You can also dock the palette without opening the Document Pane. Drag the palette tab to the Navigation Pane where other tabs appear and release the mouse button. Either way, the Fields palette is docked in the Navigation Pane.

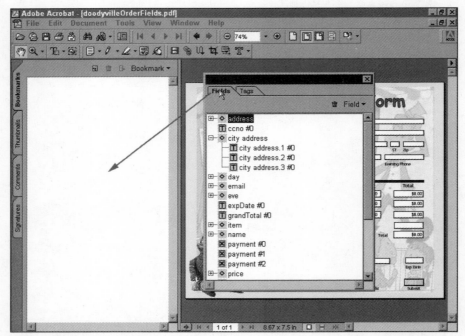

Figure 5-39: Click on the tab in the Fields palette and drag it to the Navigation Pane to dock it.

When the Fields palette tab appears in the Navigation Pane, click on the tab to open it. You can view all the fields in the scrollable window and expand or collapse field groups in the same manner as when using the Fields palette in a window. Figure 5-40 shows the Fields palette expanded in the Navigation Pane.

Tip   To undock the Fields palette and hide it from view, you must first open the palette in the Navigation Pane by clicking on the Fields tab. When the palette is open, drag the Fields tab out of the Navigation Pane and into the Document Pane. Click on the X in the top right corner for Windows or on the X in the top left corner for Mac OS.

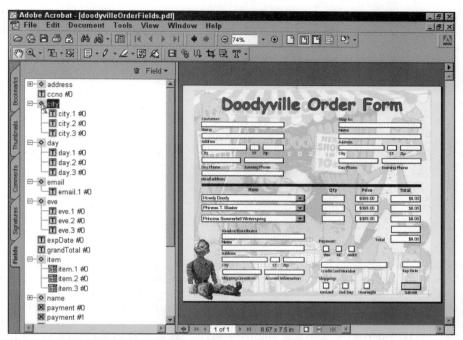

Figure 5-40: After docking the Fields palette, click on the tab to open it in the Navigation Pane.

Creating Multiple Fields Property Changes

You may have a need to create a change on all the fields on a form. Acrobat is limited in handling global changes for field properties with good reason. Different field types don't have all the same properties and therefore cannot be globally changed. However, the one common property among all fields is the Appearance settings. Assume you created fields without a key line border or background color. Or you later decide the point size for type is not large enough. These kinds of properties can be globally changed in a single access of the Field Properties dialog box regardless of what field types have been added to the form.

To change properties for all fields on a form, choose Edit ⇨ Select All or press Ctrl (Windows) or ⌘+A (Mac OS). All the fields become selected. To open the Field Properties dialog box, select Properties from a context menu or press Enter on the Numeric Pad or press the Enter/Return key. The Field Properties display Appearance properties if fields of different types are selected. If all selected fields are of the same type, you have additional opportunities for global changes in the Options properties, as shown in Figure 5-41.

Figure 5-41: When fields of different types are selected, the Field Properties dialog box displays only the Appearance properties. As an example, for Text fields you can change Appearances and Options.

In the Appearance dialog box, you can make changes for the Border, Background, Fonts, and the Common Property settings. If you see a "?" inside any color swatches, as shown in Figure 5-41, different colors are used for the respective item among separate fields. To change any properties, including those with mixed values such as colors, click on the respective item and make the necessary changes. Click OK in the Field Properties dialog box and the global changes take effect.

Tip   When changing colors where fields have been assigned different colors and you want to change all fields to a common color, deselect the Border and Background colors. Click again on the check boxes and select the color for Border and Background. Acrobat requires you to first eliminate the attributes and then reassign them.

If you select fields of common types, you can make more global changes. The Options properties are added to the Appearance settings when like fields are selected where global Options settings can be changed.

Make the changes in the Options dialog box and click OK. The changes are made globally for all like fields selected. One reason you might use this option is when changing text alignment in Text fields for a group. Make the choice in the Options properties and you can globally change text alignment for a group of selected text fields.

Summary

✦ You should exercise much care when naming form fields. When possible, you should use parent/child names in which calculation fields are positioned in columns and rows or when fields need to be duplicated in a form.

✦ You can copy and paste all field types on pages, between pages, and between documents.

✦ A context menu provides many menu commands for organizing fields and ordering them on a form. All fields are organized in reference to the anchor field.

✦ You can create tables by using modifier keys to select and drag fields to form arrays. Arrays require each duplicated field to have a unique field name.

✦ After completing a form, you should check the field tab order and readjust the order to create a logical progression through fields.

✦ Form fields can be spell-checked dynamically with Acrobat's spell check feature.

✦ You can create tool tips by adding Short Descriptions in the Field Properties dialog box.

✦ The Fields palette provides easy access to all form fields. Context menus and palette menus offer you editing control over all fields in a document.

✦ You can change properties in limited fashion for a selection of multiple fields.

✦　　✦　　✦

Calculating Field Data

The preset operations in Acrobat used for calculations are limited to a few. If you need more calculating power than Acrobat provides in the Calculation properties, JavaScripts must be used. With both the preset calculations and JavaScripts, all the numbers in your data fields need to be properly formatted before a calculation can be made. In this chapter we'll start with formatting data fields and work with some calculations using preset formulas, validating data, and resetting form fields.

Cross-Reference For calculations with JavaScripts, see Part II, "Working JavaScript," beginning with Chapter 7, "Getting Started with JavaScript."

Formatting Text Fields

As was described in Chapter 4, "Understanding Field Properties," number formats are established in the Format properties. When you begin to create form fields, you should think of how the fields will be used on the form and address the formatting as you create them. This is particularly valuable when duplicating fields or creating table arrays. If the formats are not properly defined when fields are created, you need to delete any duplicated fields, format the top row or left column fields, then repeat the duplication or recreate the array. Much time will be saved if you plan ahead and format fields as they are created. In terms of appearances, as was discussed in Chapter 5, "Creating Form Fields," appearance attributes can be globally changed on a form. However, formats for data cannot be globally changed.

Formatting dates

For the description of date formats and the following number formats discussed in this section, the `expenseDataRaw.pdf` file that is located in the Chapter 6 folder on the book's CD-ROM is used. To perform the exercises in this section, refer to the PDF file, as shown in Figure 6-1.

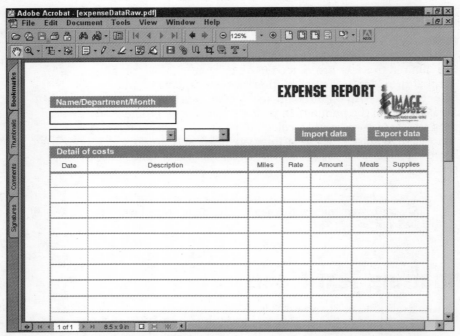

Figure 6-1: The expenseData.pdf file has a few data fields created for you with the remaining portion of the form designed for creating several field types with different formats.

On the CD-ROM   Refer to the `expenseDataRaw.pdf` file for the blank form with no fields. To see a version of the form with populated fields, refer to the `expenseData.pdf` file. Both forms are located in the Chapter 6 folder on the book's CD-ROM.

In the first column on the form that is shown in Figure 6-1, create the date fields. To create and format the field attributes, follow these steps:

1. Create a field box using the Form tool for the first date field in the left column.

2. In the Appearance settings, disable the Border and Background items and set the font size to 10 point. The name provided for the field in this example is `thisDate`. Notice the field name does not use a parent/child name. The reason for this is, when you eventually create an array, Acrobat automatically supplies child names.

3. Click on the Options tab and set the Alignment to Right, as shown in Figure 6-2.

4. Click on the Format tab.

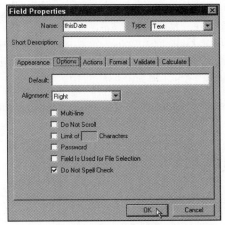

Figure 6-2: The alignment for the date entered in the field will be aligned Right.

5. Click on Date in the left column. Enter **mm/dd/yy** in the field box at the bottom right side of the dialog box, as shown in Figure 6-3.

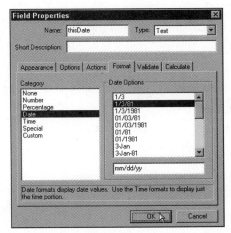

Figure 6-3: Type the date format to be used in the field box or select the date format from the scrollable list.

Note You can equally select the 01/03/81 item in the list. Acrobat provides you with two options for defining the format.

6. Click OK.

7. When you return to the form, enter text in the field box to test it. Notice, if you type a number for the current month, Acrobat provides the day and year from your system clock. Likewise, if you enter 1/1/02, Acrobat changes the date to match the format described in the Field Properties. In this example, the format was set up to express dates as 01/01/02.

8. Add a text field for the Description column and assign the same appearance formats. Eventually a table array will be created to duplicate fields down the columns. The array will be created from all the fields contained in the first row.

Formatting whole numbers

The next column on the form is for *Miles* that will be multiplied by a *Rate* to yield a *Total*. The amount of the mileage needs to be a number; however, if the format for the field is left to none, then the calculation will be made on a whole number. You can leave some fields set to the None format and create calculations; however, if the result field where the calculation is to be displayed is left to None in the Format properties, no data will appear in the field. In this example, if you format Miles for a number, format Rate for a number, and leave Amount at None, then the calculation results will not appear in the Amount field. Therefore, the most critical format is the Amount field.

As you work with forms and create calculation fields, it will save you time if you employ consistency. With regard to number formats, it is best to format each field regardless of whether the field needs formatting. Be consistent and it will save you time in having to go back and find out why a result is not being displayed in a given field.

In this exercise, rather than use a whole number for Miles, follow these steps to format numbers with one decimal place:

1. Create a field for Miles in the first row. The name provided in this example is thisMiles.

2. Click on the Format tab.

3. Select Number in the left pane and type **1** for the number of Decimal Places, as shown in Figure 6-4.

4. Click OK.

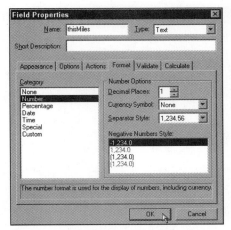

Figure 6-4: In the Format properties, set the Category to Number and set the Decimal Places to 1.

Setting number defaults

Values for fixed rates can be established in the Field Properties dialog box. There are many reasons why you may wish to use a fixed value. Among the most important is in preventing user error. Suppose you have an order form for a customer to order a product. You have a variety of items that have fixed prices. Rather than let the user supply a price in a field box, you can use a default value and lock the field against user entry. In this example, there is a fixed rate for calculating mileage reimbursement. Any row on the form a user completes will use the same rate factor to calculate the reimbursement amount.

To create a fixed rate and lock the field against user entry, follow these steps:

1. Create a field for the top row for the Rate and name the field thisRate.

2. In the Appearance properties, check the box for Read Only, as shown in Figure 6-5. When Read Only is enabled, the user cannot edit the field.

Users can open a field box and reset a Read Only field to unlock the field thereby permitting access to the field contents. If you use a Read Only field to lock out a user and to prevent changes, you need to use Acrobat Security to protect your form against user modifications.

For more on using Acrobat Security, see Chapter 11, "Using Acrobat Security."

3. Click on the Options tab. In the Default field box enter **.30**, as shown in Figure 6-6. The default supplied here becomes the value of the field. Any calculations performed when using this field use the default you add to this field box.

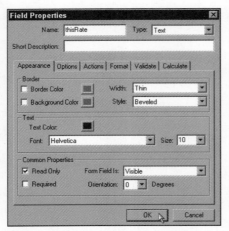

Figure 6-5: Check the box for Read Only in the Appearance properties to prevent a user from changing the rate.

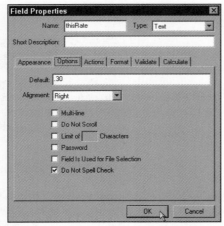

Figure 6-6: The Default described in the Options properties is used for all calculations when the field is used in a formula.

4. Click on the Format tab. Regardless of the format used as the Default, the number format established in the Format properties supercedes any other formats. Therefore, if you type .30 and select 1 for the decimal place, the field box shows 0.3 as the value. In order to display two decimal places, you need to format the field to hold the two decimal places.

5. Select Number in the Category list and enter **2** for the decimal places.

6. Click OK. When you return to the Document Pane, click on the Hand tool and view the field box. The display shows 0.30. Move the cursor over the field and you'll notice the field cannot be edited.

7. Choose File ⇨ Save to save the new edits made on the file before moving on to creating calculations.

Using Preset Calculation Formulas

The preset calculations in Acrobat offer you a limited number of field calculations that can be made from selecting the menu options in the Calculate properties. Simple math calculations like division and subtraction are missing from the preset formulas. For these and many more sophisticated operations, you need to create JavaScripts. At this time, we'll look at using some of the preset calculation formulas and learn about JavaScripts in the next chapter.

Calculating a product

As mentioned earlier, setting the format for a number is critically important for fields that acquire data through calculations. In the Amount field in this example, you need to create a calculation to produce the product of the Miles field and the Rate field. The first step is to format the Amount field and then specify the calculation in the Calculate properties. Follow these steps to complete the Amount field:

1. Create a field for the first Amount position. This field is named thisAmount.

2. Click on the Format tab and select Number for the Category. Select 2 decimal places and select a Currency Symbol. In this example a Dollar symbol is used, as shown in Figure 6-7.

3. Click on the Calculate tab. From the pull-down menu select product (x) as shown in Figure 6-8.

4. Fields can be added to the field box by typing the names and separating fields with commas. If you add fields by typing the names in the field box, be certain to place commas separating fields. You can also select the fields to be used in the calculation in the Select a Field dialog box. Click on Pick to open the dialog box.

5. Select the fields to be used in the calculation. Click on thisMiles and click the Add button, as shown in Figure 6-9. Click on thisRate and click on the Add button again. When finished adding fields, click on the Close button.

Note   If you select the parent name without a child extension, Acrobat uses all the fields with the same parent name in the formula. When creating calculations on different fields, be certain to identify the individual field names.

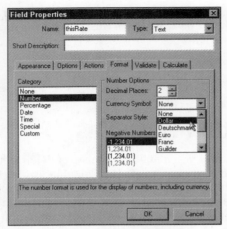

Figure 6-7: The calculation field is formatted for two decimal places and uses a currency symbol.

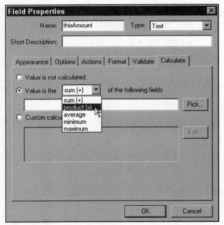

Figure 6-8: To multiply two or more fields, select product (x) in the Calculate properties.

6. Notice when you return to the Field Properties dialog box that the field names are displayed in the field box, as shown in Figure 6-10. If you wish to change an item, you can do so by editing the text or returning to the Select a Field dialog box. Also note that if you enter names without quotation marks and reopen the Field Properties dialog box, Acrobat automatically supplies quotes.

7. Click OK and test the calculation. Be certain to verify the calculation produces the correct result before moving on to duplicating any fields.

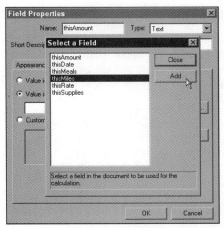

Figure 6-9: Click on the fields to be added to the calculation and click the Add button after selecting each individual field.

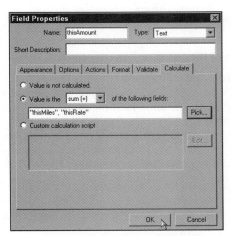

Figure 6-10: The fields added to the calculation are displayed in the Calculate properties. You can edit the names if changes need to be made.

8. The last two fields on the form are data fields to hold currency values without calculations. Add the two fields to complete the first row of data fields. In this example `thisMeals` and `thisSupplies` are used for the last two field names. In the Format properties, be certain to select two decimal places and the currency symbol as described earlier.

Creating sums

In a real-world situation you might now create the array and populate the remaining rows in the first section of the example form. Doing so enables you to test the total fields as they are created. For instructional purposes and working through a logical flow, you can postpone the field duplication until we look at more calculations to be performed in the Calculate properties.

At the bottom of the form in the Summary section, you need to create field totals for Miles, Amount, Meals, and Supplies. Each of these four new fields will use the sum (+) preset formula in the Calculation properties. To create the total for the Miles field, follow these steps:

1. Create a field in the Summary section of the form in the Miles column. Name the field `thisMilesTotal`. Notice a parent/child name is not used for the field. The total items won't need to be replicated so there is no need to add the extension to the filename.

2. Click on the Format tab in the Field Properties dialog box. To remain consistent with the fields in the Miles column, use the same number format. In the Format properties, select Number and set the Decimal Places to 1, as described earlier.

3. Click on the Calculate tab. In the Calculate properties select sum (+) from the pull-down menu options.

4. Click on the Pick button to open the Select a Field dialog box.

5. Select `thisMiles` in the list and click on the Add button. This is a temporary calculation because you do not yet have fields described with parent/child names. After you create the array, the column is added for the fields with the same parent name. For the sum of the fields, the calculation is performed for all fields using different child names that have the same parent name. Therefore, `thisMiles.1`, `thisMiles.2`, `thisMiles.3`, and so on can be summed by adding `thisMiles` in the calculate properties, as shown in Figure 6-11.

6. Click Close in the Select a Field dialog box. When you return to the Field Properties dialog box, the name selected in the Select a Field list is displayed in quotation marks. Click OK to leave the Field Properties dialog box.

7. Create a second field for the Amount total.

8. Set the Format for the field for a number with 2 decimal places and a currency symbol, then click on the Calculate tab.

9. In the Calculate dialog box, click the cursor in the field box and type **thisAmount**. Be certain to type the name exactly as used in the first field in the `thisAmount` column while observing the same letter case. Rather than use the Select a Field dialog box, you can just add the line of text.

10. Create the last two fields in the Summary for Meals and Supplies. Name the fields `thisMealsTotal` and `thisSuppliesTotal`.

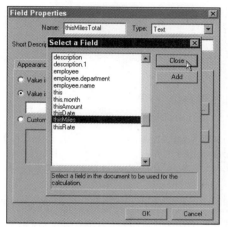

Figure 6-11: To calculate a sum of fields with different child names, the parent name is selected in the Calculate properties. The fields with the child names are created after the array is created.

Tip   To speed up the process, you can duplicate the Amount field by pressing Ctrl (Windows) or Options (Mac OS) and click-dragging to the right. With the field selected, press the Enter key to open the Field Properties. Change the field name and click on the Calculate tab. Change the parent name within quotation marks to correspond with the name of the fields to be totaled. Because the Amount and remaining fields formats are the same, it saves you time scrolling through the tabs to set the Field Properties.

Creating averages

On the example form, I want to create fields to average the amounts for all those fields that are totaled. The data is just informative for the user. For an expense account form it tells the user what the average costs for travel, meal expenses, and supply expenses are for the month. Averages can also be calculated with the preset formulas in the Calculate properties.

However, there is a caveat in using the preset average calculation Acrobat offers you. The calculation is made on the total number of fields in a group regardless of whether there are data in any fields. In this example, there are 12 rows to hold data when you create the array. If only 2 rows of data are filled in, all the averages are calculated on the 12 rows instead of 2 rows. In this case you can use the average formula and delete unpopulated fields after a form has been completed. For a better solution, you can add a JavaScript that is explained in the next chapter. Awkward as it may be for this form, to understand averages let's look at creating averages. Follow these steps:

1. Create a field for the Miles average in the first line of the History row. Name the field `thisMilesAverage`. Again there is no need to use a parent/child name.

2. Set the format to match the Miles fields. See the format for the Miles fields used above.

3. Click on the Calculate tab and select Average from the pull-down menu.

4. Use the parent name for the value, as shown in Figure 6-12.

5. Rather than repeat the same process, try another method for the next field. Press the Ctrl key (Windows) or Option key (Mac OS) and click-drag the `thisAmountTotal` field into the History row. The field is duplicated along with the Field Properties.

6. Press the Enter key to open the Field Properties dialog box. Change the field name to `thisAmountAverage`.

7. Click on the Calculate tab and select Average from the pull-down menu. No other changes are required because the parent name is the same and the Format properties match the original field. Click OK and you're ready to move to the next field. Repeat the process for the last two fields in the History row. Note: Be certain to change the name of each duplicated field.

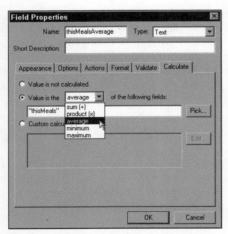

Figure 6-12: Select average from the pull-down menu and supply the parent name in the value field.

Using Arrays with Calculation Scripts

In Chapter 5, "Creating Form Fields," table arrays was discussed for easy duplication of data fields. When you have fields with calculations made from individual field names like those found in rows and columns, the calculations are made from exact field names within a given row or column. After you create an array, Acrobat adds unique field names for the new fields created in the array. However, any calculations among fields in the array are not changed to reflect the new field names. There are options available with JavaScript to simplify the process that is covered in Chapter 8, "Writing JavaScript Routines." However, without using a JavaScript routine, you need to revisit each calculation within an array and change the calculation formula individually for those fields containing calculations.

In terms of designing forms, it will always be easier and much faster to create table arrays and then go back and edit fields with calculations. To create individual fields manually and supply the proper calculation formula at the time the field is created would take much more time.

Cross-Reference For a more efficient method for adding a JavaScript that changes calculation formulas when an array is created, see Chapter 8, "Writing JavaScript Routines."

If you read Chapter 5, creating table arrays isn't new to you. The mechanics of creating an array were already explained. In this chapter, we want to look at some polish used to create the array and how to deal with fields with calculation formulas after the array has been created. The following steps walk you through the process:

1. Press the Ctrl (Windows) or ⌘ key (Mac OS) and marquee the top row of fields.

2. Press the Ctrl (Windows) or ⌘ key (Mac OS) and drag the center handle down to duplicate the fields for the array, as shown in Figure 6-13.

Tip There is no easy way to determine how far you need to drag down to create the exact number of fields to populate the form. If you drag the selection and find too many or too few rows created, Press the Esc key. Acrobat returns you to the selection without creating the fields. Drag down again to a different position and examine the number of rows created. By pressing Esc and starting again, you should be able to narrow down the area that produces the array you need. If you create too many rows, you can select the unwanted fields and delete them.

3. Press Enter to complete the array.

4. Select the fields along the bottom row and drag them down to the last row position.

5. Individually select the columns and select Distribute from a context menu, as shown in Figure 6-14.

6. At this point the task of changing the calculations is needed. The fields in the array supporting a calculation formula are the Amount fields. Select the Amount field in the first row and double-click the field rectangle or select the field and press the Enter key to open the Field Properties dialog box.

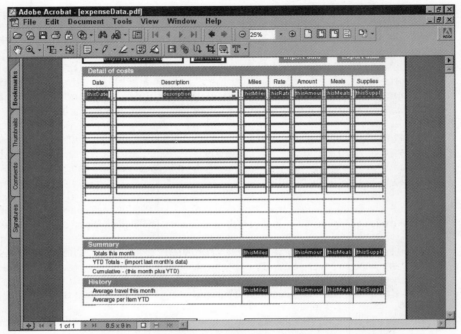

Figure 6-13: Marquee the fields to be duplicated and drag the center handle down. Press Enter to create the fields.

7. You'll notice the name provided by Acrobat for the first Amount field in the array is `thisAmount.0`. Each subsequent field in the array has a different child name. Click on the Calculate tab.

8. The calculation created earlier when the `thisAmount` field was created included the product of `thisMiles` and `thisRate`. The only thing you need to do to change the formula is add a `.0` after the field names, which results in `thisMiles.0` and `thisRate.0`, as shown in Figure 6-15.

9. Individually open each field and make the respective changes. Note that the field name for every field you open has the same extension as the changes you need to make in the Calculation properties. If you forget what child name needs to be provided in the Calculate tab, look at the field name and use the same child extension.

Be certain to test all the data fields after completing the changes in the calculation formulas. Check to see that all the calculations and totals work they way you expect.

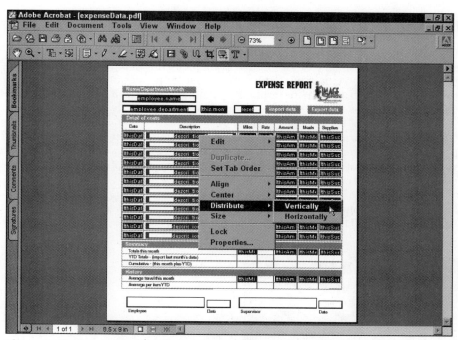

Figure 6-14: Select the fields in a column and select Distribute from a context menu. The fields are evenly distributed between the top and bottom fields for the column being distributed.

Figure 6-15: Add a .0 (dot zero) after the field names in the Calculate properties to change the formula for the first row.

Creating a Validation

On the expense report assume that company policy restricts an individual to a specific range for some expense items. Perhaps business meals have to be under a fixed amount. You can validate totals and assess the amount to see if it conforms to the validation criteria by entering the minimum and maximum values in the Validate properties.

On the expense form, open the `thisMealsTotal` field by selecting the field and pressing the Enter key. Notice the Validate attributes were not set when the field was originally created. The field and the properties were duplicated and the only edit made was to the field name.

In the Validate properties, enter **0** (zero) for the "Value must be greater than or equal to" field. Enter **500** for the "and less than or equal to" field, as shown in Figure 6-16.

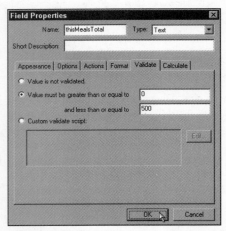

Figure 6-16: Enter the range of acceptable values in the Validate properties. If the value entered in the field is outside the range, Acrobat opens an alert dialog box.

Click OK and the range is established for the field. If the user exceeds an amount of 500, an alert dialog box opens and informs the user that the expense amount has been exceeded.

Creating a Reset Button

Reset buttons are used to assist users in filling out forms. You should try to give a little thought about where a user may wish to start over and identify fields that should be reset to help the user clear a potential error in a given area of the form. On the expense form it makes sense to keep the initial identifying data alive and not clear it when a form is reset. Also, the fields to be created for importing data should be preserved along with the signature and date fields. This leaves you with the array and the totals in the Summary and History sections. Unfortunately, you cannot predict what rows should be cleared when a user completes the form. If you set up the reset button to clear all the fields in the array and someone only wants to clear the last row, it could be frustrating for the user to watch all the data entries get wiped away.

The ideal would be to create a warning dialog box informing the user that s/he is about to clear all data. If users click OK, they know they'll loose all the entries. If they cancel out of the dialog box, they know the data are safe and they need to clear individual fields. Fortunately, you can create such a dialog box with a short JavaScript routine explained in Chapter 7, "Getting Started with JavaScript." Let's begin here to understand a little about resetting forms. Later in Chapter 7 we'll investigate how to add a little more polish with dialog boxes.

Cross-Reference   Refer to Chapter 7, "Getting Started with JavaScript," for more information.

1. Create a field at the top of the form positioned adjacent to the Import data text, as shown in Figure 6-17.

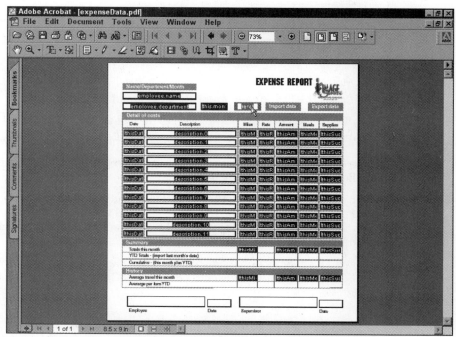

Figure 6-17: Create a field at the top of the page in some empty white space.

2. Because you don't have a graphic element on the page to use for a button, we'll let the Appearance settings create a button design. Enter a name for the field and select Button for the field Type. In this example `reset` is used for the field name.

3. Set the Appearance attributes to a Border and Background color. In the example the Border is set to black with a Thin Width, the Background Color White, and a Beveled Style, as shown in Figure 6-18.

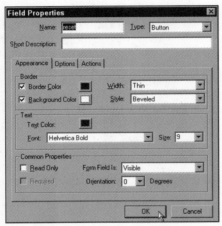

Figure 6-18: Set the Appearance items to be certain the button is visible on the document page.

4. Set the Text point size to 9 point, and then click on the Options button. Select Text Only for the Layout and enter **Reset Form** in the Text field.

5. Click Actions and click the Add button to add an action.

6. In the Add an Action dialog box, select Reset Form from the pull-down menu.

7. Click Select Fields in the Add an Action dialog box or open the Field Selection dialog box, as shown in Figure 6-19.

8. Click on All, Except and click the Select Fields button. The array contains most of the fields on the form, therefore it would take much more time to identify all the fields to be included in the reset action and much less time to just eliminate a few fields from the reset action.

9. The second Field Selection dialog box opens. Select the fields shown in Figure 6-20 in the right window and click on the Remove button to move them to the left window.

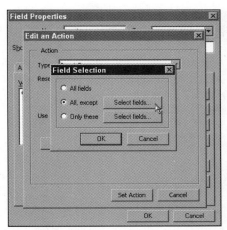

Figure 6-19: When you arrive at the Field Selection dialog box, select the button for All, Except and click the Select Fields button.

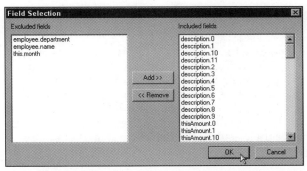

Figure 6-20: Select the fields to be removed from the reset action and click on the Remove button to move them to the opposite window.

10. When you return to the Field Properties dialog box, the Reset action is listed in the Action properties, as shown in Figure 6-21. Click OK and click on the button to see the data disappear from the fields.

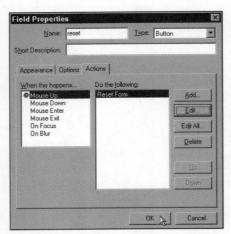

Figure 6-21: When an Action is created, the type of action is described in the Field Properties dialog box.

Setting Calculation Order

As explained in earlier chapters, the tab order for fields is determined by the order fields are created. The same order for calculations also follows the order of the fields created. In the expense form you first created the top row in the array. Tthen the summary and history fields were created at the bottom of the form. After the calculation fields were created, the array was added. In this example, the calculations for the sums are performed before the data are entered on fields 2 through 12. As a result, you need to change the calculation order so the sums occur after all data entry on the individual rows.

It is important to review calculation order after all the calculation fields have been added to a form. If the calculations are not performed in the right order, you may not see a field calculated. This is not always true. You may find calculations performed when out of the right order, but in complex forms it can create problems.

Calculation order is handled in the Calculated Fields dialog box accessed by choosing Tools ➪ Forms ➪ Set Calculation Order. Accessing the menu command does not require you to select the Form tool first as you need to do with the Set Tab Order.

The Calculated Fields dialog box opens after selecting the command. All the data fields used in calculations are listed in a scrollable window, as shown in Figure 6-22. In the example, you'll notice the fields used for summing and averaging data appear at the top of the list.

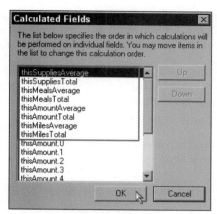

Figure 6-22: All fields used in calculations appear in a list according to the order they are calculated.

The calculation order begins with the first field in the list and follows in order from top to bottom. To reorder fields, select a field to be moved and click on the Up or Down button to move the field in the respective direction.

Select one of the fields used for summing or averaging data and click on the Down button. Keep clicking until the field is moved to the bottom of the list. Move all the summary and history fields to the bottom of the list, as shown in Figure 6-23. When the calculation order appears correct, click the OK button.

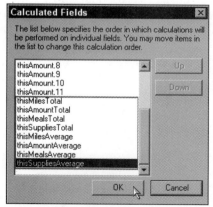

Figure 6-23: Click on a field and click the Down button in the Calculated Fields dialog box. Keep clicking the Down button until the field is moved to the bottom of the list.

Tip When selecting and moving fields in the Calculated Fields dialog box, you can select only a single field to move at one time. Each field needs to be reorganized in the dialog box individually by clicking on the ↑ and ↓ arrows. If you have a large number of fields to reorganize in a long list, it can take some time to move all the fields into the desired order. To simplify the process, you can select the fields needed to appear at the bottom of the list and choose Edit ⇨ Cut. Return to the Edit menu and select Paste. The pasted fields occupy the last order in the Calculated Fields dialog box.

Note The fields will not be pasted back in the exact location; therefore, you may need to click and drag the fields to their proper positions

Summary

✦ Text field attributes can assume many different numeric formats all accessed in the Format tab in the Field Properties dialog box.

✦ Acrobat offers you a limited number of preset calculation formulas to simplify calculating data fields.

✦ Calculations among fields in an array need to be individually edited in the Calculate Properties dialog box.

✦ The Validation tab in the Field Properties dialog box is used to validate user input in form fields.

✦ You can create buttons to clear data from form fields. You can assign Reset buttons to clear user defined fields.

✦ When creating multiple fields with calculations, it's a good idea for you to examine the calculation order and reset the order for all calculations performed out of the proper order.

✦   ✦   ✦

Working with JavaScript

Getting Started with JavaScript

♦ ♦ ♦ ♦

In This Chapter

JavaScript basics

Finding help

External editors

Duplicated
JavaScripts

Sharing JavaScripts

♦ ♦ ♦ ♦

If you're not a programmer, you may be intimidated by the thought of trying to understand a programming language. You know that JavaScript is a scripting language commonly used in Web page design and you may have seen lines of code without any understanding for what all that code means. If you consider yourself more of a forms designer rather than a programmer, you may be tempted to pass this chapter by and just deal with the design aspects of forms. Fortunately, there's good news. JavaScript in Acrobat can be learned and used without any knowledge of programming and you can learn by example.

Let me offer you a confession and set the record straight right up front. I'm not a programmer by trade and what I attempt to do in programming Acrobat JavaScript is through trial and error, examining code written by others, and gaining some help from friends. I'm certain that when I finish writing some routine, there is no doubt a better way to write the code; but if it works, I'm satisfied until I learn more about polishing up the programming. What's offered in this chapter and all other chapters dealing with JavaScript are examples of working and reworking routines to obtain desired results. Try to understand the process and use the examples from this section as a starting point to begin your own programming development skills.

Understanding JavaScript

If you have no foundation in programming, one way to help understand more about any programming language is to examine code written by others. If you look at the code for Web pages, you see pages of lines of code that immediately appear overwhelming. Try to tear apart the code to develop more understanding and you can quickly become frustrated.

With Acrobat, the structure of the document is a little different. Rather than having a long series of lines of code to create a document, there are elements such as form fields, page actions, bookmarks, links, and so on that contain scripts. Some of the scripts you find in Acrobat forms may be only a single line of code. As you move around a document and find JavaScripts, you can find routines that can be copied and pasted between documents. In some cases you may need to modify code, while in other cases you can paste fields with JavaScripts in a form without modification. As you peruse forms with JavaScripts, you begin to understand some of the language structure and eventually arrive at a point where you can write your own scripts.

The first step in learning more about JavaScript is to explore code written by others. You can browse the Internet and search for Acrobat Forms. Find forms on the Internet that contain scripts and study them. When you come across a script to produce a result, save the form to a folder where you can revisit it when you need the routine. To examine code from documents you collect, your first step is to understand where scripts are contained in Acrobat forms.

Security

To gain access to code in a PDF document, the form must not be secured against changing form fields or changing the design of the document. If you search the Internet and look for forms that contain JavaScripts, you'll want to be certain you have access to the document before saving it to disk. If security has been used in a document, you'll want to pass it by and continue the search for other files. PDFs viewed in Web browsers can be examined for security by accessing preferences before saving the file to disk. While you view a PDF in an online view in a Web browser window, open the fly-away menu in the top right corner of the browser window, as shown in Figure 7-1. Select Document Security from the menu options.

The Document Security dialog box opens. The first line of information indicating the Security Method informs you whether the file has been secured. If None appears as the Security Method, as shown in Figure 7-2, you can be certain all the JavaScripts in the document are accessible and you can open them to see the JavaScript code.

If you have a PDF open in Acrobat, the same fly-away menu with the same menu options are available. You can also examine security in Acrobat by choosing File ⇨ Document Security. Additionally, if you open a form in Acrobat and see the Form tool grayed out and inaccessible, you immediately know you cannot access any form fields and the document has been secured.

Tip   For checking security at a glance, look at the Status Bar at the bottom of the Document Pane. If you see a yellow key appearing in the Status Bar, you know the document has some level of security. However, even though a document is secure, you'll want to continue and open the Document Security dialog box. A document can be secured without locking you out of the form fields.

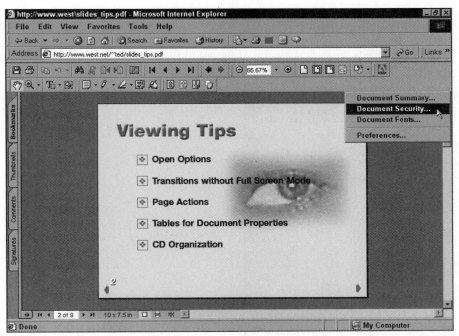

Figure 7-1: Select Document Security from the fly-away menu inside the Web browser window to open the Document Security dialog box.

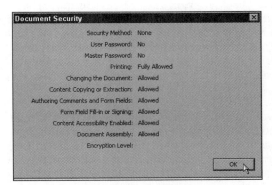

Figure 7-2: If the Security Method is None, you can be certain all JavaScripts are accessible in the form.

Field scripts

The most frequent use of JavaScript in Acrobat forms is when scripts are written for field Actions. To examine JavaScripts associated with fields, select the Form tool and open the Field Properties dialog box. Depending on the field Type, there may be several places where a script can be located. The first logical place to look is the Actions tab. For all field Types, Actions can contain JavaScripts. Click on the Actions tab to see what Actions are assigned to the field, as shown in Figure 7-3.

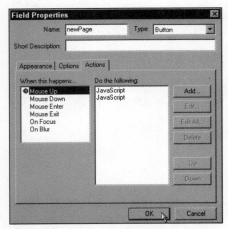

Figure 7-3: Click on the Actions tab to see if a JavaScript action has been added to the field.

If you see JavaScript assigned to a mouse behavior, click on JavaScript in the Do the Following list and select the Edit button. Acrobat opens the default JavaScript editor and displays the code written for the script, as shown in Figure 7-4. The code in the JavaScript editor can be copied from one field and pasted into the editor when assigning a script to another field. Additionally, the field can be copied and pasted into another form. When pasting fields with JavaScripts, the code is preserved in the pasted field.

With Text and Combo box fields, you can find JavaScripts in the Actions properties as well as the Format, Validate, and Calculate properties. If you are examining a form to understand how the field actions are executed, be certain to select each of these tabs to see if any custom formatting or validation is used. Click on the Format tab and look for Custom in the Category list, as shown in Figure 7-5. If Custom is highlighted, click on the Edit button where you see code in the box below either Custom Format Script or Custom Keystroke Script. In Figure 7-5, a Custom Keystroke Script is assigned to the field. Click the Edit button and the JavaScript Edit window opens.

The Validate properties offer the same options, as shown in Figure 7-6. Follow the same procedures as described above to open the JavaScript Edit dialog box.

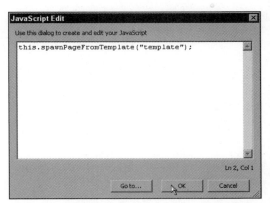

Figure 7-4: Select JavaScript in the Actions tab and click on the Edit button. The JavaScript Edit dialog box opens displaying the code.

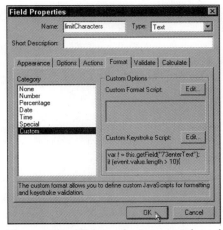

Figure 7-5: Click on the Format tab and click Edit where a script appears in the dialog box. The JavaScript Edit window opens displaying the code.

Field calculations are often handled in the Calculate tab. When JavaScripts produce data calculations, be certain to examine the Calculate properties, as shown in Figure 7-7. Not all field calculations are assigned to the Calculate tab, so be certain to check the Actions properties as well as the Calculate properties.

Figure 7-6: Click on the Validate tab and examine the dialog box. If a script is assigned to the field, select the Edit button to open the JavaScript Edit dialog box.

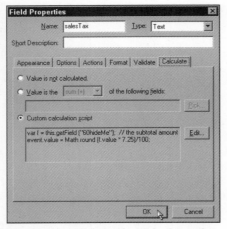

Figure 7-7: Click on the Calculate tab to see if a custom calculation script has been added to the field. If a script appears in the dialog box, click Edit to open the JavaScript Edit dialog box.

List boxes offer different properties. If a List box is used, click on the Selection Change tab. A JavaScript can be executed when a selection in the List box changes. If a script appears in the dialog box, as shown in Figure 7-8, click on the Edit button to open the JavaScript Edit dialog box.

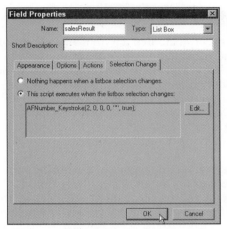

Figure 7-8: Click on the Selection Change tab in List boxes to see if a custom script is assigned to the field.

Digital Signatures can also be assigned custom JavaScripts. Click on the Signed tab for a Digital Signature field and examine the dialog box for a custom script, as shown in Figure 7-9.

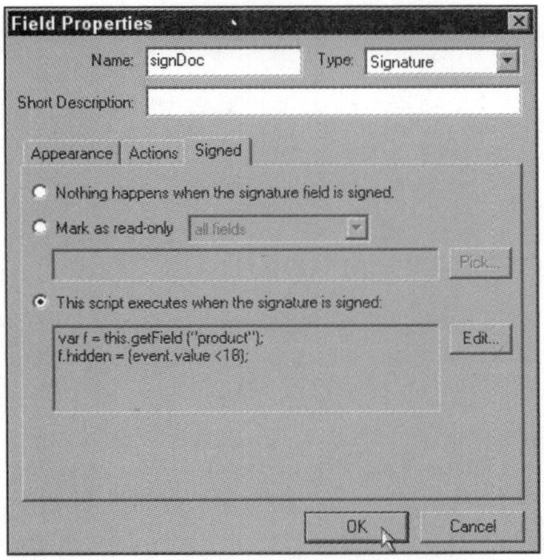

Figure 7-9: In Digital Signature fields, click the Signed tab to see if a custom JavaScript has been added to the field.

Buttons, Radio buttons, and Check boxes can only have JavaScripts added to the Actions properties. When opening these field types, click on the Actions tab described earlier.

Document Level JavaScripts

You may copy a field and paste it into another document and find an error reported when executing the JavaScript action. Notwithstanding variable names that are explained later, problems like this can be experienced because the routine in the JavaScript may be calling a JavaScript function or global action that was contained in the original document as a Document Level JavaScript. Among your tasks in dissecting a form should be an examination of any Document Level JavaScripts. To find JavaScript functions contained in a form, choose Tools ➪ JavaScript ➪ Document JavaScripts. The JavaScript Functions dialog box opens.

In the JavaScript Functions dialog box, search for any names in the box below the Script Name box. All document-level functions are listed in this dialog box, as shown in Figure 7-10. To examine a script, select the script name and click on the Edit button. The JavaScript Edit window opens where the script can be examined.

Figure 7-10: To view JavaScript functions, click on the function name in the JavaScript Functions dialog box and click on the Edit button.

Writing functions and accessing them in JavaScript code written for field actions is much more complex. If you are new to JavaScript, you may wish to start with simple scripts in form fields until you learn more about how JavaScript is coded and implemented in Acrobat. As you learn more, you can develop more-sophisticated routines that include functions.

Page Actions

Page Actions are executed when a PDF page is opened or closed. You can assign any Action type available from the Add an Action types for field actions. Among the types are also JavaScripts. When examining forms, open the Page Actions dialog box by choosing Document ➪ Set Page Action. The Page Actions dialog box opens, as shown in Figure 7-11. If a JavaScript or any other Page Action is assigned to either the page open or the page close action, a green circle (Windows) or a black asterisk (Mac OS) appears to the left of the Page Open or Page Close text in the When This Happens list.

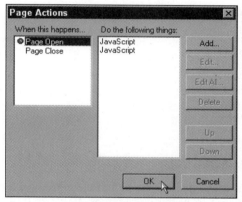

Figure 7-11: If a Page Action has been assigned to the current page in view, an icon is displayed adjacent to the Page Open or Page Close text.

Like the other dialog boxes described earlier, select JavaScript and click on the Edit button. The JavaScript Edit window opens where the JavaScript is viewed.

Document Actions

Document Actions execute JavaScripts for any one of five different Acrobat functions. On a document close, during a save, after a save, during a print, or after a print, a JavaScript action can be executed. To view any Document Actions assigned to the PDF document, choose Tools ➪ JavaScript ➪ Set Document Actions.

The Document Actions dialog box opens. This dialog box displays JavaScript assignments similar to those found with Page Actions. If a JavaScript is assigned to a Document Action, an icon appears adjacent to the action type. A script can be viewed in the dialog box, as shown in Figure 7-12, or you can open the JavaScript Edit window by selecting the action name and clicking the Edit button.

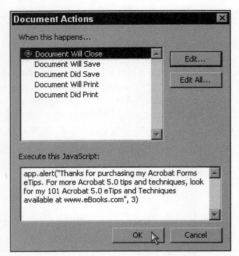

Figure 7-12: Any Document Actions assigned to the PDF are displayed with the same icon symbol found in the Page Actions dialog box.

Searching for page templates

Although not a JavaScript action, page templates can be called upon by JavaScript routines or additional fields can be created from template pages. Because templates can be hidden, the only way to examine JavaScripts on template pages is to first display a hidden template. As a matter of routine, you should search for Page Templates when examining forms.

To display a hidden template, choose Tools ➪ Forms ➪ Page Templates, as shown in Figure 7-13.

The Page Templates dialog box opens. If a Page Template is used in the PDF file, a template name appears in a list box in the Page Templates dialog box. If the Page Template is hidden, the icon to the left of the template name appears as a dash on the Mac OS. In Windows, a square appears empty when the template is hidden, as shown in Figure 7-14.

To show the template page, click on the icon adjacent to the template name. On Windows, the icon changes to an eyeball inside the square, as shown in Figure 7-15. On the Mac OS, the icon changes from a dash to a bullet.

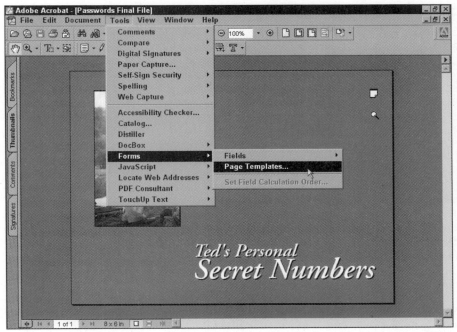

Figure 7-13: To open the Page Templates dialog box choose Tools ➪ Forms ➪ Page Templates.

Figure 7-14: If a template is included in the PDF, the template name(s) appears in a list in the Page Templates dialog box. If the template is hidden, the icon to the left of the template name appears empty (Windows) or as a dash (Mac OS).

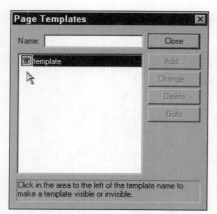

Figure 7-15: Clicking on the icon to the left of a template name for hidden templates makes the template visible in the PDF file.

The template likely appears at the end of the document. After you make a template visible, navigate to the last page in the PDF file to see the page. If form fields appear on the page, open them and examine them for JavaScripts, as described earlier.

Finding Help

Through a study of forms using JavaScripts, you can examine them and edit the code to run experiments; all of which helps you gain some skill at creating your own scripts. Observing code, however, only provides one level of understanding. For some of the theory and reasoning behind routines, you may need additional help. Or you may not have at hand any forms that execute the kind of action you want to use in your form.

For additional help, you can find a comprehensive manual available by choosing Help ➪ Acrobat JavaScript Guide. The help guide is a PDF file that is copied to your Acrobat folder when you install Adobe Acrobat.

The Acrobat JavaScript Object Specification guide opens in Acrobat, as shown in Figure 7-16. This guide is specific to using JavaScript in Acrobat. If you search the shelves of bookstores to find books about JavaScript, they won't help you as much as the JavaScript guide. Almost every JavaScript book is written for implementing JavaScript with Web pages. Acrobat's implementation of JavaScript differs from JavaScript used with HTML, so you'll find the help guide to be a much more valuable resource.

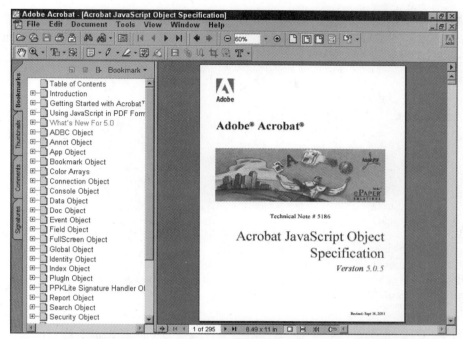

Figure 7-16: The Acrobat JavaScript Object Specification guide opens in Acrobat. You can search the PDF file with the Find command or jump to a bookmarked section by clicking on a bookmark in the Navigation Pane.

Using External Editors (Windows)

When you create or open a JavaScript document, the default JavaScript Edit window opens. The window behaves like a text editor, however, the features for the editor do not provide commands you may wish to use like search and replace, paragraph formatting, and so on. On Windows you can elect to use a text editor instead of Acrobat's JavaScript editor. To change editors choose Edit ➪ Preferences ➪ General. In the left pane, select JavaScript, as shown in Figure 7-17.

Click on External Editor in the JavaScript Editor section of the JavaScript preferences. The Choose button becomes active. Click on Choose to open the Select an Editor Program dialog box, as shown in Figure 7-18.

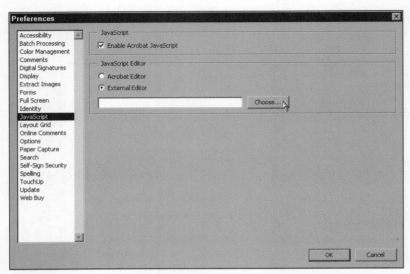

Figure 7-17: Select JavaScript in the left pane to display the JavaScript preferences on the right side of the dialog box.

Figure 7-18: In the Select an Editor Program dialog box, navigate your hard drive to find the editor to use. Select the editor and click on the Select button.

In the Select an Editor Program dialog box, navigate your hard drive to find the editor you wish to use. Acrobat acknowledges Windows Notepad and Windows

WordPad. You can also find public domain editors that can be downloaded from Web sites hosting public domain software. Download an editor and you can select it in the Select an Editor Program dialog box.

After you click Select in the Select an Editor Program dialog box, Acrobat returns you to the JavaScript preferences. In the Preferences dialog box, you can see the editor selected and the directory path where the editor is located. Click OK in the Preferences dialog box. When you review a JavaScript routine, the new default editor opens and displays the text, as shown in Figure 7-19.

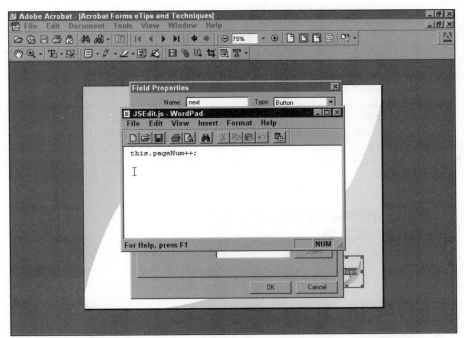

Figure 7-19: The external editor identified in the JavaScript preferences becomes the new default editor. All scripts created or viewed are handled by the text editor.

On the Mac OS, you don't have an option for choosing an external editor. If you wish to use another editor, such as BBEdit Lite, you can open the editor and copy text from BBEdit and paste it into the JavaScript Edit window. Acrobat enables copying and pasting text in the default JavaScript Edit window on both platforms.

Note

For consistency in referencing JavaScript written in an editor across platforms, I'll use the default editor for writing JavaScript code in the following pages. When I make references to open the JavaScript Edit dialog box, the default editor is used on both platforms.

JavaScript Basics

When you poke around and examine code written by others, you'll want to understand a few basics related to coding in JavaScript. There are many things to understand and you need some time in order to become a skilled programmer. Like any other skill, you need to start with some basics before advancing to complex tasks. The items listed here are offered as a few elementary points to help make some sense out of the lines of code you observe.

Comments

Many routines you find have the JavaScript code used to execute actions along with a series of comments used to help a programmer understand the routine when s/he returns to the script. If some time passes between writing a routine and revisiting it, you can find comments a benefit to help you understand what's going on with the script.

Figure 7-20 displays the characters that are used to mark comments in JavaScript. Whenever you see // or /* or * (as shown in Figure 7-20), you can interpret the text following these symbols as programmer comments. In scripts, you can eliminate comments and still have the routine execute properly. However, you should get in the habit of writing comments to help you later understand what the routines are designed to do.

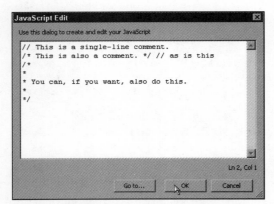

Figure 7-20: Lines of code containing special characters, such as //, /*, and in some cases *, are used to mark programmer comments.

Variables

There is much to say about variables. The thing to understand when you first begin to explore JavaScript is a variable name can be a character, a number, or a string of text containing numbers, characters, or both. Therefore, I can define a variable such as `var a = f`, `var a = product`, `var product = c`, `var total = grandTotal`, and so on. In each case, characters and strings are all variables. If I use something like `var product = "jacket"`, then `product` is a variable and `jacket` is the value of the variable. When characters or strings are placed inside quotation marks, they represent a value and not a variable.

When you start writing your own scripts, try to use variable names descriptive of the field or action you are defining. When it comes time to debug a routine, the more you know at a glance what the variables represent, the easier time you'll have in debugging a program.

Punctuation

When you examine scripts, you'll find many lines of code ending with a semicolon. You may find the exact same line of code written without a semicolon and both outines work exactly the same. The use of semicolons is necessary in some programming languages like C or Java. With JavaScript however, they are not necessary. Use of either structure works in most cases. As a matter of practice, it's a good idea to use them, as many programmers will expect to see a semicolon at the end of a statement.

Formatting

Different routines are commonly formatted with indentations for separate statements or subroutines. Breaking up a large routine to visibly show different segments apart from each other can help when debugging and when having other users review your code. In the default Acrobat JavaScript editor, pressing the Tab key moves the cursor four spaces to the right to indent a line. Pressing Shift+Tab moves the cursor four spaces to the left. As you review routines written by others, you'll develop a feel for where indentations occur. Try to emulate the formatting used by other programmers.

Using the JavaScript Console window

The JavaScript Console window is accessed by choosing Tools ➪ JavaScript ➪ Console (or Ctrl+J).

Note You can use Ctrl/Control+J on both Windows and Mac OS platforms.

In the console window, you can type a line of code to test it for errors or you can copy code from a field and paste it into the console window. To execute a segment in a routine, select the segment to be tested and press the Numeric Pad Enter key (or Ctrl+Enter in Windows). If an error is found in the code, Acrobat displays a message in the window, as shown in Figure 7-21.

Figure 7-21: When the statement is highlighted and the Num Pad Enter key is pressed, the script is executed. If an error in the coding was made, an error message is reported in the JavaScript Console window.

You can also execute a statement by placing the cursor at the beginning of the line to be executed. Press the Enter key on the Numeric Pad and the routine is run. If no error exists in the statement, no error message is displayed, as shown in Figure 7-22.

Figure 7-22: Place the cursor at the beginning of the statement. Press the Numeric Pad and then the Enter key to execute the routine. If no error is found, no error message is reported.

Using Duplicated JavaScripts

Whether you write your own scripts or find scripts in forms that are designed by others, which are available in the public domain, you can save time by reusing scripts or making simple modifications to scripts that have already been debugged. Working with any programming language means that debugging is always a factor. Whenever you use tested routines, your forms design completion will be much faster than when starting from scratch.

Copying and pasting JavaScripts

You can copy and paste text in the JavaScript Edit window when writing scripts. To do so, however, requires you to open the Field Properties dialog box for one field, select all the text in the JavaScript Edit window, close the properties, then create a new field and paste the text in the JavaScript Edit window.

Rather than move through all those motions, you can copy a field on a form and paste it into the same form or a different form. When you open the Field Properties dialog box, change the field name and make any necessary edits to the code.

If you have a series of fields with different calculations, such as a sales tax, a shipping fee, and a grand total, you can copy all the fields and paste them into another form. All the code developed for any form field is carried with the pasted copies.

Creating a script library

One means of storing commonly used scripts is to create a formula template or library. You can copy and paste fields, and add comment notes with routines to the notes for document-level scripts and Page Actions. Whenever you need to find a commonly used script, open your template and copy the field or the text from a comment note and paste it into your new form design.

In Figure 7-23, a PDF displays an assorted group of fields and comment notes with JavaScript routines. The bookmarks palette lists the names of a given routine. The view for each bookmark zooms to the fields where the scripts are written. Not only JavaScripts are used in the file. Combo and List boxes contain items like all the 50 U.S. states by abbreviation. When any one of these fields or routines are needed in a new form, they can be copied from the template to the new form.

If you build a template like the one illustrated above, create a blank page from any authoring program. To add new pages to the template, open the Thumbnails palette and select the blank page. Press the Ctrl key (Windows) or Option key (Mac OS) and drag down in the Thumbnails palette, as shown in Figure 7-24. The blank page is duplicated and ready to add more scripts on a second page. Always keep one page blank in the document to add more pages for your routines.

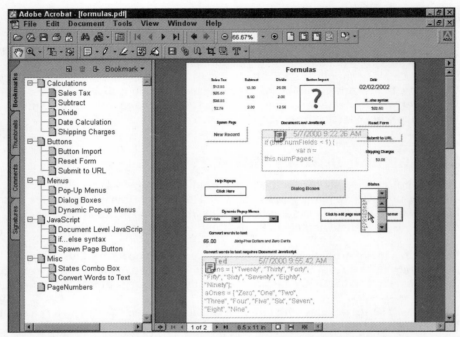

Figure 7-23: A formula template contains an assortment of scripts that are commonly used. By copying either the fields or the note contents and then pasting them into new form designs, you save time by not having to rewrite code.

Tip   You can create a new PDF document with JavaScript by adding a short line of code in the JavaScript Console. Choose Tools ➪ JavaScript ➪ Console or press Ctrl+J (Windows) or Control+J (Mac OS) to open the JavaScript Console window. Enter `app.newDoc();` in the console and press the Enter key. A new blank page is created. For custom page sizes or orientations, enter the horizontal and vertical sizes within the ( ). If you enter `app.newDoc(792, 612);` for example, a letter size page (792 points by 612 points or 11 by 8.5 inches) appears in landscape mode in the Document Pane.

Tip   In addition to creating templates, you can save PDF forms to a folder and create a search index with Acrobat Catalog. Add comments and Document Summaries. When you wish to find specific routines, you can use Acrobat Search to find the scripts needed for copying and pasting.

Cross-Reference   For more on Acrobat Catalog and Document Summaries, see bonus Chapter 17, "Organizing Real-World Workflows," which you'll find on the book's CD-ROM.

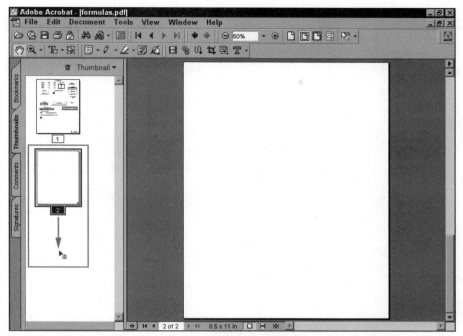

Figure 7-24: To duplicate a PDF page, press Ctrl (Windows) or Option (Mac OS), click on the thumbnail, and drag the page down in the Thumbnails palette.

Sharing JavaScripts

When searching out to find scripts, be certain that all those you use and modify are in the public domain. If you find forms that carry a copyright symbol, avoid using content on copyrighted forms. As a matter of ethics, you should respect the rights of others even if the scripts may not be an issue for a copyright suit. There are plenty of forms available to you without endangering yourself or your company in a copyright violation.

As you design forms and host them on the Web, try to host your forms without security protection. Unless there is a need for copyright and security, you can be a participant in a larger community that generously shares information and time. Many PDF experts around the world provide assistance and offer demonstrations freely to others. As a segment of the high technology community, the PDF people tend to be a generous group who liberally offer tips and techniques to others. You can be a participant and help other PDF forms designers learn from your own experiences.

As a forum for sharing any kind of information on PDFs and Acrobat forms, visit the www.planetpdf.com Web site. You can be a contributor and offer your own tips to one of the best PDF resources available. If you need help with scripting problems or any other kind of PDF related question, posting problems on the Web site forum will get you answers from some of the most renowned PDF experts.

Summary

✦ When you examine JavaScript routines that have been developed by other users, the first check point is to determine if any security has been applied to a form.

✦ JavaScripts can be found within fields, Document Level actions, Page Actions, and Document Actions.

✦ The JavaScript specification guide is accessed from the Acrobat Help menu. This guide is the most comprehensive source available for the Acrobat implementation of JavaScript.

✦ External JavaScript editors are available to Acrobat users on Windows computers.

✦ You can copy and paste JavaScripts into the JavaScript Edit dialog box or in an external editor. Fields containing JavaScripts can be copied and pasted between PDF pages and between PDF documents.

✦ An effective means for storing frequently used scripts is to create a formula template and paste fields containing scripts on the template pages.

✦ ✦ ✦

Writing JavaScript Routines

The last chapter dealt with some basic information related to the Acrobat implementation of JavaScript. Now it's time to begin using JavaScript in real-world forms. The exercises explained in this chapter walk you through writing scripts.

On the CD-ROM You'll find most of the scripts that are addressed in this chapter in the Chapter 8 folder on the book's CD-ROM.

Understanding JavaScript and Mouse Behaviors

JavaScripts can be used for an infinite number of actions. Before attempting to write a script, think about exactly what you want a script to do. With calculations, it's relatively simple. If I need to subtract one field of data from another, it is obvious what the script needs to do. If, on the other hand, I want to do something simple like sound a warning beep, then I need to think about why the beep will sound and on what kind of mouse behavior the sound is executed. I might use a warning beep to alert a user that a field contains no data, that the data that are supplied are not in the proper format, or some other kind of alert that aides the user in filling in the form.

Warning beeps are but one example of a need to understand the various mouse behaviors used to invoke a JavaScript action. Depending on the form, the kind of field used, and the action invoked, there are circumstances when one behavior over another may be better suited.

Using Mouse Up mouse behavior

Mouse behaviors associated with JavaScript actions are often applied to buttons. When a button is clicked, either the Mouse Down or Mouse Up action executes a script. By default, a user expects a button action to be executed on a Mouse Up behavior. Unless there is a special reason to use a Mouse Down behavior, be certain button actions are executed when the mouse button is released—thus Mouse Up. This gives the user a moment to think when the mouse button is pressed and still move away from the button before invoking the action. If the mouse moves out of the field before the mouse button is released, the JavaScript won't execute. Users expect this kind of behavior when they approach a button.

Using Mouse Down mouse behavior

If there is a special reason a Mouse Down behavior would better suit a button action, then the option is available. The main thing to avoid is combining random Mouse Up and Mouse Down behaviors in the same form. Doing so confuses users. Above all, try to be consistent when assigning button actions to mouse behaviors.

Using On Enter mouse behavior

An On Enter mouse behavior invokes an action when the mouse cursor enters a data field or button. You might use On Enter to alert a user all fields have not yet been completed on the form when the cursor moves over a submit button or a save button. In this example you could use a conditional statement that may be something like: If x, y, z fields contain no data, open an alert dialog box and inform the user the fields need to be completed.

Using On Exit mouse behavior

Perhaps the data field needs to have a specific format such as a credit card number with the dashes between every four digits. If the user doesn't enter the correct format, an alert dialog box opens asking the user to reenter the data. The alert box opens when the cursor exits the field—thus Mouse Exit.

Using On Focus mouse behavior

On Focus mouse behaviors are used when a user presses the Tab key to enter a field (or clicks in the field). If a specific format is required for the data entry, you can open an alert dialog box informing the user of the proper format. You may also have a user enter data in a response dialog box. When the user clicks the OK button, the data typed in the response dialog box are moved to the field.

Using On Blur mouse behavior

On Blur behaves like the On Exit mouse behavior. When the user tabs out of a field (or clicks somewhere else), a script is executed. A similar kind of effect may be used with On Blur as you use with On Exit.

Creating Calculation Scripts

The preset math calculations provided by Acrobat are limited to summing numbers and producing a product. If you need to subtract or divide numbers, a JavaScript is needed. When you wish to calculate the result of a formula for calculating fields like a sales tax, shipping fees, or more complex calculations, JavaScript is also needed. With almost any kind of calculation script, there are some common statements that are always essential. These include:

✦ **Variables.** The variables to be used need to be identified. If values are calculated from field data, the field values need to be assigned to variable names.

✦ **Formulas.** The variables are used in the formula to produce a calculation. Syntax used in creating the formula needs to be precise.

✦ **Results.** The destination for the result needs to be stated. Where will the result of the calculation be placed?

Let's take a look at creating some simple calculations where the statements above are used to produce the result of the calculation and the result is stored in a field.

Subtracting values

To subtract one value from another a JavaScript is needed. Suppose you have a form where a discount is subtracted from a subtotal to render a total amount for a line item. Each line on an order form might have a discount applied to each purchase and the discount amounts might vary according to each item purchased. To create a formula that subtracts one value from another and places the result in a field, follow these steps:

 You'll find the `clockOrder.pdf` file in the Chapter 8 folder on the book's CD-ROM.

1. Create the fields for an amount, discount, and total. Use the `clockOrder.pdf` file in the Chapter 8 folder on the book's CD-ROM. The form has fields where an amount and a discount are calculated according to the quantity of items ordered for each product, as shown in Figure 8-1. In this example, three fields are created across the first row and named `amount.1`, `discount.1`, and `total.1`.

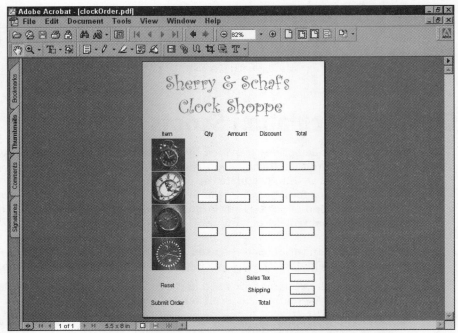

Figure 8-1: The clockOrder.pdf form contains spaces for fields for amounts, discounts, and totals. The total is calculated by subtracting the amount field from the discount field, and the result is placed in the total field for each line item.

Note On the example form, fields have been created with calculations and a quantity field also appears in each row. To perform the steps in this example, you can delete the fields on the example form and ignore the quantity fields.

2. Open the Field Properties dialog box for the `total.1` field. Click on the Calculate tab. The Calculate tab is where the formula for the calculation is added.

3. Select the radio button for Custom Calculation Script in the Calculate tab. Click on the Edit button to create a Custom calculation script, as shown in Figure 8-2.

4. The JavaScript Edit dialog box opens. Enter the following script in the JavaScript Edit dialog box.

```
var a = this.getField("amount.1");
var b = this.getField("discount.1");
event.value = a.value - b.value;
```

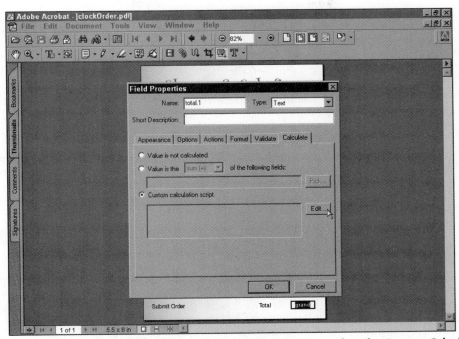

Figure 8-2: To add a JavaScript to calculate the subtraction, select the Custom Calculation Script radio button and click on Edit.

Figure 8-3 shows the statements entered in the JavaScript Edit dialog box.

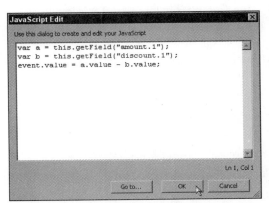

Figure 8-3: Enter the statements in the JavaScript Edit dialog box and click OK.

When you return to the PDF form and enter arbitrary vales for an amount in the `amount.1` field and add a discount amount in the `discount.1` field, the difference is calculated in the `total.1` field.

The JavaScript above first identified the variables. The first line in the script assigned `amount.1` to a variable called a. The second line of code assigned the field `discount.1` to a variable called b. The calculation was the value of a (`a.value`) minus (-) the value of b (`b.value`). The destination for the calculation is `event.value` that stores the result in the field where the script is created.

The variable names in the above formula are random uses of characters. You could also use names for variables such as `var amount` and `var discount` resulting in the last line of code reading as `event.value = amount.value - discount.value`. When assigning variable names, realize you can use text strings to express a variable name.

Dividing values

Division is a little more complex and requires some awareness of the data format used for the values in the fields calculated. If you attempt to divide the contents of one field with another, the result must match the number of decimal places defined in the Format properties. If the dividend is greater than the number of decimal places permitted in the Format field, Acrobat reports an error in the calculation. In many cases you will often choose to round off a number to the number of decimal places determined in the Format properties. A good example for such a calculation is when calculating a sales tax.

To divide values in a formula where a sales tax is calculated, follow these steps:

1. Complete the remaining fields for amount, discount, and totals on the `clockOrder.pdf` file and test the calculations by adding amounts and discounts in each row.

2. Create a new text field anywhere on the form. In this example, a field is created to the left of the sales tax field.

3. In the Field Properties dialog box, enter **subTotal** as the field name.

4. Click on the Format tab and click Number. Select 2 decimal places for the Decimal Places field.

5. Click on the Calculate tab and select the Value Is the radio button.

6. Select sum (+) from the pull-down menu and enter **"total"** in the field box, as shown in Figure 8-4.

7. This field will be used as a container to temporarily hold the subtotal of all the total fields. It is not created for user input and offers no benefit to the end user in terms of displaying the contents. Therefore, you can hide the field from view, while still using the contents to calculate the sales tax. To hide the field, click on the Appearance tab.

Figure 8-4: Create a field to calculate the subtotal of all the total fields.

8. Select Hidden from the pull-down menu, as shown in Figure 8-5, and click OK in the Field Properties dialog box.

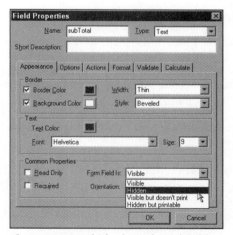

Figure 8-5: To hide the subtotal field, click on the Appearance tab and select Hidden from the Form Field Is pull-down menu.

9. Create a field and name it tax.

10. Click on the Calculate tab in the Tax Field Properties dialog box and select the Custom Calculation Script radio button.

11. Click Edit to open the JavaScript Editor and enter the following code:

```
var f = this.getField("subTotal");
event.value = Math.round (f.value * 7.25)/100;
```

12. Click OK in the JavaScript Editor dialog box and OK in the Field Properties dialog box.

13. Test the formulas to be certain the results are reported accurately. You should see the form without the appearance of the subtotal field.

In this example, the last statement uses the reserved words Math.round to round off the calculation. The 7.25 item is the sales tax rate of 7.25 percent. The /100 divides the subtotal times the 7.25 rate by 100 to produce the tax with two decimal places. If you multiply .0725 times the subtotal, the calculation will be incorrect because the rounding off of the numbers looses the data past two decimal places.

Tip   If you create forms for sales in which tax rates vary according to customer residences, you can add a field for a user-supplied tax rate. In the JavaScript to calculate the rate, you assign a variable to the tax rate field, such as var r = this.getField("taxRate");. In the formula, substitute the 7.25 item in the formula with r.value. The rate is calculated on the amount the user adds to the tax rate field.

Calculations with Table Arrays

In the above example, we had to edit four individual fields and supply the JavaScript for each of the total fields. You can duplicate a field and have the formula change by either pressing Ctrl (Windows) or Option (Mac OS) + drag, or when creating arrays (as I explained in Chapter 6). For multiple rows, you need to edit each calculated field individually when the variables change.

Cross-Reference   For more information about arrays, see Chapter 6, "Calculating Field Data."

You do have a workaround when using JavaScript and you can create a formula that changes variable names for all fields created in rows or columns developed from an array. In this example, a calculation can be used with a loop that cycles through all the fields after the array creates them. To understand how calculation formulas are added to fields in an array with JavaScript, follow these steps:

On the CD-ROM   In this exercise, the veggiecalc.pdf file is used that you'll find in the Chapter 8 folder on the book's CD-ROM.

1. Create the first row of fields on a form. (In this example, the veggiecalc.pdf file is used from the book's CD-ROM in the Chapter 8 folder. If you use this file, the first three fields have been created, as shown in Figure 8-6.

Figure 8-6: The `veggiecalc.pdf` file on the book's CD-ROM contains the first three fields in the top row for a table.

Note

No child names are used for the first row of field names.

2. If you need to fix any values, such as an item amount, and don't want the user to change the price, open the Options tab and enter the price for the Default, as shown in Figure 8-7. In the Appearance properties, select the Read Only check box. If the PDF is secured with Acrobat Security, the end user cannot change the price.

Cross-Reference

For more information about Acrobat Security, see Chapter 11, "Using Acrobat Security."

3. Create the calculation for the `total` field. In this example, each `amount` field is to be multiplied by each `quantity` field. Open the `total` field and click on the Calculate tab. Select the Custom Calculation Script radio button, click the Edit button, and enter the following formula in the JavaScript Edit dialog box:

```
var fieldOneName = "amount."; // include the period!
var fieldTwoName = "qty.";
var fieldSumName = "total.";

var numberOfFields = 8;

for (var i = 0; i < numberOfFields; i++)
{
var one = getField(fieldOneName + i).value;
var two = getField(fieldTwoName + i).value;
getField(fieldSumName + i).value = one * two;
}
```

This script is your first introduction to a loop. The statement beginning with `for (var i = 0; i < numberOfFields; i++)` contains the instructions for Acrobat to loop through the number of fields as long as the `i` value is less than the `numberOfFields` value. Remember, JavaScript is zero-based; therefore, the loop begins with zero (0) and continues through 7 resulting in a loop through 8 fields. The statement `var numberOfFields = 8` tells Acrobat there are 8 fields. As the loop begins, the first field values are `fieldnames + 0`. These names change with 1, 2, 3,and so on until `fieldnames.7` are reached.

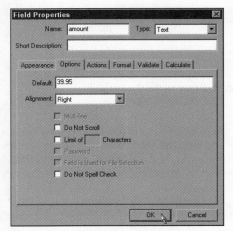

Figure 8-7: To fix a default price, enter the amount in the Default field box in the Options properties.

4. Click OK in the JavaScript Edit dialog box. The JavaScript Console dialog box opens and reports an error. Don't be concerned about the error. This is normal because you do not yet have fields identified with parent/child names. Acrobat supplies the names when you create a table array. Click Close in the JavaScript Console dialog box.

Note   If you have trouble coding the script in the JavaScript Edit dialog box, the script has been provided in a Comment note on the sample form contained on the book's CD-ROM. Open the Comment note in the top left corner of the form and copy the note contents. Paste the contents in the JavaScript Edit dialog box.

5. It's now time to create the table. This part is tricky. You need to create seven additional rows precisely if the formula is to work properly. Shift+drag (Windows) or ⌘+drag (Mac OS) to marquee the three fields. Press Control (Windows) or ⌘ (Mac OS) and drag the center handle down to a position where seven rows are created. If you drag too far or not far enough for creating exactly seven rows, press the Esc key and start again. You should see seven blue boxes below the first row, as shown in Figure 8-8.

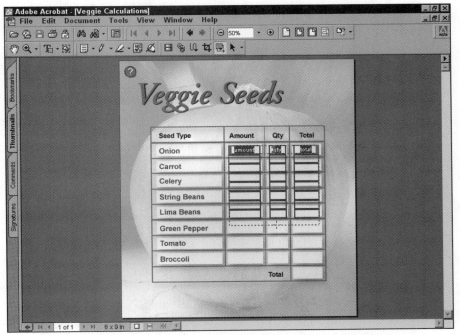

Figure 8-8: For the formula to work properly in this example, exactly seven additional rows need to be created below the first row. Press the Enter key when the new rows equal seven.

6. Press the Enter key to create the table. Move the last row into position and distribute fields to align them, as shown in Figure 8-9.

 Cross-Reference   See Chapter 5, "Creating Form Fields," for more on using the Distribute command.

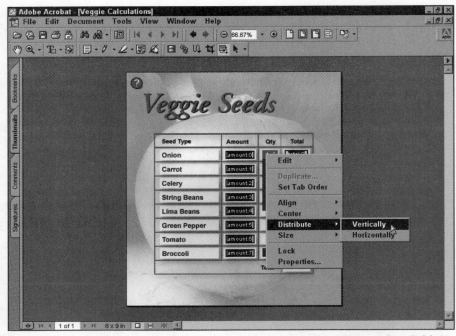

Figure 8-9: After creating the table, move the last row into position. Select fields in a column and choose the Distribute ➪ Vertically command from a context menu to move the fields into position.

7. Test the calculations. Enter a quantity amount in each row. If the script was coded properly, no errors are reported and the calculations are made correctly for each row total field.

The one item that may require manual editing field by field is the default value for the first field in each row. If you need to change the default values, you need to individually open each field and edit the Default text in the Options tab.

Creating Viewer Options Warning Alerts

There are some circumstances where it will be helpful for users to know the limitations of completing your forms before they attempt filling in data fields. If users open your forms in Acrobat Reader, they cannot save the data after filling in the form. In other cases, some scripts you add to a form cannot be performed in either Reader or Acrobat Approval. Some examples of such scripts may be adding a Comment note from a button action or spawning a page from a template. These actions require Acrobat. In other cases, new features in Acrobat 5 make some actions unusable to users with viewers earlier than Acrobat 5. Therefore, you may wish to assess the viewer type and viewer version when a user opens your forms. If a version or viewer type cannot be used with the form you created, you can alert the user immediately when the file opens.

Cross-Reference

For more on adding fields with JavaScripts, see "Adding fields based on user responses," later in this chapter. For more on spawning pages from templates, see Chapter 9, "Creating Templates and Spawning Pages."

Creating Viewer Type Alerts

A viewer type is the Acrobat viewer used to view the PDF form. Acrobat Reader, Acrobat Approval, and Acrobat are the viewer types that are used in filling out PDF forms. If you have forms submitted via an Internet connection, any viewer type is capable of submitting data if you have the proper server-side programming and create a button to submit the data to a URL.

Cross-Reference

For more on submitting data, refer to Chapter 13, "Submitting and Distributing Forms."

In a local environment where PDF forms may be completed on local hard drives or network servers, users of the Reader software may not be aware that they cannot save the form data after completion. If a user realizes this only after filling in a long form, the user will become annoyed and frustrated. To help the user out, follow these steps to create an alert dialog box informing the user that the current viewer type has limitations:

1. Open a PDF file and navigate to the default page view when the file is opened. Choose Document ⇨ Set Page Action. The warning message you create appears immediately after a user opens the PDF form. To ensure the message is displayed upon opening the file, be certain to navigate to the opening page. Unless the default has been overridden in the Document Open Options dialog box, the opening page is the first page in the PDF file.

Cross-Reference

For more about using Open Options, see bonus Chapter 17, "Organizing Real-World Workflows," which you'll find on the book's CD-ROM.

2. The Page Actions dialog box opens. Select Page Open and click on the Add button.

3. In the Add an Action dialog box, select JavaScript from the pull-down menu for Type. Click on the Edit button to open the JavaScript Edit dialog box.

4. Enter the following code in the JavaScript Edit dialog box:

```
//is Reader (as opposed to Acrobat)
if (typeof(app.viewerType)!="undefined")
 if(app.viewerType == "Reader")
```

```
{
var msg = "To save form data you need to purchase Adobe
Acrobat or Acrobat Approval. This form can be completed and
printed from Reader; however to save the data, you need one
of the viewers noted above.";
 app.alert(msg);
 }
else
 {
//do nothing
 }
```

This routine begins with a comment denoted by // in which a programmer's comment is added to the script. The if statement assesses the viewer. If the viewer type is equal (==) to Acrobat Reader ("Reader"), an alert dialog box opens app.alert(msg). The variable msg is defined in the var msg statement. Therefore, the variable msg value appears when the alert dialog box opens. If the viewer type is not Reader, the else statement instructs Acrobat to do nothing because no instructions are provided after the else statement.

Note   You can eliminate the else statement. It is not necessary. It is illustrated here in the event you wish to add more code if the viewer type is not Reader.

5. Click OK in the JavaScript Edit dialog box and OK in the Page Actions dialog box. Save the file and close it. Open the file in Acrobat Reader and you see an alert dialog box open when the file is launched, as shown in Figure 8-10.

Creating viewer version alerts

You may create JavaScripts to perform actions that are not available in earlier versions of Acrobat. The newer Acrobat 5.0 implementation of JavaScript adds many more statements and reserved words than earlier versions. If it is essential for a user to complete your form in Acrobat 5, you can add a Page Action and inform the user in an alert dialog box that Acrobat 5 is needed to complete the form.

In other cases, you may have a few actions that require Acrobat 5, but maybe a workaround can be used if the user opens your form in an earlier version of Acrobat. As an example, assume you have a button that creates a Comment note when the button is selected. You design your form to make it easy for the user to add a comment. However, creating a Comment from a button action is available only in Acrobat 5 or greater. In this regard, you can alert a user that Acrobat 5 is needed to use the button action, but you can inform the Acrobat 4 user that the Comment tool can be used to add the message.

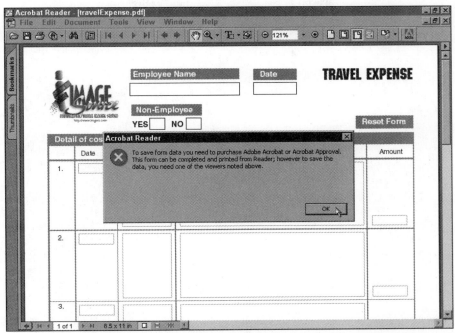

Figure 8-10: When the PDF file is opened in Acrobat Reader, the alert dialog box displays the message created in the JavaScript routine.

Using the above example for creating a comment, create a JavaScript action on a field. When the user tabs out of the field, an approval stamp comment is created. However, if the user is viewing the form in an Acrobat viewer less than version 5, the user is instructed in an alert dialog box that the Stamp Comment tool needs to be selected and used to manually create the comment. Follow these steps to produce the results:

On the CD-ROM

In this exercise, the `empApplication.pdf` form is used that you'll find in the Chapter 8 folder on the book's CD-ROM.

1. Create a Text field on a form. (For this example use the `empApplication.pdf` form in the Chapter 8 folder on the book's CD-ROM.

2. Create a text field where the Approved item appears in the lower-left corner of the form. Name the field `approved`.

3. Click on the Actions tab and select On Blur for the mouse behavior. Click on the Add button to open the Add an Action dialog box.

4. In the Add an Action dialog box, select JavaScript for the Type and click on the Edit button to open the JavaScript Edit dialog box.

5. Enter the following code in the JavaScript Edit dialog box:

```
//is Reader (as opposed to Acrobat)
if (typeof(app.viewerType)!="undefined")
 if(app.viewerType == "Reader")
 {
var msg = "Acrobat Reader does not support creating Comments.
Please use Acrobat to complete this form.";
app.alert(msg);
 }
else
 {
if (typeof(app.viewerType)!="undefined")
 if(app.viewerVersion < 5.0)
 {
var msg = "To add Comments in Acrobat versions lower than
5.0, select the Stamp tool from the Tool palette and create
an Approval Stamp.";
 app.alert(msg);
 }
else
 {
var name = this.getField("approved");
var annot = this.addAnnot
({
page: 0,
type: "Stamp",
name: "Standard",
popupOpen: false,
rect: [360, 725, 520, 760],
contents: "Application approved",
AP: "Approved"
});
annot.author = name.value;
 }
}
```

This routine has three parts. From the first line of code to the first else statement, the subroutine determines whether Acrobat or Reader is the current viewer. The second part determines what type of viewer is used (app.viewerVersion). After the second else statement, the instructions direct Acrobat to create a Stamp Comment. The line of code var name = this.getField("approved") stores the value the user enters in the field created at the beginning of this exercise. At the end of the routine, annot.author = name.value takes the contents of the approved field and uses it for the comment author. The page: 0, line instructs Acrobat to create the stamp comment on the first page in the document. The rect: [360, 725, 520, 760] determines the coordinates where the Stamp is drawn. The line contents: "Application approved", places the text in quotation marks in the note window for the Stamp comment.

Cross-Reference For using aids when adding coordinate locations for fields and comments, see Chapter 2, "Using Authoring Applications," in which using grid templates were discussed. If you want to move the Stamp comment in the script above to a new location, review Chapter 2 to help you determine precise coordinate values.

6. Click OK in the JavaScript Edit dialog box and Set Action in the Add an Action dialog box. Click OK in the Field Properties dialog box.

7. Test the action by clicking in the field and typing your name. When you tab out of the field or click the mouse button in another field, the approval stamp appears, as shown in Figure 8-11.

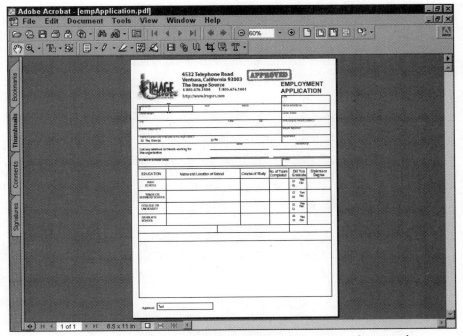

Figure 8-11: When you tab out of the field, the Stamp comment is created.

8. Double-click on the Stamp comment with the Hand tool to open the note. The title of the note window displays the name entered in the `approved` field and the contents for the note is derived from the text added in the JavaScript.

If a user exits the field from an Acrobat viewer less than version 5, an alert dialog box opens informing the user that s/he needs to create the comment manually. If Acrobat Reader is the viewer, an alert dialog box opens and informs the user that comments cannot be created in Reader.

Working with Fields and JavaScript

You may find a need to create a new field on a form based on a user response or when a need arises to create fields across a number of pages. The JavaScript addField statement enables you to add fields on a form from another field action. You may have a form that requires one user to add data to existing fields, and based on a response, perhaps another field is added where additional data are supplied. In other circumstances, you may wish to add fields across all pages in a document. Perhaps a manual created from several authoring programs needs to have page numbers added after the final PDF has been developed.

Adding fields based on user responses

The travelExpense.pdf file in the Chapter 8 folder on the book's CD-ROM has a field for an employee name. If an employee in the organization completes the form, the employee enters his/her name in the field box and selects the No box under non-employee, as shown in Figure 8-12.

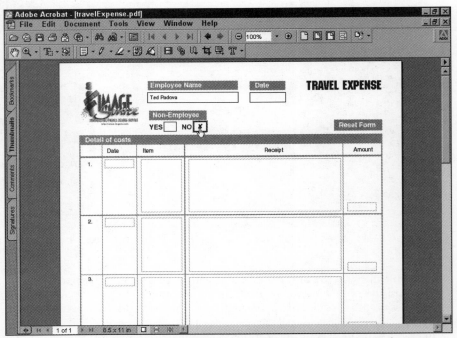

Figure 8-12: If an employee selects the No check box, no new fields are added to the form.

On the CD-ROM You'll find the `travelExpense.pdf` file in the Chapter 8 folder on the book's CD-ROM.

When a non-employee completes the form, the Yes check box under Non-Employee is selected. When a user selects this box, two new fields are added to the form. A read-only field is added instructing the user to supply *Your Name* and a data field is added where the user types his/her name. In addition, the data *Non-Employee* is added to the Employee Name field at the top of the form, as shown in Figure 8-13.

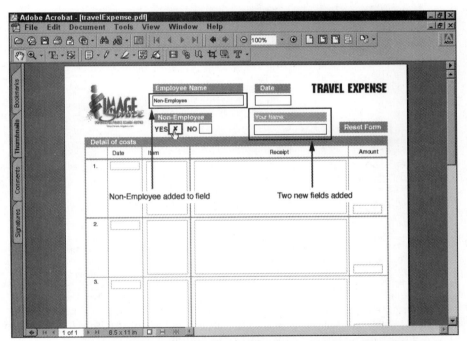

Figure 8-13: If the user selects the Yes check box, two new fields are added to the form and the text *Non-Employee* is added to the Employee Name field.

When the data are exported from the file, the data can be filtered for all employees versus non-employees. To add fields like those shown in Figure 8-13, follow these steps:

Note In this exercise, use the Yes check box on the `travelExpense.pdf` file that you'll find in the Chapter 8 folder on the book's CD-ROM.

1. For a check box JavaScript action, you will create two check boxes. Open the Field Properties dialog box on the check box where the action adds new fields to the form. In this example, use the Yes check box on the `travelExpense.pdf` file.

2. Add a JavaScript action and enter the following code in the JavaScript Edit dialog box:

```
//add non-employee to the name field
var a = this.getField("name.employee")
a.value = "Non-Employee";

//add a field for a title and make it Read Only
var f = this.addField("title", "text", page =
this.pageNum,[338, 686, 468, 703])
 f.textSize = 10;
 f.textfont = font.HelvB;
 f.textColor = color.white;
 f.fillColor = new Array("RGB", .7, .7, .7);
 f.alignment = "left";
 f.multiline = false;
 f.value = "Your Name:";
 f.readonly = true;

//add the data field for the non-employee name
var g = this.addField("titleName", "text", page =
this.pageNum,[338, 662, 468, 681])
 g.textSize = 10;
 g.textfont = font.Helv;
 g.textColor = color.white;
 g.borderColor = color.black;
 g.fillColor = color.transparent;
 g.alignment = "left";
 g.multiline = false;
```

This routine has three parts. The first part zeros out any data in the Employee Name field and enters the text Non-Employee to the field.

The second part creates a field for the description for the data field to instruct the user what to enter in the field box when it is added. This description is a read-only field that prevents a user from adding any data to the field. The properties for the field text attributes, field box attributes, and the field contents are listed after the addField statement.

The last part of the routine creates a second field for the data to be supplied by the user. Different attributes are assigned to this field, as shown in the items also following the addField statement.

3. Click OK and set the action. Test the button to be certain the script runs properly.

Adding page numbers with JavaScript

If you merge PDF pages created from different PDF authors or from different authoring programs, it may be difficult to know exactly where the page numbers fall on the completed work while laying out the document in the authoring applications. In some cases, it may be easier to add the page numbers after the PDF file has been assembled and approved. To add page numbers to a document, use the addField statement discussed above and use a loop to increment the page numbers. Follow these steps to add page numbers in a multiple-page document:

1. Open a multiple-page PDF file with dimensions set to 8.5x11 inches in a portrait view.

2. Create a Button field and open the JavaScript Edit dialog box.

3. Enter the following code:

```
// place page number 1/2 inch from upper right corner
// for standard letter portrait documents
var r = [612-36, 792 - 36, 612, 792];

for (var i = 1; i < numPages; i++) {
var f = this.addField(String("page"+i),"text",i,r);
f.textSize = 12;
f.textColor = color.blue;
f.fillColor = color.transparent;
f.textFont = font.HelvB;
f.borderStyle = border.s;
f.strokeColor = color.transparent;
f.value = String(i+1);
}
```

4. Select the Hand tool and press the new button. All the page numbers are added to the document.

5. Delete the Button field after the page numbers have been added.

The routine above adds a field box to the top-right corner on a standard portrait letter size page one half inch down and one half inch to the left of the right page edge (612-36 and 792-36 subtract 36 points or one half inch from the top right and right edge respectively). The loop begins at page 1 (var i = 1). The page numbers actually begin to appear on the second page. JavaScript is zero-based; therefore, all page numbers begin with page zero. To eliminate a page number on the cover page, the routine starts the numbering on page 2 (page 1 according to JavaScript). A blue, 12-point text entry is incremented on each page as the loop runs to the end of the document. All fields have unique field names defined by the ("page"+i) statement.

Tip   This routine may be a frequent operation you wish to perform on many documents. You can copy the Button field containing the script and paste it into a formula template discussed in Chapter 7, "Getting Started with JavaScript." When you wish to add page numbers to a document, copy the Button field from the template and paste it into the document where the page numbers are to be added. Delete the button after creating the page numbers.

Changing field attributes

As was illustrated in previous examples when we created fields, the field attributes such as font, point size, color, and so on were defined in the JavaScripts. If you have fields existing on a form and wish to change attributes, you can write routines permitting these changes. If, for example, you have accounting information where negative values are more desirable when the text changes color, you can analyze the data for a field and change color according to the value.

Figure 8-14 shows an expense report calculation. A monthly expense account is provided to an employee. When the total claims reported on the form are greater than $1,000, the employee is responsible for the amount over $1,000. Additionally, there are times when the employee may purchase a company product or service that is not charged against the expense account. Therefore, company purchases need to be deducted from the total expenses. If the value of the total minus company expenses exceeds $1,000, the amount due the employee is reported as a negative value and the color of the text is changed from black to red.

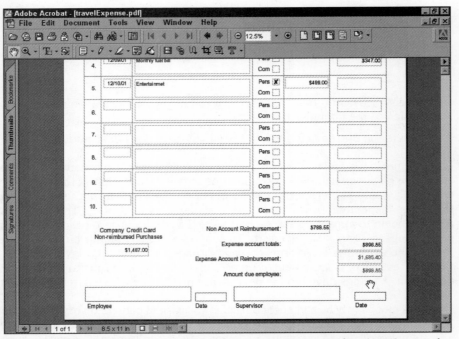

Figure 8-14: Negative values for the total amounts are reported as negative numbers in red text.

On the CD-ROM

For the following exercise, use the `employeeReimbursement.pdf` form that you'll find in the Chapter 8 folder on the book's CD-ROM drive.

To understand how the text changes are made on this form, follow these steps:

1. Select the Form tool and right-click on the `tempCalc` field to open a context menu and select Properties or double-click the mouse button on the field to open the Field Properties dialog box.

2. In the Field Properties dialog box, click on the Format tab.

3. Click on Custom in the Category list.

4. Click on the Edit button for Custom Format Script, as shown in Figure 8-15.

Figure 8-15: In the Format properties, click on the Edit button for Custom Format Script to open the JavaScript Edit dialog box.

5. Enter the following code in the JavaScript Edit dialog box:

```
var f = this.getField("expenseReimburse");
var g = this.getField("amountDue");
if (f.value >1000){
  f.textColor = color.red;
  g.textColor = color.red;
}
else
{
  f.textColor = color.black
  g.textColor = color.black
}
```

On this form, if the field called `expenseReimburse` is greater than $1,000, the text changes to red for the field contents and the `amountDue` field contents. If the amount is less than $1,000, the text changes to black.

Note   The default color is black. However, if an item is entered that changes the total to more than $1,000 and later the item is edited, you need to instruct Acrobat to change the color from red to black. The last part of the routine changes text from red to black in case a user makes an edit and the amount is reduced below $1,000.

For similar text attribute changes, use the Format tab and select the Edit button to open the JavaScript Edit dialog box. In most cases, you'll use the Format tab for these changes rather than the Calculate tab.

Importing images

Acrobat forms can appear with more polish when adding image elements to the data fields. You may have an employee form where a photo of the employee is imported along with other employee data. You may wish to import scanned images for receipts on a claims form to organize documents that can be easily retrieved, or many other similar uses for scans or digital camera photos.

When you design a form, you can write a script to import an image so the user doesn't have to maneuver the Field Properties dialog box. The user can easily click on a button to open the Browse dialog box and search for an image to import. There are three issues to deal with when using button imports. First, the field where the image is to appear needs to be set up properly. Secondly, if you want users to scan and import images into forms, you need to have a desktop scanner configured and Acrobat installed if you want to scan directly into Acrobat. Finally, you need to set the field attributes with the proper script in order to import images. If users have Acrobat Reader or Acrobat Approval, they can import images saved to disk as PDF files from scans or digital camera archives, but they cannot scan directly into either of these programs. Depending on your workflow, you can decide how users access data—for example, either through image archives saved as PDF files or via Acrobat Scan. To understand the full range of opportunity with Acrobat, let's first look at scanning, than we'll look at the forms design.

Note   When Acrobat Reader users import images in a form, the data obviously cannot be saved from Reader. However, an image can be imported and printed from the Reader software. With Acrobat and Acrobat Approval, the button imports can be saved after importing the images.

Scanning in Acrobat

Acrobat Scan is a plug-in installed with Acrobat when installed on either Windows or Mac OS computers. To access Acrobat Scan, choose File ➪ Import ➪ Scan. The dialog box that opens is the scanner software dialog box outfitted with your scanner via a TWAIN (Technology With An Important Name) driver. You have access to all the controls for image resolution, brightness, image cropping ,and so on, as you would if scanning through an image-editing program. Figure 8-16 shows a dialog box for the Agfa ScanWise software that is used with an Agfa SnapScan desktop scanner.

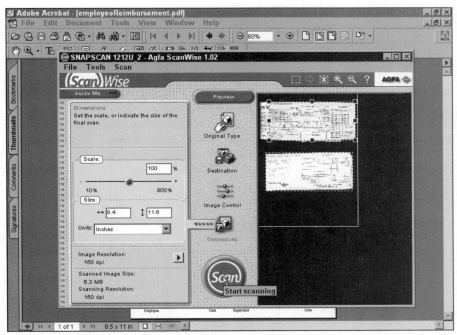

Figure 8-16: When scanning from within Acrobat, you have all the controls accessible for image scanning provided by your scanner manufacturer's scanning software.

Note

For information regarding TWAIN access and using Acrobat Scan with your brand of scanner, see your scanner documentation for TWAIN driver installations or visit your scanner manufacturer's Web site. Access to your scanner from Acrobat requires proper scanner configuration and appropriate software installation. If Acrobat Scan does not function, the problem is with your scanner configuration.

Make the necessary brightness and image resolution adjustments in your scanner dialog box and click on the Preview button. Marquee the area you want to scan and click on the Scan button.

Note

Button names vary between software plug-ins according to the scanner manufacturer. You may have a button for Import or Acquire instead of Scan. If in doubt, consult your scanner manufacturer's reference guide for acquiring scans.

When you acquire the scan, Acrobat prompts you in a dialog box if you want to create a new document or append the scan to an open document. If no document is open, the scan automatically appears in a new untitled document window. For the purposes of using an image with a button import, be certain to create a new PDF file from the scan.

Save the scan and continue if you have more images to convert to PDF.

If you intend to use multiple scans for button imports, you can append new scans to the first image converted in Acrobat. When it comes time to select images to be imported, the Browse dialog box explained on the next pages enables you to scroll through pages in a PDF file to select any image within the document.

Creating a button import

On a PDF form, the field to import the scan is a Button type. The field will be designed so that a user with Acrobat, Reader, or Acrobat Approval can import a PDF file into the field. To set up the field, follow these steps:

In the following exercise, use the `travelExpense.pdf` form that you'll find in the Chapter 8 folder on the book's CD-ROM.

1. Create a new field on an existing form or use the `travelExpense.pdf` form in the Chapter 8 folder on the book's CD-ROM. Use the Form tool and drag open a rectangle.

2. In the Field Properties dialog box, provide a name for the field and click on the Options tab. For the Layout, select Icon Only from the Layout pull-down menu, as shown in Figure 8-17.

3. Click on the Actions tab and click on the Add button with the Mouse Up behavior selected.

4. Select JavaScript in the Add an Action dialog box and click Edit.

5. In the JavaScript Edit dialog box, enter the following code:

```
event.target.buttonImportIcon();
```

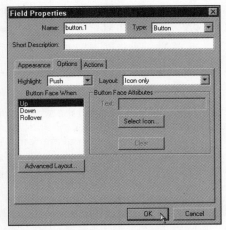

Figure 8-17: Click on the Options tab and select Icon Only from the Layout pull-down menu.

6. Click OK and click Set Action. Click OK in the Field Properties dialog box. The button is now ready to import an image.

7. Click on the button with the Hand tool selected.

8. The Select Appearance dialog box opens. Click Browse in the Select Appearance dialog box.

9. The Open dialog box appears. Navigate your hard drive and find the PDF file to import. (In the example, the `receipts.pdf` is used, which is included in Chapter 8 of the CD-ROM.)

On the CD-ROM You'll find the receipts.pdf file in the Chapter 8 folder on the book's CD-ROM.

10. Select the file to import and click Select in the Open dialog box.

11. When you select an image to import, Acrobat returns you to the Select Appearance dialog box and a preview of the file to be imported is displayed, as shown in Figure 8-18. If the file is not the file to be imported, click on the Browse button again to navigate to another file.

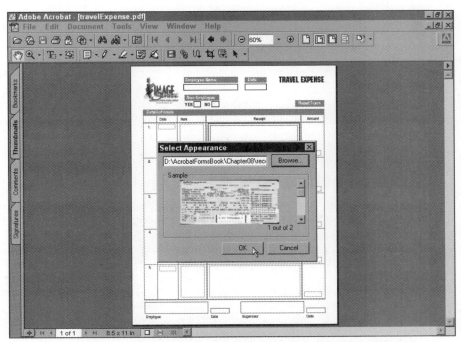

Figure 8-18: After selecting a file to import, the Select Appearance dialog box displays the image selected for import. Click OK to accept the image or click Browse to search for another image.

12. After importing images, the form displays the imported PDFs at the size of the field dimensions. By default, the image is centered in the field box and proportionally sized. Figure 8-19 shows two fields where files have been imported into the field boxes.

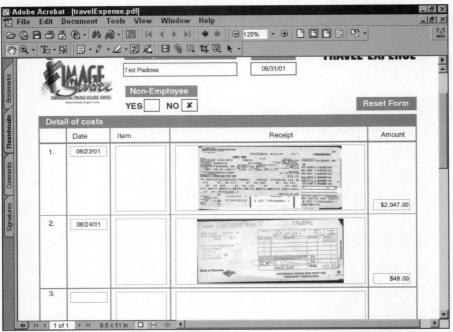

Figure 8-19: After importing images, the images appear sized proportionally within the field boxes.

Securing button imports

If you have a need to secure a field against unauthorized image imports, you can side step Acrobat Security and use a JavaScript to add a level of security for the user who changes a button image. If you protect the document with Acrobat Standard Security and prevent a user from adding or changing fields, the password security you provide secures a form against any changes. However, if you wish to add a password to a button field in order to prevent unauthorized changes to images, you can supply a second level of security. Assume a user adds a receipt to a button field. You want to ensure no other user can change the image, but you don't want to give the Acrobat Standard Security password that protects the form to other users so they can't change any calculation fields. In this example, you can add a password with JavaScript to permit only authorized users to change scanned images of receipts without giving the user the master password to change the document.

Cross-Reference   See Chapter 11, "Using Acrobat Security," for using Acrobat security.

In this example, we'll look at creating an alert beep when a button is clicked, then opening an alert dialog box to ask for confirmation for changing the button appearance. If the user clicks No, the alert dialog box closes and nothing happens. If the user clicks Yes in the alert dialog box, a response dialog box opens in which a password is supplied. If the password is wrong, another alert dialog box opens, informing the user that s/he typed the wrong password in the response dialog box. If the password is entered correctly, the Select Appearance dialog box opens. Here's how to do it:

1. Create a field for the button import and set the attributes, as described earlier, for importing images.

Note   You can use the `travelExpense.pdf` file from the last exercise.

2. Create another button field (name the second button field `imageField`), add a JavaScript Action, and enter the following code in the JavaScript Edit dialog box:

```
var f = this.getField("imageField"); //button field where
image is imported
app.beep(2);
var n = app.alert("Change image?",2,2);
 if (n == 4) {
var i = app.response("Enter your password");
 if (i == "roadrunner") {
        f.buttonImportIcon();
 }
else{
        if (i!= null) {
        app.alert("Wrong password!");
        }
 }
 }
```

The code above opens an alert dialog box when the mouse button is clicked on the button field containing the JavaScript action, and the question "Change Image?" is displayed in the alert dialog box. If the user clicks Yes, a response dialog box opens where the password is entered. If the password is "roadrunner," the `buttonImportIcon()` statement opens the Select Appearance dialog box. If the wrong password is typed in the response dialog box, another alert dialog box opens with the message "Wrong password!"

3. Set the Field Properties and return to the document window. Click on the button to invoke the action. The first alert dialog box opens, as shown in Figure 8-20. Click No, and nothing happens.

Figure 8-20: The first alert dialog box opens when the button containing the JavaScript is selected.

4. Click Yes, and the response dialog box opens. You must enter the correct password contained in the JavaScript. In this example, the password is **roadrunner** in lowercase letters, as shown in Figure 8-21.

Figure 8-21: The response dialog box permits you to type a password. Enter the correct password in this dialog box to proceed to the Select Appearance dialog box.

5. If you type the wrong password, another alert dialog box opens indicating the password was not correct. If you enter the correct password, the Select Appearance dialog box opens.

The dialog boxes opened with the above script use dialog box titles created from Acrobat defaults. You can add more polish to the dialog box appearances by adding a title to the alert and response dialog boxes.

To see more-sophisticated scripts that are used for application alerts and response dialog boxes, read Chapter 10, "Creating Advanced Form Designs," and Chapter 16, "Creating Forms for Real-World Uses."

Using Document Actions

Document Actions are actions from JavaScript routines that can be implemented when a file is printed, saved, or closed. Rather than using a button to execute an action, Acrobat executes the action during one of five conditions. A Document Action can be executed when a file closes, when a file is saved, after a file is saved, when a file is printed, and after a file is printed. There are many uses for executing actions on one of the Document Action items. You may wish to delete unused fields on a form, delete all page templates, or perhaps offer a message to the user after a form has been saved or printed. In environments where Acrobat Reader is used, alert dialog boxes can be displayed from Reader on all of the Document Action types.

Using Did Print Document Actions

If forms need to be routed in printed form, you can offer a user instructions on what to do with the form after it finishes printing. You may have Acrobat Reader users who cannot save data and find it necessary to circulate printed documents. In this case, you can set up a Document Action after a file has finished printing. You are assured the user sees the message because the form needs to be printed as the last step in completing the form.

Here's an example for creating an alert dialog box with a message to instruct a user what to do with a form after it has printed:

1. Open a PDF file and choose Tools ➪ JavaScript ➪ Set Document Actions.

2. The Document Actions dialog box opens. Select one of the five items in the list box for the type of action to be used. In this example, use Document Did Print as the action type. After the form prints, the action is executed by Acrobat.

3. Click Edit in the Document Actions dialog box. The JavaScript Edit dialog box opens.

4. Enter the following code:

```
app.alert("Please submit the printed form to the accounting
In box in the main office complex.",3)
```

5. Click OK in the JavaScript Edit dialog box.

6. The Document Actions dialog box displays an icon adjacent to the action type and the code appears in the window below Execute This JavaScript, as shown in Figure 8-22. If you later wish to delete the script, click on the Edit button and highlight the text. Press Delete (Backspace) on the keyboard to eliminate the text.

7. The Document Action type was the Document Did Print action. After the PDF file finishes printing, the dialog box shown in Figure 8-23 opens.

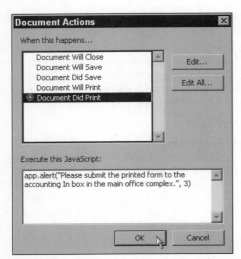

Figure 8-22: When you return to the Document Actions dialog box, the action type that you use is denoted by an icon that appears adjacent to the action type name. The JavaScript for the action appears in the lower window.

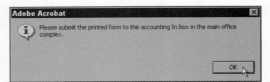

Figure 8-23: When the PDF file has finished printing, the application alert dialog box displays the message coded in the JavaScript routine.

Using Did Save Document Actions

If there are Acrobat or Acrobat Approval users who route forms electronically in your environment, you may wish to prevent other users from editing a file after it has been submitted to a department. There are a number of things you can do for protecting a file against unauthorized data entries among which include hiding data fields, locking data fields, deleting data fields, using digital signatures, and so on.

Using the same form from the last exercise, suppose all data entries must be typed in an Acrobat viewer. No data entry is permitted from handwritten forms. The amount fields in the form exist for user entry for each line item and the total field shown in Figure 8-24 is automatically calculated. If the user only fills in two lines like the example in Figure 8-24, you can hide the empty amount fields so no user can add more data reflected in the total calculation.

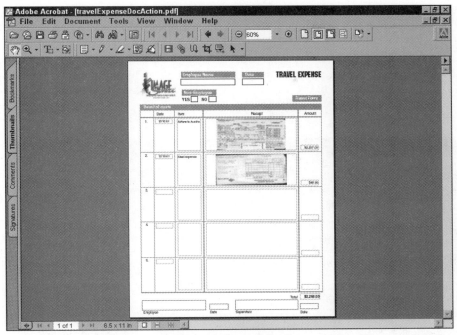

Figure 8-24: Two rows are filled in with data while the remaining three rows are empty. If the amount fields are hidden after completing the form, the total amount cannot be changed.

In this example, you can hide the fields for the last three amount data fields. Because the total field is locked and Acrobat Standard Security can prevent a user from changing the document, the file is secured after adding the Did Save Document Action. Follow these steps to hide the fields on the Document Action:

1. Choose Tools ➪ JavaScript ➪ Document Actions.

2. Select Document Did Save from the list of action types.

3. Click Edit to open the JavaScript Edit dialog box.

4. Enter the following code:

```
for (var i = 0; i < 5;i++) {
var f = this.getField("amount."+i);
  if (f.value == "")
    f.hidden = true;
}
```

In the preceding code, the loop cycles through all the amount fields (amount.0, amount.1, amount.2,and so on) for the five fields. The value of the amount.i field is assessed and if the amount field contents are empty (==""), the field is hidden (f.hidden = true;).

5. Click OK in the JavaScript Edit dialog box. You are returned to the Document Actions dialog box. If you use the Document Did Print script from the previous exercise, then two Document Actions are listed with an icon adjacent to the respective action type.

6. Exit the Field Properties dialog box and save the file. After saving, you'll notice the fields in the amount column below the last field containing data are hidden, as shown in Figure 8-25.

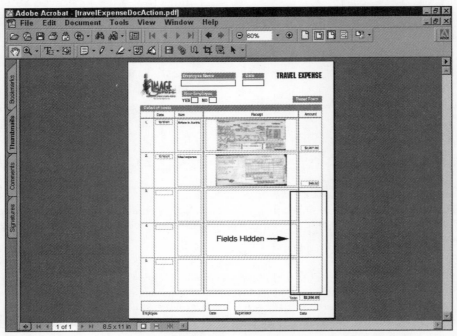

Figure 8-25: After saving the PDF file, the empty fields that are identified in the JavaScript are hidden, thereby preventing any data entry or a change the total value.

Document Actions can be set to individual, multiple, or all action types. When creating Document Actions, you must be certain the script actions can be implemented by the viewer being used. Obviously, there are many actions that won't work with some viewers. As an example, if you attempt to delete fields in Acrobat Reader, the function is not available to Reader users. You may wish to add the app.viewerType statement (which I mentioned at the beginning of this chapter) to guide users to select an appropriate viewer that can execute the Document Actions you create.

Summary

✦ You can associate actions with a number of different mouse behaviors. When using JavaScript, the routines are invoked according to the assigned mouse behaviors.

✦ JavaScript routines are used for performing calculations that are not available in the preset calculations that Acrobat provides.

✦ You can use JavaScripts in Page Open actions to alert users when an Acrobat viewer version or viewer type is not compatible with the actions that you've made available through JavaScripts on your forms.

✦ You can add new form fields to PDF forms through JavaScript.

✦ You can import images from button actions that use JavaScript to open a dialog box in which PDFs can be located and added to button field face appearances.

✦ You can add routines to Document Actions in which an action can be instructed to run during print and save operations.

✦　　✦　　✦

Creating Templates and Spawning Pages

You use templates in PDF forms to hold pages with or without fields that may be used for creating additional pages and extending a document. From a template, pages can be spawned to form new pages in the PDF form. When pages are spawned from templates with form fields, Acrobat creates a new page; then Acrobat renames the fields so unique field names are added to the new pages. This ensures that the fields from one page to another are unique and unique data can be added to fields appearing on all pages. Spawning pages is handled with JavaScript. Before a page can be spawned, however, you must first have a template.

Working with Templates

Templates are created from one or more pages in a PDF document. You can produce the PDF document with a page that becomes a template or you can create a separate PDF document and insert the page, then convert it to a template. Any PDF document with one or more pages can have a template made from a given page. Templates in PDF documents can be visible or hidden. If you have a single-page PDF file and wish to make the page a template, Acrobat creates a duplicate page and makes the duplicate a template. At least one page in a PDF file must remain visible; therefore, a duplicate page is necessary when creating a template from a single-page PDF file. If you have more than one page in a PDF file, Acrobat converts pages to templates without duplicating them.

Creating custom stamps from templates

In addition to creating new pages from a template page, there are some other uses you can find with templates that can assist you in working with forms. Templates also afford us an opportunity to create custom stamp libraries in which icons and symbols can be imported into PDFs for use in your forms. In Chapter 8, "Writing JavaScript Routines," we created a Stamp comment from a JavaScript to display an approval stamp. The stamp icon that was used was imported from the default stamp library provided with the Acrobat installation.

 Cross-Reference Refer to Chapter 8, "Writing JavaScript Routines," for a discussion about creating Stamp comments with JavaScript.

You may find that the standard stamps provided by Adobe don't suit your needs and you may wish to use a variety of custom stamp icons for use with your forms. In this regard, you can create a library of custom stamps that can be used with the Stamp Comment tool and share them with all Acrobat users in your company.

Creating a custom stamp library involves three steps:

✦ First, you create PDF files to represent the stamp icons and to produce a single PDF file.

✦ Next, you create page templates and name the category that you want displayed in the Stamp Properties dialog box.

✦ Finally, you save the PDF file to a specific location in the Acrobat folder so the stamps can be selected in the Stamp Properties dialog box.

Creating templates

To start creating custom stamps, you need to have a PDF file with the icons, images, and/or text to be used for each stamp. In this exercise, use the `stamps.pdf` file in the Chapter 9 folder on the book's CD-ROM. The file contains four pages, as shown in Figure 9-1.

 On the CD-ROM You'll find the stamps.pdf file in the Chapter 9 folder on the book's CD-ROM.

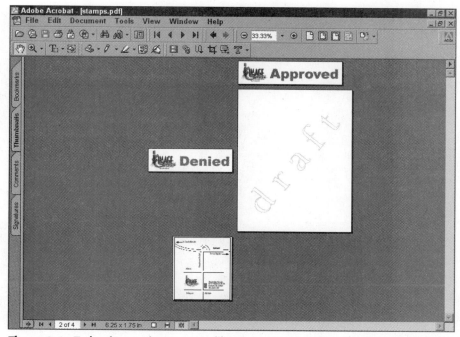

Figure 9-1: To begin creating a stamp library, you start with a PDF file with pages to be used for each individual stamp.

1. Open the `stamps.pdf` file or any document with several pages to be used as custom stamps. Begin on the first page and choose Tools ➪ Forms ➪ Page Templates, as shown in Figure 9-2.

2. The Page Templates dialog box opens. Enter a name in the Name field in the Page Templates dialog box, as shown in Figure 9-3. The name you provide here is the template name and also the name listed in the Stamp Properties dialog box in a list below the Category listing. Use a descriptive name for the stamp.

3. Click on the Add button to add the current page in view to the list in the Page Templates window. Before the template is added to the list window, an alert dialog box opens, as shown in Figure 9-4.

4. Click Yes and the template is added to the list in the Page Templates dialog box.

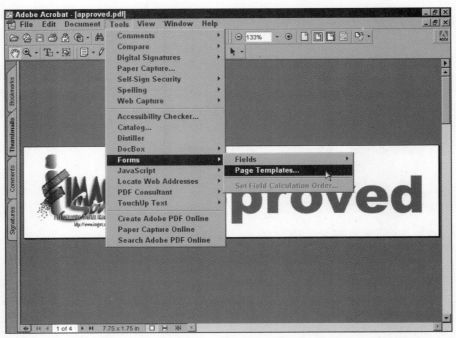

Figure 9-2: To create a Page Template, choose Tools ➪ Forms ➪ Page Templates.

Figure 9-3: Add a name for the template and click on the Add button.

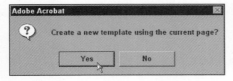

Figure 9-4: A dialog box opens asking you to confirm creating a template from the current page in view in the Document Pane. Click Yes to create the template.

5. Navigate to Page 2 and select the menu command to create a template from the page in view. Follow the same steps above by providing a name and clicking Yes to confirm adding the page as a template. Continue the same procedure until page templates have been created for all four pages. After creating a template for the last page, the list in the Page Templates dialog box displays all template names, as shown in Figure 9-5.

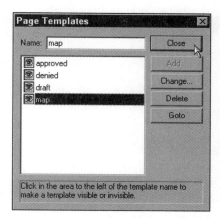

Figure 9-5: All page templates are listed in the Page Templates dialog box.

6. The names for the page templates appear in the Stamp Properties dialog box as a list like the one shown in the Page Templates dialog box. Stamps also have category names, so you can select a category from a pull-down menu and display all the stamps in a given category. The category name is derived from the Title field in the Document Summary dialog box. To add a category name, choose File ⇨ Document Properties ⇨ Summary. In the Document Summary dialog box, add a name to the Title field to be used as the category name in the Stamp Properties dialog box, as shown in Figure 9-6.

Cross-Reference For more information on using Document Summaries, see bonus Chapter 17, "Organizing Real-World Workflows," which you'll find on the book's CD-ROM.

Saving PDFs to the Stamps folder

In order for the stamps to be recognized in the Stamp Properties dialog box, the file with the template pages needs to be saved to the Stamps folder on your hard drive. To save the file to the proper location, follow these steps:

1. Choose File ⇨ Save As after you've created the template pages and added a category name in the Title field of the Document Summary dialog box.

2. The file needs to be saved to the Stamps folder nested below several folders in the Acrobat Folder. The directory path is Acrobat 5.0: Acrobat: Plug_ins: Annotations: Stamps, as shown in Figure 9-7.

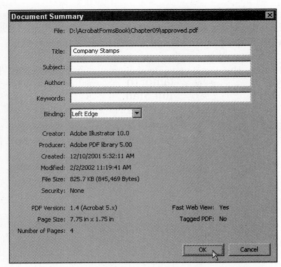

Figure 9-6: Add a descriptive name in the Title field in the Document Summary dialog box.

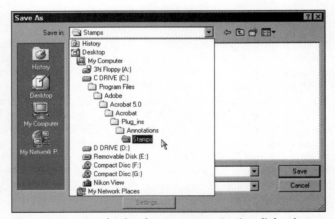

Figure 9-7: In order for the Stamp Properties dialog box to recognize custom stamps, they need to be saved to the Stamps folder nested below several folders in the Acrobat folder.

3. Open the Stamps folder, provide a name, and click Save in the Save As dialog box. The name you provide for the filename has nothing to do with the listings in the Stamp Properties for either stamp names or the category name. Feel free to name the file as you wish.

The custom stamp library has been created and saved to the proper location and can now be used for adding Stamp Comments from this library to your PDF forms.

Using custom stamps

When you use the Stamp tool and create a stamp, the default stamp appearance is displayed in the document window. The default Stamp is determined by Acrobat from the last stamp you used. When you change the stamp appearance, it becomes the new default. To change Stamp Properties and use your custom stamps, follow these steps:

1. Select the Stamp tool in the Acrobat Command Bar and drag open a rectangle.

2. To change the stamp appearance, right-click (Windows) or Control+click (Mac OS) to open a context menu and select Properties.

3. The Stamp Properties dialog box opens. Select the pull-down menu for Category to display the menu items. In this list you should see the library created in the previous exercise. The name appearing for the Category is the same name you supplied for the Title field in the Document Summary dialog box. In this example, the Company Stamps is used for the Title field. When you open the pull-down menu to list My Categories, Company Stamps appears, as shown in Figure 9-8.

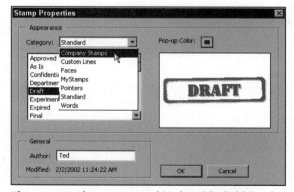

Figure 9-8: The name used in the Title field for the Document Summary information is displayed as a category name in the Stamp Properties dialog box.

4. Select the Category name for the custom stamp library. In the list box below the Category name, each page template name appears. Select a stamp to use and click OK. Acrobat returns you to the Document Pane and the stamp image you selected appears on the PDF page, as shown in Figure 9-9.

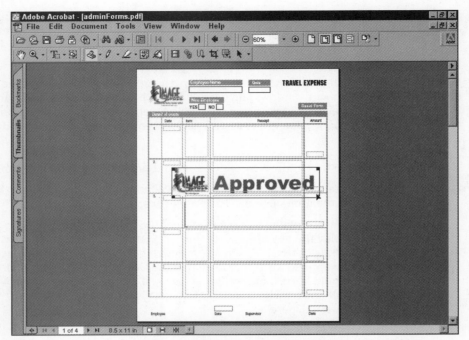

Figure 9-9: Select a stamp in the list window from the Stamp Properties dialog box and click OK. The new stamp appearance is displayed on the page.

Changing stamp attributes

Images and vector objects cannot be changed in Acrobat. Text, on the other hand, can be modified in Acrobat. If you use text for symbols, icons, or when combined with raster or vector objects, you can change the text attributes. If you create stamp icons with text and later wish to change text attributes such as text color, font, or point size, you can modify the attributes and resave the stamp library. When changes are made to stamps, the file needs to first be saved with the updated edits before you can use the stamps with the new attributes. To change the color of text as an example, follow these steps:

1. Open the PDF file saved to the Stamps folder, and navigate to the page to be edited.

2. Select the TouchUp Text tool from the Acrobat Command Bar.

3. Drag the tool across the text on the stamp to select the text to be changed.

4. Open a context menu on the selected text. Select Attributes from the menu options, as shown in Figure 9-10.

5. In the Text Attributes dialog box, click on the color swatch for the fill color to open a pop-up menu, as show in Figure 9-11. Select a color to change the appearance of the text.

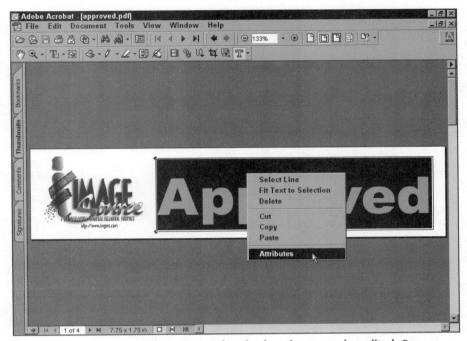

Figure 9-10: Use the TouchUp Text tool and select the text to be edited. Open a Context menu and select Attributes.

Tip

When you create the original PDF files that you want to use in a custom stamp library, use one of the base 13 fonts or a font that has been loaded on all the computers in your company. Some fonts may be embedded and treated as a subset. You may not be able to edit the text attributes if the font is not loaded on your system.

6. Choose File ➪ Save to update the file in the Stamps folder. When you return to the Stamp Properties, the edits are reflected in the stamps listed under the Category.

Note

You may need to close any open PDF files and reopen them to use stamps when the attributes have been changed.

Tip

You can add more pages to an existing library. Each page added to the file must have a new template created. Create the templates and save the file to update it. When you open the Stamp Properties, all new template names are undated in the Stamp Properties dialog box.

7. Select the Stamp tool and drag open a rectangle. The last stamp used appears as the image for the new stamp.

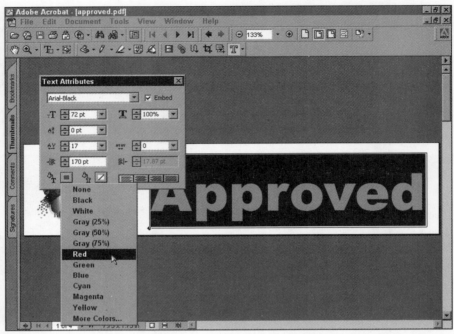

Figure 9-11: Select the attributes to change in the Text Attributes dialog box. For color fill changes, select the first color swatch at the bottom of the dialog box and make a new color selection.

8. In order to change stamp icons, you need to open the Stamp Properties dialog box. Open a context menu from the selected stamp and select Properties.

9. In the Stamp Properties dialog box, select the stamp where the text attributes were changed and click OK. The new stamp reflects the changes made to the text attributes.

Creating templates from pages with fields

If you have a page with fields that needs to be converted to a template, Acrobat provides the means for producing pages from a template with unique field names. Each page spawned from a template produces fields with parent/child names much like Acrobat offers you when creating table arrays. The procedures for creating a template when fields are present on a form follow the same steps as above. In this exercise, create a template that will later be used to spawn pages. Follow these steps to first create the template:

On the CD-ROM

You'll find both the `courseEval.pdf` **file and the** `courseEvalPage2.pdf` **file in the Chapter 9 folder on the book's CD-ROM.**

1. For this exercise, use the `courseEval.pdf` file in the Chapter 9 folder on the book's CD-ROM. After opening the file, choose Document ⇨ Insert Pages. The PDF file is a single-page document and the template to be used is another single-page PDF document to be inserted in the first file opened.

Cross-Reference

For more on inserting pages in PDF documents, see Chapter 2, "Using Authoring Applications."

2. The Select File to Insert dialog box opens. For this exercise, use the `courseEvalPage2.pdf` file located in the Chapter 9 folder on the book's CD-ROM. Select the file to open and click on the Select button.

3. The Insert Pages dialog box opens. In this dialog box you determine where the page is inserted and how many pages are to be inserted. Because both files are single-page documents, no decision needs to be made for the number of pages to insert. For the location of the inserted page, select After from the pull-down menu and select the Last radio button, as shown in Figure 9-12.

Figure 9-12: Select After from the pull-down menu for Location and select the Last radio button. Click OK to insert the page at the specified location.

4. The four fields at the top of the first page are used on the template. To duplicate the fields, select all the fields and open a context menu. From the menu choices, select Duplicate.

Cross-Reference

For more on duplicating fields, see Chapter 3, "Understanding Field Types," and Chapter 5, "Creating Form Fields."

5. The Duplicate Field dialog box opens. Select From Page 2 To Page 2 in the dialog box.

6. Navigate to page two by clicking on the Next Page tool in the Acrobat Command Bar. Open the Field Properties dialog box and change the names for the fields. In this example, use `comments` to append the existing field names, thus: `comments.course`, `comments.date`, and so on.

7. Create additional fields to be used on the template. In this example, there are three areas for student comments. Create a text field for each of the three areas and set the Field Properties in the Options tab to Multi-line, as shown in Figure 9-13.

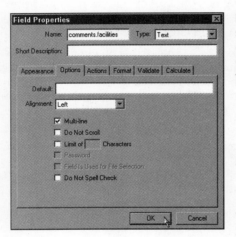

Figure 9-13: For the comment fields, select Options in the Field Properties dialog box and click on the Multi-line check box to enable user input in the field for several lines of data.

8. When all the fields have been created and the attributes defined, it's time to create the template. Choose Tool ➪ Forms ➪ Page Templates, as used in the earlier exercise.

9. The Page Templates dialog box opens. A PDF file can have more than one page template, therefore each new template needs to have a unique name. In the Name field, type a name for the template. In this example, `comments` was used for the name.

Note   Page template names are case-sensitive.

10. Click on the Add button in the Page Templates dialog box to add the page as a template. A warning dialog box opens asking you to confirm creating a template from the page in view in the Document Pane. Click OK in the Adobe Acrobat dialog box.

11. Acrobat returns you to the Page Templates dialog box and shows the template name listed as a new template. By default, the template is visible.

   In Windows, the template visibility is denoted by an eye icon inside a square to the left of the template name. On the Mac OS, the icon appearance is a bullet to the left of the template name. You can choose to have templates remain visible or hide them. To hide a template, click on the eye icon (Windows) or bullet (Mac OS) in the Page Templates dialog box.

12. Click on the icon to the left of the template name and hide it.

   In Windows, the icon changes from an eye to an empty square. On the Mac OS, the bullet changes to a dashed line. When you examine the Page Templates dialog box, you can immediately see all the templates listed and whether they are currently visible or hidden, as shown in Figure 9-14.

Figure 9-14: When hiding templates, the icon adjacent to the left of the template name changes appearance. The template page is immediately hidden before you exit the Page Templates dialog box.

13. Click OK in the Page Templates dialog box. The template is hidden when you click on the icon in the Page Templates dialog box. When you return to the document window in this example, notice the status bar reports 1 of 1 pages in the PDF file. Acrobat does not report the hidden templates for the page count in the PDF file.

At this point, the template has been created. In order to duplicate pages from the template, you need to add a JavaScript action to spawn a page from the template.

Spawning Pages from Templates

Spawning pages from a template is an Acrobat feature that you can find useful for many different kinds of forms. For forms to be completed by users, spawning pages can offer a simple short form more flexibility by adding pages based on user responses. You can design forms and templates with description fields for amplifying responses if a user is inclined to supply more information. The base form can be designed to solicit responses without overwhelming a user with a long complicated form. In other situations, you might use Acrobat forms for creating filing systems, address books, records maintenance tools, or other documents where pages appear the same and the data fields change for each new page.

Creating a new page from a template

Using the example with the template, start with a simple routine to create a new page from the template. In this example, the evaluation form used in the last exercise requests user input for multiple-choice questions. If a user wishes to add a narrative, the option for adding the page where the open-ended questions appear is created as a new page. To offer the choice for the user, create a button field with a JavaScript to spawn a page from the template. Follow these steps to set up the button:

On the CD-ROM You'll find the `courseEval.pdf` file in the Chapter 9 folder on the book's CD-ROM.

1. Open a PDF file with a template. For this example use the `courseEval.pdf` file with the template created in the last exercise.

2. Drag open a field rectangle with the Form tool. Name the field and select Button for the field Type. Set the Appearance and Options properties as desired. Click on the Actions tab and add a JavaScript action.

3. In the JavaScript Edit dialog box, add the code below:

   ```
   this.spawnPageFromTemplate("comments");
   ```

   The addition of "comments" is the name of the template. If you used a different name, enter the name between the quotation marks.

4. Click OK.

5. Click OK to close the Field Properties dialog box and click on the button when you return to the Document Pane.

6. Notice how a new page is created from the template. When a user clicks on a button to add a new page, typically the user will want to begin filling in data. When this page is spawned, you need to navigate to the new page. To help the user find the new page immediately after spawning it, add another line of code to the button field. Select the Form tool and open the Field Properties dialog box.

7. Select Actions and click on the JavaScript item in the right window. Click on Edit to open the code in the JavaScript Edit dialog box.

8. Append the JavaScript routine and add a second line of code. The complete script appears as:

```
this.spawnPageFromTemplate("comments");
this.pageNum++;
```

9. Click OK to close the JavaScript Edit window. Click OK to close the Field Properties dialog box. When you return to the Document Pane, click on the button. A page is spawned from the template and the new page opens in the Document Pane, as shown in Figure 9-15.

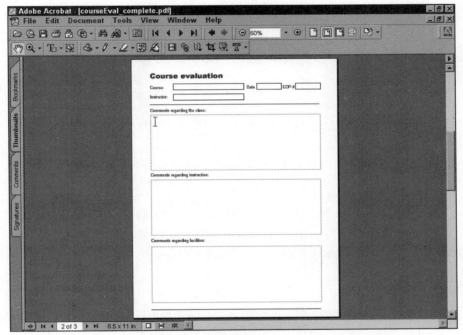

Figure 9-15: When a user clicks on the button, a new page is created from the template and Acrobat navigates to the page immediately after spawning it.

In this example, a page was added to the PDF file. You can use a similar routine to imprint a page to superimpose an image or text over an existing page much like a watermark or stamp.

Imprinting pages

You may have legacy files that need to be updated for changes in your company. Something like changing a logo, adding a Web site, altering header or footer information, or similar kinds of tasks can often be easier to perform in Acrobat than returning to authoring applications and recreating PDF files. In other cases, you may wish to add a watermark, symbol, or directive to a PDF file containing many pages. Perhaps an employee manual needs to be routed to management as a draft document. If the manual was created from several applications with illustrations, graphs, text, and layout content, adding the word *draft* to all the pages could take some time. With a modification to the code discussed above, you can use a page template and imprint all pages with the content of the template page.

To superimpose the data from a template to all pages in a PDF file, follow these steps:

You'll find the `adminForms.pdf` file in the Chapter 9 folder on the book's CD-ROM.

1. Open a PDF file with several pages. For this example, I use the `adminForms.pdf` file in the Chapter 9 folder on the book's CD-ROM. This file is a collection of a few forms used in earlier exercises. Presume you want to circulate some draft forms to a management committee for approval. The forms should not be used in the company until all appropriate personnel have reviewed and approved them. Therefore, we will watermark the pages with the word *draft*.

2. Create a PDF file to be used as the template. For this example, use the `draft.pdf` form in the Chapter 9 folder on the book's CD-ROM, as shown in Figure 9-16.

You'll find the `draft.pdf` form in the Chapter 9 folder on the book's CD-ROM.

3. Insert the page `draft.pdf` in the open PDF file containing the forms and choose Tools ⇨ Forms ⇨ Page Templates. (For inserting pages, see the previous exercise.)

Make sure you navigate to the page that you want to use as a template before addressing the Page Templates menu command.

4. In the Page Templates dialog box, provide a name for the template and click on the Add button. Click OK in the confirmation dialog box, as described in the earlier exercise. Click on the icon adjacent to the template name to hide the template. In this example, use the word `draft` for the template name.

5. Click Close in the Page Templates dialog box.

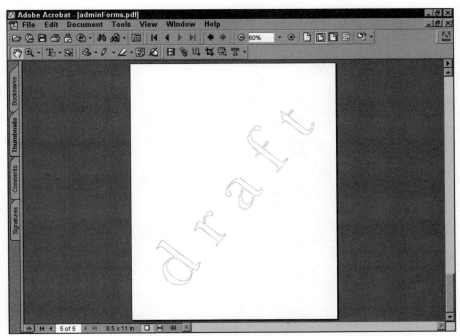

Figure 9-16: Insert the page to be used as a template. (In this example, I used the `draft.pdf` file that you'll find in the Chapter 9 folder.)

6. Add a button field to the first page and add a JavaScript action. In the JavaScript Edit dialog box, enter the following code:

```
var iNumPages = this.numPages;
  console.println(iNumPages);
for (i = 0; i < iNumPages; i++)
{
  console.println(i);
  this.spawnPageFromTemplate("draft", i, true);
}
```

In the above code, the loop moves through all pages and spawns the template page data. However, the spawned page superimposes the template page on all four pages determined by the loop and the (`"draft", i, true`) items at the end of the routine.

7. Click OK in the Field Properties dialog box to set the properties and return to the Document Pane.

8. Select the Hand tool and click on the button. You should see the template data imprinted on each page, as shown in Figure 9-17.

9. Delete the button field and the template before saving the PDF and distributing the document.

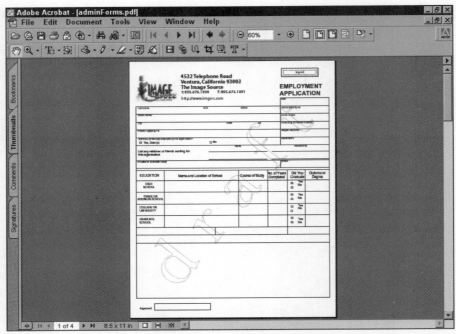

Figure 9-17: After clicking on the button, the template data appears on each page.

Spawning pages from multiple templates

You may have a need to spawn a page from a choice between several templates. If one condition exists, template(1) is used. If another condition exists, template(2) is used. You can set up a button or response in a field to make a choice between one of several templates to be used for creating a new page. In other circumstances, you may wish to create forms for personal documents such as filing systems, address books, calendars, or similar files that may use several templates. Depending on the button action, a choice is made for which template is used to spawn the page.

The addrBook.pdf file in the Chapter 9 folder on the book's CD-ROM is a sample of a file to be used as an address book. This document contains only the first few pages for adding names in the A to C categories. If a button is selected on the A page, the button action spawns a page from the A template. If a button is selected on the B page, the B template is spawned, and so forth. To illustrate how choices for spawning pages from different templates are made, use the example shown in Figure 9-18.

You'll find the addrBook.pdf file in the Chapter 9 folder on the book's CD-ROM.

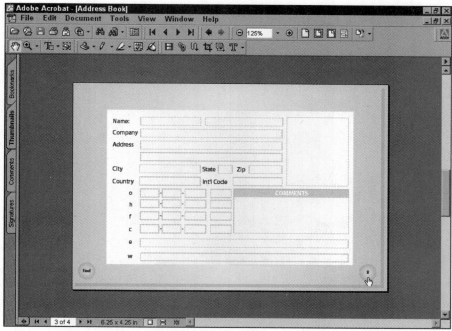

Figure 9-18: The addrBook.pdf file contains three templates. Each of the buttons on the address pages spawns a page from one of the three templates.

The opening page of the address book file has a cover page, as shown in Figure 9-19. On the cover page are links that link to pages for the A to C categories. Click on the A link and view the changes to a form in which the letter A appears in the lower-right corner of the page. Click on B and the letter B appears on the page, and so forth.

When a page has been filled in, a button in the lower-right corner is used to spawn a page from a template. (In this example, the button field rests atop the alpha character on each page.) If another name beginning with B is to be used, then clicking on the button to spawn a page on the B page pulls the B template and places the page immediately after the page in view. This behavior keeps all the like alpha characters together. It doesn't alphabetize the pages, but does keep the pages with the same characters together.

If you examine the Page Templates, you can see from Figure 9-20 that the file has three templates with the respective alpha character as the name for the template. Notice all Page Templates are hidden.

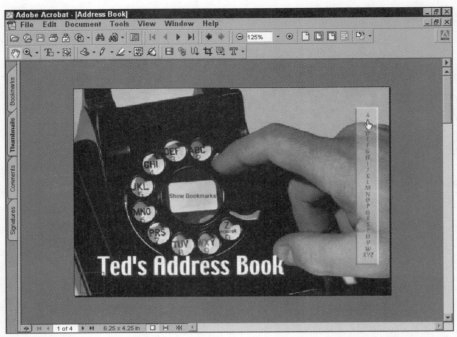

Figure 9-19: The cover page has links from the A to C characters that link to the respective pages.

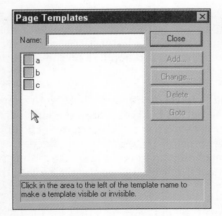

Figure 9-20: The three template names are named according to the respective pages for the alpha order.

If you navigate to the B page and open the field in the lower-right corner to display the Field Properties, the Action tab shows a JavaScript on the Mouse Up behavior, as shown in Figure 9-21.

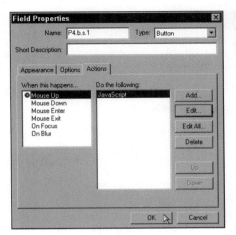

Figure 9-21: Each page has a button field with a JavaScript used for spawning a page from one of the templates.

The following code is the script that is used for the B page:

```
this.spawnPageFromTemplate({
cTemplate: this.getNthTemplate(1),
nPage: this.pageNum + 1,
bRename: true,
bOverlay: false
});
this.pageNum ++;
```

The first line of code triggers spawning a page from a template. The this. getNthTemplate(1) item uses template number 1. The templates are chosen according to the position displayed in the Page Templates dialog box. The first template is (0), the next (1), and so forth. The this.pageNum +1, item places the spawned page after the current page (for example, this page viewed plus 1). Using true and false tells Acrobat to change the field names on the spawned page and to create the page as a new page in the document. If you use false and false, the field names don't change. If you use true and true, the field names change, but instead of creating a new page the page is superimposed on the page where the button was selected. The final line of code navigates to the spawned page.

In the above example, pages are spawned from a given template from the button selected on each page. The three templates all contain the buttons used to spawn the pages, so when a new page is added, the respective button is included on the new page. Therefore, additional pages can be spawned to keep all the alpha characters together. In other forms, you may wish to use if, else statements where if one condition exists, spawn template (0). If another condition exists, spawn page (1). Regardless of how the form is designed, keep in mind the selection of a particular template is made from the this.getNthTemplate(N) statement where N equals the number order of the template in the Page Templates dialog box.

Summary

✦ You can convert a PDF page into a page template for creating custom Stamp libraries and adding new pages to a PDF document.

✦ You can make page templates visible or invisible.

✦ Spawning pages from a template is handled with a JavaScript routine.

✦ You can add pages to a PDF document as well as use the PDF document for imprinting pages with watermarks and page content.

✦ ✦ ✦

Creating Advanced Form Designs

Some forms you work with may be single-page forms simplified for user input and routing data. Other forms may be more complex in which a little automation can help users complete a form.

You may wish to force data decisions, auto tab fields, swap data between forms, add audio directives, or other similar actions that distinguish your forms from more-static designs. In this chapter, we'll take a look at adding a little flair to a form to assist users in understanding a form and filling in the data fields with ease.

Adding Audio Messages to Forms

Business workers in the twenty-first century are constantly bombarded with visual stimuli and audio messages and are becoming increasingly more dependent on these methods over spending time reading text. Adding audio or motion to forms designs can reduce the amount of time a user needs to complete a form and at times make your forms more interesting. As you introduce effects, such as audio sounds, be aware that too much defeats the purpose of simplifying a form and each audio message adds significantly to the file size.

Finding sound creation applications

Audio messages are imported from sound files. In order to import a sound, you must first create the sound in a sound editing application. The Audio comment tool in Acrobat is used for creating sounds and importing them as comments. However, if you wish to repurpose sounds for Page Actions or field actions, you need to use another tool to first create the sound and save the sound as a separate file. Once saved as a file, the sound can then be imported through action types other than the Audio comments.

If you are so inclined, you can purchase a commercial application for editing sounds and saving recordings to files that Acrobat can recognize. If recording sounds is an infrequent task and does not warrant purchase of expensive commercial software, you can find sound recording applications as shareware and in the public domain that can satisfy almost any need you have for using sounds on forms.

Web sites change frequently, so you may need to do a search for public domain software for your computer platform. As of this writing, you can find applications at www.freewarefiles.com (Windows) or www.macupdate.com (Mac OS). Public domain software applications downloaded from these sites enable you to record sounds and save them in formats acceptable to the platform you use that can then be recognized by Acrobat. The most common of the file types recognized by Acrobat is .wav for Windows and .aiff for Mac OS, or any sound format compliant with Apple QuickTime.

Recording sounds

Be certain you have a microphone properly connected to your computer according to your computer's user manual. Launch the application you downloaded from a Web site distributing public domain software or use a commercial application if you have made a purchase. Most programs offer you a record button similar in appearance to a tape recorder or VCR. Click the Record button and speak into the microphone. When finished recording, click the Stop button. Depending on the application, you may be prompted in a dialog box to save the file or you may see a window where the sound can be further edited, as show in Figure 10-1.

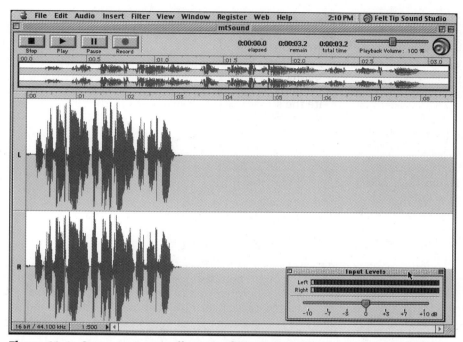

Figure 10-1: Some programs offer you editing features for the sounds recorded. After the recording and any editing you wish to make, save the file in a format acceptable to Acrobat.

If a dialog box does not prompt you to save the recording, select Save or Save As from a menu option. Typically, the commands are under the file menu, but these may vary depending on the program used. When you save the file, be certain to save in a format acceptable to Acrobat. You can import in Acrobat a .wav or .aif (Windows) or .aiff (Mac OS) file format, or any file type acceptable to the Apple QuickTime format, but be careful of any file compression that you applied to the file when you saved it. You may need to test various format options in order to find a format that Acrobat can recognize. After choosing the format, supply a name for the file with the proper extension, as shown in Figure 10-2.

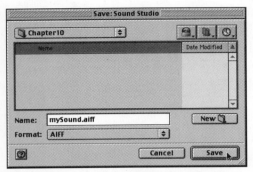

Figure 10-2: Select the proper format and save the sound file to disk.

Adding sounds to page actions

A sound may be added to a Page Open or a Page Close action to inform a user about either some information about completing the form or what to do with the form after filling in the data fields. In order to add a sound to a Page Action, you must have the sound file saved to disk, as described above. To add a sound to a Page Action, follow these steps:

1. Be certain your sound file is available in a directory on your hard drive and choose Document ⇨ Set Page Action. The Page Actions dialog box opens.

2. Select either the Page Open or Page Close item in the left window in the Page Actions dialog box and click on the Add button.

3. The Add an Action dialog box opens. From the pull-down menu for Type, select Sound, as shown in Figure 10-3.

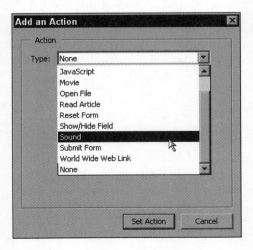

Figure 10-3: Select Sound from the pull-down menu choices for Type.

4. Click on Sound in the Add an Action dialog box.

5. The Open dialog box appears. Navigate your hard drive to find the sound to import and select it in the Open dialog box. Click Open.

6. Acrobat may pause momentarily. The sound file imported in Acrobat is converted during the import. When a sound is imported in a PDF file, the sound can then be played across platforms. Therefore, a .wav file can be played on a Mac OS computer and an .aiff file can be played on a Windows computer. Click OK in the Add an Action dialog box and you are returned to the Page Actions dialog box.

7. Click OK in the Page Actions dialog box.

After saving the PDF file and reopening it, the sound is played. You may add a sound for a Page Open action that informs a user that all fields need to be completed and a digital signature is required before submitting the form, or some sort of similar message. On a Page Close action, you may alert the user as to when an order can be expected or processed. When the user quits Acrobat or closes the file, the sound message plays.

Adding sounds to field actions

Of the mouse behavior types, you may find that a Mouse Enter, On Focus, or On Blur mouse behavior works better in some cases than the other behaviors. As an example, you might have a message play to add a description to a button when the cursor is placed over the field before the user clicks the mouse. Or, you may wish to invoke a sound when the user tabs out of a field as a reminder to verify their data entry. In these situations and any other similar conditions you wish to use, the sound is played from a mouse behavior related to a field action. To understand how to use sound actions with mouse behaviors, follow these steps:

You'll find the golfClassic.pdf form in the Chapter 10 folder on the book's CD-ROM. In a subfolder titled "sounds," you'll find four sound files that can be imported in the example form.

1. For this example, use the golfClassic.pdf form in the Chapter 10 folder on the book's CD-ROM, as shown in Figure 10-4. On the form there are four check boxes for sponsor contributions. When the mouse enters one of the four check boxes for the sponsor selection, a message plays informing the user of the advertising benefit relative to the level of sponsorship. On this form, use four separate recordings. Use an application to make four different recordings as examples for informing a user of the benefit of sponsorship.

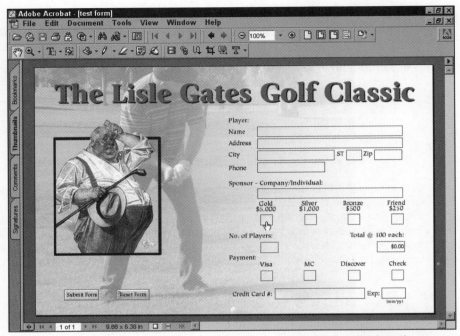

Figure 10-4: The form has four check boxes for sponsorship level. When the mouse cursor enters one of the four check boxes, a sound is played.

2. Open the Field Properties dialog box for the first check box for Gold sponsors. Select the Actions tab.

3. Select Mouse Enter from the "When this happens . . ." list or category in the Actions tab.

4. Click on the Add button to open the Add an Action dialog box.

5. Select Sound from the pull-down menu for Action Type, as described earlier in Figure 10-3.

6. Click on the Select Sound button to open the Open dialog box and select the sound to import for the first check box. In this example, the sound file `gold.aiff` was added for the Gold sponsor check box. Click Open. Select Set Action after the sound is imbedded.

7. When you return to the Add an Action dialog box, the Mouse Enter mouse behavior displays an icon to the left of the text.

8. Click OK in the Add an Action dialog box and OK again in the Field Properties dialog box.

9. Repeat the same steps using the same Mouse Enter behavior for the remaining three check boxes and use the sound files respective to the sponsorship check boxes on the form.

All sounds are found in the Chapter 10 folder inside the Sounds folder.

When the mouse enters one of the check boxes, the respective sound plays. The sound plays completely even if the cursor leaves the field. Sounds added to forms either for Page Actions or field actions can be played from any Acrobat viewer.

Adding Motion Effects to Forms

Movies can be imported in Acrobat PDF documents. The problem with using a movie file for an animation effect is the movie file is a link to the PDF. Whereas all other file types are embedded in a PDF document, a movie file needs to accompany the PDF in order for it to be played in Acrobat; and the directory path where the movie is located needs to be fixed to a designated location when the file is imported. All this creates a problem when downloading files from Web servers or copying files across networks.

Rather than use a movie file for an animation effect, you can use button icons and some JavaScript to create an animation. For PDF forms, you may wish to have some sort of animation used to inform a user that a field needs to be completed or amplify the importance for making the correct choice for a field entry.

The kind of animation effect you create with button icons are a simulated motion where one button appears and then disappears and the next button appears, then disappears, and so forth. To create such an effect, you need to approach it in two steps. First, the motion objects need to be created and imported as buttons in the sequence they are to appear in the animation. Second, you need to write the JavaScript to display and hide the button icons as well as set an interval for the speed in which they are displayed.

Creating motion objects

The first step in creating an animation is to first create the objects to be used in the animation. Because a movie file won't be imported, you need to create each individual frame for the animation. In some cases, the objects may change appearance or design, while other effects can be created from a single image duplicated and offset from each other. When each frame is displayed and hidden, the result appears as an animation. For example, an arrow that moves across the screen starts with a single image in view on the left side of the screen; the image is then hidden, then the next image is displayed. At an interval cycle, all images appear momentarily then hide from view, thus giving the illusion of an animated sequence.

In the following example, use an arrow icon to move horizontally across the form. If a user clicks on a submit button without supplying a credit card number, the arrow moves from the submit button to the credit card number field. After the last arrow image is displayed, a message box opens informing the user that the credit card number field needs to be completed.

To create the animation for the preceding example, follow these steps:

1. Create an icon or image in any authoring application and export the file to PDF. In this example, an arrow created from a text character from the Zapf Dingbats font is used, as shown in Figure 10-5.

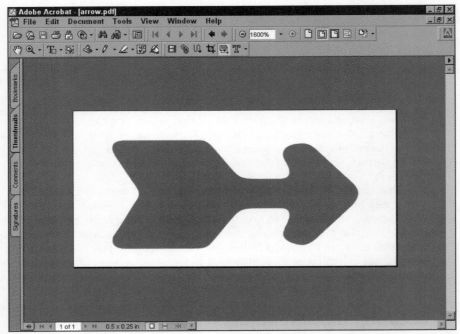

Figure 10-5: An arrow is created in an authoring application from the Zapf Dingbats font and saved as PDF.

2. Create a button field and import the image created above in the Options tab, as shown in Figure 10-6. The Layout should be Icon Only and the field rectangle size should be sized to suit a single animation frame.

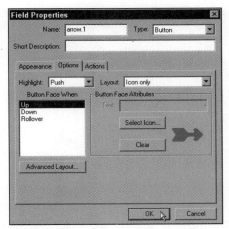

Figure 10-6: Add the icon or image to
be used for the animation in a Button field.

For more on creating button face appearances, see Chapter 4, "Understanding
Field Properties."

3. Click on the Appearance tab and select the Read Only check box.

4. Duplicate the field. You can either create an array or use parent/child names
and Ctrl+Shift drag (Windows) or Option+Shift drag (Mac OS) to duplicate a
field, press the + (plus) key to change the field name, then repeat the process
for each field created.

For more on duplicating fields and creating arrays, see Chapter 5, "Creating Form
Fields."

5. Distribute the fields. If you create an array, move the last field created to the
end of where the animation sequence is to stop. Select all fields and open a
context menu. From the menu choices, choose Distribute ➪ Horizontally, as
shown in Figure 10-7.

For more on distributing fields, see Chapter 5, "Creating Form Fields."

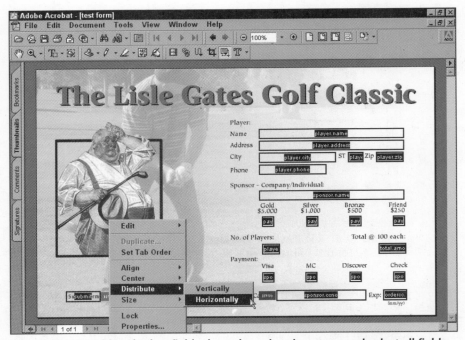

Figure 10-7: Position the last field where the animation stops and select all fields. Distribute the fields using a menu choice from a context menu.

6. Create a message field. In this example, an arrow is moved horizontally across the form from left to right to remind a user to fill in the credit card information. The arrow moves and stops at the field box where the credit card number needs to be entered. When the animation stops, a message box opens telling the user not to forget to fill in the credit card information. Create a button field for the message and supply the message text in the Button Face Attributes in the Options field properties, as shown in Figure 10-8.

7. Select the Appearance tab and check the box for Read Only.

8. Click OK in the Field Properties dialog box.

After all the fields have been created and positioned, save the file. You are now ready to write the JavaScript routine to create the motion effects.

Scripting motion effects

For this example, use the image created above with the golfAnimation.pdf file in the Chapter 10 folder on the book's CD-ROM. The Submit button contains the script to run the animation. Follow these steps to create the button that runs the motion:

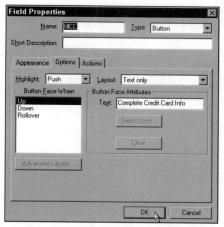

Figure 10-8: Create a field to be used for a message. Select the Options tab and enter your text message in the Button Face Attributes field box.

On the CD-ROM You'll find the `golfAnimation.pdf` file in the Chapter 10 folder on the book's CD-ROM. Note that the Submit button on the sample form already contains the script that's listed in the following section.

When you add a new button, see if you can follow the code (below) to recreate the button. If you run into difficulties, you can examine the code already supplied for the button field on the form. Create a button field with a JavaScript action and enter the following code:

```
//JavaScript Function can be at document level
function moov () {
var show = eval ("frame" + i);
show.display = display.visible;
if (i == 1) {
 frame15.display = display.hidden;
 }
else {
 var hide = eval ("frame" + (i-1))
 hide.display = display.hidden;
 }
i++
if (i == 16) {
 app.clearInterval (y); //stop
 msg.display = display.visible; //show msg
 }
}
//script for running the animation
```

```
var msg = this.getField("fillCC");
var cc = this.getField("sponsor.ccno");
if (cc.value =="") {
var frame1 = this.getField ("arrow.1");
var frame2 = this.getField ("arrow.2");
var frame3 = this.getField ("arrow.3");
var frame4 = this.getField ("arrow.4");
var frame5 = this.getField ("arrow.5");
var frame6 = this.getField ("arrow.6");
var frame7 = this.getField ("arrow.7");
var frame8 = this.getField ("arrow.8");
var frame9 = this.getField ("arrow.9");
var frame10 = this.getField ("arrow.10");
var frame11 = this.getField ("arrow.11");
var frame12 = this.getField ("arrow.12");
var frame13 = this.getField ("arrow.13");
var frame14 = this.getField ("arrow.14");
var frame15 = this.getField ("arrow.15");
i=1;
}
y = app.setInterval ("moov ()", 75);

if (cc.value !="") {
   app.clearInterval (y);
   ccData.hidden = false;
}
```

The script uses three subroutines. The first part is the function that controls the field displays. After reaching the last frame, the interval is cleared (app.clearInterval).

The second subroutine starts by checking the credit card field. If the field is empty (cc.value ==""), the routine is executed. The code begins by assigning the variables for the 15 frames. The last line of code in the second subroutine uses the function (moov) and sets the interval (75). You can change the number to run the motion faster or slower. A lower value results in a faster display of the fields. A higher value takes more time to display and hide fields, thereby slowing down the motion.

The function from the first subroutine takes care of stopping the animation and showing the message field at the end of the interval. Notice the interval stops when (i == 16). After the 15th frame is displayed and hidden, the interval is cleared.

The third subroutine examines the credit card field. If data are entered in the field, the interval is cleared and another message box opens. This subroutine is needed to halt the animation and prevent it from falling into an endless loop when a user adds data to the credit card field and clicks on the submit button.

When the Submit Form button is selected on the form and the credit card field does not contain any data, the arrow moves from the Submit Form button to the credit card field. Figure 10-9 shows one of the frames in between the beginning and the end of the sequence.

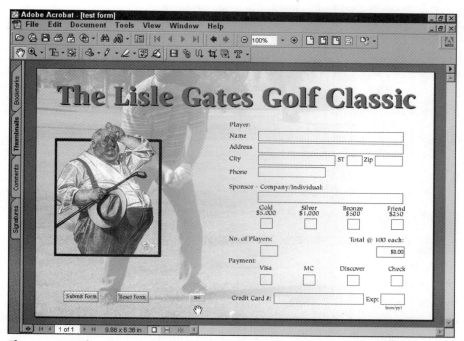

Figure 10-9: The arrow moves from left to right when the credit card field contains no data and the Submit Form button is selected.

After the 15th frame is displayed and hidden, the routine stops and the message field is displayed, as shown in Figure 10-10. In order to control the visibility of the message field, you might include a line of code in the routine to hide the message after data has been entered in the credit card field. You can also add a Page Action to hide the field when the document opens, in the event the file is saved after the user clicks on the Submit Form button.

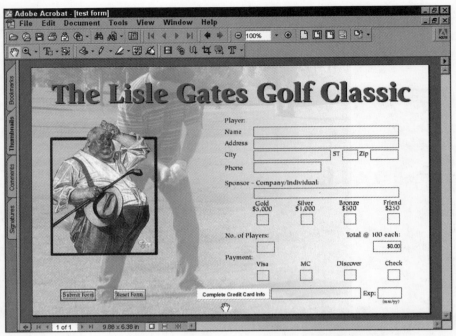

Figure 10-10: After the sequence ends, the message field is displayed.

The above example is a simple animation that can be easily created in Acrobat. You can copy and paste the JavaScript from the sample form and embellish it to add other animation effects with scrolling text, changing objects, and simulated animations that render movielike appearances.

This routine works for the example form where only one page exists on the form and the animation is used with a single button field. Assume for a moment you have several pages and you create similar effects for different pages. To eliminate redundant coding, you can move the subroutine for the function to a Document Level JavaScript where each field can use the function. To learn how to create Document Level functions, see the discussion on Document Level JavaScripts later in this chapter.

Cross-Reference   To understand more about creating more animation effects and using Document Level JavaScripts, see Chapter 16, "Creating Forms for Real-World Uses."

Creating Application Pop-Up Menus

Application pop-up menus have a similar appearance to Combo boxes. You can create application pop-up menus that help you conserve space on a form and offer a user options for opening files, jumping to pages in a multi-page form, or executing other actions that you develop in the JavaScript edit dialog box.

Application pop-up menus can be created with nesting so submenus offer choices within category listings much like a parent/child relationship. A parent item is listed as a category, and the child items for each parent appear as submenus or nested selections. For purposes of page navigation, submenus are linked to named destinations. Before you create an application pop-up menu, you first need to create named destinations for all the menu links.

Creating named destinations

A Destination is similar to a bookmark, and the method for creating a destination is handled like a link or bookmark. The name provided to the destination is the name, including case sensitivity, used in the JavaScript when you link a menu choice to a destination page.

To create a Destination, you first start with viewing the Destinations palette. Choose Window ➪ Destinations to open the Destinations palette. Before a Destination can be created, you must scan the document for existing destinations. Click the Scan icon in the Destinations palette to scan the document for destinations. (The Scan document icon is shown in Figure 10-11 to the left of the Create new destination icon.) Even if the form you use is a new document and contains no destinations, you must first start by scanning the document to add new destinations.

The second step is to navigate to the page where the destination is to be created and click on the Create New Destination icon in the Destinations palette, as shown in Figure 10-11. When you create a new destination, Acrobat automatically names the destination Untitled. Type a name for the destination and press the Enter key. Make note of the name and be certain to observe the case sensitivity. The name of the destination is used when you wish to open a file from a button on a form and navigate to a specific page or when you use an application pop-up menu and wish to open pages associated with the destinations. In Figure 10-12, the destination appears in the palette after creating and naming it.

Figure 10-11: To create a destination, navigate to the page where the destination is to be created and click on the Create New Destination button in the Destinations palette.

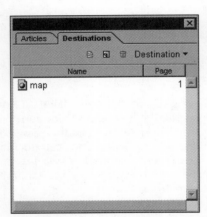

Figure 10-12: When naming destinations, use a consistent naming style for case sensitivity. The name you provide in the Destinations palette is used in the JavaScript that navigates to the destination pages.

Navigating to a destination

If you wish to open a file from a button and navigate to a specific page in the file all from a JavaScript routine, you first open the destination file and create a Named Destination, as described above. In another file, create a button field and add a JavaScript to open the PDF document and page where the destination was created. The following code illustrates an example of how to open a specific page in another document:

```
var employeeID = app.openDoc ("c/mydir/employee.pdf");
employeeID.gotoNamedDest("map");
```

In the above code, you must specify the directory path for where the file resides on your computer. If no directory path is specified, Acrobat only looks in the same directory as the file containing the button. If the file to open resides in the same directory, you can eliminate the path and just use the file name between the quotation marks. If you want the original file containing the button to close when the second file opens, use the following statement at the end of the routine:

```
this.closeDoc();
```

Creating a pop-up menu

Application pop-up menus can help users navigate through a long form and find pages easily through menu selections. In Figure 10-13, an application pop-up menu is designed with three categories. For each category, a submenu contains menu choices for pages to open in the PDF document. This form was designed for an insurance claim to be used by an adjuster in the event a claim is made on a homeowner's policy. From the opening page, an adjuster can select a menu choice to open a page where the detail on a given item is explained.

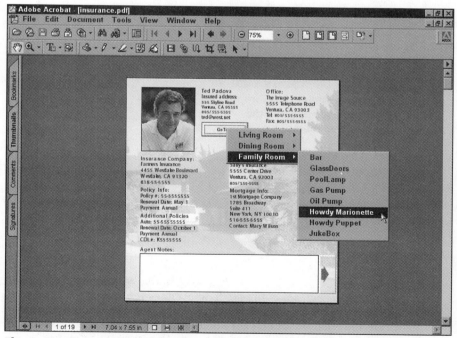

Figure 10-13: On the opening page in the PDF document, an application pop-up menu displays the categories and submenu items that are linked to page destinations.

To create an application pop-up menu similar to the one shown in Figure 10-13, follow these steps:

1. Create Named Destinations for all pages that are to appear in the application pop-up menu. When you view the Destinations palette, you can list the destinations by name in alphabetical order or by page, as shown in Figure 10-14.

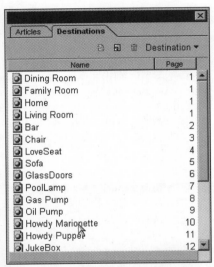

Figure 10-14: Create destinations for all menu choices to appear in the application pop-up menu.

2. Create a button field and add the following JavaScript code in the JavaScript Edit dialog box:

```
var c = app.popUpMenu
(["category1", "dest1", "dest2", "dest3"],
(["category2", "dest4", "dest5", "dest6"],
(["category3", "dest7", "dest8", "dest9"]);
this.gotoNamedDest (c);
```

The JavaScript for the example form shown above appears in Figure 10-15. The first item within each set of brackets determines the parent name or category. The following items separated by commas and contained within quotation marks are the child or subcategory names linked to the specific destinations. The last line of code instructs Acrobat to go to a named destination.

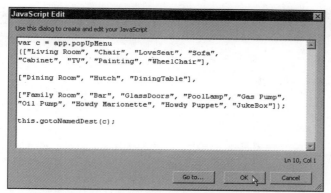

Figure 10-15: The parent category appears as the first name following the left bracket. The subsequent names following the category name are the named destinations.

3. Test the menu options. Select a category and a submenu item. If the coding is correct, you should navigate to the page corresponding to the destination name. If a page does not open when making a menu selection, double check the destination name and the name used in the JavaScript.

Creating Help Messages

If directions and messages are needed to help users complete a form, you can choose to add text in the design of the document or add text to fields that can be triggered for display from buttons, field entries, or Page Actions. To reduce clutter on a form, a pop-up type of help menu can be effective when a user needs some clarity on how to complete a form or fill in specific fields. By using the Show/Hide field action types, you can easily create text fields that can be displayed or hidden on a page. In addition, you also have the opportunity to add JavaScripts for displaying or hiding fields.

Adding Help text to fields

If help comments are to be hidden until a user activates a button to display a help note, you first need to set up the fields containing the messages. In Figure 10-16, a button resides on the form for Help with additional comments on an employee application form. Before scripting the button field, you need to create the help field(s).

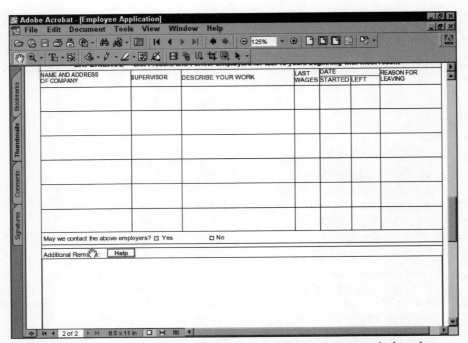

Figure 10-16: A help button is used on a form to open a message window that provides a user information about filling in a data field.

In this example, use Mouse Enter and Mouse Exit behaviors to display and hide two fields, respectively. One field is used as a title for the help message and the other field is used as the message contents. When the cursor enters the help button, the two text fields shown in Figure 10-17 appear. When the cursor leaves the help field, the fields disappear.

The `employeeApplication.pdf` form in the Chapter 10 tutorial folder on the book's CD-ROM is used in this example. Follow these steps to create the fields for the help title and help message:

You'll find the `employeeApplication.pdf` form in the Chapter 10 tutorial folder on the book's CD-ROM. Note: The fields have been created on the sample form. Try to add new fields similar to the examples appearing on the form.

1. Create a Text field for the title. In this example, the field was named `helpTitle`. In the Appearance properties, select the appearance options for Border and Background that contrast with the form design. Select a black thin border and a light color fill for the Background. The Style is beveled and the font chosen is Helvetica Bold.

2. Click on the Options tab. Set the Text Alignment to Center.

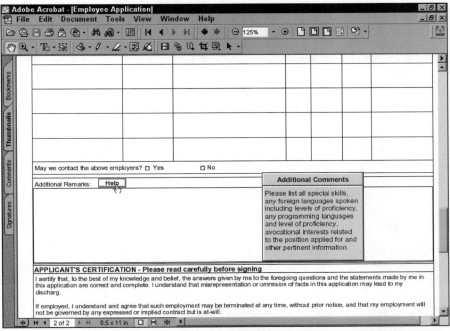

Figure 10-17: On the Mouse Enter mouse behavior, the help title field and the help message field are displayed. When the mouse cursor leaves the help button, the fields are hidden.

3. Click OK in the Field Properties dialog box. Create a second Text field for the help contents. In this example, the field is named `helpContents`.

4. In the Options properties, set the Alignment to Left and select the Multi-line check box.

5. Click OK in the Field Properties dialog box to return to the Document Pane. Select the Hand tool and enter the title text and message in the fields.

Position the fields in an area that is easily viewed by a user when the help button is activated to display the help fields. After the fields have been arranged and the messages supplied in the fields, you are ready to script the actions to hide and display the fields.

Hiding and displaying fields with JavaScript

Create a button field close to the help fields in a logical area for the user to recognize that the help applies to the field to be completed. The button uses an action for the Mouse Enter and Mouse Exit mouse behaviors for displaying and hiding the fields, respectively. Inasmuch as the fields are currently visible, you can write the JavaScript code to invoke the actions without hiding the fields.

Follow these steps to create the scripts that show and hide the fields:

1. Open the Field Properties for the button field and select Actions.

2. Add a JavaScript Action for the Mouse Enter mouse behavior and add the following code in the JavaScript Edit dialog box:

```
var f = this.getField("helpTitle");
var g = this.getField("helpContents");
f.hidden = true;
g.hidden = true;
```

3. For the Mouse Exit behavior, the true statements are change to false, as indicated for the script on the Mouse Exit:

```
var f = this.getField("helpTitle");
var g = this.getField("helpContents");
f.hidden = false;
g.hidden = false;
```

The preceding scripts accomplish the job. However, one caveat in using these scripts is when a user opens the PDF document and views the help messages, then closes the document without making any changes, Acrobat prompts the user to Save changes. To eliminate the warning dialog box when no changes are made to the PDF form, rewrite the scripts as shown below:

```
var f = this.getField("helpTitle");
var g = this.getField("helpContents");
var bDirty = this.dirty;
f.hidden = false; //true for Mouse Exit script
g.hidden = false; //true for Mouse Exit script
this.dirty = bDirty;
```

After adding the JavaScript, the Actions properties display an icon to the left of the Mouse Enter and Mouse Exit behaviors. Click OK in the Field Properties dialog box.

Test the button by placing the cursor over the button, then move the cursor away from the button. If you scripted the actions correctly, the fields should appear and disappear as the mouse cursor enters and exits the button field.

Tip

If you need to edit text in a hidden field and use the Field Properties dialog box to display the hidden field, all the text in your field is lost when you return to the Document Pane. Any changes made to the Field Properties dialog box, including Appearance settings, empties out all field contents. In order to preserve text and make edits to existing text, modify the Mouse Exit script to *show* the field(s) when exiting a button. The Mouse Enter displays the field and it won't *hide* on the Mouse Exit due to your modified script. Make the edits in the field, then return to the Mouse Exit action and modify the script to *hide* the field. With long messages, this workaround can save you time by eliminating a need to re-key all the field contents.

Using Document Level JavaScripts

Document Level JavaScripts are routines developed at the top level and they can be accessed anywhere and anytime by other scripts you write for page actions, bookmarks, links, and fields. (Additionally, they can be used to initialize conditions when eForms open.) Rather than writing the same code over many times, you can use one routine or function and address it whenever the file is open. The example with animation effects, which was discussed earlier in this chapter, is a good example in which a Document Level JavaScript can be helpful. As another example, assume you wish to perform numeric averaging among a group of fields on a page and then do the same on other pages in a PDF file. By using a Document Level JavaScript, you can include all the code necessary to do the numeric averaging and include the script on each page where the averaging routine is needed. Yet another example is using a nice feature in Acrobat called Custom Keystroke Filtering, which you may use to auto tab fields as each field is filled in.

There are many uses for adding functions to the document level. In terms of real-world usage, let's take a look at a few functions you may wish to use in your Acrobat forms. The following examples are used to explain more about how functions are created at the document level.

Checking for empty fields

Suppose you have a form that needs to be completed in entirety and no text fields can remain blank. You want to ensure the user completes all fields before submitting the form. You can also extend this example to document saves or prints with the Document Actions that are described in Chapter 8.

 Cross-Reference For more information about Document Actions, refer to Chapter 8, "Writing JavaScript Routines."

Assume further that individual pages on a multi-page form can be printed if all the fields on a given page are filled in or the entire PDF can be printed or submitted after all fields are filled in properly. To assess each page for any blank fields means you would use a function to look at each field and determine if it was left blank. Rather than re-writing the same function over several times, you can use a Document Level JavaScript to check the fields on a page or on the entire PDF document. The same function would be used several times for each button for printing or submitting a page or the entire form. In this example, you need two scripts. One script is created for the function at the document level and the other script uses the function in a field action.

Adding a Document Level function

For this example, use the `id.pdf` file in the Chapter 10 folder on the book's CD-ROM, as shown in Figure 10-18. The file is a single-page PDF form for a user to complete identifying information and submit the data to a URL on a company Web site.

You'll find the `id.pdf` file in the Chapter 10 folder on the book's CD-ROM. You'll notice that the form contains the scripts noted in the following section. You can delete the scripts and reenter the code for practice or use one of your own custom forms.

Before the data are submitted, we want to ensure all fields are filled in and the form is complete. If a field is left blank and the submit button is selected, an alert dialog box opens to inform the user not all fields have been completed. The routine in the script for the submit button uses a document level JavaScript function.

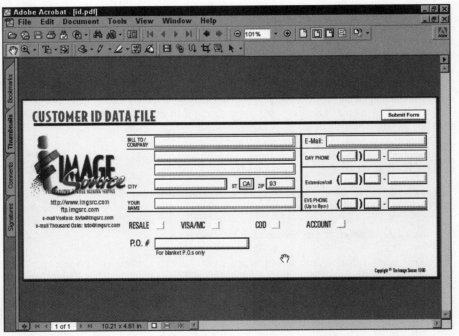

Figure 10-18: The Submit Form button contains a JavaScript that uses a Document Level JavaScript function for assessing all fields. If any field is left blank, the data won't be submitted to the specified URL.

The first step is to create the Document Level JavaScript. Using the sample form, follow these steps to create the JavaScript function at the document level:

1. Choose Tools ➪ JavaScript ➪ Document JavaScripts.

2. The JavaScript Functions dialog box opens. Type a name in the Script Name field box. For this example, use `checkField` for the script name.

3. Click on the Add button shown in Figure 10-19 to open the JavaScript Edit dialog box. Add the following code in the dialog box:

```
function checkField(aField)
{
  if (aField.value == "") // empty field
  {
  var msg = "No fields can be left empty.";
  app.alert(msg);
  return 0;
  }
return 1;
} // end of function
```

This function assesses a field's contents. If the field is empty, an application alert message reports to the user that No fields can be left empty.

4. Click OK in the JavaScript Edit dialog box and you are returned to the JavaScript Functions dialog box. In this example, the name of the function is the same name used for the script name. The function appears in the list window below the script name after you create the code in the JavaScript Edit dialog box, as shown in Figure 10-19.

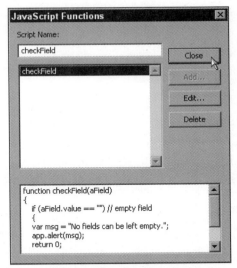

Figure 10-19: After a function has been added, the name of the function appears in the scrollable list window. In this example, the script name and the function name are identical.

5. Click Close in the JavaScript Functions dialog box and you are returned to the Document Pane.

The function is now ready to be used with any script in the form. When writing the code for a field action, the code from the function can be included and addressed by any field on any page in a PDF form.

Including functions in field scripts

With the id.pdf file still in view, add a submit button. In the JavaScript action for the submit button, several actions will be performed. First, a loop is added to assess all text fields on the page and the button fields will be skipped. The function created above is included in the script so that when a field is found without data, the function opens the alert dialog box. If all is well, the script also contains a statement for what to do with the data. In this example, the data is routed to a URL and submitted to a server.

Cross-Reference   For more on submitting and routing data to URLs and Web servers, see Chapter 13, "Submitting and Distributing Forms."

Create a button field and in the JavaScript Edit dialog box add the following code:

```
var okToSubmit = true;
// loop over all fields:
 for (var j = 0; j < this.numFields; j++)
{
 var fieldname = this.getNthFieldName(j);
 var theField = this.getField(fieldname);
 if (theField.type != 'text')
continue; // get past button fields
 //include function
 var valid = checkField( theField );
 if (!valid) // valid == 0? Halt!
 {
okToSubmit = false; // set flag
break; // exit loop prematurely
 }
}
//if no fields are left blank, submit data
var myurl = "http://www.west.net/cgi-bin/process.pl";
if (okToSubmit)
   this.submitForm(myurl, false);
```

The comment lines (//) give you an idea of what's going on with the script, and should be self-explanatory. If a text field is left blank and the submit button is selected, an alert dialog box, like the one shown in Figure 10-20, opens.

Figure 10-20: If a text field is left blank and the submit button is selected, an alert dialog box opens.

If all the text fields contain data, the last statement sends the data to the specified URL and is directed to the CGI script called process.pl. Notice that the data submission is contained in the JavaScript rather than using an Action type for Submit Form. If you attempt to use a Submit Form action, the data are submitted before you can check them. In this case, the data are submitted from within the JavaScript.

Auto tabbing fields

If you have fields with fixed character lengths such as phone numbers, social security numbers, employee id numbers, credit card numbers, and so on, you may wish to set up fields to automatically tab to the next field after each field is completed. On the autoTab.pdf form in the Chapter 10 folder on the book's CD-ROM, there are fields for a phone number and social security number, as shown in Figure 10-21.

You'll find the autoTab.pdf form in the Chapter 10 folder on the book's CD-ROM.

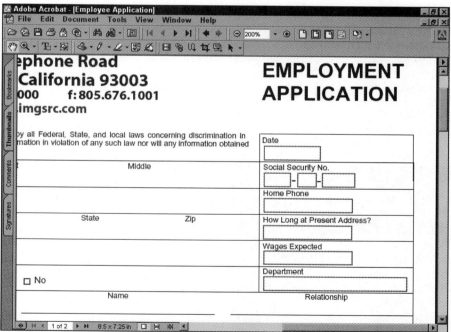

Figure 10-21: The social security number field is broken up into three fields in which to enter numbers.

As you can see in Figure 10-21, the social security number has three separate fields. In this example, you can have a user enter the necessary data for each field box and have the cursor automatically tab to the next field. To set up the auto tabbing, you need to first create a Document Level JavaScript function, then add a routine for a custom keystroke filter.

Cross-Reference For more on auto tabbing fields, look at the examples for Comb forms in Chapter 15, "Understanding the Real-World Forms Market."

Adding a document level function

Follow the same steps explained earlier for creating a Document Level JavaScript function. In the JavaScript Edit dialog box, enter the following code:

```
function goNext(item, event, cName)
{
 AFNumber_Keystroke(0, 0, 0, 0, "",true);
   if (event.rc &&
   AFMergeChange(event).length ==
   event.target.charLimit)
   item.getField(cName).setFocus();
}
```

The preceding function uses item, which is the field assessed for the character length, event is the character length assessment, and cName represents the field the cursor moves to after the character limit has been reached. The character limit is determined in the Field Properties dialog box in the Options tab. The statement containing set.focus() instructs Acrobat to go to the next field.

Click OK in the JavaScript Edit dialog box and you are returned to the JavaScript Functions dialog box. The new script appears in the list, as shown in Figure 10-22.

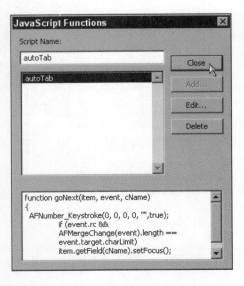

Figure 10-22: After the function is created in the JavaScript Edit dialog box, the script appears in the list window in the JavaScript Functions dialog box.

Adding a keystroke filter

Keystroke filters can examine in real time the keystrokes added to fields. The value `event.change` is examined and the consequences of the change are reported as you determine. For example, you may want a field to be filled in with data other than using a word like `other`. Assume you have an open-ended question that requires an answer. You may wish a user to respond on how they heard about your company, like newspaper advertising, referral, radio broadcast, and so on, but you don't want a user to respond with `other`. The way to code a keystroke filter is to open the Validate properties, select Custom Validate Script, and add a Custom validate script.

For this example, you might enter

```
var forbidden = "other";
var str = event.value + event.change;
var illegal = str.match(forbidden);
if (illegal) //a non-null value was returned
{
app.alert("The value'" + illegal + "'is notallowed.");
event.rc = false; //disallow the change
}
```

The routine above analyzes the text in real time as a user completes a field. If the word "other" is typed in the field, the application alert dialog box opens and informs the user that: The value `other` is not allowed.

Cross-Reference For an example of this routine, open the `forms_eTips.pdf` file found in the Chapter 14 folder of the book's CD-ROM. Navigate to tip number 67 on page 73.

In the example at hand, we want to tab to the next field instead of open an alert dialog box. You obviously cannot assess each field for correct data because there is no way of knowing whether the telephone number or the social security number is correct. However, you can determine the character length and move the cursor to the next field when the number of characters that are needed for each field have been added by the user. To finish the auto tab routine, follow these steps:

Cross-Reference For an example of the code that is used in the following steps, open the `form_eTips.pdf` file in the Chapter 14 folder on the book's CD-ROM and navigate to tip number 75 on page 81.

1. Open the Field Properties dialog box for each field for the social security number. In the Options tab, check the box for Limit of ___ Characters and add the number of maximum characters in the field box. (For the social security number, the field lengths are 3, 2, and 4, respectively.)

2. Open the first field box to add the keystroke filter. On the example form, the first field to address is the first social security field. I named this field `ss.1` and the next two fields `ss.2` and `ss.3`.

3. Click on the Format tab and select Custom from the Category list. Click on the Edit button for Custom Keystroke Script.

4. The JavaScript Edit dialog box opens. Add the following code in the dialog box:

```
goNext(this, event, "ss.2");
```

This script calls the `goNext` function created earlier. The item `this` is the field where the script is created—in this example the `ss.1` field. Event is the character length, which was determined in the Options properties. When the length is reached, the event changes and thus invokes the `getField(cName)` statement in the function. The `cName` item is the name of the field you want to tab to. In this example, the cursor needs to move to the field `ss.2`. Thus, the last item within the parentheses is `"ss.2"`.

5. Click OK and you are returned to the Format properties.

6. Repeat the same steps for each field noting the name of the next field to jump to in the keystroke script.

7. Test the fields. If you type the data within the corresponding fields, the cursor moves to the next field determined for the `cName`.

Note
If you work with Comb forms in which fields are designed to support single characters, the approach may be better served with different scripts. For a detailed explanation for designing forms with Comb fields, refer to Chapter 15, "Understanding the Real-World Forms Market."

Creating Smart Forms

One of the advantages of using electronic forms is the ability to create *smart forms* that aid the user in accurate completion and minimize the chances for error. Rather than leave decisions to the user for things like pricing sales items, calculating sales tax, completing totals, or making item choices from category listings that have fixed results, you can design an intelligent form that helps the user avoid potential calculation errors.

Some of the routines you have worked through thus far can contribute to the development of a smart form. In addition, you'll want to add things like locking out data that does not need user input, such as a sales price on a given item and forcing data choices from options based on different item choices. To begin, let's look at locking out fields that are fixed and don't require user-supplied input.

Locking data fields

The `golfOrder.pdf` file in the Chapter 10 folder on the book's CD-ROM has five columns for placing an order. The Item and Type columns are for user decisions on the products to be purchased. The Qty column enables a user to specify a quantity for items selected. The Price column is automatically calculated on the form from the item selection made by the user. In addition, the totals, sales tax, shipping, and grand total are all automatically calculated for the user. Figure 10-23 shows the form with two items chosen for an order.

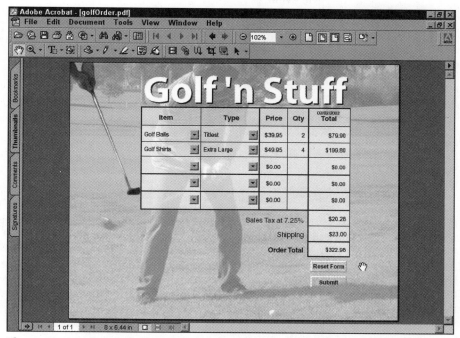

Figure 10-23: The user supplies the quantity for items selected and the remaining fields are locked and cannot be changed by the user.

The fields representing the calculated amounts are locked. When the form is protected against user changes with Acrobat Standard Security, no changes can be made in the pricing or calculation fields. Locking a field is relatively easy and only requires you to open the Appearance properties and select the check box for Read Only, as shown in Figure 10-24.

Cross-Reference For more on using Acrobat Standard Security, see Chapter 11, "Using Acrobat Security."

Figure 10-24: When you select a field as Read Only and secure it with Acrobat Standard Security, the field cannot be changed by anyone.

If the price field is locked, the data for pricing based on the user choice for Type needs to be calculated in a JavaScript. In this example, the complete script lists all items and the price respective to each item. The first line of code gets the `type.0` field and looks at the contents. If the value equals the item selection, the respective price is added to the field. If the field is blank, $0.00 (zero) is added to the field. The code listed below is the script for adding the price for a selection for the `type.0` field.

```
var c = this.getField("type.0")
{
if
 (c.value == "")
   (event.value = 0);
else
if
 (c.value == "Titlest")
   (event.value = 39.95);
else
if
 (c.value == "MaxFli")
   (event.value = 29.95);
else
if
 (c.value == "Pinnicle")
   (event.value = 19.95);
else
```

```
if
  (c.value == "Small")
    (event.value = 29.95);
else
if
  (c.value == "Medium")
    (event.value = 39.95);
else
if
  (c.value == "Large")
    (event.value = 39.95);
else
if
  (c.value == "Extra Large")
    (event.value = 49.95);
else
if
  (c.value == "Navy")
    (event.value = 19.95);
else
if
  (c.value == "White")
    (event.value = 19.95);
else
if
  (c.value == "Green")
    (event.value = 19.95);
else
if
  (c.value == "25")
    (event.value = .95);
else
if
  (c.value == "50")
    (event.value = 1.95);
else
if
  (c.value == "100")
    (event.value = 3.95);
else
  (event.value = 89.95);
}
```

The same code is added to the remaining price fields, except `type.0` is changed to `type.1`, `type.2`, and so on for each respective row. Once again, when the fields are locked and the form is secured, no user changes can be made.

Note The above script is added for the individual fields here for illustration purposes only. You can add a document level JavaScript and eliminate some redundant code.

Forcing data choices

Using the same form as above, when a user makes a choice for an Item, the options for Type are limited to only those Types available for a given Item, as shown in Figure 10-25. In this example, if a user selects Golf Shirts as an item, then the Type choices include four options for the shirt sizes. If the user selects an item like Golf Shoes, the Type choices change to reflect different size options. Obviously, the right shoe size is important to the individual ordering the product. To eliminate errors for making the correct choice for the Type respective to an Item, you can force the Type options based on the user Item selection.

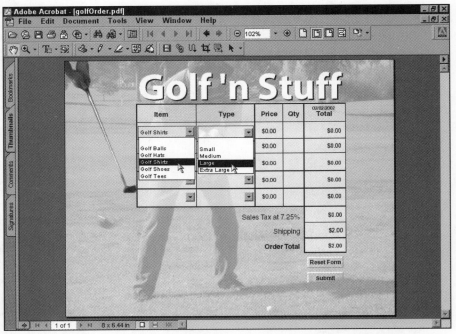

Figure 10-25: When a user makes a selection for Item from the pull-down menu choices, the Type items in the menu change to the respective Item options.

To set up the fields, use a Combo box for both the Item and Type selections. The Combo box for Item choices is shown in Figure 10-26. The different Item choices are listed in the Combo box as you would expect with this field type. The first option is a blank line, so no data are exported without a user selection for a product order.

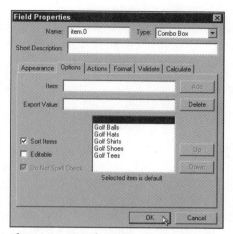

Figure 10-26: The Item Combo box lists the Item types that a user can order.

The Type field is also a Combo box. This field, however, does not contain any items in the Options properties. If you list all option choices for Type, the user can make a mistake by ordering a set of Golf Shoes and choosing a type like a hat size. To prevent this kind of error, let a JavaScript routine decide the types to supply for the option choices in the Combo box, based on the Type choice made by a user—or, in essence, you'll force the user to make only restricted choices for a given Item.

To offer the choice selections from the Type pull-down menu for a given Item selection, return to the Item field where the current Combo box has a list of Item selections. Select the Format tab in the Field Properties dialog box and click on the Edit button for the Custom Keystroke Script. In the JavaScript Edit dialog box, enter the following code:

```
if (!event.willCommit) {
  var a = this.getField("type.0");
  a.clearItems();

  switch (event.change) {
        case "Golf Balls":
a.setItems(["", "Titlest", "Pinnicle", "MaxFli"]);
        break;
        case "Golf Hats":
                a.setItems(["", "Navy", "White", "Green"]);
        break;
```

```
        case "Golf Shirts":
a.setItems(["", "Small", "Medium", "Large", "Extra Large"]);
        break;
        case "Golf Shoes":
a.setItems(["", "Size 9", "Size 9.5", "Size 10", "Size 10.5",
"Size 11", "Size 11.5", "Size 12"]);
        break
        case "Golf Tees":
                a.setItems(["", "25", "50", "100"]);
        break;
    }
}
```

In this example, the routine starts by calling out the `type.0` field, therefore all item listings in this script apply only to the `type.0` field. The statement `case "Golf Balls":` is the Golf Balls Item selection in the Item field Combo List. The next line of code `a.setItems(["", "Titlest", "Pinnicle", "MaxFli"]);` lists the items to be displayed when the Golf Balls Type is selected. Each subsequent *case* applies to the respective list in the Item Combo box. The remaining fields, type.1, `type.2`, and so on, have the same code with the exception of the second line in which the respective `type.n` is used.

As you examine this form, the user only has a few choices to make with regard to placing an order—the Item, a restricted list for the Type, and the Quantity of the Items to order. All other decisions are intelligently calculated.

Merging Form Data

If you have a product catalog that describes all the purchase items a consumer can buy from your company, you may wish to have an order form separate from the catalog. In this example, you would have two PDF documents—one for the catalog and another for the order form. If a user wants to purchase an item, s/he can click a button to place a given item in a shopping cart. After browsing the catalog, the user can review the shopping cart, accept all the items, or perhaps choose to delete some items, then move the data to the order form with the click of a button.

The data handling in this example routes data between pages in an open PDF file, then directs data to a second PDF form. To see how you might approach handling data in both situations, we'll first look at taking data supplied in an application alert dialog box and move it to a page used for the shopping cart. In the second example, the data are moved from the shopping cart page to a second PDF file used as an order form.

Adding data from Application Response dialog boxes

In the Chapter 10 folder on the book's CD-ROM, the `clockBrochure.pdf` file has three pages. The second page in the file is the catalog page where descriptions of the products are found, as shown in Figure 10-27.

On the CD-ROM

You'll find the `clockBrochure.pdf` file in the Chapter 10 folder on the book's CD-ROM.

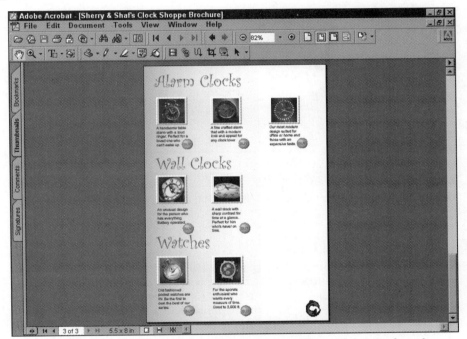

Figure 10-27: The product brochure contains a page where all the purchase items are displayed and a description of each product is detailed.

For each item there is a Buy button. When a user clicks on the button, an application response dialog box opens and asks the user how many of the selected items are to be purchased. When the user enters a value and clicks OK, the quantity is placed on the shopping cart page, shown in Figure 10-28. If the user cancels the dialog box, an application alert dialog box opens and confirms the cancellation.

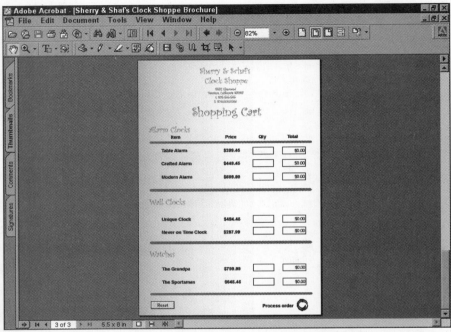

Figure 10-28: When a user clicks on a Buy button and supplies a quantity in an application response dialog box, the value is placed on the shopping cart page.

The total fields on the shopping cart page calculate the quantity of ordered times and the fixed price for the respective items. This is all handled in the Calculation properties for the individual total fields. The issue at hand remains with the `Buy` button on the catalog page. This button controls the appearance of dialog boxes and moving data from the application response dialog box to the shopping cart page. To understand how this is accomplished, follow these steps:

1. Create a button field surrounding the first `Buy` icon on the catalog page (page 2 in the PDF file).

2. In the Field Properties dialog box, click on the Actions tab and add a JavaScript Action. In the JavaScript Edit dialog box, enter the following code:

```
if (typeof(app.viewerType)!="undefined")
if(app.viewerVersion < 5.0)
{
var msg = "Acrobat 5.0 or greater is required to run this
script.";
app.alert(msg);
}
else
{
```

```
var t = this.getField("qty.0"); // target field
var cResponse = app.response({
cQuestion: "How many do you wish to purchase?",
cTitle: "Quantity to purchase"});
{
if ( cResponse == null){ // if Cancel is selected
app.alert ("Cancel order for this item?");
  cResponse = 0;
}
else
app.alert("You ordered, \""+cResponse+"\".. it's noted on the
shopping cart page.",2);
}
t.value = cResponse; // places the data from the dialog to
the target field
}
```

In the preceding script, the first section determines what application viewer version is handling the catalog form. If the viewer version is lower than Acrobat 5, then an alert dialog box opens to inform the user that this routine can't run on earlier versions of Acrobat.

After the else statement, assign variable t to the "qty.0" field on the shopping cart page. This quantity field relates to the first item in the top left of the catalog page. An application response dialog box contains the cQuestion that appears below the dialog box title. The cTitle item places a title in the response dialog box, as shown in Figure 10-29.

Cross-Reference For more information on creating Response dialog boxes, see Chapter 16, "Creating Forms for Real-World Uses."

Figure 10-29: The application response dialog box has a title and a question above the field entry box.

If the response is null (the Cancel button is selected in the response dialog box), the response dialog box closes and an alert dialog box opens confirming the cancellation. If the cResponse is not null, the routine moves to the second else statement that means the user entered a value in the response dialog box. When the user clicks OK in the response dialog box, an application alert dialog box opens and confirms the quantity ordered, as shown in Figure 10-30.

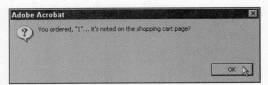

Figure 10-30: The value placed in the application response dialog box is reported in the application alert dialog box.

At the end of the routine, the `t.value` is equal to the `cResponse` value and places the data in the `"qty.0"` field on the shopping cart page.

3. Test the button to be certain it works properly and review the shopping cart page to ensure the data you enter in the application response dialog box is placed in the first total field.

4. Copy the JavaScript for the first button (or duplicate the field and open the Field Properties). Create a second button and paste the routine in the JavaScript Edit dialog box. Change the `"qty.0"` item to `"qty.1"` and repeat the steps for all items on the catalog page.

5. After clicking a few buttons, open the last page in the catalog document. You should see the quantity and total fields filled in for the items ordered. In this example, three different items were ordered.

Swapping data

After a user completes the orders for the shopping cart, the data needs to be transposed to a separate PDF file used as the order form. When a user prints the order or submits it electronically, the complete catalog is not needed, especially if the document is a large file. In this example, use the `orderForm.pdf` file in the Chapter 10 folder on the book's CD-ROM, as shown in Figure 10-31.

You'll find the `orderForm.pdf` file in the Chapter 10 folder on the book's CD-ROM.

Opening secondary files with Page Actions

To add data from one PDF file to another, a second file needs to be opened in Acrobat. If you have separate PDF files, there is no need to open a second file until the user is ready to click a button to add the data to a second file. Therefore, in this example, the order form file doesn't need to open until the user arrives at the shopping cart page. When the user does arrive at the shopping cart page, the secondary file is opened and remains in the background so the order can be processed. To accomplish this, assign a Page Action so the order form file only opens when the shopping cart page is viewed.

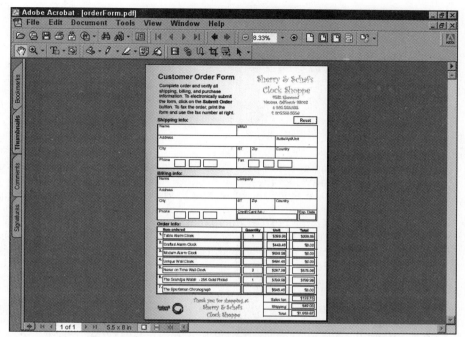

Figure 10-31: The order form is a second PDF document. When the user clicks on a button to process the order in the catalog file, the form is populated from the data on the shopping cart page. In this example, three items were ordered that are reflected in the order form when the order is processed.

Tip   Page Actions are not the only means you can use to open secondary files. If you wish to have the current file close as another file opens in which the result data are to be placed, you can also use a button field and a JavaScript routine to open the second file, close the open document, and transpose the data. For a detailed description of this process, see Chapter 16, "Creating Forms for Real-World Uses."

To set up a Page Action to open a secondary file, add a JavaScript to the Page Open Action. Be certain you create the Page Action on the page that needs to use the secondary form. In this example, the shopping cart page is where a button is created to move data to the order form. Therefore, this page needs the Page Action. To create a Page Action that opens another file, follow these steps:

On the CD-ROM   You'll find the clockBrochure.pdf file in the Chapter 10 folder on the book's CD-ROM.

1. Navigate to the shopping cart page in the clockBrochure.pdf file.

2. Choose Document ➪ Set Page Action.

3. Select Page Open in the left window and click the Add button.

4. Select JavaScript for the Action type and enter the following code in the JavaScript Edit dialog box:

```
if (app.viewerVersion < 5)
  app.alert("Version 5.0 required. Some features will not
work.");
else {
  this.slave = app.openDoc("orderForm.pdf",this);
  this.bringToFront();
}
```

In the above routine, the first part once again determines the viewer version. A user warning is reported if the version is less than Acrobat version 5. After the `else` statement, a slave document is identified and the name of the slave document is `our order` form. The `app.openDoc` opens the file. The last statement tells Acrobat to take the current document (the `clockBrochure.pdf` file) and move it to the front of the Document Pane after the other file opens. Because the Page Action opens the file, you still need to click a button on the shopping cart page to move data to the new open PDF document. Therefore, you don't want to confuse a user by allowing the opened file to come to the front.

One more script needs to be added before the job is completed. Open the `orderForm.pdf` file and select Tools ➪ JavaScripts. Enter a name for the JavaScript function, something like *initialize* and click Add. In the JavaScript Edit dialog box enter the following code:

```
this.disclosed=true;
```

Click OK and click Close in the JavaScript Function dialog box. Save the file and then return to the `clockBrochure.pdf` to execute the first script created earlier. If the JavaScript function is not added to the order form file, Acrobat may not open the secondary document on the Page Action. Whenever you access a secondary document be certain to add the same function to all documents where the `app.openDoc()` statement is used.

Tip　The use of *slave* to reference the second file is not a reserved word in JavaScript. You can easily use `this.myFile = app.openDoc(...)` or any variable name you wish to use. When opening secondary files, it can often be helpful to use a common variable name to help eliminate confusion. In this regard, the term *slave* is used to refer to secondary files that are opened. You'll note this naming convention is consistent for the same scripts used in Chapter 16. Maintaining consistency can help you design your JavaScript code with fewer potential errors.

Copying data between forms

Now that the order form page is open and the shopping cart contains the items to order, it's time to move data from the shopping cart to the order form. Follow these steps to finish the job:

1. Create a Button field at the bottom of the shopping cart page on which `process order` is located.

2. Add a JavaScript action on a Mouse Up behavior and enter the following code:

```
for (var i = 0; i < 7;i++) {
var quantity = this.getField("qty."+i);
var result = this.slave.getField("orderQty."+i);
     result.value = quantity.value;
}
slave.bringToFrontZ();
```

This routine loops through the `qty.n` fields. The variable `quantity` is assigned the value of the `qty.n` fields. The variable `result` is assigned to the `orderQty.n` fields on the order form. The `result.value` is equal to the `quantity.value`, which takes the value of the `qty.n` field and places the value in the corresponding `orderQty.n` field. After the loop finishes, the slave (`orderForm.pdf`) document is moved to the front of the Document Pane so the user can complete the order form and submit the data or print the form.

The calculations could be added to the order form document; however, the only essential information is the item that a user orders and the quantity. In this example, the calculations on the order form are contained in JavaScripts for all the fields requiring calculations, such as the total amounts, sales tax, shipping, and so on.

In this example, we worked with a product brochure and an order form. The process, however, is obviously not limited to these kinds of forms. You can use similar methods for human resource forms, financial reports, personalized documents, or any other PDF documents in which transposing data eliminates redundant data entry.

Cross-Reference For more ideas and examples on populating data on secondary forms, look over the examples in Chapter 16, "Creating Forms for Real-World Uses."

Summary

✦ You can import audio files into PDF forms and use them to help end-users clarify the form fill-in process. In order to import audio files, you must first create sound recordings and save the audio files in formats acceptable to Acrobat.

✦ You can use JavaScript routines to create an animation on a PDF form without the need to import a movie file. Animation effects can help users clearly understand some aspects for properly filling in data fields.

✦ You can use application pop-up menus for page navigation. In order to navigate pages from application pop-up menus, you first need to create named destinations.

✦ You can design help messages to appear when a user needs help in filling in a form or specific fields. The help fields can remain hidden until needed, thereby reducing clutter on a form. Use of a JavaScript routine to show/hide fields eliminates the need to have an Acrobat alert dialog box prompt a user to save changes to a file when no edits have been made.

✦ You can include Document Level JavaScripts in scripts for individual fields. The same functions created at the Document Level enable you to reuse the code with several fields, thereby reducing redundant coding on a form.

✦ Smart forms help end users prevent errors and intelligently supply data based on user choices. You can use JavaScripts to force item selections and auto calculate fields when user input is not needed for fixed results.

✦ You can merge data between PDF forms with simple short JavaScript routines. Data exported from a larger PDF file, such as a product catalog, can be transposed to a smaller PDF form that is used for submitting data to place an order.

✦   ✦   ✦

Distributing Forms

P A R T

◆   ◆   ◆   ◆

In This Part

Chapter 11
Using Acrobat
Security

Chapter 12
Working with
Accessible and
Tagged PDFs

Chapter 13
Submitting and
Distributing Forms

◆   ◆   ◆   ◆

Using Acrobat Security

There are two types of security to deal with in regard to forms. You can secure the PDF file and protect the design, content, and all the scripts created on the form in two different levels of security, and you can create security with Acrobat Self-Sign Security and digital signatures. Securing PDF files requires no special configuration. Self-Sign Security requires you to create a signature profile and distribute and/or acquire public certificates for the purposes of securing documents and verifying signatures. Acrobat offers quite a bit in regard to security and signatures. This chapter details all you need to know about securing PDF forms, using Acrobat Self-Sign Security and using Digital Signatures.

Securing PDF Files

The first of the two types of security to be discussed is Acrobat Standard Security. The standard security is used for password protection for opening and viewing PDF files and/or securing them against any unauthorized changes. Preventing changes in a document means the form design and the form fields including JavaScript routines are protected. Two levels of standard security are available for protecting documents, 40-bit encryption and 128-bit encryption. Before you examine the different encryption methods available to you, it is important to understand a little bit about security in general.

Understanding password protection

During recent times there has been much discussion about security and breaking password codes in electronic documents and in particular breaking codes in PDF files. A few companies have claimed to have developed software that can crack security in PDF files and Acrobat eBook Reader files. Many people became concerned over the potential loss of their digital rights and a few stories made headlines, resulting in a global concern over PDF protection.

The bottom line on password security, like anything else electronic, is: If it can be made, it can be broken. How security is broken is important to understand. Software designed to decrypt files use algorithms to try character and number combinations searching for the security code to crack the file. This is like an odometer beginning with zero and continuing to spin through all the permutations of ASCII characters until the password(s) are broken.

If you use a password containing three characters, all the permutations for getting the right number of characters are relatively few and a password with a sophisticated cracking program can break through the security in little time. As you add another character to the password, the permutations rise geometrically and it takes more time to break the code. The odometer keeps spinning at the same rate, but it has more iterations to run through as additional characters are added.

When you add eight characters to a password, the most sophisticated programs on the fastest dual processor computers will take years to run through all the permutations. Jump up to 12 characters and it will take several lifetimes to break a code. Therefore, the bottom line on securing documents is to be certain to use at least 8 or more characters for your passwords if you think there is a risk in having codes broken on documents that need the utmost security. You can be certain that Adobe Systems provides you with a product that can be used confidently if you design your forms following a few simple guidelines.

Using 40-bit encryption

Acrobat Standard Security affords you either of two levels of security from which to choose according to the kind of security you wish to add to your PDF files. The first of these levels is 40-bit encryption, which was part of the Acrobat family prior to version 5.0. If you intend to share files with users of earlier versions of Acrobat, you must use the 40-bit encryption. If you secure documents with 128-bit encryption, users cannot open the documents with Acrobat viewers lower than version 5.*x*.

With regard to forms, you may wish to prevent users from changing the form fields and the values associated with fields. To secure a PDF form with 40-bit encryption and protect your form fields against any changes, follow these steps:

1. Open the form to be secured and choose File ➪ Document Security.

2. The Document Security dialog box opens. In this dialog box you determine what kind of security is to be applied to the document. From the pull-down menu select Acrobat Standard Security, as shown in Figure 11-1.

3. The first items to address are the Specify Password items. If you want to secure a file against anyone viewing the PDF, select the check box for Password Required to Open Document, as shown in Figure 11-2. Supply a user password and only those people who know the password can open the file.

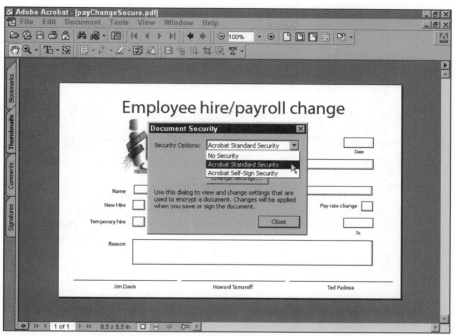

Figure 11-1: Select Acrobat Standard Security from the pull-down menu.

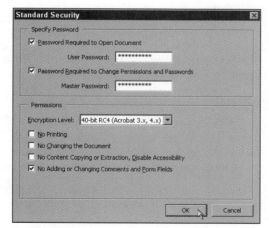

Figure 11-2: The Standard Security dialog box offers options for adding a User Password and a Master Password.

4. The second password is used to protect the document against changes. Supply a Master Password and be certain to use a different password than the User Password. If the same password is used for both fields, Acrobat prompts you with a warning dialog box and forces you to supply different passwords.

5. The default Encryption Level is 40-bit. Leave the default setting at 40-bit.

6. The four check boxes at the bottom of the Standard Security dialog box are used to determine what is to be protected. With respect to forms, you'll want to protect the file against any form field changes. Select the box for No Adding or Changing Comments and Form Fields, as shown in Figure 11-2.

7. Click OK.

8. A confirmation dialog box opens. The first Password dialog box asks you to supply the User Password. Be certain to use the same letter case and type the password identical to the User Password entered in the Document Security dialog box. Click OK and the Password dialog box for the Master Password opens. Type this password identical to the original Master Password and click OK.

9. Click Close in the Acrobat Standard Security dialog box.

10. Save the PDF file by choosing File ➪ Save.

Document Security has been added to the PDF. The security, however, does not take effect until the file is saved, closed, and reopened. If you add both a User Password and a Master Password, the PDF can be opened using either password.

Using 128-bit encryption

Securing files with 128-bit encryption is not used to make your files more secure, it is used to offer different options for protecting your document. If you are certain that users of Acrobat viewers lower than version 5 will not view your PDFs, you can use the 128-bit encryption and choose different options.

1. Open the Standard Security dialog box, as described earlier. Leave the User Password field empty and supply a Master Password. When the file is saved, anyone can open the PDF, but a user would need the Master Password to change the document.

2. Select 128-bit RC4 (Acrobat 5.0) from the Encryption Level pull-down menu.

3. Open the Changes Allowed pull-down menu and select General Editing, Comment and Form Field Authoring from the menu choices, as shown in Figure 11-3.

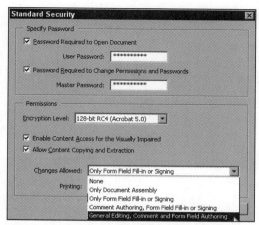

Figure 11-3: 128-bit encryption offers different security options found by opening the pull-down menu for Changes Allowed.

4. Click OK and confirm the Master Password in the separate dialog box Acrobat opens for password confirmation. If the password is not correctly typed in the Password dialog box, the Adobe Acrobat dialog box opens with a warning message. If you see this dialog box, the password you typed in the Password dialog box did not match the password entered for the Specify Password items. Click OK and be certain to check your Caps Lock key before retyping the password.

5. Click Close in the Standard Security dialog box and save the file. When you reopen the document, you'll notice the Form tool is inactive in the Command Bar. A Master Password is needed to activate the tool and change the form.

The 128-bit encryption enables you to secure your form fields against any changes; however, users can add comment notes and markups. Notice the tools for changing fields and adding links are grayed out while all the Comment tools remain active, as shown in Figure 11-4.

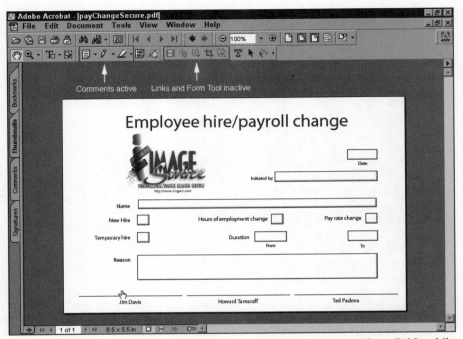

Figure 11-4: The 128-bit encryption options enable you to protect form fields while keeping the Comment tools active.

Opening secure files

If a User Password has been added to the encryption options, a password is required to open the file. If both a User Password and a Master Password have been used, you can open the file using either password. If you open the PDF with the User Password, all the encryption protection prevails. Tools may be grayed out and you cannot make changes according to the kind of protection enabled when the document was encrypted.

If you open a PDF using a Master Password, you still need to change the security settings in order to edit the file. Select Change Settings in the Document Security dialog box and you'll be prompted again for your password. Type in the password and change the document. Reapply the security settings before saving the file and the document returns to the same level of security.

When you open a PDF file where a password was used to encrypt the file, a dialog box opens prompting you to supply a Password. In this dialog box, you type either the User Password or the Master Password if two passwords have been used. Obviously, any user who does not know the Master Password can only open the file if the User Password is known.

If you change passwords frequently when securing PDF files, you may need a guide or help file to log all the passwords you use. If you forget a password, you won't be able to reopen your file. In Chapter 16, a PDF document is used for the purpose of cataloging passwords. Look at Chapter 16 and use a similar file to store all your passwords. Protect the file with a user password you can commit to memory and save the file on your hard drive. Be certain to make backup copies. You can also keep a copy on your Web site so the file can be retrieved from your office, home, and while on the road.

Changing security

If you want to change any security settings or eliminate security from a file, open the Document Security dialog box. The button for Change Settings is used to change the security options. From the pull-down menu, you can select No Security to eliminate all encryption. Regardless of whether you change security or eliminate it, you must know the Master Password.

If you open a PDF with a User Password when a Master Password was also used and select either the Change Settings button or the No Security menu option, a dialog box opens asking for your Master Password. If you open the file with the Master Password, Acrobat does not prompt you for a password to change settings or eliminate security.

If prompted for a password, enter the Master Password and click OK. Acrobat then opens another dialog box. If you wish to continue, click OK in the confirmation dialog box. Acrobat returns you to the Document Security dialog box. Click OK and save the file. All the changes take effect when the PDF is saved, closed, and reopened.

Using Self-Sign Security

The Acrobat Standard Security was the first method discussed and the two encryption levels are subsets of the Standard Security. The second type of encryption that Acrobat offers you is Self-Sign Security. Self-Sign Security has two primary uses. First, you can secure a file that can be opened by a selected group of individuals. Each individual can be assigned different permission options. When using Self-Sign Security, you don't need to supply a user password. The files are accessible by only those you determine when self-signing the document. This is handled through the use of public certificates.

Although not necessarily a subset of Self-Sign Security, the common attributes used to develop a self-signed document are also used with Digital Signatures. When applying a digital signature, you have options for securing individual fields on a document. Securing fields is not necessarily dependent on securing the PDF file.

All of this may at first appear a little confusing, so we'll work through all the steps to handle the means of using Self-Sign Security and Digital Signatures. The first step in the process is to create a signature profile.

Creating a signature profile

A signature profile is your personal profile that you create and add your own password. The password you use is only known by you and not distributed to others. The profile information is used in securing a document with Self-Sign Security or when you digitally sign a document. If you sign a document and send the PDF to other users, they see your signature; however, they don't know if you signed the file. In order to have another user authenticate the document and verify that indeed you signed the file, the person needs a Public Certificate for the purposes of authentication. The Public Certificate is generated from your signature profile, but it does not include your password. You send your public certificate(s) to all users who need to verify your signature.

When you use Acrobat Self-Sign Security, you determine who can open your PDF and what changes, if any, they can make to the document. In order for you to distribute self-signed PDFs to other users, you need to acquire their public certificates. From a list of public certificates you collect, you determine who among the group can open a given PDF file. Therefore, the use of Digital Signatures and Self-Sign Security starts with first creating your own personal signature profile and then sending public certificates to other users. Let's start with creating your own personal signature profile.

Creating a new user profile

If you have not yet used Digital Signatures or Acrobat Self-Sign Security, you must begin by creating a User Profile. User Profiles can be created with or without a PDF file open in the Document Pane. To create a User Profile, follow these steps:

1. Choose Tools ➪ Self-Sign Security ➪ Log In.

2. The Security – Log In dialog box opens. If you have a profile, you can open the pull-down menu and select any one of all previous profiles you created. If this is your first profile, click on the New User Profile button, shown in Figure 11-5.

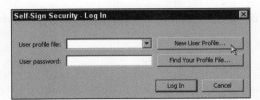

Figure 11-5: To create a new profile, click on the New User Profile button in the Self-Sign Security – Log In dialog box.

3. The Create New User dialog box opens. In this dialog box you supply your personal password. The password used here is the password you use with a Digital Signature or when self-signing a document. This password never travels with Public Certificates you share with others—notice I reiterate this point so you know your public certificate does not compromise your security. Enter your password in the Choose a Password field box and retype the same password in the Confirm Password field box, as shown in Figure 11-6.

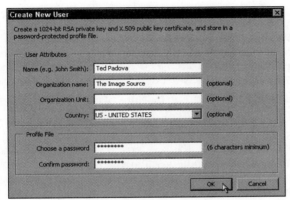

Figure 11-6: Enter a password and retype the same password in the two field boxes at the bottom of the Create New User dialog box.

4. Click OK in the Create New User dialog box.

5. Acrobat now prompts you to save your personal profile by opening the New Acrobat Self-Sign Security Profile File dialog box. The file extension for profiles is `.apf`. Select a folder on your hard drive and enter a name for the profile and click Save.

Tip

Create a folder on your hard drive where your personal profile and all your public certificates are stored. You can create a folder in the Acrobat folder and name it `DigitalSignatures`. Be certain to back up this folder every time you add a new certificate or profile. Make two copies of the backup if using external media cartridges or floppy disks. If your profile is lost, you need to create a new one and send all users who have your public certificate a new copy generated from the new profile. Backup with digital signatures is essential to save you time in the event you loose your hard drive.

6. After you save your profile, the Acrobat Self-Sign Security – Alert dialog box opens. The dialog box confirms your logon as the user for the profile you created. At this point you can click OK and either use a Digital Signature or Self-Sign a PDF file.

Creating a public certificate

If you stay in the Acrobat Self-Sign Security – Alert dialog box, you can click on the User Settings button to open the Self-Sign Security – User Settings for *yourname* (in which *yourname* is the name you provided when you created your user profile). Note: Hereafter, for simplicity, I'll refer to the dialog box as the User Settings dialog box. If you don't click on User Settings in the dialog box, you can later select User Settings from a menu option. When distributing public certificates, you need to address the User Settings. To open the user settings for creating a public certificate, follow these steps:

1. Assume you are now logged on and you closed the User Settings dialog box. To log out as a user, choose Tools ➪ Self-Sign Security ➪ Log Out *yourname*. Further assume we'll start from scratch as if you need to follow the same procedures when you first open Acrobat and you're not yet logged on.

2. Choose Tools ➪ Self-Sign Security ➪ Log In. Note: You can only address the Log In menu command after your have created a signature profile like the one created above.

3. The Self-Sign Security – Log In dialog box opens. If you have more than one profile, you can select it from the pull-down menu. If you have a single profile, the default User Profile File is the profile you created above, as shown in Figure 11-7. Type your password in the User Password field box and click OK.

Note   Acrobat always prompts you for a password when logging on as a user. This protection ensures you that no one without your password can sign a document from your computer.

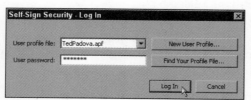

Figure 11-7: When the Self-Sign Security – Log In dialog box opens, enter your password and click OK.

4. The Self-Sign Security – Alert dialog box opens again. At this point, you'll want to change the User Settings. Click on the User Settings button, as shown in Figure 11-8.

Figure 11-8: Click on User Settings to open the User Settings dialog box.

Tip

> If you need to open the User Settings dialog box after you have logged on as a user, you can open the dialog box by choosing Tools ➪ Self-Sign Security ➪ User Settings.

5. The default selection in the left panel is User Information. While User Information is selected, the options on the right side of the dialog box provide you options for e-mailing your public certificate to another user or exporting the certificate to a file, as shown in Figure 11-9. If you select E-mail, Acrobat opens your default e-mail program and attaches the certificate data to a new e-mail message. You supply the recipient information and send the e-mail.

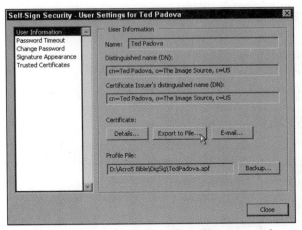

Figure 11-9: The User Information offers you options for e-mailing your public certificate or saving the certificate to a file.

6. If you want to save you public certificate to a file that can later be copied across a local network or e-mailed to another user, click Export to File.

7. The Export Certificate As dialog box opens. The default file format for public certificates is .fdf (Form Data File). Find the location where you store your digital signature files and click on the Save button.

Tip

If securing files for Web browsers or e-mail applications, you can choose another file format by opening the pull-down menu for Save As Type when saving your certificate. Select the item for Certificate Message Syntax – PKCS#7 (*.p7c) and click Save in the Export Certificate As dialog box.

The file you save is your public certificate. You can freely distribute this file to any other user without compromising your digital signature security. If another user applies Acrobat Self-Sign Security to a document intended for your viewing, the other user needs this file in order to apply your user permissions for accessing the file. In addition, if you digitally sign a document, other users need your public certificate to authenticate your signature.

Changing the profile appearance

When a document is signed, the default appearance for your signature is a check mark and some text related to the signature information, as shown in Figure 11-10. This appearance can be changed to a custom display for your signature. You can, for example, sign a piece of paper and scan your signature. Once scanned, the image can be used together with the default signature information. The appearance used with a digital signature has nothing to do with the authenticity of the signature. It merely acts as a design element. However, if you create a more recognizable appearance, users are able to easily distinguish your signature from others on a form at a quick glance—especially when viewing PDFs in a Fit in Window mode.

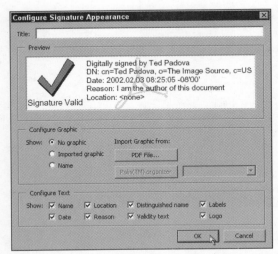

Figure 11-10: The default display for a signature is a check mark, some text related to the signature information, and the name you used when creating your profile.

To create an appearance with your analog signature, you first need to scan your signature and save the scan as a file. Save the scanned image as a PDF file. The file format needs to be a PDF document or a file format that is acceptable to the Open as Adobe PDF file formats. When your signature is saved as one of these formats, follow the steps below to change the appearance.

Cross-Reference For more on scanning with Acrobat Scan, refer to Chapter 8, "Writing JavaScript Routines." For more on Open as Adobe PDF file formats, see Chapter 2, "Using Authoring Applications."

1. Open the User Settings dialog box. If you are not logged on, choose Tools ➪ Self-Sign Security ➪ Log In. After logging on, click on the User Settings button. If you are already logged on, choose Tools ➪ Self-Sign Security ➪ User Settings.

2. In the User Settings dialog box, select Signature Appearance, as shown in Figure 11-11.

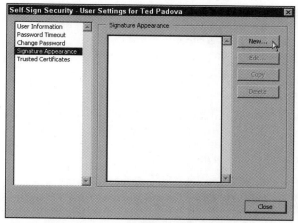

Figure 11-11: In the Self-Sign Security – User Settings dialog box, select Signature Appearance, then click on the New button to create a new appearance.

3. Click on the New button to open the Configure Signature Appearance dialog box.

4. In the Configure Signature Appearance dialog box, add a Title (I used my first name as the title), select the Imported Graphic radio button, and click the PDF File button, as shown in Figure 11-12.

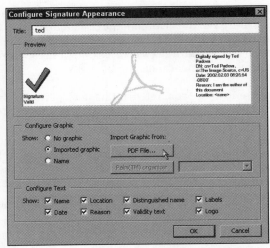

Figure 11-12: Click on PDF File to import your scanned signature that has been saved as a PDF document or a file format that is compatible with the Open as Adobe PDF command.

5. The Select Picture dialog box opens.

6. Click on the Browse button and locate the file to be used for the appearance. Select the file and click Select in the Open dialog box. When you return to the Select Picture dialog box, the appearance of the image to be used is displayed in the dialog box, as shown in Figure 11-13.

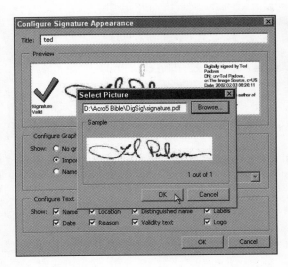

Figure 11-13: After selecting the PDF that you want to import and opening the file in the Open dialog box, a sample of the selected PDF file appears in the Select Picture dialog box.

7. Click OK and you are returned to the Configure Signature dialog box. Click OK again and you are returned to the User Settings dialog box. When the Signature Appearance has been created, the Title you typed is listed in the Signature Appearance.

The new signature appearance is now ready use. Click Close in the User Settings dialog box and you can begin signing documents. If you use Acrobat Self-Sign Security for the purpose of securing documents for a select group of users, you now need to add the user public certificates to your User Settings.

Adding public certificates to the user settings

Public certificates acquired from other users need to be locally stored on your hard drive in order to secure documents for a user or group of users with Acrobat Self-Sign Security. When you open the User Settings dialog box and select Trusted Certificates, the button settings on the right side of the dialog box offer you options for importing a certificate and sending an e-mail request to acquire a certificate from another user, as shown in Figure 11-14.

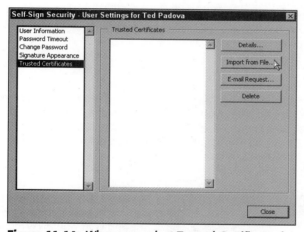

Figure 11-14: When you select Trusted Certificates in the left panel, the button options for Import from File and E-mail Request appear on the right side of the dialog box.

If you don't have a public certificate from a user and wish to request one, click on the E-mail Request button. The E-Mail Certificate dialog box opens. You supply the recipient address in the dialog box and if you wish to have the user call you for verification, you can add your phone number. The subject line for the e-mail and your return address are added to the request, as shown in Figure 11-15.

Figure 11-15: When you click on the E-mail Request button in the User Settings dialog box, the E-Mail Certificate dialog box opens. Click on the E-Mail button and your request is sent to your default e-mail application.

After all the information is supplied in the E-Mail Certificate dialog box, click on the E-Mail button and Acrobat automatically launches your default e-mail program. The request information, subject line, recipient address, a message, and your public profile are all added to the e-mail, as shown in Figure 11-16. Click the Send button and your request is e-mailed to the recipient.

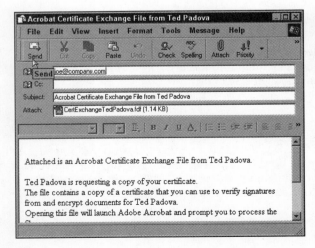

Figure 11-16: The information from the E-Mail Certificate dialog box and your public certificate are included in the e-mail request.

Users can attach public certificates to e-mail messages without using the E-mail Request in Acrobat. Locate your public certificate and attach it as a normal file attachment and you can send it along to any user. Other users likewise can do the same. Regardless of how you acquire a certificate, once you have one or more Public Certificates from users, you can add them to your Trusted Certificates list. To create a Trusted Certificates list, follow these steps:

1. In the User Settings dialog box, select Trusted Certificates, as shown previously in Figure 11-14. Click on the Import from File button on the right side of the dialog box.

2. The Import Certificate dialog box opens. Select a certificate to import and click Open.

3. The Verify Identify dialog box opens. The dialog box displays encryption information for review purposes only. You cannot change any of the encryption data. Click Add to List to add the user to your Trusted Certificate list.

4. An alert dialog box opens informing you the user has been added to your Trusted Certificates list.

5. If you have more users to add to your Trusted Certificates list, click Import from File again. Follow the same steps to add more users. The User Settings dialog box displays all users you add to the Trusted Certificates list, as shown in Figure 11-17. When you complete adding users, click on the Close button.

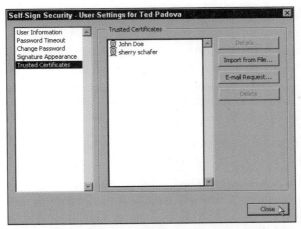

Figure 11-17: When you return to the User Settings dialog box after each public certificate is added, the user profile appears in the Trusted Certificates list.

All of the steps outlined here are your initial configuration for Digital Signatures and Self-Sign Security. You need to create your profile before you can digitally sign a document and you need to add the trusted certificates before you use the Self-Sign

Security for other users. Creating a signature profile is optional, but all the other steps followed in this section need to be completed before you can use the methods described next.

Securing a PDF with Acrobat Self-Sign Security

You may have files that need to be viewed and reviewed by a select group of people in your organization. Perhaps proofing a human resources form or any kind of PDF document that needs to be accessed by only a select group. If you use the Acrobat Standard Security covered earlier in this chapter, you run the risk of having someone learning the password and opening your file. When you use Acrobat Self-Sign Security, only those you determine from your Trusted Certificates list can open the file. When a user attempts to open a document that has been secured with Acrobat Self-Sign Security, the user password needs to be supplied before the file can open. Therefore, even if another user acquires a public certificate, it will be useless without the password.

Acrobat Self-Sign Security also offers permissions consistent with the 128-bit encryption permissions discussed at the beginning of the chapter. You can prevent users from changing your form fields but still let users comment on a form. You can also set different permissions for different users. You may wish some users to comment without changing a form while offering other users full permission rights.

All the above options are available when you have acquired Trusted Certificates and you have your own User Profile created. To understand more about encrypting PDF files with Acrobat Self-Sign Security, follow these steps:

1. Be certain you have added at least one Trusted Certificate to your User Settings.

 If you don't have any certificates available, use the public certificate in the Chapter 11 folder on the book's CD-ROM. Add the certificate to your Trusted Certificates list as described earlier.

2. Choose File ➪ Document Security. In the Document Security dialog box, select Acrobat Self-Sign Security from the pull-down menu choices.

3. A Self-Sign Security dialog box opens.

4. Select a Trusted Certificate in the left window and click on the Add button. If you have more users to add, click on the Trusted Certificate and then the Add button for each user. As users are added, the certificates appear in a list in the right window, as shown in Figure 11-18.

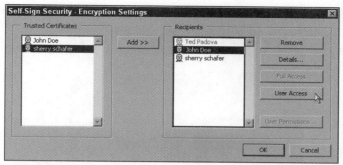

Figure 11-18: As Trusted Certificates are added to the Recipients list, they appear listed in the window.

5. To assign specific user permissions to a given user, select the user name in the Recipients list in the right window and click on the User Access button, then click on the User Permissions button, as shown in Figure 11-19.

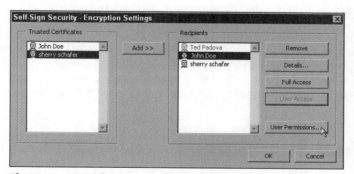

Figure 11-19: Select a user name in the Recipients list and click on the User Access button, then click on the User Permissions button.

6. The User Permissions dialog box opens. From the pull-down menu, select the permissions changes you wish to allow for the user, as shown in Figure 11-20. Click OK after making your choices.

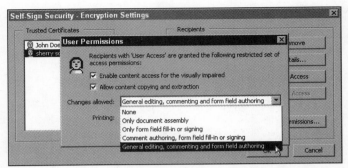

Figure 11-20: Select the permissions to allow by opening the pull-down menu and making the desired choice for the user selected in the Recipients list.

7. When you return to the Encryption Settings dialog box, select another user in the Recipients list and add the user's permissions. If you want the user to have full access to the PDF, select the username and click on the User Access button, then click OK. The default setting enables full access.

Click OK in the Self-Sign Encryption Settings dialog box and you are returned to the Document Security dialog box. Click Close and save the PDF. Acrobat Self-Sign Security has been added to the PDF. The only people who have access to the PDF are those identified in the Recipients list and you as the author of the document. When you open the self-signed document, you need to log on with your user password.

Using Digital Signatures

When you design forms, you can include fields used for digitally signing a document. A digital signature can act much like an analog signature for the purposes of signing forms or a digital signature can add a level of security to a form. You can design Signature fields that lock out field data after form fields have been filled in. The only person who can change the data is the owner of the password for the profile created for the digital signature used.

Signing a document is one step in properly using digital signatures. The second step is verifying a signature for authenticity. If you receive a form signed by another user, you will want to verify the signature to be certain the authorized individual completed the form. Therefore, you need to acquire the public certificates from all those who sign your forms. The public certificates you acquire are the same as those explained earlier in this chapter.

With regard to digitally signing a document, there are three common uses apart from the Self-Sign Security explained earlier. You can sign a PDF with your digital signature, you can verify signatures for authenticity, and you can use a Signature field for encrypting fields.

Digitally signing forms

Digital Signatures can be added either from a Signature field or a signature added to a form by a user without a Signature field appearing on the form. To add a digital signature, you must be logged on as a user. Acrobat enables you to log on as a user or invoke a command for digitally signing a document, and subsequently prompts you for a log on.

To sign a document without a Signature field added to a form, choose Tools ➪ Digital Signatures ➪ Sign Document. Acrobat selects the Digital Signature tool from the Command Bar for you and prompts you with a dialog box informing you the tool has been selected and ready for use. Click OK in the Digital Signatures alert dialog box.

The next step is to create the Digital Signature field. Click and drag open a rectangle to create the field in the area where the signature is to appear in the document. If you are not logged on as a user, then a dialog box opens prompting you to log on. Supply your password and click Log In.

An alert dialog box opens confirming your logon. Click OK and the Self-Sign Security – Sign Document dialog box opens, as shown in Figure 11-21. Confirm your password and click on the Save button.

Note   You may have to select the Show Options button to see all the options that are available, as shown in Figure 11-21.

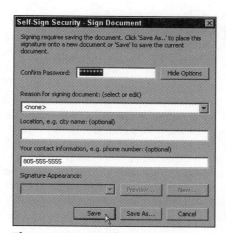

Figure 11-21: Confirm your password by typing it in the Confirm Password field box and click Save to sign the document.

A confirmation dialog box again opens, this time informing you the document has been signed. Click OK in the Self-Sign Security Alert dialog box.

When you view the signed document, the digital signature appears with the Appearance setting created for your user profile, as shown in Figure 11-22. The document is both signed and saved automatically by Acrobat.

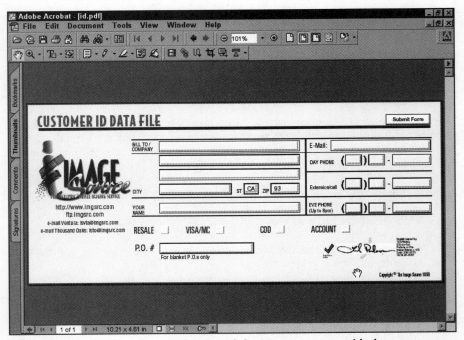

Figure 11-22: The signature on the signed document appears with the appearance setting created for your user profile.

If you close the PDF without saving, your digital signature is still saved in the file. Acrobat performs a *blind* save when you access the menu command and sign a document. If you close the PDF without selecting the Save or Save As command, Acrobat won't prompt you to save the file if no other edits have been made. If you want to eliminate your signature, you need to clear signatures from the document, then manually save the updates. Signature fields can be cleared in two ways. You can select the Form tool and click on the signature field and clear like any other field either from a context menu or by pressing the Backspace (Windows) or Delete (Macintosh) key.

You may have a form where a digital signature field has been added as part of the form design. Perhaps the field needs to remain on the form, but the signature needs to be cleared. When you choose Tools ➪ Digital Signatures ➪ Clear All Signature Fields, the signatures on the document are cleared, but the fields remain undisturbed.

Invisibly signing forms

Invisible signatures offer you a means of signing a document without the appearance of a form field. Invisible signatures are handled with a menu command by choosing Tools ➪ Digital Signatures ➪ Invisibly Sign Document.

If you are not logged on, Acrobat prompts you for a logon and password confirmation, the same as described with digitally signing a document. However, with invisible signatures, the Digital Signature tool is not selected and you do not have to draw a field box. After logging on, Acrobat signs the document without creating a field box. A dialog box opens confirming your signing.

If you select the Form tool, you cannot find the invisible signature on the document page. If you want to access the signature properties, you can open the Fields palette and find the signature, as shown in Figure 11-23.

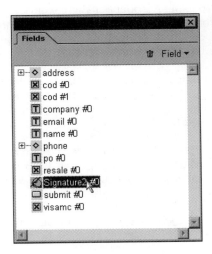

Figure 11-23: Invisible signatures are not shown in the document when the Form tool is selected. Open the Fields palette and you can gain access to the signature properties.

By using a context menu, you can delete the Signature or access the Field Properties. However, if you select Go to Field in the Fields palette, Acrobat cannot take you to the field because the field is invisible. You can clear the Signature from the document by selecting the Clear All Signature Fields command explained earlier or open a context menu in the Fields palette and select Delete field(s).

Securing Form Fields

Up to this point, the discussion related to signatures has involved securing a PDF or signing a PDF. These conditions apply to the entire PDF document and can be used with forms or a PDF created for any other purpose. With respect to Digital Signature fields, you can also protect any field or group of fields against unauthorized changes.

Assume for a moment you have a user complete a form that then needs to be sent to a supervisor for approval. The user signs the document after completing all the form fill-in. The form is then sent to a supervisor who first verifies the signature, then approves the document by signing it. When the supervisor signs the document, all the form fields can be locked against changes. This ensures any other department personnel the form has met approval and, regardless of who views it, the data have not been changed since the supervisor's signature.

Locking fields in an Acrobat form is similar to using Acrobat Self-Sign Security; except, rather than the entire form being protected against changes, only selected fields are protected. The only way the fields can be unprotected is when the user has the password for the signature field used to lock the other fields.

In Figure 11-24, the `poSignatures.pdf` form that is found in the Chapter 11 folder on the book's CD-ROM contains areas for three signatures. Each of the individuals can approve a purchase order. When an employee completes the purchase order, all the fields that appear above the signatures need to be secured. The fields at the bottom of the page need to be accessed by an accounting clerk who spreads the costs to departments according to items purchased. In this example, we don't want the accounting personnel making changes on the purchase order after it has been approved, but we do want the accounting department to access the fields needed to complete their job.

To understand how fields are individually protected when using digital signatures, follow these steps:

 On the CD-ROM To follow the steps below, use the `po.pdf` file in the Chapter 11 folder on the book's CD-ROM. To observe signature fields created on a similar form, open the `poSignatures.pdf` file from the same folder on the CD-ROM.

1. Create a digital signature field by using the Form tool and dragging open a field box.

 Note The Form tool, not the Digital Signature tool, is used to create the field. If you use the Digital Signature tool, you create the field box *and* sign the document. In this example, we want to create the field box for later signing by a user.

2. Provide a name for the field and select Signature for the Type.

3. Click on the Signed tab. In the Signed properties, select the radio button for Mark As Read-Only. From the pull-down menu, select All Fields Except These, as shown in Figure 11-25.

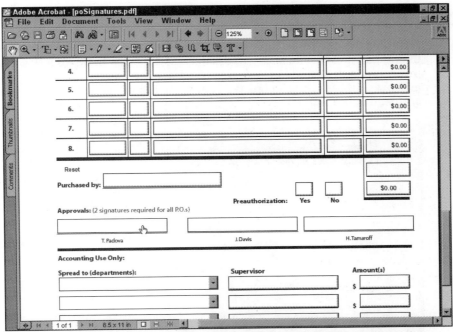

Figure 11-24: The purchase order form has three signature fields for supervisor approval. All the fields above the signatures need to be locked, but the accounting department needs to access the fields below the signatures.

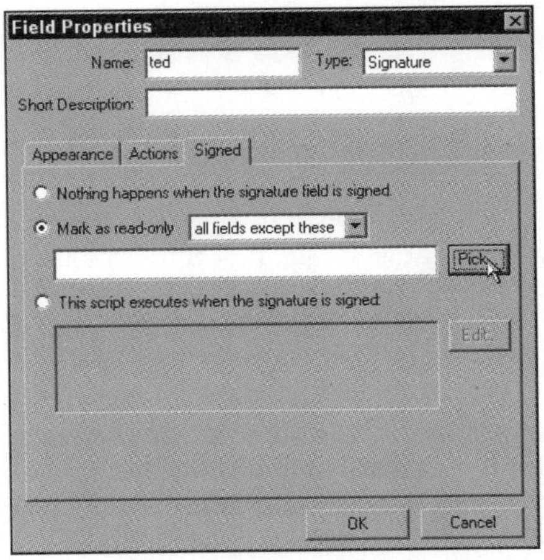

Figure 11-25: In the Signed properties dialog box, select All Fields Except These from the pull-down menu choices.

4. Click on the Pick button on the right side of the dialog box.

5. The Select a Field dialog box opens. Select an item to be excluded from the read-only list. In this example, since more fields are going to be protected than those that remain accessible, select all the fields to be excluded from protection. Click on the field name to be excluded and click Add, as shown in Figure 11-26. Keep selecting fields in the list that belong to the excluded group and click Add after each selection.

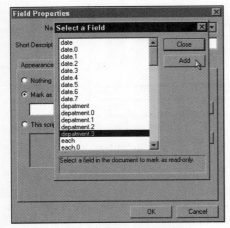

Figure 11-26: Select a field to be excluded in the list and click on the Add button. Keep clicking on the fields to be excluded from protection and click Add after each field has been selected.

6. Click Close. All the fields are listed in the Signed properties dialog box. Click OK to return to the document window.

When you examine the form, notice all fields are accessible. If you fill in data to complete the form for a purchase order and then sign the document, all the fields above the signatures cannot be changed. Those fields below the signatures can be selected and edited, as shown in Figure 11-27.

If more than one signature is needed on a form, apply the same settings in other signature fields and be certain to exclude all the signature fields from the read-only list. When you finish designing the form, you can use Acrobat Standard Security to prevent any user from changing the form and editing the signature fields.

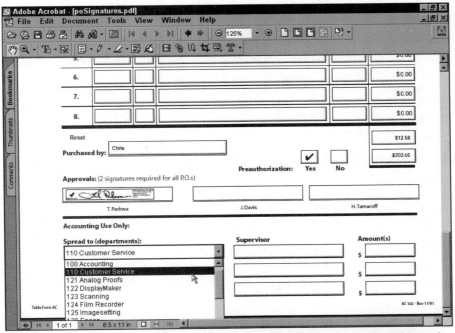

Figure 11-27: After signing the document, the field exceptions are accessible and editable.

Securing signed documents

One point of clarification needs to be made with regard to using a signature field and securing a document with Acrobat Standard Security. If you design a form with a signature field and sign it or digitally sign a document using the Tools ⇨ Digital Signatures ⇨ Sign Document or Tools ⇨ Digital Signatures ⇨ Invisibly Sign Document menu commands, and then try to protect your document with Acrobat Standard Security, Acrobat opens a warning dialog box and prohibits you from securing a signed PDF. In short, you cannot first sign a document, then use Acrobat Standard Security.

To secure a file against any changes or other Acrobat Standard Security options, first open the Document Security dialog box. Apply all the security settings in the Standard Security dialog box. Return to the Document Pane, then sign your document. The file is saved and the security is applied. It is important to follow the proper sequence when adding security and digital signatures.

Verifying Signatures

A digital signature is meaningless unless it can be authenticated. Anyone can create a digital signature and return a form to you digitally signed. When you open a file that has been signed by a user, the digital signature field appears with a yellow question mark. The question mark on the signature field informs you that the signature has not yet been verified. To verify a signature, you first need to acquire the user's public certificate.

Authenticating a signature

When you open a PDF file that has been digitally signed by a user, the first appearance of the signature field shows a yellow question mark on the signature, as shown in Figure 11-28. Acrobat informs you the file has been signed but the signature has not yet been verified. To verify a signature, follow these steps:

1. Open a signed PDF file. The signature field displays a question mark within the signature. To verify a signature, you must have acquired a public certificate from the user who signed the form. Assuming you have the public certificate, choose Tools ⇨ Self-Sign Security ⇨ Log In, as shown in Figure 11-28.

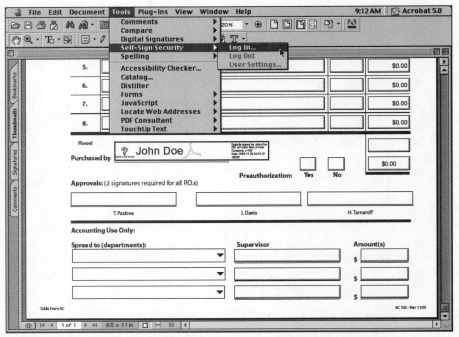

Figure 11-28: In order to verify a signature, you must first log on as a user.

2. The Self-Sign Security Log In dialog box opens. Enter your password and click Log In.

3. Acrobat informs you the logon is complete in an alert dialog box. From the Self-Sign Security Alert dialog box, you can immediately access the User Settings if you need to add the current user to your trusted certificates. If you already have the user who signed the document added to your Trusted Certificates list, you can click on the OK button in the Self-Sign Security-Alert dialog box. If you need to add the user to the Trusted Certificates list, click on the User Settings button and follow the steps for adding Public Certificates to the User Settings, explained earlier in this chapter.

4. Choose Tools ➪ Digital Signatures ➪ Verify All Signatures.

5. A Digital Signatures – Alert dialog box opens. If you have several pages in the PDF and several signatures on a form, the verification of the signatures may take some time. Acrobat informs you that it may take awhile to verify the signatures. If you design single page forms with a few signatures, the time it takes to verify the signatures is relatively short. Click OK in the alert dialog box to proceed.

6. Acrobat surveys your form and searches for all the signatures, then matches them against the Trusted Certificates list. When the verification is complete, another Alert dialog box opens. Click OK in the Digital Signatures – Alert dialog box.

7. When you view the PDF document, the signature field(s) displays a check mark within the signature appearance, as shown in Figure 11-29. Acrobat informs you the signature has been authenticated and matches the Trusted Certificate.

Comparing changes after signing documents

Depending on how you design a form and the attributes used for securing fields when a form is signed, you may wish to examine any changes in a document after a signature has been added. For example, you may not secure a form with Acrobat Standard Security and you may choose to not lock fields after a user has signed a document. In this case, any user can return to the form and enter more data in the unprotected fields. Acrobat provides you a means of comparing a document from the time it was originally signed and any changes that may have occurred after the file was signed.

To compare changes to a document, choose Tools ➪ Compare ➪ Two Versions Within a Signed Document.

The Compare Document Revisions dialog box opens. The document to be examined is listed in the Document pull-down menu. From the Compare pull-down menu, select the version last signed. From the To pull-down menu, select Current Version, as shown in Figure 11-30.

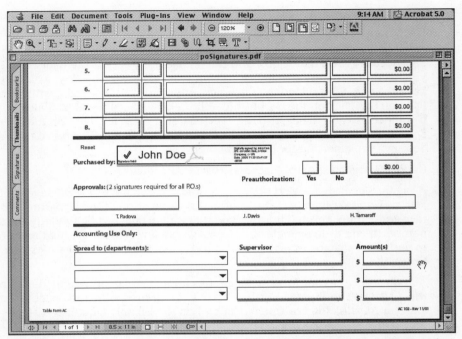

Figure 11-29: When you examine the signature(s) in the PDF after verification, the signature appearance(s) changes the question mark to a check mark indicating that the signature(s) has been verified.

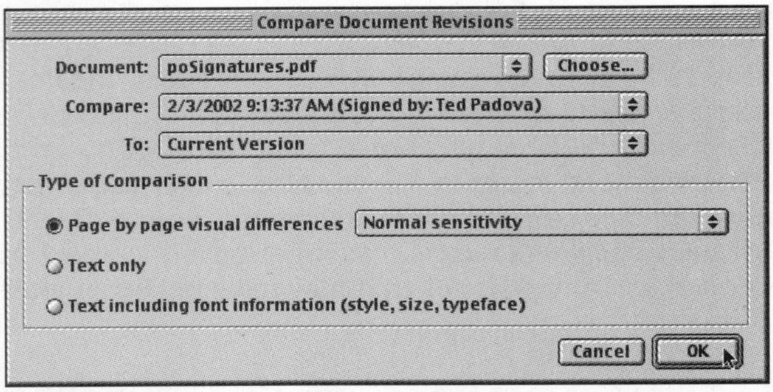

Figure 11-30: Select the two documents to compare from the pull-down menus.

If several people have signed the document, you can compare the originally signed versions against any user signature. If anyone has changed the document since it was originally signed, the Compare feature in Acrobat reports the results in a window displaying the original signed version and the changes made by another user.

After clicking OK in the Compare Document Revisions dialog box, Acrobat creates a PDF file with pages showing the originally signed document and pages where all the changes since the signature have been made. The display shown in the new PDF is in double-sided facing pages mode where the pages in the file can be examined beside each other, as shown in Figure 11-31. Both documents are displayed with Pencil Comments highlighting the changes.

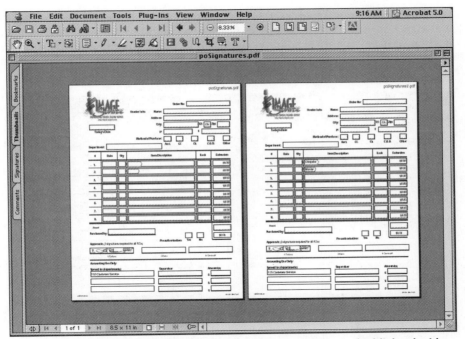

Figure 11-31: When the document is compared, all changes are highlighted with Pencil Comments with a magenta color.

Tip You can use the Compare Documents menu command to compare two different versions of your PDF forms. If you are uncertain whether changes have been made between two different files designed to be the same form, choose Tools ➪ Compare ➪ Two Documents. The same comparison applied to comparing signed documents is used where the files appear beside each other and Acrobat marks the differences between the documents. This method offers you a comparison without signing the documents.

Using the Signatures palette

The Signatures palette offers many of the same menu commands found under the Tools menu and a list of all signatures displayed conveniently in the Navigation Pane or a floating palette. If you dock the Signatures palette in the Navigation Pane, you can view signatures much like you would review comments, bookmarks, and thumbnails.

Cross-Reference   For more on docking palettes in the Navigation Pane, see Chapter 5, "Creating Form Fields."

As Digital Signatures are added to a PDF, they are listed in the Signatures palette, as shown in Figure 11-32. The display of the icon adjacent to the signature informs you at a glance if a signature is valid. In Figure 11-32, one signature appears valid and the other signature needs verification.

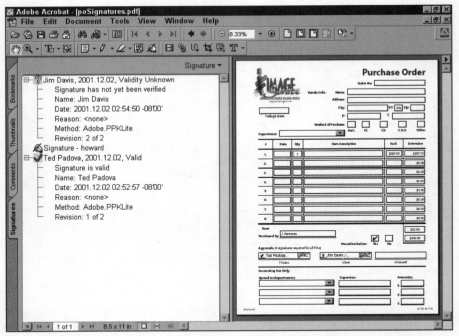

Figure 11-32: Icons appear next to signatures in the Signatures palette indicating whether they are valid or need verification.

From the palette menu you can make menu choices the same as those offered in the Tools ➪ Digital Signatures menu. Open the pull-down menu, as shown in Figure 11-33, to display the menu options.

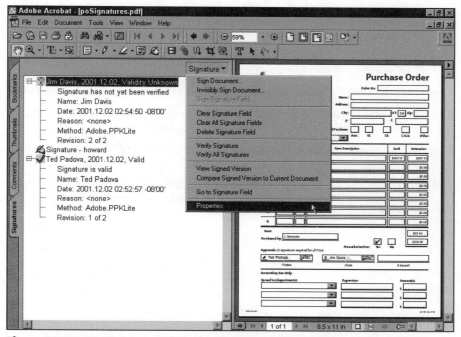

Figure 11-33: Menu commands in the Signatures palette display the same menu choices as the Digital Signatures submenu command from the Tools menu.

Likewise, context menus offer the same menu options as when you open a context menu on a digital signature field. If you invisibly sign a document, the signature appears in the Signatures palette. Like the visible signatures, you can open the signature properties or delete a signature.

Summary

✦ Acrobat Standard Security provides you with two levels of encryption: 40-bit encryption enables all viewer versions access to PDFs when a password is known and 128-bit encryption is only available to Acrobat viewers 5. 0 or greater.

✦ Acrobat Self Sign Security enables you to encrypt files for selected groups of users. In order to use Self-Sign Security for protecting files for select users, each user's Public Certificate needs to be acquired.

✦ Different appearance settings for signatures are determined by importing PDF images or images that are compatible with the Open As Adobe PDF command. These are represented as icons, symbols, scans, and other types of image content.

✦ Before a user can digitally sign a document, the user needs to create a Personal Profile and log on as a user.

✦ You can sign PDF forms with a Digital Signature, Invisibly signed, or Self-Signed.

✦ Digital Signatures can protect individual fields against unauthorized access that would enable users to change field contents.

✦ You authenticate Digital Signatures through access of the signer's Public Certificate.

✦ You can compare PDF forms between the last signed document and any changes after a document has been signed, or between two different versions of a PDF form.

✦   ✦   ✦

Working with Accessible and Tagged PDFs

Adobe Acrobat 5 is compliant with U.S. Federal code Section 508 of the American Disabilities Act that regulates document accessibility for vision- and motion-challenged persons. What this means is screen readers can interpret the PDFs that you create to read aloud a PDF file. Through an extensive set of keyboard modifiers available in Acrobat, almost anyone with vision or motion challenges can be included in sharing your documents and working with your forms.

Accessibility may not seem important to you if you think that your work won't be used by persons with vision or motion challenges; for the moment, however, stop and think about the fact that all of us are not immune from potentially challenging conditions. One automobile accident or an unexpected event can place any of us in a situation in which we may need to rely on document accessibility for our work and leisure activities. Therefore, accessible documents are not just for an audience of people with current challenges; understanding more about Accessibility may be preparing for your own or a loved one's future. Let's hope not, but realize that the possibility does exist and we all share a mutual interest in knowing as much as we can about document accessibility.

In order for a document to be accessible, you must use authoring applications capable of delivering a document's structure to Acrobat. Hence, you need to know something about the internal structure of documents and what programs are used to create the structure required by Acrobat to make a document accessible. In this chapter, we'll look at creating and working with structured and tagged PDF files not only for accessibility, but also for document repurposing.

Creating Accessible Documents

Thus far, these terms of document accessibility, structure, and tagged PDFs may be confusing to you. If the term "accessibility" is new, then you need to begin with an understanding of what accessible documents are before you can go about working with them. Once you know more about document accessibility, you can move forward and look at how to create an accessible document. Then you can look at how Acrobat can manage accessible documents. Therefore, there are three areas to work with: understanding accessibility, creating accessible documents from authoring programs, and finally working with accessible documents in Acrobat. Let's begin with a basic understanding of accessibility.

Understanding Accessibility

For sighted people, when we view a document on our computers or read a printed page, we can easily discern the difference between titles, subtitles, columns, graphic images, graphic elements, tables or tabular information, and so on. With regard to Acrobat forms, we can easily see the difference between background designs and form fields, and we typically see visual clues to know where buttons and fields exist.

With regard to hardware devices dependent on software to generate audio output from an Acrobat form or other PDF file, the software used by readers isn't intelligent enough to distinguish differences based on visual clues. A document with three columns of text, for example, may appear to a screen reader as one continuous column and the reader may interpret the text from left to right across all three columns row by row. Obviously, the output will be confusing and useless to the end user working with a screen reader. Headings, subheadings, and tables are interpreted by readers the same as body copy, offering no distinction in the structure unless the reader has some clue that these items are different from the body text.

When you create PDF files from authoring programs, some programs provide an opportunity to deliver the underlying structure of a document that can be retained in the resultant PDF file. With a series of tags and a capture of the document structure, a screen reader can use alternative text to make distinctions in the document much like the visual user would interpret a page. The document flow, alternate text for graphic elements, distinctions between headings, and so on, can all be managed in Acrobat when the internal structure of the document structural tree is included in the PDF export. When files are not exported with the document structure, a free Acrobat plug-in is available from Adobe Systems to convert an unstructured and untagged PDF file to accessible content. In order to make it possible for people with screen readers to navigate your PDF forms or other PDF documents correctly, the underlying structure must be present.

To gain more of a grasp on what is meant by using terms like structure and tagged PDF files, a definition is warranted. PDF files fall into three categories when we speak of a document's structure. The categories include:

✦ **Unstructured PDF Files.** Screen readers cannot interpret unstructured PDF documents. When exporting the PDF to other formats, such as a Rich Text File (RTF), the basic paragraph structure is preserved, but tables, lists, and some text formatting are lost. PDF files can be repurposed, enabling handheld devices and various-sized monitors with a document reflow capability to view them. You cannot reflow unstructured documents, however.

✦ **Structured PDF Files.** Screen readers can read structured PDF files, but the reliability is much less than the next category of tagged PDF documents. When exporting files to other formats, more structural content is preserved, but tables and lists can be lost. Additionally, structured documents like the unstructured documents above do not support content reflow for different sized devices.

✦ **Tagged PDF Files.** Tagged PDFs contain both the document structure and a hierarchical structure tree in which all the internal structure about the document's content is interpreted. Tagged PDFs have the highest reliability when repurposing files for screen reader output and saving files in other formats such as RTF, HTML, XHTML, and XML. In addition, tagged PDF files support document reflow for viewing on different-sized devices and accommodating any zoom level on a monitor. For more on reflowing documents, see the use of the Reflow tool later in this chapter.

The goal for you when creating PDF forms for accessibility is to be certain you use PDF documents that are not only structured, but also tagged PDFs. Once you create tagged PDFs, you can work with the structure tree and modify the contents for optimum use. In terms of making Acrobat forms accessible, there are several things you should consider when optimizing documents that can be handled effectively by screen readers. These include:

✦ **Assessing Accessibility.** Fortunately, Acrobat provides tools for determining whether a PDF file is an accessible document. As a first order of business, you should plan on assessing the file for accessibility. If you work with legacy files or files that are created from authoring programs that don't support the export of the document structure, you need to make certain to first make the document accessible before following the remaining steps.

✦ **Logical reading order.** The underlying text apart from the form fields should follow a logical flow. Column text needs to be properly defined in terms of the path that a screen reader follows (for example, down one column, then begin at the top of the second column, and so on). Headings and subheadings should be marked for distinction.

✦ **Alternative text descriptions for image and graphic elements.** Those familiar with HTML know that you can code an HTML document with alternate tags so users with text-only browsers can understand the structure of Web pages. The same principle for accessible documents applies. Alternate text needs to be inserted so the screen reader can interpret graphic elements.

✦ **Form field descriptions.** Form fields need to be described with text to inform a user with a screen reader that a form field is present. A description of each field needs to be identified with a text statement.

✦ **Field tab order.** We know that setting the logical tab order for fields on a form is important for the visual user. With screen readers it is essential. The logical tab order for fields should be strictly followed.

✦ **Document security.** If documents are secured with Acrobat security, you must use the Acrobat 5 compatibility and 128-bit encryption. If you use compatibility less than Acrobat 5 or 40-bit encryption, the PDF is secured, however form fields won't be protected.

✦ **Links and interactivity.** Use form fields for link buttons with descriptions so the user knows that another destination or a link action is invoked if the field is selected.

✦ **Document language.** Screen readers typically deliver accessible documents in only one language. Screen readers and the software to run them may change with new models. To protect your documents against inoperability with new devices, specify a document language when creating accessible forms. Document language specification is also important when using tools in Acrobat for checking accessibility.

Creating structured and tagged forms

Not all authoring programs currently support creating accessible PDF documents. This phenomenon may change with new upgrades to software, so what is said today, may change tomorrow. As of this writing, the programs offering the best support for document accessibility include Microsoft Word version 2000 or higher, Adobe PageMaker 7.0 or higher, and Adobe InDesign 2.0 or higher. If you use other authoring applications, you do have another option with the Make Accessible Plug-in offered by Adobe Systems. Let's first take a look at making accessible documents from authoring applications, then later move on to making existing PDFs accessible.

Creating accessible documents from Microsoft Word 2000

Microsoft Word may not be the ideal authoring tool for creating forms, but if it serves your forms needs, you can derive great benefit when making your forms accessible from Word documents. Word files can be exported with structure and tagged information. To effectively create accessible documents from Microsoft Word, follow some of these recommendations:

✦ **Use styles.** For all text in your Word file, be certain to use style sheets and identify all categories, such as body copy, headings, subheadings, and so on, with different style names. Use paragraph properties, such as space before and space after, to add spacing rather than using the Enter or Return key to add space between paragraphs and headings.

✦ **Use Word's columns definitions.** Define columns in Word and preview the pages to be certain the columns fall as you intend to have them appear in the PDF. Don't use the tab key to tab body text when creating columns.

✦ **Add alternate text.** When it is feasible, try to use alternate text in Word before creating the PDF file. You can use the Web tab in the illustrations properties for creating alternate text. (Setting Web attributes for alternate text is discussed on the following pages.) Use this tool when images or graphic elements are introduced in your documents.

✦ **Use Word's table and drawing features.** When you create a table in the Word file, use the Insert Table command or the Draw Table tool when possible. Using these methods is preferred over using styles for tabbing text across columns and using carriage returns for rows.

✦ **Group objects.** If you introduce icons and graphic elements, such as an object and a key line, or use Word's drawing features to create multiple objects, use the Group command to group the objects. Word interprets the group as a single illustration as opposed to multiple elements, thereby making the alternate text description much less complicated.

✦ **Use PDFMaker to produce the PDF file.** Be certain to use the PDFMaker supplied by Acrobat when installed on a computer containing MS Office applications. Avoid printing a PostScript file and distilling in Acrobat Distiller.

Note If you use a Microsoft Word version less than Word 2000, be certain to upgrade your MS Office applications. Word 2000 has much more improved accessibility features and you will want all your older Word files to be opened and updated to the newer version before converting to PDF.

Following the guidelines above, let's take a look at creating an accessible document from Microsoft Word 2000. To create an accessible document from Microsoft Word, follow these steps:

1. Design the form in Word using style sheets for all the text and use the Insert Table command for any tables used in the form. In this example, use the `accessibleApplication.doc` file in the Chapter 12 folder on the book's CD-ROM, as shown in Figure 12-1.

On the CD-ROM You'll find the `accessibleApplication.doc` file in the Chapter 12 folder on the book's CD-ROM.

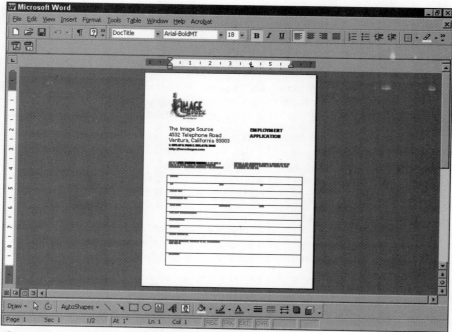

Figure 12-1: The form in Microsoft Word uses style sheets and defined tables.

2. For any graphic images, be certain to provide alternate text. In the example, you need to add alternate text for the logo appearing in the top-left corner of the form. To add alternate text in Microsoft Word, right-click the mouse button (Windows) and select Format Picture from the context menu.

3. The Format Picture dialog box opens. Click on the Web tab and add the alternative text in the field box, as shown in Figure 12-2. Click OK after adding a description of the object.

4. In Microsoft Word, select the Acrobat menu and select Change Conversion Settings.

5. The Acrobat(R) PDFMaker 5.0 for Microsoft (R) Office dialog box opens. Click on the Office tab and select the check box for Embed Tags in PDF (Accessibility, Reflow), as shown in Figure 12-3.

6. If Bookmarks are to be included in the PDF document, click on the Bookmarks tab and identify the styles to be converted to bookmarks. If you have a single-page form, you will not likely need bookmarks. Be certain to disable bookmarks in the Bookmarks tab if they are not needed in the PDF.

7. Click OK. The PDF file is produced. In Acrobat, open the file and choose Window ➪ Tags. The Tags palette displays the structural items contained in the PDF file, as shown in Figure 12-4.

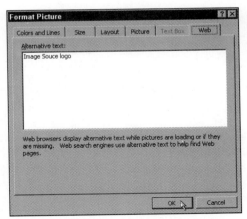

Figure 12-2: Open the Format Picture dialog box and click on the Web tab. Enter text in the field box for Alternative Text.

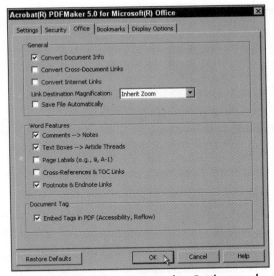

Figure 12-3: Click on Conversion Settings and check the box for Accessibility.

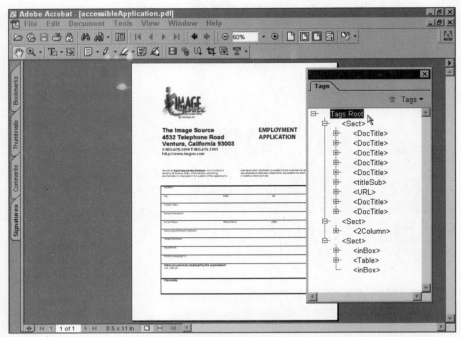

Figure 12-4: Open the Tags palette and view the structural items that are contained in the PDF file. If no tags appear in the palette, the document is not tagged or accessible.

At this point, you have successfully created a tagged and accessible PDF document. The use of the Tags palette and discussion on managing accessibility is covered later in this chapter. Before you move on to using Acrobat tools with accessible documents, take a look at how Adobe PageMaker creates accessible PDFs.

Creating accessible documents from Adobe PageMaker

Adobe PageMaker 7.0 and above support accessibility. If you use earlier versions of PageMaker with the PDF Export filter, you won't produce accessible documents, so be certain to upgrade PageMaker to version 7.0 or higher. Newer releases of layout applications are likely to support accessibility, so if you use another program, stay abreast of all new releases and look for the same support.

Accessibility in PageMaker 7 is supported across platforms. Keep in mind you need to do the same with PageMaker as when using Microsoft Word in regard to producing the PDF file. Don't print to PostScript and distill the file. PageMaker 7 supports direct export to PDF without the use of additional plug-ins and, like Word, creates tagged PDF documents. To see how a PageMaker file exports an accessible document, follow these steps:

1. Create a document in PageMaker and be certain to use styles much like those used in Microsoft Word. The same form used above was created in PageMaker, as shown in Figure 12-5.

On the CD-ROM

You'll find the `accessibleApp.pmd` file in the Chapter 12 folder on the book's CD-ROM.

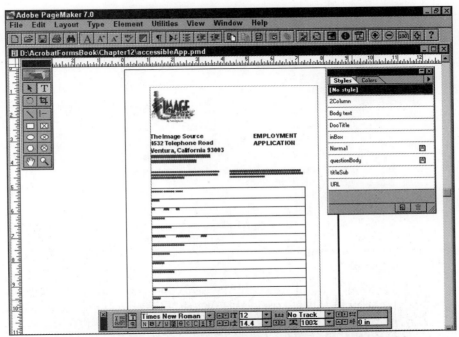

Figure 12-5: A PageMaker 7.0 form is created with all the text defined with PageMaker styles.

2. Save the document and choose File ➪ Export ➪ Adobe PDF. The PDF Options dialog box opens, as shown in Figure 12-6. At the bottom of the General PDF Options settings, select the check box for Embed Tags in PDF (For Accessibility and Reflow).

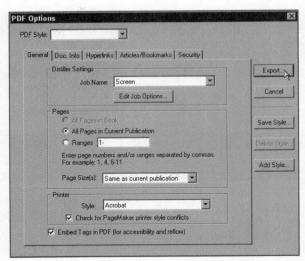

Figure 12-6: Choose File ⇨ Export ⇨ Adobe PDF to open the PDF Options dialog box. Select the check box at the bottom of the General PDF Options dialog box to include accessibility.

3. Click Export and the Export PDF As dialog box opens. Supply a filename and choose a destination for the resultant PDF file. If you want the PDF to be viewed in Acrobat immediately after the PDF is created, check the box for View PDF.

4. Click Save in the Export PDF As dialog box. A PostScript file is printed to disk and also distilled in Acrobat (transparent to the user). After a momentary pause, the PDF is displayed in Acrobat.

5. Open the Tags palette to display the document tags and structure. Click on the TouchUp Order tool in the Acrobat Command Bar. (The tool displays a selection arrow with 1,2,3 adjacent to the arrow, as shown in Figure 12-7.) For more on using the TouchUp Order tool, see "Changing the reading order," later in this chapter.

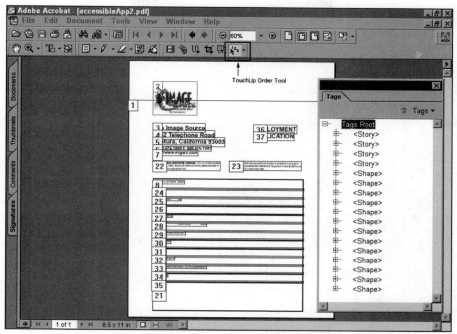

Figure 12-7: Open the PDF in Acrobat to view the Tags palette. After you select the TouchUp Order tool, you can see the document tags and text flow.

Creating PDFs with structure from an authoring application provides you with a one-step process for creating accessible PDFs. You may not use either Word or PageMaker to create your forms or you may have files already in PDF format that you wish to make accessible. Fortunately, Acrobat provides a solution with the Make Accessible plug-in.

Making existing PDFs accessible (Windows only)

If you have PDF forms that you wish to make accessible, returning to an authoring program can be time consuming and potentially unnecessary. Unfortunately, the solution provided by Adobe as of this writing is only available to Windows users. The solution is in the form of a plug-in you can download free from Adobe's Web site at `www.adobe.com/support/downloads/88de.htm`. Look for the Make Accessible plug-in, download it, and follow the installation instructions. Once installed, you can open a PDF file and access the Document ⇨ Make Accessible command (shown in Figure 12-8) to add accessibility to any existing PDF file.

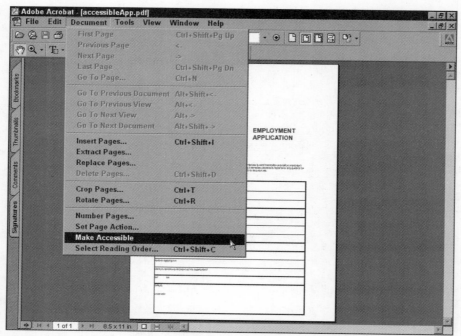

Figure 12-8: After the Make Accessible plug-in has been installed, open a PDF file and choose Document ⇨ Make Accessible.

If your document is already accessible (or contains Tags) and you try to run the Make Accessible command, Acrobat opens a warning dialog box, as shown in Figure 12-9, and informs you the document is already accessible.

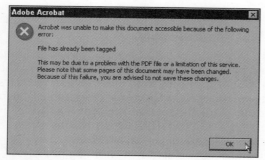

Figure 12-9: If a document has been tagged and you select the Make Accessible command, Acrobat reports to you in a dialog box that the document has already been tagged.

If you have some internal structure that can't be interpreted by Acrobat, another dialog box warning appears. If a PDF has a font problem or other anomaly, you may need to return to the authoring program and recreate a PDF file, then go back to Acrobat and try to make it accessible if the authoring program does not support exporting the necessary structure. For the most part, the plug-in is seamless, and making accessible documents from existing PDFs is a simple task.

Tip   You can use the Make Accessible plug-in on a tagged PDF file by untagging a file. Open the Tags palette on a tagged PDF document and deselect Document is Tagged PDF in the palette menu. The Make Accessible Plug-in can then be used to rescan the document.

Batch processing for document accessibility (Windows only)

Using the Make Accessible plug-in via a menu command is sufficient for creating accessible documents for a few files. If you have many forms that you want to convert, you can use Acrobat's Batch Processing mode to convert a collection of PDFs from user-defined folders.

To create a batch sequence used for making PDFs accessible, be certain the Make Accessible plug-in is installed. Choose File ➪ Batch Processing ➪ Edit Batch Sequences to open the Batch Sequences dialog box. Click on the New Sequence button in the dialog box and provide a name for the sequence when the Name Sequence dialog box opens. (Name the sequence Make Accessible.)

The Batch Edit Sequence dialog box opens. Click on the Select Commands button and the Edit Sequence dialog box opens. Select the Make Accessible command from the list of commands in the left window, as shown in Figure 12-10.

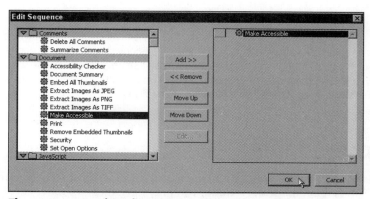

Figure 12-10: In the Edit Sequence dialog box, select the Make Accessible command and click on the Add button to add the sequence to the list on the right side of the dialog box.

Click on the Add button to add the command to the list of sequences on the right side of the dialog box. Click OK and you are returned to the Batch Edit Sequence dialog box. In this dialog box, you can determine what folder is used for the files to convert and the destination where the converted files are saved. If you elect to be prompted when the command is accessed, leave the first pull-down menu option set to Ask When Sequence is Run, as shown in Figure 12-11.

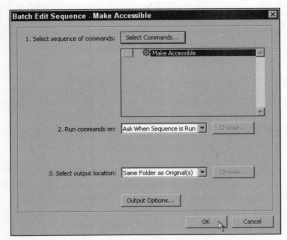

Figure 12-11: Select Ask When Sequence is Run from the pull-down menu for Run Commands On and you are prompted to identify the source files when you select the command to run the batch sequence.

Click OK and your new sequence is added to the file menu for the Batch Sequences. If you want to run the sequence, choose File ➪ Batch Processing ➪ Make Accessible (or the name you provided for your sequence). Acrobat prompts you in a dialog box to locate the files to be made accessible. Select the files to convert and Acrobat runs the Make Accessible command in a batch mode.

Verifying Accessibility

When you work with PDF forms that require accessibility, you'll first want to check and see if the PDF has been made accessible. You may have files that have no structure, tags, or alternative text and need to use the Make Accessible plug-in; and in other cases, you may wish to analyze the document for accessibility, reading order, modify alternate text, or insert alternate text for items that need definition. The first step in working with accessibility in existing PDF files is to check the file for document structure.

Checking the accessibility of a form

When you open a PDF file and wish to determine whether the document is accessible, a simple view of the Tags palette enables you to determine whether you're working with a tagged PDF. In addition, Acrobat has a menu command that provides you with more information and also gives you an idea of whether the content can be made accessible. To check for accessibility, choose Tools ➪ Accessibility Checker.

The Accessibility Checker Options dialog box opens. If you wish to have comments generated in the PDF to display any problems associated with the file and the ability to make it accessible, select the check box for Create Comments in Document, as shown in Figure 12-12. If you elect to not have comments displayed in the document, you can have Acrobat create a log file and write the comments to a text file that can be opened in any text editor. Where the log file is saved can be established by clicking on the Choose button in the Accessibility Checker Options dialog box.

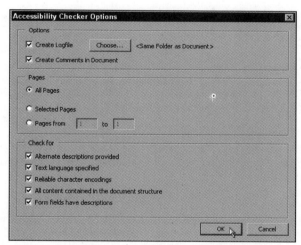

Figure 12-12: After selecting the Accessibility menu command, the Accessibility Checker Options dialog box opens. Make the choices for what to check for in this dialog box and click OK.

At the bottom of the dialog box are check boxes for what Acrobat checks for in assessing the open document. By default, all options are enabled. Leave the check boxes as they appear and click OK. Acrobat assesses the file and reports back in an Adobe Acrobat dialog box a description of the analysis, as shown in Figure 12-13. In this example, the document may have problems when trying to make it accessible. If you encounter problems such as this, you return to the authoring program and recreate the PDF. In some cases, you can gain a clue from the report as to how to fix the problem. In other cases, you may have to experiment and try to produce a good quality PDF file.

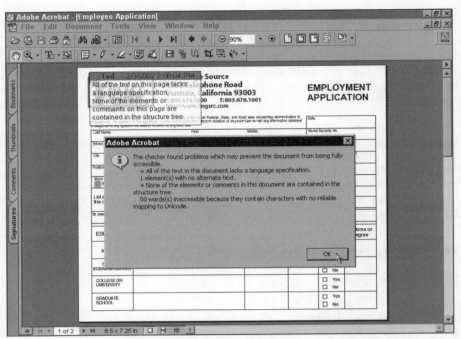

Figure 12-13: The results of the Accessibility Checker are reported in a dialog box.

In addition to the report in the dialog box, the comments display messages for found problems, and some form elements are highlighted as a further indication of which problems are found.

If you run the Accessibility Checker on a PDF document with no accessibility problems, a different dialog box opens informing you that no problems exist. When you see a dialog box that doesn't report any problems, you can assume that using the Make Accessible plug-in produces an accessible document that is optimized for screen reading.

Changing the reading order

The order in which a screen reader reads a PDF document follows a similar example, as was observed when setting the tab order for form fields. You can easily display the reading order in a tagged PDF file by selecting the TouchUp Order tool from the Acrobat Command Bar. When the tool is selected and an accessible document is viewed in the Document Pane, the reading order of the elements are displayed with numbers indicating the order the file will be read, as shown in Figure 12-14.

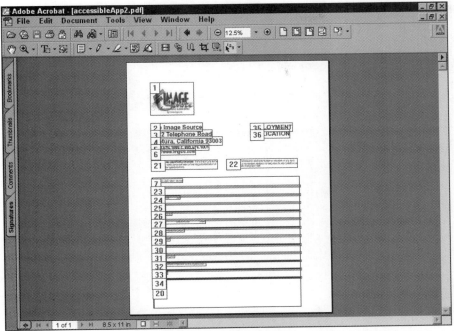

Figure 12-14: Open an accessible document and select the TouchUp Order tool from the Acrobat Command Bar. The reading order is shown with the appearance of the numeric order by which the screen reader will read the file.

Much like you can change the tab order of form fields, the reading order of a document can also be changed. In the example shown in Figure 12-14, the title of the form is Employee Application. The text for the title appears as numbers 35 and 36 in the reading order. On this form, the form title should be the first item- read after the alternate text for the logo. Therefore, these two lines of text need to occupy the number 2 and number 3 order. To change the order, click on the item to appear as the first in the sequence. Then click on successive numbers in the desired order. In this example, when the order of the first two items is changed, they appear as shown in Figure 12-15.

The structure of the PDF file contains not only the order of the elements, but also an order of layered items. If you find difficulty in changing the order of items, it may be due to one element appearing on a top layer in which the element that you want to change lays behind another item. You can make choices for handling the ordering of the elements by opening a context menu and adjusting the layering, as well as a few other choices for organizing the sequence, as shown in Figure 12-16.

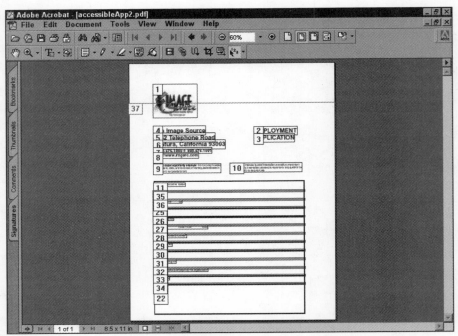

Figure 12-15: After using the TouchUp Order tool, the first two lines of text are changed to read first in the document after the logo.

Figure 12-16: When an item appears behind another element, you can change the layer position from choices in a context menu.

At best, the use of the TouchUp Order tool is awkward and needs some serious improvement. You may find a struggle at first, but with practice you can come to understand how to reorder the structure on an accessible document.

Tip

When using authoring programs, be certain to design forms with the order and layers in mind. As you move items around a document page, pay particular attention to the elements appearing in front of and behind other elements. Try to design forms with a logical structure that reduces the amount of time needed to reorder items in Acrobat.

Adding alternate text

Graphic elements need alternate text for the user of a screen reader to interpret graphic elements on a page. When you have a tagged PDF file, you can easily add alternate text for the graphic elements that have no text descriptions. Using the example described above, the logo appearing at the top of the page is a raster image. When a screen reader reads the form, no specific instructions are contained in the document to interpret this image. As an option, we can create alternate text so a visually challenged person knows a graphic element exists on the page. To add alternate text in a tagged PDF document, follow these steps:

1. Open a tagged PDF file and choose Window ➪ Tags to open the Tags palette.

2. Click on the Tags Root icon to the left of the text. On Windows, a minus (-) symbol appears adjacent to the text. On the Mac OS, a right pointing arrow appears next to the text. Clicking on the icon opens the tags tree.

3. Find the element in which you want to add the alternate text. In this example, open the child tags and find a description for InlineShape. To be certain you are working with the element in which you intend to add the alternate text, you can ask Acrobat to highlight the items selected in the Tags palette. From a context menu opened on the tag in question, select Turn On Associated Content Highlighting, as shown in Figure 12-17.

4. The element on the page that is associated with the tag that is selected in the Tags palette appears highlighted. Be certain the tag is correctly selected by verifying the highlighted object on the page.

5. Before you can edit a tag's properties, you need to turn the highlighting off. When you open a context menu again in the Tags palette, you only have one option to choose, as shown in Figure 12-18. Notice in the figure that the graphic image is highlighted with a key line border.

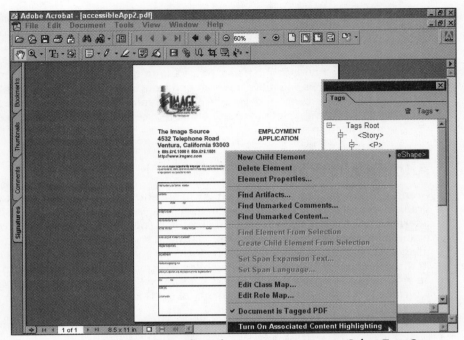

Figure 12-17: Select the tag to edit and open a context menu. Select Turn On Associated Content Highlighting at the bottom of the menu.

6. Select the menu option for turning off the highlighting and open the context menu again with the cursor positioned on the tag to be edited.

7. From the menu items, select Element Properties.

8. The Element Properties dialog box opens. Add a title for the tag, a mention of the image type, the alternate text, and choose a language version from the pull-down menu choices. The edits made in this example are shown in Figure 12-19.

9. The text added for Alternate Text in the Element Properties dialog box is handled by the screen reader. Click OK and you've completed adding alternate text to a graphic element.

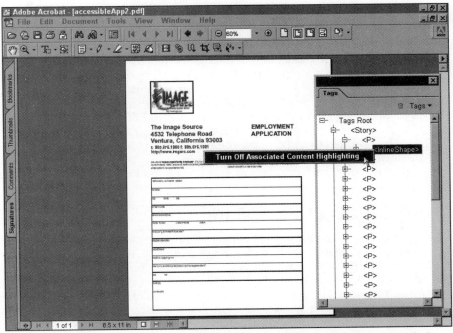

Figure 12-18: When you open a context menu after the highlight is activated, the only menu choice available is to turn off the highlighting.

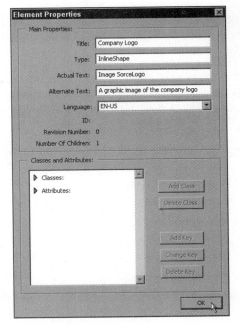

Figure 12-19: Fill in the desired fields in the Element Properties dialog box. Be certain to add a description for the Alternate Text.

Making Forms Accessible

Forms differ from other PDF collections you wish to make accessible because they require you to add more content after a PDF has been created. Unless you create static forms with no form fields, the editing you perform in Acrobat needs to be made accessible as well as the background content that was made accessible in an authoring application. Ideally, a form that is to be accessible will have been created in an authoring program that produces a tagged PDF file. If there are no tags in the PDF file, then your first step in making the form accessible is to add tags. After tags have been added to a PDF form, you need to provide descriptions for each field on the form. Therefore, there are two steps in making a form accessible. First create the tags, then add form fields with descriptions or add descriptions to existing fields.

Adding tags to a PDF form

Adding tags can be handled in two ways. For Windows users, you can use the Make Accessible plug-in described earlier in his chapter. For Mac OS users, you need to manually create tags individually on each form. The method for creating tags manually can be used on either platform. There are two steps in creating tags for a PDF form. You need to create tags for the background text in the PDF form and you need to add tags for the field elements. For Windows users, if you use the Make Accessible plug-in or use a form that already has tags, you don't need to be concerned with adding tags to the background text. The only task for you is to add tags for the form fields.

Adding tags to background text

Background text relates to all the content created in the authoring application. All fields on a form are excluded when I refer to background text. For Mac OS users, this step is your first after creating a PDF for making a form accessible. Windows users can follow the same steps, but you would be best served by first using the Make Accessible plug-in to add accessibility to your file and have Acrobat automatically create the tags for you. Of course, adding tags to the background text assumes you are working with a form that cannot have tags added by your authoring program, or you're working with a legacy file created without tags.

To understand how tags are added to a PDF form for the background content, follow these steps:

1. Open an untagged PDF form in Acrobat and choose Window ⇨ Tags. The Tags palette shows no tags currently exist in the PDF document, as shown in Figure 12-20.

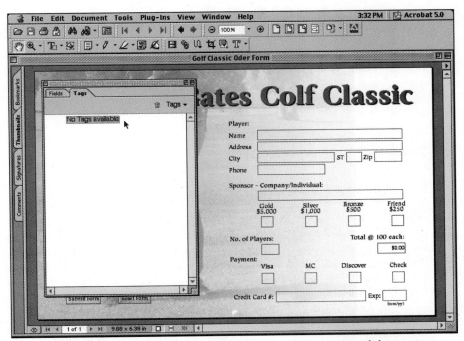

Figure 12-20: When the Tags palette is displayed with a PDF containing no tags, the palette reports No Tags Available.

2. Open a context menu in the Tags palette and select Create Tags Root, as shown in Figure 12-21. You can also use a menu command from the pull-down menu in the Tags palette. When no tags exist in a PDF file, the menu options for either menu contain only a single choice.

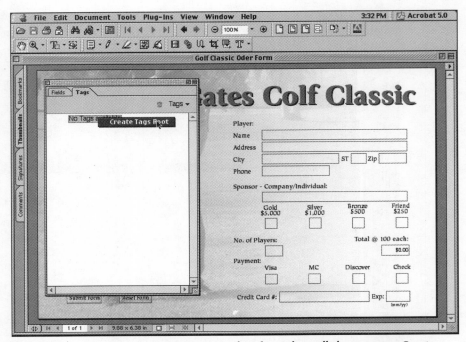

Figure 12-21: Open a context menu or select from the pull-down menu Create Tags Root.

3. Select the Column Select tool from the Acrobat Command Bar. Drag across the first line of text on the form. There is a title for the form appearing at the top of the page. Select the title text with the Column Select tool by dragging through the text.

4. Click on the Tags Root text in the Tags palette and open a context menu. Select New Child Element from the menu selections. Make a choice for the kind of text displayed in the document. Select Heading Element, as shown in Figure 12-22.

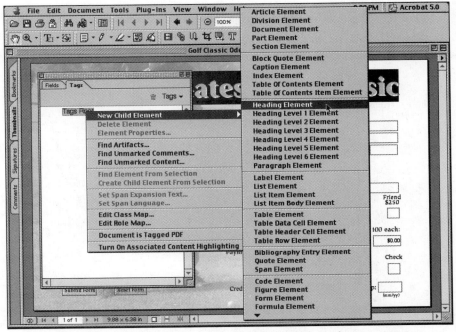

Figure 12-22: Select the Tags Root text in the Tags palette and open a context menu. Select New Child Element and a submenu choice closely approximating the text being tagged from the list of menu options.

5. The new element is added as a child element below the Tags Root. Select the next text block with the Column Select tool.

6. Select the Tags Root if the new element is to be a child under the root. Select the previous tag if the new element is to appear as a child element under the last tag. Create a new element below the Heading tag created above. All the text will be created under the title tag.

7. Open a context menu and make a choice for the new tag. Create a Heading Level 1 Element, as shown in Figure 12-23.

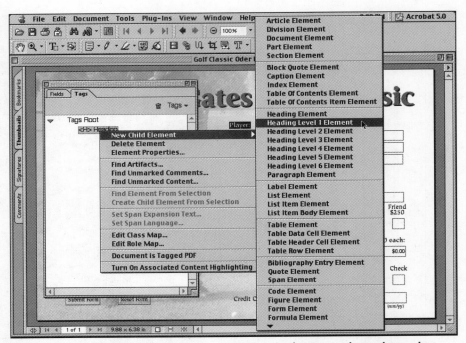

Figure 12-23: Select the tag to be the parent tag in the Tags palette, then select New Child Element and make a choice from the submenu options for the type of tag to be created.

8. When you arrive at text used for form titles, make a selection for Form Element, as shown in Figure 12-24. Create a subheading for the Players text, then add another tag for the Name text and use a Form Element as the tag choice.

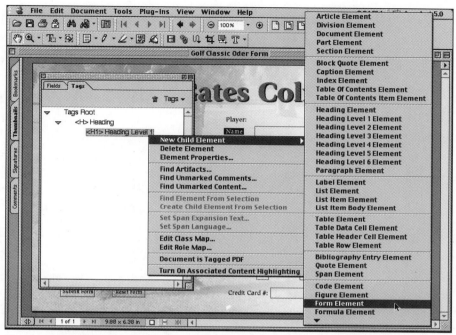

Figure 12-24: Choose Form Element for the text in which a form field is to appear.

9. Continue creating tags for the remaining text on the form. When you wish to have a child element below a subheading, select the subheading in the Tags palette and then create a New Child Element. Whenever a tag is selected in the Tags palette, the next tag created appears as a child element below the selected tag. When you finish creating tags and open the parent items, the Tags palette should appear similar to the one shown in Figure 12-25.

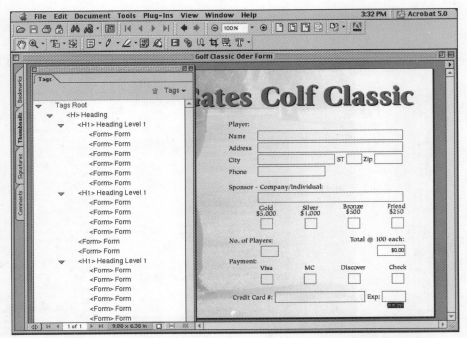

Figure 12-25: After creating all tags, open all the parent items by clicking on the plus (+) key (Windows) or right arrow (Mac OS) to display all the child items.

Adding tags properties

The properties for the tags, such as title, type, alternate text, language specification, and so on, can be added at the time the tag is created or after you finish creating all the tags. For complex forms, it may be best to add tags properties as each tag is created. In my example, I use a simple form and discuss the properties apart from the section above for the sake of clarity.

To change tags properties, follow these steps:

1. Select a tag in the Tags palette and right-click (Windows) or Control+click (Mac OS) to open a context menu.

2. From the menu selections, choose Element Properties. The Element Properties dialog box opens, as shown in Figure 12-26.

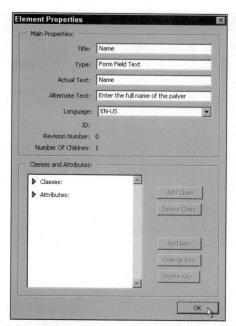

Figure 12-26: Select the tag and then open a context menu. Choose Element Properties to open the Element Properties dialog box.

3. The Title for the tag is viewed adjacent to the type of tag described. Enter a name in the Title field that describes the text tagged in the document. For the name field, add Name for the Title in Figure 12-26. Type is the type of tag used. Use Form Field for the Type. Actual text is the actual text on the PDF. If you have a paragraph or large passage, add a few words to describe the block of text. A screen reader will read the Alternate Text. Try to make this text clear so the end user knows exactly to what the tag relates. As a final step, choose a language from the pull-down menu items.

Note The remaining items in the Element Properties dialog box relate to a style dictionary referred to as a Class Map. When creating tags in a PDF file, you won't have a Class Map or associated Attributes available for editing. These items are added from styles in an authoring application that supports accessibility. If you start with an unstructured document, you cannot add a new Class Map or Attributes.

4. Click OK in the Element Properties dialog box and continue adding the property attributes for all tags in the palette. When you complete the edits, your Tags palette should appear like the one shown in Figure 12-27.

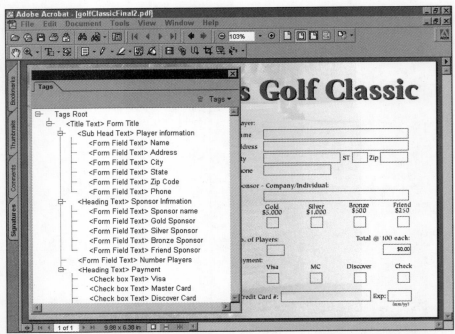

Figure 12-27: The Tags palette reflects all the Element Properties information for the edited tags.

Tip   If you wish to edit the name appearing in the Tags palette, select the tag to be edited. Click again with the mouse cursor and the cursor appearance changes to an I-beam. Insert the cursor in the selected text and edit the line. The edits you make on the tag name are updated in the Element Properties dialog box.

Adding tags to form fields

Up to this point we have been concerned with tagging the PDF content apart from form fields. For optimum accessibility, form fields also need to be tagged. You can tag a form field after creating tags on your form or after all the form fields have been added and the document remains untagged. Form field tagging cannot be performed by the authoring application. Because the fields are created in Acrobat after processing the PDF, you need to tag the fields manually. If the Make Accessible plug-in is used after fields have been created, some fields may have been tagged and others may have been missed. As a matter of habit, you should review all fields in the Tags palette and determine if the Make Accessible plug-in skipped any fields. In most cases, you need to manually tag some fields.

To understand how field tagging is performed, follow these steps:

1. Open an accessible document. In this example, continue with the same form used in the previous exercises.

2. Select the first field on the form.

3. Select the tag used for the text describing the field selected above. This text lies on the PDF background adjacent to the respective field. The text has been tagged, but the field box has not yet been tagged.

4. Open a context menu and choose New Child Element ➪ Form Element.

5. The new tag appears in the tags palette as a child element below the text used to describe the field. Continue tagging all fields by first selecting a field, then adding a new child element for the respective tag in the Tags palette.

6. When you complete all field tagging and expand the hierarchy, it should look similar to Figure 12-28.

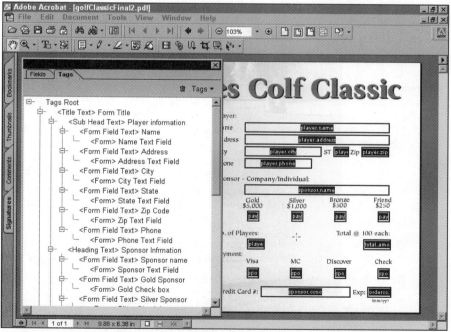

Figure 12-28: After tagging all fields, the Tags palette displays the new hierarchy.

Part one of the field tagging has been accomplished. For the next step, you need to add field descriptions explained in the next section.

Organizing tags

The hierarchy of the tags and how they are reorganized is similar to a bookmark hierarchy and bookmark methods for reorganization. After all tags have been created, you may wish to reorganize the parent/child relationships of the tags. Working in the Tags palette, you can move the tags around and reorganize their positions and relationships. To move a tag up or down in the hierarchy order, click on the tag and drag it up or down in the palette. A horizontal bar appears similar to the way you organize Bookmarks in the Navigation Pane. When the bar appears in the desired location, release the mouse button. The tag now appears in a new location.

To change the parent/child relationship, drag a child tag to the left and it assumes a new parent position. Drag any parent tag to the right and it assumes a new child position. If you wish to move a parent tag with associated child tags below it, click on the parent tag and drag it to a new position. The child tags move together with the parent. By clicking and dragging the tags in the palette a few times, you can easily understand how to reorganize the tag hierarchy.

Adding field descriptions

Thus far, the screen reader has been able to interpret the content of the PDF form, however, you still do not have the individual fields tagged for recognition by the reader. The previous exercises added the structure to the PDF, but you still need to apply a few more steps to complete the field tagging. There are two steps in making the form fields accessible. First you need to create a description for the field and then tag it for recognition. To understand how descriptions are created and fields are tagged, follow these steps:

1. Open the Field Properties dialog box for the first field on the PDF form.

2. Click on the Options tab and enter a Short Description in the field box, as shown in Figure 12-29. The text entered in this field box is what the hardware reader interprets.

3. Continue adding Short Descriptions for all fields on the form. When initially creating a form, this step can be performed at the time the fields are created.

4. After all Short Descriptions have been added, select the Form tool then open a context menu from the Tags palette and select Find Unmarked Comments from the menu options.

5. The Unmarked Comments dialog box opens. Click on the Find Next button in the dialog box.

6. The first field is highlighted. Add a Tag Title in the field box at the bottom of the dialog box and select Form from the Tag Type pull-down menu.

7. Find the associated tag in the Tags palette and select it. It is important you first select the tag in the Tags palette that parents the new tag you create. With the tag selected and the Unmarked Contents dialog box placed adjacent to the Tags palette, click on the Create Tag button in the Unmarked Content dialog box, as shown in Figure 12-30.

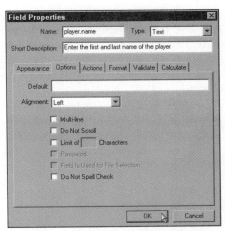

Figure 12-29: Enter a Short Description
for the field in the Options properties.

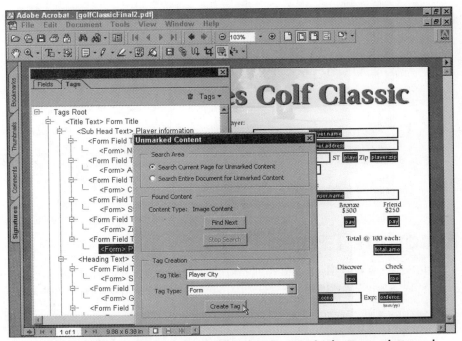

Figure 12-30: Select the tag for the field description text in the Tags palette and
click on the Create Tag button in the Unmarked Content dialog box.

8. Click on the Find Next button. The next field is highlighted on the form. Repeat the steps above for adding the Tag Title and selecting the associated tag in the Tags palette. Click on the Create Tag button, then move to the next field, and so on. Complete all field tags and save the file. You now have an accessible PDF form. When you view the Tags palette with the parent items expanded, your view should appear similar to Figure 12-31.

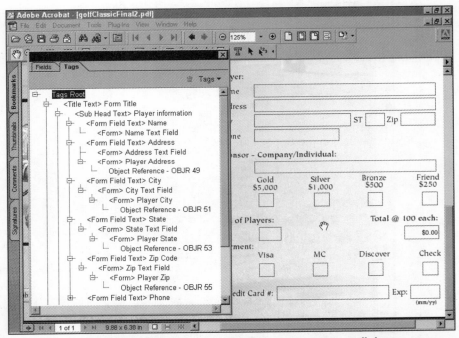

Figure 12-31: The items denoted as Object Reference represent all the new tags created for the fields.

Exporting Tagged PDFs

All of what was discussed thus far related to accessibility for screen readers. In addition to document accessibility, creating tagged files can also help you repurpose your PDF forms for other displays. Tagged PDFs are the best source for converting a file back to a word processor or layout application, creating Web pages from PDF forms, and porting PDFs to other devices, such as handheld PDAs and eBook readers. For converting the file format, you'll need a little help from a plug-in that is available as a free download from Adobe's Web site.

Using the SaveAsXML plug-in

A free download called the SaveAsXML plug-in is available from Adobe's Web site. When you download the file, double-click on it to install it in your Acrobat Plug-Ins folder. This plug-in not only handles XML exports from PDFs, but also several versions of HTML and a text accessible format.

To use the plug-in, you must start with a tagged PDF file. Choose File ➪ Save As to open the Save As dialog box that is shown in Figure 12-32. Open the pull-down menu for Save As Type and the additional file formats appear as new menu choices. In addition to the default Acrobat formats, HTML-3.20 Accessible, HTML-3.20 without CSS, HTML-4.01 with CSS-1.00, Text (Accessible), XHTML-1.00 with CSS-1.00, and XML-1.00 without styling are added to the menu commands. The reference to CSS in the formats applies to Cascading Style Sheets.

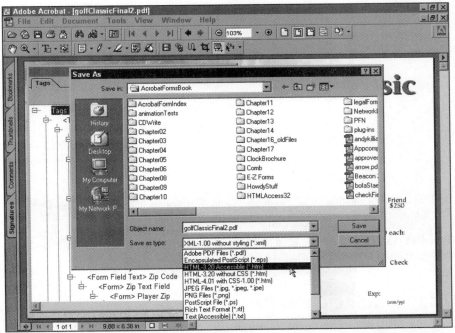

Figure 12-32: After loading the SaveAsXML plug-in, new file formats are introduced in the Save As Type pull-down menu.

Choose a format and save the file. If you save in one of the HTML formats, the images from the PDF form are converted to JPEG files and an HTML file contains all the markups to display the document as a Web page.

Saving accessible PDFs as RTF files

The structure and integrity of PDF files exported as RTF files contain more document structure than untagged PDFs. If you need to export a PDF for re-editing in an authoring program, more of the document structure is preserved when saving in RTF. Tables and lists are preserved from tagged PDFs exported as RTF. Figure 12-33 shows a PDF file exported as RTF and opened in Microsoft Word.

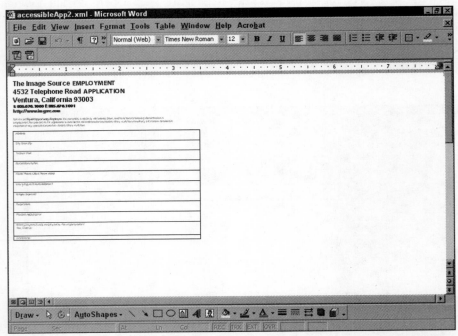

Figure 12-33: Tagged PDFs saved as RTF preserve the document integrity including columnar data, tables, and lists.

Using handheld devices

Tagged PDF files can conform to any display by using the Reflow tool from the Acrobat Command Bar. Files ported to handheld devices, in particular, take advantage of the document reflow capabilities in Acrobat. However, the Reflow tool only works on tagged PDF files. Be certain your document is a tagged PDF file, then click on the Reflow tool in the Acrobat Command Bar. As you size the zoom level, the document reflows text and resizes graphics. This accommodation can effectively display PDFs on small devices.

To illustrate how document reflow works, take a look at Figures 12-34 and 12-35. Figure 12-34 displays a PDF form in a "Fit in Window" view. When the Reflow tool is selected, the document reflows to fill the entire screen, as shown in Figure 12-35.

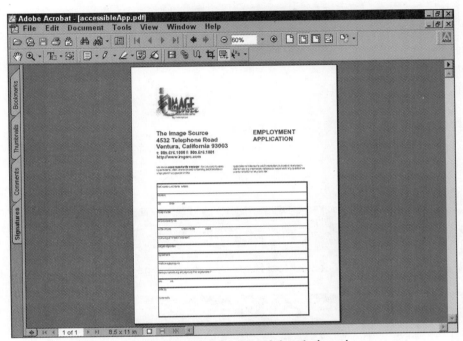

Figure 12-34: A PDF is opened in Acrobat in a Fit in Window view.

As you zoom in on a document and use the Reflow tool, the content conforms to the screen view. In Figure 12-36, the PDF is viewed at 200% size without document reflow. In Figure 12-37, the Reflow tool is selected and the content conforms to the current zoom level. Notice the two columns of text have been formed into a single column in Figure 12-37.

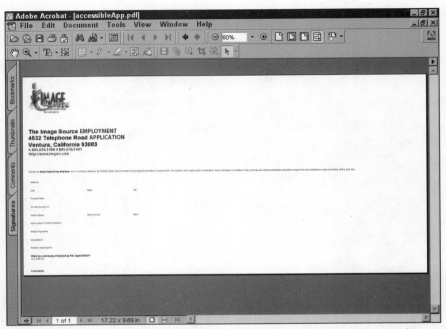

Figure 12-35: When the Reflow tool is selected, the document reflows to the screen size.

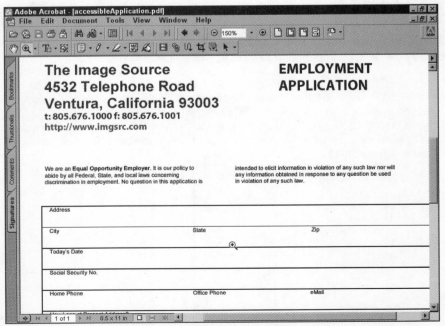

Figure 12-36: A PDF is zoomed to 200% without reflow.

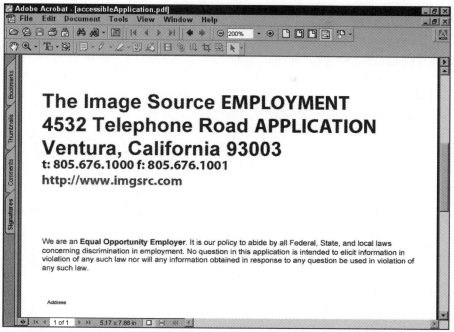

Figure 12-37: The same document at the same view with the Reflow tool used changes the content display to conform to the screen size.

Summary

✦ Screen readers can interpret accessible PDF forms for audio output for people with vision and motion challenges.

✦ Microsoft Word, Adobe PageMaker 7 and higher, and Adobe InDesign 2.0 and higher are capable of creating tagged and accessible PDF forms.

✦ The Make Accessible plug-in, offered as a free download from Adobe Systems, can add tags and structure to legacy files that were created without accessibility.

✦ Both Mac OS and Windows users can manually create tagged PDFs in Acrobat by adding tags in the Tags palette.

✦ Field Descriptions should be added for files needing compliance with accessible standards. Screen readers can interpret Short Descriptions that are added to the Options properties for form fields.

✦ Tagged PDFs are a benefit when needing to export text back to an authoring program. When saving in RTF, tagged PDFs support exporting more reliable structure than untagged files.

✦ The SaveAsXML plug-in that is offered as a free download from Adobe Systems, supports saving PDFs in a number of different formats including XML and HTML.

✦   ✦   ✦

Submitting and Distributing Forms

The distribution of forms and form data can be handled several ways. If your forms are Web-based, you have choices for what data are to be submitted and how the data are handled when the data gets to a server. If you e-mail forms and have data e-mailed back to you, then there are different considerations. Furthermore, if you elect to distribute forms on CD-ROMs for client use, then there are some other considerations to think about. In this chapter, we'll look at the many different ways PDF forms and data can be exchanged between you and your clients and colleagues.

Using FDF Data

FDF (Forms Data Format) is a proprietary format native to Acrobat for storing information that can be imported or exported from a PDF document. Data from form fields and comments can be extracted and saved as a separate file in FDF. Once saved as FDF, the data can be reintroduced in a PDF form. Hence, if you have users submitting data as a file to a Web server or as an e-mail attachment, or saving the FDF data locally on a hard drive, the file size is significantly reduced compared to the PDF in which the data were created.

In terms of data recognition, Acrobat can also understand delimited text data and import data created from spreadsheets or database managers capable of exporting delimited text. This data, of course is not FDF. However, it does belong with a discussion on data handling; therefore, we'll also take a look at importing text data in this section. To begin an understanding for how Acrobat manages FDF and text data, we'll start by looking at how data are imported and exported in and out of PDF forms.

Importing and exporting data

One of the great benefits for importing and exporting data is the ability to eliminate redundancy in recreating common data used in different forms. Among the most common redundant data entries is your personal identifying information. The numbers of times you enter your name, address, phone number, and so on on forms is no doubt a frequent task. In an environment where you need to supply your personal identity information, you can keep an FDF file on your hard drive and load it into different PDF forms, thereby eliminating the need to re-key the data.

In order to swap data between forms, there is one precaution you need to observe. All data fields used to import FDF data must have identically matched names to the fields from which the data were exported, including case sensitivity. Therefore, the data from a field called Name in a PDF that exports to FDF cannot be introduced in a PDF with a field called name. Setting up the fields is your first task, then you can move on to data exports and imports. To understand this further, let's break it down to, first, design forms with common fields, then, export and import data.

Creating common fields

To be certain your field names match exactly between two forms, the easiest and most efficient way to duplicate the fields is to copy fields from one form and paste them into another form. In Figure 13-1, a form (customerID.pdf) is used for customer identity. In Figure 13-2, a form (orderBlank.pdf) uses the same data for customer identity. As yet, the fields on this form have not been created. The customer identity form has all the identifying information, but nothing specific to placing an order. This form is designed to be the source for a customer's individual identity. From this form, we want to take the data and place it on all order forms when the customer places an order. To do so requires all forms having the exact same field names for the identity information.

On the CD-ROM You'll find the customerID.pdf and orderBlank.pdf files in the Chapter 13 folder on the book's CD-ROM. The orderScanning.pdf form contains form fields that match the customerID.pdf form.

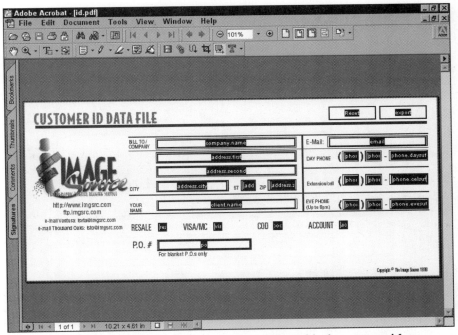

Figure 13-1: The customerID.pdf file contains all the fields that are used for a customer's identity. These same field names need to be used on all forms in which the data exported from this form are imported to other forms.

To ensure the field names have an exact match in other files, we'll copy and paste the fields. Open the document where the fields are to be pasted and keep it in the background. On the form containing the fields, select all the fields by pressing Ctrl (Windows) or Shift (Mac OS) and marquee the fields to be copied. When the fields are selected, open a context menu and choose Edit ⇨ Copy from the menu choices or choose the Edit menu and select Copy.

Tip
If all fields on the form need to be copied, click on the Form tool and press Ctrl+A (Windows) or ⌘+A (Mac OS) to select all fields. Press Ctrl+C (Windows) or ⌘+C (Mac OS) and all the selected fields are copied to the clipboard.

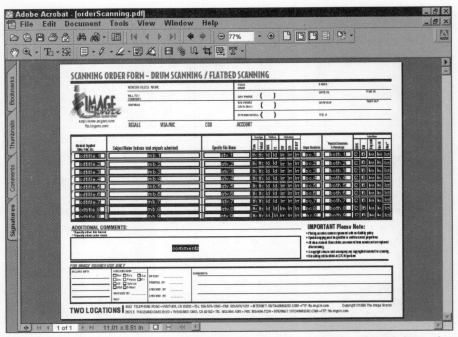

Figure 13-2: The order form (orderBlank.pdf) uses the same identifying information. As yet, the form contains no fields for the customer identity.

Choose Window ➪ *filename* in which filename is the name of the file in which you will paste the fields. When the destination PDF appears in the Document Pane, choose Edit ➪ Paste. You need to move the fields to the proper location and may need to change appearances if the form designs are different. Click and drag the group into position or nudge the fields with the arrow keys on your keyboard. Be certain to keep the fields selected if they are close to existing fields on the page. In Figure 13-3, the fields were pasted fields the `customerID.pdf` form to an order form (`orderScanning.pdf`) and then moved into proper position.

The appearance of the fields may change with different forms designs. In this example, a beveled style is used on the `customerID.pdf` form. The order form has much less space for fields and a beveled style crowds the form too much. Therefore, a solid style is used on the order form to occupy less space. As a result, the appearance of the fields needs to be changed. With all the fields selected, press the Enter key and the Field Properties dialog box opens. The appearance can be changed for multiple fields, as shown in Figure 13-4. To change appearances, click on the Border and Background color swatches. Make the desired changes and select Solid from the Style pull-down menu.

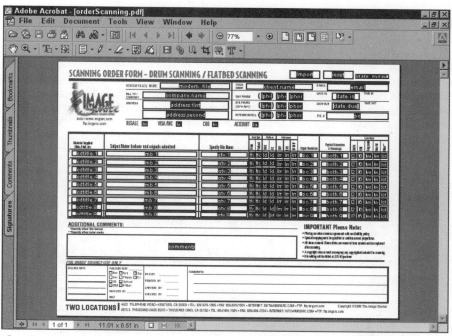

Figure 13-3: After pasting the fields, move them into position on the form. The pasted fields have the identical names as the fields in the document where they originated.

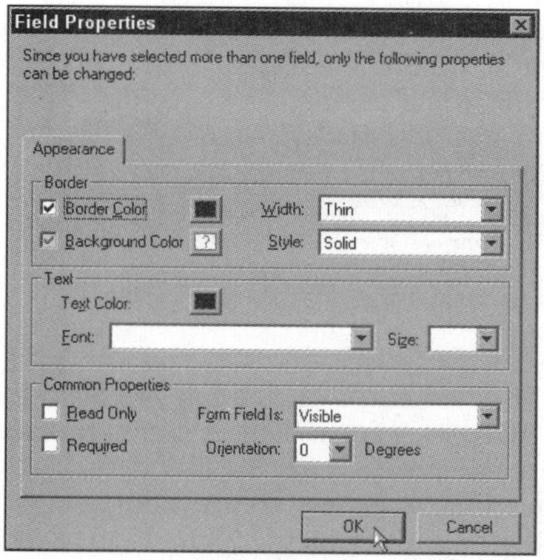

Figure 13-4: With multiple fields selected, press the Enter key to open the Field Properties dialog box. Change the attributes for the desired appearance.

Cross-Reference   For more on global Appearance changes, see Chapter 5, "Creating Form Fields."

Exporting FDF data

After the forms have been created with matching fields, complete a form and fill in all the data fields like the example shown in Figure 13-5. If you have some fields on one form that have been excluded on a second form, Acrobat ignores any field data where it can't find a matching field name. Therefore, you need not worry about exact matches for the same number of fields being equal on both documents.

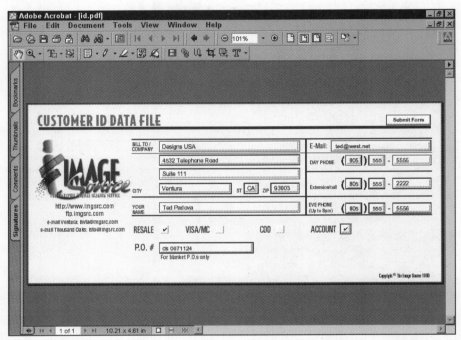

Figure 13-5: Fill in a form and you are ready to export the data as an FDF file.

Exporting data from a PDF file is handled with a menu command. If you wish to export the data from a form, choose File ➪ Export ➪ Form data. A dialog box opens where you can name the file and designate a destination for the FDF data. If you want a user to be able to export data from a button action, create a button field on the form. Add an Action in the Actions tab and select Execute Menu Item from the Type pull-down menu.

Click on the Edit Menu Item button and the Menu Item Selection dialog box opens (Windows) or an alert dialog box opens on the Mac OS informing you to make a menu selection. On Windows, choose File ➪ Export ➪ Form Data from the dialog box, as shown in Figure 13-6. On the Mac OS, use the top-level menu bar and choose File ➪ Export ➪ Form Data.

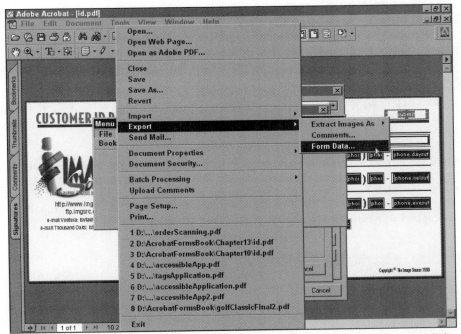

Figure 13-6: Choose the menu command File ➪ Export ➪ Form Data from the dialog box (Windows) or top-level menu bar (Mac OS).

Click OK and you are returned to the Add an Action dialog box. The menu selection is displayed in the dialog box below the Edit Menu Item button. Verify the menu selection is correct and click Set Action in the Add an Action dialog box. Click OK again in the Field Properties dialog box and the button is ready to export form data.

When you click on the button or select the menu command, the Export Form Data As dialog box opens. By default, the name of your PDF file and an fdf extension are supplied in the Object name field box. This name is used as the FDF filename. If you wish to change the name, edit the Object name, but be certain to leave an .fdf extension after the filename. Click Save and the file is saved as a Forms Data Format file.

The file you save as FDF contains only the data from the form fields. Therefore, the file size is considerably smaller than the PDF that produced the data. The file can be stored on a local disk or network server, or sent as an e-mail attachment to another user. If another user has a PDF with the same field names, the data can be imported.

Importing FDF data

Like the form data exports, importing FDF data in PDF forms is handled with menu commands. You can choose File ➪ Import ➪ Form Data or create a button like the export button mentioned above. In either case, the Select File Containing Form Data dialog box opens where you can navigate your hard drive and find the FDF file to import.

To create a button, follow the same steps used for exporting form data. In the Menu Item Selection dialog box (Windows) or the top-level menu bar (Mac OS), choose File ➪ Import ➪ Form Data.

Click Set Action in the Add an Action dialog box and OK in the Field Properties dialog box to complete creating a button field. When you click on the button, the Select File Containing Form Data dialog box opens, as shown in Figure 13-7. The default file type from the Objects of Type pull-down menu is Acrobat FDF Files (*.fdf). When the dialog box opens, only files saved as FDF appear in the window list.

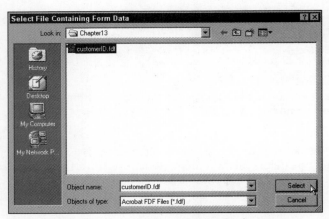

Figure 13-7: When you click on the Import button or select the menu command for importing form data, the Select File Containing Form Data dialog box opens. Select the file to import and click Select to import the data.

Select the FDF file for the data to be imported and click on the Select button in the dialog box. When you import data, the data are imported in fields with matching names with respect to the file that exported the data.

Protecting form data

If there are forms that you use frequently, such as an order form discussed above, you may wish to keep a record of all the orders you place. Therefore, each time you fill out a form, you may wish to save a copy and avoid the possibility of inadvertently overwriting a form with existing data. In essence, you need a template file that needs to be protected against saving data entries. To create a template and protect it against accidental overwriting, follow these steps:

1. If you work in a group where different people may place orders and the identifying information changes according to user, then leave the identity information empty on the form. If you use the same identity information, you may wish to add this data before protecting your file. When the form has the data that remains consistent for all uses, open the folder on your desktop where the PDF is stored.

2. Select the file and right click the mouse button (Windows) and select Properties from the menu items, as shown in Figure 13-8. On the Mac OS, select the file and choose File ➪ Get Info or press ⌘+I.

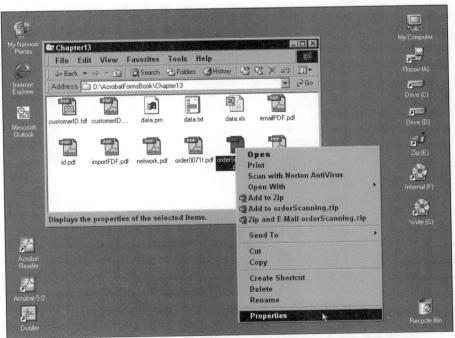

Figure 13-8: On Windows, select the file to be protected and open a context menu by right-clicking the mouse button. Select Properties from the menu options.

3. The document Properties dialog box opens (Windows) or the Info dialog box opens (Mac OS). In the Properties dialog box (Windows), select the check box for Read Only, as shown in Figure 13-9, or select the check box for Locked (Mac OS), as shown in Figure 13-10.

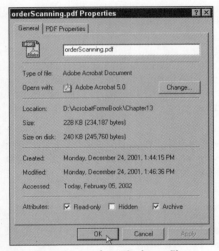

Figure 13-9: In the Windows file Properties dialog box, select the check box for Read Only.

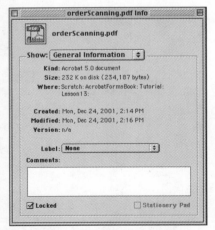

Figure 13-10: In the Mac OS Info dialog box, select the check box for Locked.

4. When the file opens, fill in the fields and import data as you would with any PDF form. If you attempt to save the file by choosing File ➪ Save, Acrobat disallows the command thus preventing you from overwriting the protected document. To save the data, choose File ➪ Save As. The Save As dialog box opens.

5. Provide a new filename and click the Save button. A copy of the file with the data fields populated is saved to disk while the original PDF file remains protected.

Importing FDF data with JavaScript Actions

In earlier examples buttons created from the Execute Menu Item selections were used to export and import FDF data. If you wish to automate the process, you can use a JavaScript to automatically import FDF data when a file opens. Furthermore, you can protect a file and still use a JavaScript to import data into a Read Only or Locked file. The only requirement in this example is the FDF file needs to remain in the same location when you write the script. Because you designate the directory path in the script, moving the FDF file cannot automatically import the data because Acrobat won't know where to look for the file. To import FDF data when a file opens, follow these steps:

1. Using the `orderScanning.pdf` file in the Chapter 13 folder on the book's CD-ROM, choose Document ➪ Set Page Action.

On the CD-ROM

You'll find the `orderScanning.pdf` file in the Chapter 13 folder on the book's CD-ROM.

2. In the Page Actions dialog box, add a Page Open action and select JavaScript from the Type pull-down menu.

3. In the JavaScript Edit dialog box, add the following code:

```
this.importAnFDF("/d/AcrobatFormsBook/Chapter13/
customerID.fdf");
```

The `this.importAnFDF` statement directs Acrobat to import an FDF file. The `/d/AcrobatFormsBook/Chapter13/customerID.fdf` item specifies the directory path. In this example, a hard drive D is used. At the root level of the D drive a folder called `AcrobatFormsBook` resides and inside this folder another folder called `Chapter13` is present. The name of the FDF file to be imported follows the directory path. In this example, the filename is `customerID.fdf`.

Note

You can eliminate the directory path and Acrobat will methodically search several directories to find the FDF file. Acrobat searches 1) the Acrobat installation directory/folder; 2) the Windows directory (Windows only); 3) the current directory/folder; 4) the current directory path. If the file is not found, the Select File Containing Form Data dialog box opens enabling you to browse your hard drive to find the file.

4. Click OK in the JavaScript Edit dialog box, click Set Action in the Add an Action dialog box, and select OK again in the Page Actions dialog box. When you save the form and reopen it, the Page Open action imports the FDF data just like the import resulting from a button click or menu item selection.

Tip

If Acrobat cannot find the FDF file from the directory path specified in the JavaScript action, an error is not reported. A dialog box opens as described in the note above and the end user has an opportunity to search a drive to locate the FDF file. If you create PDFs to be distributed to other users, eliminate the directory path and the user can access an FDF file by navigating the Select File Containing Form Data dialog box.

Importing text data

The discussion thus far has been limited to FDF data in Acrobat Forms. Because the task is related to importing and exporting data, you should know that you have other options available with different data types. You may receive data files created in database managers or spreadsheets that you wish to use in your Acrobat forms. Hence, you can import data saved as text-delimited data to populate Acrobat form fields.

To understand how Acrobat supports text data, we'll look a creating data in a spreadsheet and importing the data in a PDF form. Begin by following these steps:

1. **Create a database.** You can use any program capable of exporting data as a text file. In this example, Microsoft Excel is used to create a data file with three records. For the first record (first row in a spreadsheet application), add the exact same names as the field names used in the Acrobat form. All subsequent records (rows) contain the data like the example shown in Figure 13-11.

2. **For fields like check boxes,** the data to be used to denote a checked box is equal to the Export Value associated with the field in Acrobat. In this example, there are several check boxes on the form where the data are imported. When you open the Field Properties dialog box for a check box and examine the Export Value, you know what data needs to be added to the spreadsheet to enable a check box. In Figure 13-12, the Options properties show the Export Value for the check box field denoted as Yes. All the check boxes have the same Export Value. Therefore, when completing the spreadsheet data, enter Yes in all fields relating to check boxes where you wish to have the check box enabled. If the check box is to be disabled, leave the cell in Microsoft Excel blank.

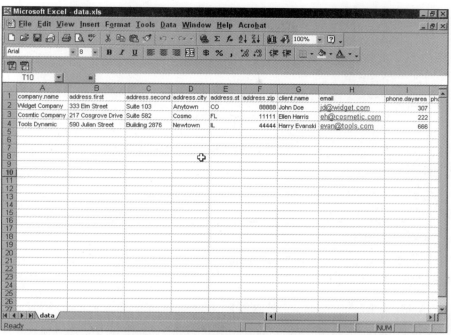

Figure 13-11: A data file is created in Microsoft Excel with three records. Each row is a separate record and the cells across each row represent the field data for the respective record.

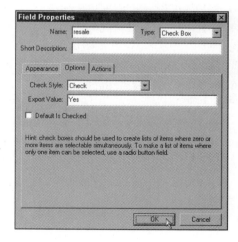

Figure 13-12: Enter the same value in Microsoft Excel as the Export Value for check boxes in the Acrobat Form. In this example, all cells containing Yes check the corresponding fields in the Acrobat form when the data are imported.

3. Save the spreadsheet as tab-delimited text only from your database manager. Choose File ➪ Save As and select Text (tab delimited)(*.txt) in the Microsoft Excel Save As dialog box.

4. Quit your database manager and open the form to import the data in Adobe Acrobat.

5. Choose File ➪ Import ➪ Form Data.

6. The Select File Containing Form Data dialog box opens. From the Objects of Type pull-down menu, select Text Files (*txt). Find the file exported from the database manager and select it. Click Select to open the file.

Note Each time you address the File ➪ Import ➪ Form Data menu command, Acrobat defaults to the *.fdf Object name expecting you to select an FDF file. Be certain to select Text Files (*.txt) from the Objects of Type pull-down menu when importing text data. You need to manually access the pull-down menu each time you want to import data other than FDF.

7. The Import Data From Delimited Text File dialog box opens. In the dialog box, you see the names of the fields appearing at the top of the dialog box. Below the title fields are the records in the database. Only one record can be imported in the form. Therefore, you need to tell Acrobat which record is to be imported. Click on the first field in a record row to select the desired record, as shown in Figure 13-13. In this example, the second row is selected for import.

Figure 13-13: Select a record to import by clicking on the first field in the record row you wish to import.

8. Click OK and the data are imported in your form, as shown in Figure 13-14.

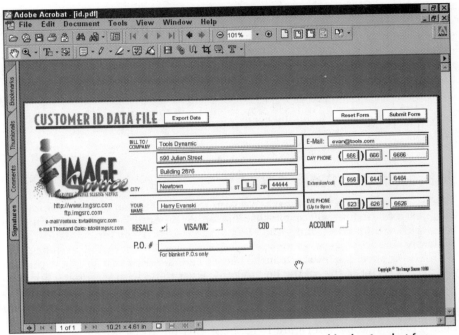

Figure 13-14: The data for the selected record are imported in the Acrobat form.

Creating and Using Submission Buttons

All the previous discussions for importing and exporting data work well on local hard drives and network servers. When you use the Internet for data transfers and extend the data submission to users of the Acrobat Reader software, you need to use other measures. Users of any Acrobat viewer can submit Acrobat form data, which provides you with a powerful tool when collecting data from any computer user. Because the Acrobat Reader is a free download from Adobe Systems, you can be assured any user can place orders for your products or any employee can remotely complete any form you create and submit the data to you.

The primary thing to understand with regard to submitting data to Web servers or across the Internet via e-mail attachments is once the data leaves Acrobat, Acrobat is no longer in control of the data. Whatever programming you add to a PDF file, remember that after Acrobat executes its action to throw out the data to a destination, some other form of programming is needed to collect the data and route it to the proper location. If you find errors in submitting PDFs or FDF data on servers and the submissions appear to be lost and disappear, you most likely have a problem in the programming outside of Acrobat. Look to your system administrator or individual responsible for server-side programming to help you troubleshoot a problem.

Submitting data to URLs

Data from a PDF form can be sent to a Web server in several different formats and with different attributes. You can also use either an Acrobat built-in action type or a JavaScript action. The submission of data, regardless of the format exported, is a relatively simple process. Things get more complex with scripting actions, however the real complexity is involved at the server end. In terms of a simple explanation, you need a script at the server end to know what to do with your data. For the server side issues, you can find a wealth of information on the Web related to CGIs (Common Gateway Interface) and scripting languages like Perl, which is one of the more-popular scripting languages for writing CGI scripts. Start your browsing by logging on to `www.perl.com` and download the free Perl software for your platform. Next, log on to `www.planetpdf.com` and search for Perl on the Web site. There are examples of how to process PDF data and how to use a Perl script for collecting PDF data. If Planet PDF doesn't answer your questions, start searching the Web for PDF and Perl or PDF and CGIs. There are many sites that offer sample code and documentation to help you get started. In addition, you can find many examples in the FDF Toolkit from Adobe Systems. Log on to Adobe's Web site at `http://partners.adobe.com:80/asn/developer/acrosdk/forms.html` and download the Software Development Kit (SDK) and supporting files. If you are a forms designer and not a programmer, you'll be best served by passing on the above information to your system administrator. The task at hand is not to be concerned with what happens at the server end, but how to get the data from the PDF file on your computer to the server. In this regard, we'll look at using a Submit Form action and some JavaScript actions.

Using the Submit Form Action type

You create a Submit action by making a choice in the Add an Action dialog box and then selecting Submit Form from the Type pull-down menu. You can create a button field, use a Page Action, or use a Document Action to invoke the Submit Form Action. Most often you'll want to use a button field so the user knows when the data are submitted to the server. Submit buttons work equally from all Acrobat viewers and you can submit any of the data types from the free Acrobat Reader software.

To create a submit button on a PDF form, you create a button field and then select the Actions tab. Click on the Add button and select Submit Form from the Type pull-down menu. Click on Select URL in the Add an Action dialog box.

At the top of the Submit Form Selections dialog box, enter the URL where the data are to be sent. Include the script name for the script that will process the form data. Under the Export Format section on the left side of the dialog box, you have four data type options from which to choose, as shown in Figure 13-15.

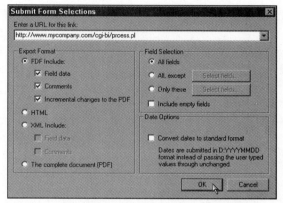

Figure 13-15: The Submit Form Selections dialog box enables you to supply the URL where the form data are sent and the type of Export Format options available.

The four data options include

- ✦ **FDF Include.** The FDF data are sent to the server. The three options below the FDF Include item offer you choices for sending the Field data; Comments, which includes any comments created on a form; and Incremental Changes to the PDF, which should be used when digital signatures have been used to save updates. Any one or all of the selections can be made for this data type.

- ✦ **HTML.** The data are sent in HTML format. Much like you may create a form on a Web page using HTML and JavaScript, the HTML option processes the same data type.

- ✦ **XML Include.** The data are sent in XML format. Two options are available for sending the Field data or the Comments data, or both.

- ✦ **The complete document (PDF).** This option enables you to submit the PDF populated with the field data — it is also very useful for submitting a PDF when a digital signature has been included.

On the right side of the dialog box, you have options for including all or selected field data in your submission. If there are fields to be eliminated, click on the All Except button and then click on the Select Fields button. The Field Selection dialog box opens, as shown in Figure 13-16. From the list on the right side of the dialog box, select an item to be eliminated from the submission and click on the Remove button. All removed items move to the list on the left side of the dialog box. You might use this option for eliminating unnecessary data such as the submit button itself, reset buttons, navigation buttons, and other similar data fields that don't need post processing. If button faces include images important for the form, you must include these buttons in your submission and not select them for exclusion.

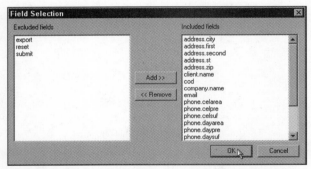

Figure 13-16: The Field Selection dialog box enables you to eliminate data fields unnecessary to process a form.

Click OK and you are returned to the Field Selections dialog box. Another option is available for converting dates to standard formats. If the resultant script uses a standard format for date calculations, select the check box. Click OK, click Set Action, and click OK again in the Field Properties dialog box. When the user clicks on the button, the form data from the choices you made in the dialog box are sent to the specified URL.

Using a JavaScript Action

One of the best reasons to use a JavaScript action over a Submit Form action is that part of the JavaScript routine can check your form and validate it prior to submitting the data. If you wish to verify all fields have been completed, you can instruct Acrobat via JavaScript to check the form. If the form is complete, a JavaScript instruction submits the data in any format you specify in the JavaScript code. If the form is not completed properly, you can instruct Acrobat via JavaScript to halt the submission action and advise a user what problem needs to be overcome before the data are submitted.

The first part of a routine to check for empty fields was detailed in Chapter 10, in which functions in JavaScripts were covered.

Cross-Reference   If you need to review the code for checking for empty fields, refer to Chapter 10, "Creating Advanced Form Designs."

After the statements to check for empty fields, you can add one of the following routines for the various data types to be submitted:

✦ **Submit FDF Data.** Use the following:

```
this.submitForm("http://www.mycompany.com/cgi-
bin/process.pl#FDF");
```

The #FDF item instructs Acrobat to submit FDF data. If you add

```
this.submitForm({
cURL: "http://www.mycompany.com/cgi-bin/process.pl#FDF",
bFDF: true,
bAnnotations: true,
bIncrChanges: true
});
```

the three button options for FDF data are enabled.

✦ **Submit HTML Data.** Use the following:

```
this.submitForm("http://www.mycompany.com/cgi-
bin/process.pl", bHTML:true);
```

✦ **Submit XML Data.** Use the following:

```
this.submitForm({
cURL: "http://www.mycompany.com/cgi-bin/process.pl",
bXML: true,
bAnnotations: true,
});
```

✦ **Submit a PDF file.** Use the following:

```
this.submitForm({
cURL: http://www.mycompany.com/cgi-bin/process.pl,
bPDF: true
});
```

Any one of these routines would be placed after a loop that checks for empty fields. If the fields are populated, you instruct Acrobat to continue to one of the instructions above according to the data type you want to submit. If empty fields are found, you break out of the loop and stop the execution. You might also add an application alert informing the user why the routine stopped without submitting the data. Once again, the scripts to check for empty fields are covered in Chapter 10.

Submitting Attachments to E-mails

You may have a need to ask a user to fill out a form and return the populated form to you or another user. A user could fill out a form and attach it to an e-mail message like any other file. However, by using a little JavaScript, you can help the user out by creating a button that automatically launches the default e-mail application and attaches the data to a message window when the user clicks on a button field. Depending on your need, you can choose to send the complete PDF file or an FDF file. In order for a user to see the FDF data, the PDF form is needed at the recipient end so the data can be imported. Conditions vary, so it's a good idea to become familiar with both methods. Note: You must have Acrobat or Acrobat Approval to e-mail FDF data or a populated PDF document.

Attaching PDF forms to e-mails

At the user end, the user can select the Send Mail tool in Acrobat or choose File ➪ Send Mail, and the current active PDF document is attached to an empty e-mail message ready for the user to type the message and send off the e-mail. The same effect occurs when creating a button field and a JavaScript action. Once again, by using a JavaScript, you can check the form for empty fields before the button action is invoked. By adding a button, a user unfamiliar with the Acrobat tools or menu commands can easily send an e-mail attachment by clicking on the button you create on the form.

To understand how button fields can be used to attach a PDF file to an e-mail message, follow these steps:

1. Create a button with a JavaScript action on a PDF form.

2. In the JavaScript Edit dialog box, enter the following code:

```
if (typeof(app.viewerType)!="undefined")
 if(app.viewerType == "Reader")
 {
 var msg = "You must use Acrobat or Acrobat Approval to send
the application back to us. You can download Acrobat Approval
for $39 US from Adobe's Web site at: http:www.adobe.com.";
 app.alert(msg);
 }
else
 {
```

```
this.mailDoc(true, "management@company.com",
"supervisor@company.com", "ceo@company.com",
"Employment Application Form");
  }
```

The preceding routine starts by examining the viewer version. If the user is attempting to e-mail the file from Acrobat Reader, an application alert dialog box opens informing the user that either Acrobat or Acrobat Approval is needed to submit the form. The user is instructed on where to acquire Acrobat Approval to submit the form properly.

If the user's viewer is either Acrobat or Approval, the statement after else is executed. this.mailDoc instructs Acrobat to attach the active PDF document to an e-mail message. The three items in quotation marks begin with the recipient, the cc recipient, and the bcc recipient, respectively. The last item in quotation marks is the subject title for the e-mail message. If you wish to eliminate a cc and a blind cc, the code would read as:

```
this.mailDoc(true, "management@company.com", "", "",
"Employment Application Form");
```

If you wish to add multiple recipients, cc, or bcc recipients, just add a comma after the name of the recipient within the quotation marks for the respective recipients. An example for multiple recipients might be:

```
this.mailDoc(true, "management@company.com, joe@company.com,
alice@company.com", "", "", "Employment Application Form");
```

3. Click OK in the JavaScript Edit dialog box, click on the Set Action button in the Add an Action dialog box, and click OK again in the Field Properties dialog box.

4. Click on the button and your e-mail application is launched with the active PDF file attached and the specified recipients placed in their respective locations, as shown in Figure 13-17.

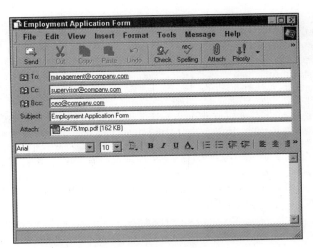

Figure 13-17: When you click on the submit button, your default e-mail application is launched, the PDF file is attached, the recipients are designated, and the subject line is filled in.

If the user attempts to submit the file from Acrobat Reader, the dialog box shown in Figure 13-18 opens.

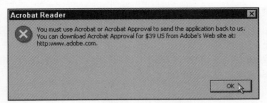

Figure 13-18: If the user attempts to submit the form from Acrobat Reader, an application alert dialog box opens with a message to inform the user that Acrobat or Acrobat Approval is needed to properly complete the form.

Attaching FDF data to e-mails

In the above example, an e-mail attachment was used to submit an employee application form to several users. The entire PDF file was distributed to various parties. As a practical measure, it makes sense to submit the entire form because some parties may not have the original PDF at hand. In other cases, you may not need the original PDF document. For example, suppose an employee application form is routed to the human resources department, which screens all applications. The HR department certainly has the original PDF file and therefore only needs the data from the form that they can import into an empty employment application form. In this regard, the company personnel need only receive the FDF data. Sending the data will require much less storage space and the file transfer will be much faster, especially if the form is complex and contains many pages.

To send the data instead of the PDF file, you need to make just one slight change in the JavaScript. Using the previous example, enter the following code after the routine to determine the application viewer type:

```
this.mailForm(true, "management@company.com", "", "",
"Employment Application Form");
```

Suppose an employee completes a form on a home computer or on the road on a laptop computer. Assume for a moment that the employee has a different e-mail address for office and home or on the road. If you wish to offer an option to enable the employee to e-mail a copy of the FDF data to a second e-mail address, you might wish to ask for the address in a dialog box. The response from the dialog box can be placed in the cc line of the e-mail message. This way, you can use a generic form suited for all employees.

To send FDF data with a cc to an address specified from a dialog box, follow these steps:

1. Create a button field and a JavaScript action. In the JavaScript Edit dialog box enter the following code:

```
var cResponse = app.response({
cQuestion: "To copy yourself, enter your email address. Click
cancel to send data without sending a copy to yourself",
cTitle: "emailAddress", }); // title of the dialog box
{
if ( cResponse == null)
  this.mailForm(true, "finance@company.com", "", "", "Purchase
Order");
else
  this.mailForm(true, "finance@company.com", cResponse, "",
"Purchase Order");
}
```

   The beginning of the routine asks the question. Do you want to copy yourself? If no, click on the Cancel button in the response dialog box and the data are sent to the recipient (finance@company.com). If yes, an address is typed in a dialog box; and when the OK button is selected, the data from the response dialog box are posted in the cc line of the e-mail message.

2. Click OK in the JavaScript Edit dialog box and OK again in the Field Properties dialog box.

3. Click on the button and the dialog box shown in Figure 13-19 opens.

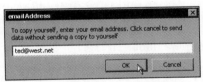

Figure 13-19: A response dialog box supplies the e-mail address that you want to use in order to send a copy of the FDF data.

4. Add an e-mail address and click OK. The e-mail message window appears with the FDF data attached, and the cc line includes the address from the response dialog box, as shown in Figure 13-20.

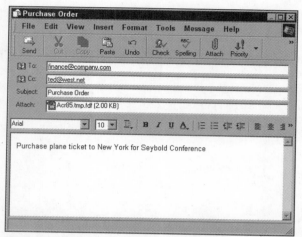

Figure 13-20: The data from the response dialog box are placed in the cc line of the e-mail message.

Distributing Forms

Forms for access by clients, employees, and other parties can be distributed in several ways. Obviously, in a work environment, you may wish to host forms on network servers. You can also host forms on Web servers where employees or clients can access them. As another means, you may have a large repository of forms for catalog orders and documents, which may be an option for distribution on CD-ROMs. With each method of distribution, you have some different considerations. If forms are Web hosted, how do you get them on a server? If forms are distributed on CD-ROMs, how do you keep them updated?

For network servers, the previous chapters demonstrate how users complete forms and what viewing tools are needed to work with Acrobat forms. If users are limited to the Acrobat Reader software, you need to have forms posted on Web servers to enable Reader users the ability to submit form data. In regard to Web hosting and CD-ROM replication, let's take a look at some considerations for each method for preparing files for distribution.

Hosting forms on Web servers

In terms of hosting PDFs on the Web, you have two considerations. First, you need to get the PDF file on the Web server. Secondly, you need to create a link from a Web page to a PDF file. To send the PDF file to a Web server from a remote location, you need a software application program that enables you to submit files to Web servers. Most of the programs used today for submitting PDFs to Web servers are found in the public domain. You can find Web sites hosting software applications as shareware or public domain programs and download them to your computer. For Windows, visit `www.tucows.com` for an extensive list of programs for almost any purpose. Among the programs available are ftp client software applications designed to ftp files to Web servers. The list is extensive, so read the comments and try out a few to find one that you can easily understand and use.

On the Mac OS, the most popular ftp client is Fetch. You can find Fetch available on many different Web sites available as a free download. Download the program and install it. When you launch an ftp client application on either platform, you are prompted for identifying the following: Host (`http://mycompany.com`—this is the URL in which your company Web site is located), User ID (typically this is your name used in your e-mail address or your authorization to gain access to your Web pages), Password (your password to access your Web site), and Directory (in most cases the root directory is *public_html* + a sub folder where you wish to send your files). If you experience difficulty, contact your system administrator for the directory where your files should be delivered.

After sending files to the Web server, you enter the URL in HTML on a Web page for a button action that opens the PDF file. For example, you may have text or a button with a hypertext link (in a simplified version) specified as `< a href = "http://www.mycompany.com/directory/file.pdf">` `text or button goes here` `</a>`. This code instructs the browser to go to the company Web site (`mycompany.com`), to a directory you specify (`/directory`), and open the PDF file specified (`/file.pdf`).

Getting PDF files on your Web server and creating hypertext links to the files is the easy part. Where you encounter problems is with many users who experience difficulties in viewing your PDFs. These problems are generally on the user end and not with your hosting of the PDF files. Web hosted PDFs may be designed for inline viewing. That is, a PDF file viewed inside the browser window. If users aren't seeing the PDFs as online views, they most likely have a configuration problem on their end. In other cases, you may wish to have a user download a file from your Web site and use it offline. In such cases, you'll want the user to be able to save a file to disk.

The best way to overcome problems users may experience in working with your PDF forms is to design several help pages in HTML describing how your forms are viewed as online files, how they are saved as copies from the Acrobat Reader software, and special considerations for completing your forms online and offline. Try to address viewing PDFs from several browsers and different versions in your help files. With a little guidance for the end user, you can minimize the numbers of inquires users may have regarding accessing your forms.

Writing forms to CD-ROMs

You have an advantage in hosting PDF forms on the Web with the ability to keep them updated and current as they are changed. With CD-ROMs, you loose this advantage. However, CD-ROMs have their own advantages that you can't duplicate with Web-hosted forms. For example, you can eliminate any problems for users accessing your forms and you can create search indexes that enable users to find a given form quickly by loading an index file and invoking a search. You can eliminate long download times for large files and you can minimize confusion when several forms are interactive and need to be housed in the same directory to work properly. With some of these advantages, you may find replicating CD-ROMs a viable solution for distributing your forms.

If you replicate CD-ROMs for distributing your Acrobat forms, you'll want to exercise some care in creating a master CD that works properly and provides users with all the features you want them to enjoy. In this section, we'll look at some considerations you may wish to make when creating a CD-ROM to be replicated.

Organizing a CD-ROM collection of PDF forms

When organizing your documents to be copied to a CD-ROM, there are two important measures to consider. First, you must preserve the directory path for all actions that open and close files. If you use a button, a Page Action, a Bookmark, a Link, or any interactive element that opens another file, the path that Acrobat searches is absolute. If you relocate files on the CD-ROM to different paths, Acrobat won't be able to find the linked files. The best way to prevent against a potential problem is to create a single folder on your hard drive, then nest subfolders below the main folder. Create the links and test them thoroughly before creating a master used to replicate the CD-ROMs. You can copy all the files and subfolders from the main folder on your hard drive to the root location on the CD-ROM, but don't move any files from the subfolders. The folders and folder names need to be preserved.

The second precaution is to ensure all filenames are preserved when copying PDFs to a CD-ROM. This issue is related to the software used to write the CD. You must use mastering software that preserves long names. It's always best to write CDs for a cross-platform audience. Therefore, if you use a Mac OS, be certain the filenames are not disturbed when viewing on a Windows machine and vice versa. As a final step, you should test a CD-ROM before replication on both platforms.

Adding search indexes

The details of creating search indexes and the necessary steps to relocate index files are covered in bonus Chapter 17.

Review bonus Chapter 17, "Organizing Real-World Workflows," which you'll find on the book's CD-ROM, before you attempt to replicate a CD-ROM with a search index.

The issue for preserving directory paths is equally important to search index files as it is to linked documents.

Replicating CD-ROMs

If you have a limited number of CD-ROMs to copy, a personal CD-R device can satisfy your needs. These devices come with different interfaces where the write speed varies greatly according to the interface type. USB devices are extremely slow, while FireWire drives are the top of the line. Even if your CD-ROM write needs are occasional, you'll appreciate the much faster completion time of a FireWire drive.

If your CD-ROM replication involves writing many CDs, then you will want to use a replication center. The cost of replicating CD-ROMs can be reduced to less than $1.00 apiece depending on the number of CDs you order. For a replication source, search the Internet and compare the costs of the services. When you find a service, send them a CD-ROM of the PDF forms you want replicated. In order to ensure the filenames and directory paths are properly specified on the destination media, you can thoroughly test your own CD to be certain everything works properly before submitting the files to the replication center.

Adding a Web page for updates

Once you distribute a CD-ROM to clients or employees, you have no idea how long people will use the files. You may go through several iterations of the same files before someone updates your CD to the latest version. To guard against obsolescence, create a folder with an HTML file. For all the button and text links, make the hypertext references to the pages on your Web site where updates are routinely reported. You can add a *readme* file or a PDF to instruct users they should frequent your Web site for updated forms. Be certain to keep the directory paths fixed on your Web site so even a user with an antiquated CD can easily access the pages without having to search your site.

Creating a welcome file

A file that describes the CD, its contents, and a general statement about visiting your Web site can be made as a text-only file or a PDF document. If you create a PDF file, then the user needs to have an Acrobat viewer installed on his/her computer. Any computer user can read a text file, so you may wish to add both.

Unfortunately, Readme files won't be viewed by everyone. Some users will avoid them and jump right into your documents. If you want to ensure the fact that every user sees your welcome file at least one time, then you can add an Autoplay file that automatically launches your welcome file when the CD-ROM is inserted in the CD drive. The creation of an Autoplay file and how you set it up are explained in the next section.

Adding Acrobat Reader

Before I explain about the inclusion of the Acrobat Reader software, you should always check with Adobe's Web site for the current rules and licensing restrictions before copying software like Acrobat Reader. The distribution policy can change at any time, so what is said today may not be true tomorrow.

As of this writing, Adobe permits you to copy the Acrobat Reader software installer to a media source for distribution. You must comply with the licensing policy and include all licensing information with the installer application. For specifics related to the distribution of the Acrobat Reader software, visit Adobe's Web site at www. adobe.com/products/acrobat/distribute.html for the most recent copy of Acrobat Reader and the current distribution policy.

If you include the Acrobat Reader installer on a CD-ROM, also create a Web page that is linked to the download page of the current Reader software. If your CD is out for a long time, Reader may go through several versions before a user updates to your latest CD-ROM version.

Setting up an Autoplay

An autoplay directs the operating system to launch an application or a document within an application at the time the CD-ROM is read by the system software. You have no doubt seen autoplays on CDs you have purchased for application software. A window opens and directs you to the installer buttons to install software or browse a CD for the contents. You can create a similar effect by adding your own autoplay to the CD-ROMs you distribute and giving them a professional look.

For a more professional look, you may wish to add a few bells and whistles to your CD-ROM by developing an autoplay, creating a custom icon, and perhaps even detecting a hard drive to see if an Acrobat viewer is installed. Let's take a look at some of the options available to you for creating an autoplay with some of these features.

Creating an Autoplay

Autoplays are created differently according to your platform. On the Mac OSMac OS, you create an autoplay at the time the CD-ROM is written. Autoplay features are available in newer versions of CD writing software. Not all software is capable of creating an autoplay, so be certain to check the features of software before you make a purchase. If you already have software to write CDs and an autoplay feature is not available, you'll need to acquire a new application. One popular program used for writing CDs is Toast by Roxio (formerly Adaptec).

Another issue relates to Mac OSMac OS users that may need mention in a Readme or PDF file. The autoplay feature can be turned off in the Mac OSMac OS QuickTime settings. If users disable the autoplay feature, the autoplay you set up on the CD won't run. Therefore, you may need to inform a user to choose Apple ➪ Control Panels ➪ QuickTime Settings. In the QuickTime Settings dialog box, select the pull-down menu and choose AutoPlay. Select the check box for Enable CD-ROM AutoPlay, as shown in Figure 13-21.

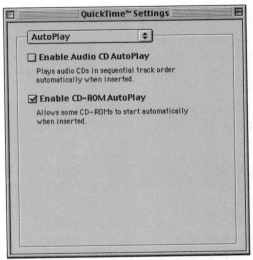

Figure 13-21: Mac OS users need the Enable CD-ROM AutoPlay option checked in the QuickTime Settings dialog box in order for an autoplay feature to work.

Windows users have more flexibility in adding an Autoplay to CDs you write. A very simple method is to create a text file in any text editor and add the following code:

```
[AutoRun]
open=C:\Program Files\Adobe\Acrobat 5.0\Acrobat\Acrobat.exe
welcome.pdf
icon=myicon.ico
```

In the preceding code, AutoRun tells the operating system to launch the following lines of code. The line beginning with `open=` specifies the location of the application and the executable application to be launched. The document name `welcome.pdf` is the file that opens in an Acrobat viewer.

Note A space separates the executable application name and the document filename.

The last line of code is optional. This line specifies the icon that appears on the CD drive when the CD is inserted in the drive. When you finish writing the code, save the file as text only as `autorun.inf` (be certain to use an `.inf` extension). Write the text file, along with your other files, to a CD. When you insert the CD in the CD drive, Acrobat launches the `welcome.pdf` file.

The above routine is fine if you're working with your own system and you know you have Acrobat installed and you know the absolute directory path for the application. However, when distributing CDs, you won't know the directory path for the user and you won't know if they have an Acrobat viewer loaded. Thus, your welcome file won't be launched.

You can write all the code necessary to search a user's hard drive for an Acrobat viewer, prompt the user to install an Acrobat viewer if one does not exist, and find a viewer through a search if one does exist. Writing the routine is more complex, but you can write the code in a text editor. Fortunately, there's an easier way.

There are a number of applications designed specifically for creating an .inf file based on criteria you supply in dialog boxes. When you finish responding to all the options, the file is written for you. Among the many applications available is GS Technologies AcroPDF Launch 2. This program specifically addresses PDF documents. The product sells for $59.00. A fully functional demonstration version is available for download from the Internet. As an example, download the demo version from www.autorun-autoplay-tools.com and follow these steps:

1. After installation, launch the program. The easy to use directions are supplied in the dialog boxes you navigate to supply the attributes for your autorun file. The first screen appears when you launch the program, as shown in Figure 13-22.

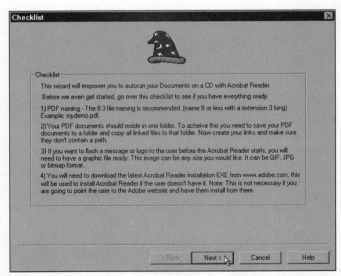

Figure 13-22: The dialog boxes offer step-by-step instructions for how to create the autorun file.

2. As you move through the dialog boxes, you are prompted to identify files to be included on the CD. You can copy files to the folder from the desktop or add them in the dialog boxes offered by AcroPDF Launch 2. When you move on to the next screen after loading files, you are prompted to identify the file to be used as the launch file when the CD is inserted.

3. The next dialog box enables you to identify the Acrobat Reader installer. If you intend to add the Reader installer, you specify the name of the installer in the dialog box. Figure 13-23 shows the dialog box to acquire the Reader installer and a message that opens to inform a user that the Reader software will be installed. If you wish to change the message, edit the text in the field box at the bottom of the dialog box.

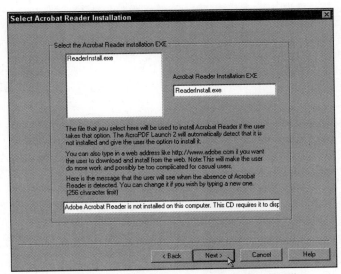

Figure 13-23: You can add the Acrobat Reader installer to the autorun file. If autorun does not detect an Acrobat viewer, a dialog box opens prompting the user to install Acrobat Reader from the CD-ROM.

4. When you finish with all the attribute settings, the autorun files are written to the folder where the PDFs are contained that you ultimately copy to the CD-ROM.

5. After writing a CD and copying all files from the designated folder, insert the CD in your CD drive. A dialog message box opens if you are using the evaluation copy of AcroPDF Launch 2. The dialog box is a reminder that the software is an evaluation copy. If you purchase the product, no dialog box opens.

6. An option to include a Flash graphic is also available in the options settings when you create the autorun file. If you elect to use a graphic, it is displayed on-screen and subsequently the PDF identified for launch opens in an Acrobat viewer. In my example, I use a file to open in Full Screen mode, as shown in Figure 13-24. The buttons launch other PDFs where individual files can be selected for opening. When a user inserts my CD-ROM, the first screen that appears is the welcome file, where central navigation can open any of the forms installed on the CD. An exit button is available for the user to bail out of Full Screen mode.

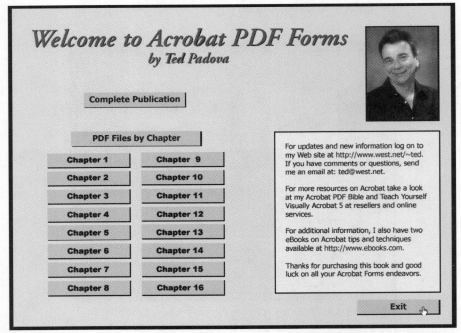

Figure 13-24: When the CD-ROM is inserted, the designated PDF file opens. By setting the Open Options to Full Screen mode, the file is displayed in the full screen display.

Creating image icons

There are many applications available for creating custom icons you can use for the display of your CD-ROM when it is inserted in the CD drive. Search for *icon maker* or *icon editor* and literally hundreds of utilities can be found for creating custom icons for both Mac OS and Windows systems. On the Mac OS, you can designate a custom icon to be used in the CD writing application. On Windows, you can include the icon in the .inf file, as described earlier.

To create an icon for use in Windows without the use of an editor, you can select a file with an icon appearance you wish to use. If you save files from Adobe Photoshop with the icon included, the icon appearance is displayed on the file when viewed as an icon on the Desktop. Create a shortcut for the file with the icon to be used and right-click the mouse button on the shortcut to open a context menu. Select Properties from the menu options. In the Shortcut to the *<filename>* Properties dialog box, click on the button for Change Icon, as shown in Figure 13-25.

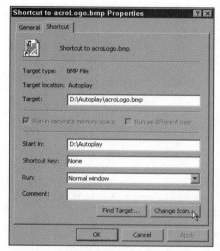

Figure 13-25: Click on the Change Icon button in the Shortcut Properties dialog box to select the icon to be displayed.

Another dialog box opens where you can select a system icon or click on the Browse button to browse your hard drive and find the file to use as the icon. Select the file and click OK in the Change Icon dialog box. The new icon is displayed and ready for use, as shown in Figure 13-26. Add the line of code mentioned earlier to use the new icon for the display on the CD-ROM when it is mounted.

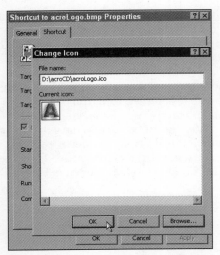

Figure 13-26: Click OK in the Change Icon dialog box. The new icon is now ready to be included in the autorun routine.

Summary

✦ You can export form data from populated PDF forms to an FDF file. The data can be introduced into any form that has field names that match the field names in the form from which the data were exported.

✦ You can create button fields to submit form data from any Acrobat viewer. Once the data leaves an Acrobat PDF file, a server-side application needs to collect and route the data.

✦ Submitting data from JavaScripts offers the ability to check forms for required data before submitting the data to a server.

✦ You can attach data and PDF forms to e-mail messages from JavaScript button actions.

✦ CD-ROMs provide an economical opportunity for distributing large collections of PDF forms. A CD-ROM can be designed professionally with "Welcome" messages, auto launches, and autoplays that have been enabled to detect installation of Acrobat viewers.

✦   ✦   ✦

Working with Real-World Forms

Using Form Design Assistants

In This Chapter

Dedicated form
design applications

Acrobat plug-ins

In addition to the authoring applications that were covered in Chapter 2, there are other tools you can use to design forms that eventually get converted to PDF, and tools that can help you once you begin to work in Acrobat. These tools come in two flavors. The first set of tools discussed in this chapter falls in the category of dedicated form design applications. The second category involves Acrobat plug-ins that have been developed by Adobe and third-party manufacturers.

Depending on the kind of forms you create and the work you need to accomplish in Acrobat, you may want applications or utilities that can complement your authoring programs and form designs in Acrobat.

Cross-Reference Refer to Chapter 2, "Using Authoring Applications," for more information about commercial authoring programs that are available.

Using Dedicated Form Design Applications

There are a number of software programs available specifically for designing forms. At the low end, many of these applications are Windows based and many are available at costs ranging from $19.99 to $39.99. For more sophisticated design applications, you can find programs offering many more features in the $400–$700 price range. If you are not a graphic designer or forms designer, then starting off with a program specific to forms design can be quite helpful. Depending on your needs, you can choose from among the low-end design programs or the more robust applications. With any application you elect to use, you'll want to be certain some degree of compatibility exists with Acrobat PDF.

Using low cost design programs

Some applications offer you the capability for creating forms with fields supporting data entry, however, these programs defeat the purpose for using Acrobat forms. With the low-cost form design programs, the applications are intended to help you create a design suited for printing and photocopying. Applying these designs to Acrobat PDFs means that instead of printing and photocopying forms, we'll use a program to help us design a form, then convert it to Acrobat PDF where the form fields are added.

Converting designs to PDF

There are number of programs available in the low-end market and they vary according to features and pre-designed templates. Although the programs vary, the process for generating PDFs is the same, so you need not spend a lot of time researching one program's power against another. What's important to understand here is the process for how you use a low-cost application to help you out with a design. In this regard, I use an off-the-shelf design application to illustrate the point.

Form Tool Express, by IMSI (www.imsisoft.com/), is a low-cost forms design tool you can purchase for less than $30 as of this writing. The program is impressive for a low-cost application and offers both a design program and many pre-designed templates. The templates are organized in several folders, as shown in Figure 14-1.

Figure 14-1: When you launch the Form Tool Express application and choose File ➪ Open, pre-designed templates can be selected from those installed in the Forms folder.

If a pre-designed form exists to suit your needs, you can open the template and modify it in the application. The program used in this example offers an easy user interface and many tools for creating forms elements such as boxes, rules, type, and so on, as shown in Figure 14-2.

If you prefer to perform editing in another program after the PDF is created, you can convert the form to PDF and modify the design by using the Edit Object command discussed in Chapter 2. If the form design helps you create the design you want, convert the file to PDF and add the form fields in Acrobat. Either way, the first step is to convert the document to PDF.

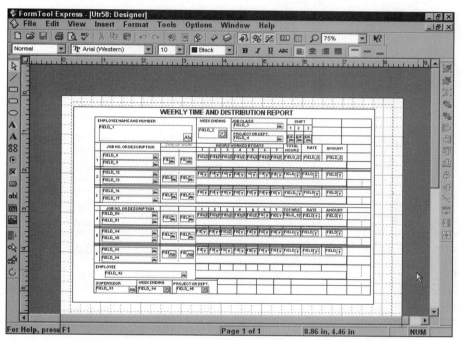

Figure 14-2: Form Tool Express is a feature-rich program offering many tools for creating or editing a form's design.

Cross-Reference   For more on modifying PDF content, see Chapter 2, "Using Authoring Applications."

Almost any low-cost application you use for designing forms won't have an export directly to PDF. Therefore, you need to print a PostScript file and distill the file in Acrobat Distiller, use the Acrobat Distiller printer in Windows, or use Create Adobe PDF on the Mac OS. In this example, Form Tool Express is a Windows application, therefore choose File ➪ Print and choose the Acrobat Distiller Printer.

For more on using the Distiller application to convert PostScript files to PDF, see Chapter 1, "Getting Started with Acrobat Forms."

Once converted to PDF, you can further edit the form in a design application that supports the Edit Objects menu selection shown in Figure 14-3. As discussed in Chapter 2, the default program used with the Edit Object command is Adobe Illustrator.

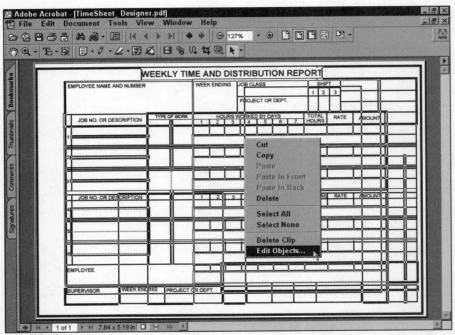

Figure 14-3: If you wish to edit the form in another authoring application, select all the objects with the TouchUp Object tool and choose Edit Objects from a context menu.

In this example, Adobe Illustrator is used to add a company logo, adjust the page size, and add a few design elements, as shown in Figure 14-4. In most cases you won't have an opportunity to copy/paste between a design program and an authoring program. Therefore, converting to PDF may be the only way to get a design into your favorite design tool.

Rather than dynamically update the existing PDF form, you can save a new copy to disk from Adobe Illustrator as a PDF file. If you change page sizes and perform a radical change to the form as opposed to editing a few objects, the results will be better by saving the file as a new PDF. When the final file is saved to PDF and opened in Acrobat, as shown in Figure 14-5, you can proceed to create the form fields and add form features in Acrobat.

If you retrace the steps above and compare all the design elements for text and rules in the template form compared to drawing these elements in an illustration program, you can easily see that starting with a template saves time. With some programs, the templates may be ideal for a given form. With others, you may need to make some alterations in the form designer or an illustration program like Adobe Illustrator. For the low cost of such programs, you can often find the time saved by creating new forms well worth the purchase price.

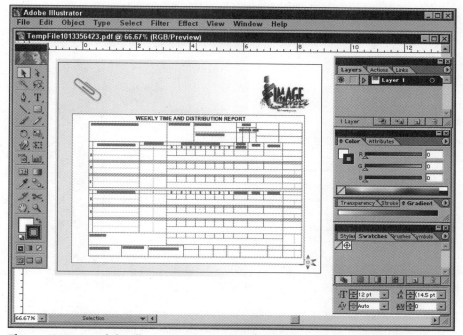

Figure 14-4: In Adobe Illustrator, some enhancements are made on the form and the page size is adjusted to accommodate a larger page size.

Using PDF template forms

There are a few off-the-shelf packages that offer you templates as PDF files. When you search for these kinds of products, be certain that the forms are *open* and the form fields are accessible. You can find some form kits that use PDF files with complex JavaScript code. In some cases, the forms offered in PDF format may be applicable to your needs and in other cases you may wish to redesign the form and copy/paste the JavaScripts.

PDF templates can be used across platforms and design changes can be made with the Edit Object command as long as the PDF has not been secured. An example of forms in this category is from EZ-Forms (www.ezx.com/). When you open any of the PDF files that are contained on the installer CD-ROM, you'll immediately notice that the form fields and JavaScript code are accessible, as shown in Figure 14-6.

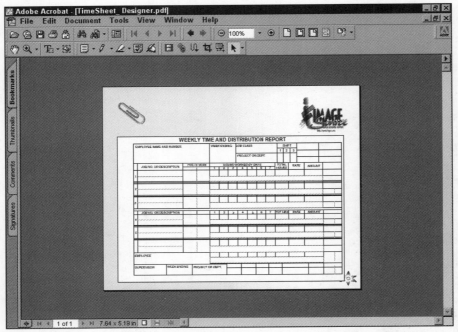

Figure 14-5: After saving as a new PDF file, the document is ready to add all the form fields in Acrobat.

Using OmniForm

A much more sophisticated approach to designing forms is handled with a professional dedicated form design tool. Among the best on the market is OmniForm Premium by ScanSoft (www.scansoft.com). In addition to providing you with a form design tool capable of creating forms with fields and rendering PDFs, OmniForm is designed to help you convert analog forms to electronic forms via scanned documents. It you have a need to convert printed documents to electronic forms, then OmniForm's easy-to-use and feature-rich application is the program for you. For users requiring industrial-strength applications, OmniForm can help you save much time in converting paper forms to PDF forms.

OmniForm is a powerful tool, but is easy to use for almost any level of user. Follow a simple installation process and OmniForm guides you through configuration of the program and communication with your scanner. When you launch the program after the configuration is complete, the Form Assistant dialog box opens asking if you want to take control over the form design or just scan it in for a quick fill-in. Click on the Next button, as shown in Figure 14-7, and OmniForm opens your scanner dialog box.

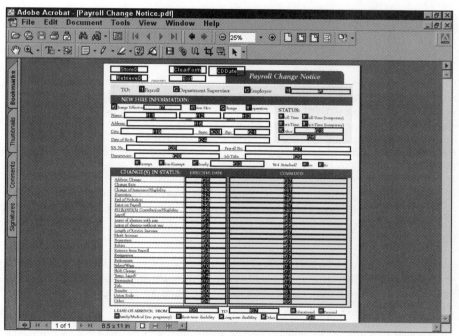

Figure 14-6: EZ-Forms is a form kit that offers PDF forms in which all the form fields and JavaScript code can be examined and modified.

Be certain to scan your file at the appropriate resolution and color mode. The scanner resolution needs to be set to 300 ppi (Pixels Per Inch) and the mode must be either Color or Line Art (Black and White, not grayscale). If a color mode is used, it needs to be checked in a dialog box in OmniForm before addressing the scanner software.

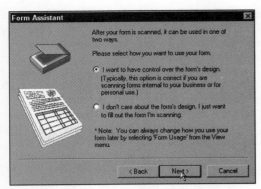

Figure 14-7: Launch OmniForm and select
one of the two choices in the Form Assistant
dialog box. Click on the Next button and your
scanner software dialog box opens.

Click on the Scan button in your scanner software dialog box and your scanner
software produces the scan that is delivered to OmniForm. If your computer or
scanner pauses, be patient, because the OCR (Optical Character Recognition)
capability in OmniForm may take a few moments to interpret the text. When the
scanner finishes, you'll be returned to OmniForm where the form opens in an
OmniForm document window. All the fields on the form are highlighted, as shown
in Figure 14-8.

If you want to fill in the form, you can use OmniForm's fill-in feature to populate
fields. Click on the Form Filler tab at the top of the document window and click in
the first field box. Enter data in the field and tab through the fields adding more
data, like the example shown in Figure 14-9.

If you want to convert the OmniForm document to PDF, OmniForm supports saving
directly to PDF without a need for file conversion. Choose File ⇨ Save As and the
Save As dialog box opens. Select PDF from the Save As Type pull-down menu.
Name the file and save it to your hard drive.

After saving as PDF, open the file in Acrobat. Because all the text was converted
with OmniForm's OCR, the text is selectable. You can use either the TouchUp Text
tool or the Column Select tool, as shown in Figure 14-10, to select text.

Click on the Form tool and you see all the fields created by OmniForm and
preserved in the PDF file, as shown in Figure 14-11. The steps used in this example
were elementary and simple to illustrate the ease of working with OmniForm.
There is much more to the product and much more sophistication can be employed
with converting hard copy forms or designing forms in OmniForm before producing
a PDF.

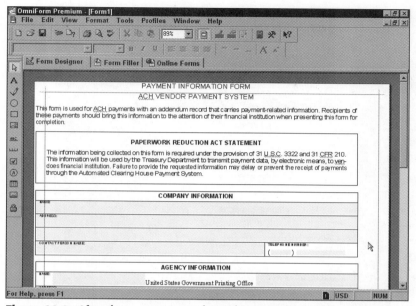

Figure 14-8: After the scanner completes the scan, the form is opened in an OmniForm document window. All fields are highlighted in yellow.

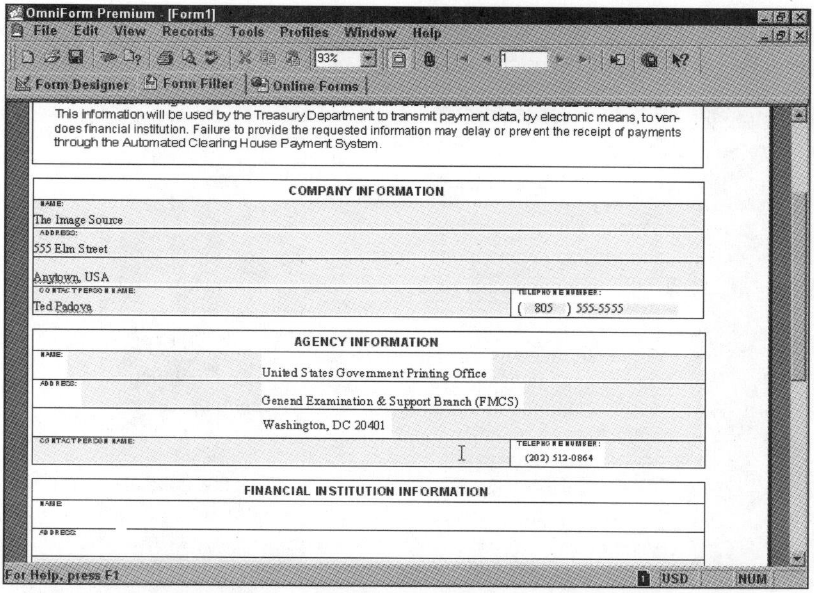

Figure 14-9: OmniForm offers a fill-in feature where the scanned form can be completed in the OmniForm program.

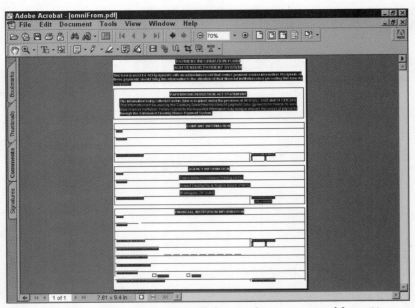

Figure 14-10: OmniForm captures all the text from a scanned form. You can select and edit text with the TouchUp Text tool.

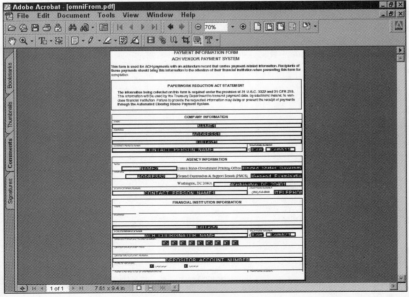

Figure 14-11: When you click on the Form tool, you can immediately see all the fields created by OmniForm.

Using Acrobat Plug-Ins

The numbers of third-party plug-ins that support extended features in Acrobat are no less then astounding. It's hard to find a problem with manipulating a PDF document where a third-party solution doesn't exist. With regard to Acrobat forms, I place the plug-ins offered by third-party manufacturers in five categories. These include:

✦ **Using plug-ins as design tools or design assistants.** These tools help you edit the background design in a PDF file.

✦ **Editing PDF files.** When the TouchUp tools are not doing the job, there are many plug-ins that offer some more-sophisticated editing features than those provided by Acrobat.

✦ **Exporting PDF structure.** When you need to return to an authoring program to edit a PDF, sometimes there is a need to get the content back out to an authoring application with the document integrity preserved. In other cases, you may have a need to repurpose documents for other uses such as HTML. All of these tasks are included in this category.

✦ **Managing data.** Plug-ins used for importing and exporting data are covered in this category.

✦ **Enterprise solutions.** Submitting data to servers and managing data in enterprise environments is what is included with these tools.

The foregoing list is not necessarily inclusive, but you can get an idea of many of the tools available to you as add-ons via Acrobat plug-ins from third-party vendors. If you have a problem and don't see one of the products mentioned in this chapter as a potential solution, try visiting the Planet PDF online store at `www.epublishstore.pdf`. Planet PDF operates an online store where all of the following plug-ins can be purchased and trial versions can be downloaded.

Creating/Designing PDF forms

Plug-ins in this category are examples of third-party solutions, which are used in the PDF creation process. They are also tools to help you with form design issues. If you use software applications that don't support exporting directly to the PDF format, some of the tools that are listed in this section can help simplify document conversions to PDF.

activePDF DocConverter

Vendor: activePDF

Platform: Windows

URL: `http://activepdf.com`

Demo file size: 8.48MB

Full version: 8.48MB

Cost: $299.00

Description: activePDF DocConverter converts Microsoft Office 97 and WordPerfect documents to PDF. With an easy drag-and-drop interface, you can convert these file types to PDF while preserving structure. Heads, TOC, and index entries are converted to bookmarks and links. For the WordPerfect user, DocConverter is an easy, affordable solution for creating PDF files. The demo version is fully functional for a one-day trial period.

FormBar

Vendor: Actino Software

Platform: Windows

URL: www.actino.com

Demo file size: 160K

Full version: 160K

Cost: 75 EUR = $65 US (approximate)

Description: FormBar is a nifty little tool that offers you a small toolbar where tools appear for aligning, scaling, distributing, arranging form fields, and setting tab stops. Although all these functions are available in Acrobat, FormBar places the functions in a floating toolbar easily accessible during your editing sessions. FormBar is particularly helpful when designing forms with many fields and when a quick access to the functions is needed. FormBar is only one of the many plug-in offerings by Actino. Take a look at their Web site for other plug-ins providing many different PDF solutions.

PageForm

Vendor: MapSoft Computer Services

Platform: Windows and Adobe PageMaker 6.52 and PageMaker 7.0

URL: www.mapsoft.com

Demo file size: 1.7MB

Full version: 3.0MB

Cost: $149.00

Description: For users of Adobe PageMaker, PageForm is an ideal tool for converting PageMaker documents to Acrobat forms. A separate dialog box is used to specify field types and attributes directly within PageMaker before the file is converted to PDF, as shown in Figure 14-12. You have complete access to page handlers, Page Actions, and JavaScript routines in PageForm. The trial version is completely functional for a three-day trial period. Check the MapSoft Web site at www.mapsoft.com for the new update that supports PageMaker 7.0.

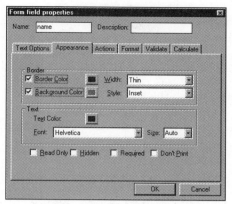

Figure 14-12: PageForm offers a dialog box similar to the Field Properties dialog box in Acrobat in which form field attributes are created in PageMaker prior to PDF conversion.

SimplePDF

Vendor: Tangent Software

Platform: Windows

URL: www.simplepdf.tangentially.com

Demo file size: 1.2MB

Full version: 1.2MB

Cost: $35.00

Description: There are several PDF converters in the marketplace. The SimplePDF shareware application is perhaps one of the most cost-effective solutions available for converting text documents to PDF. Now, SimplePDF is also available online as a workflow solution for corporate environments, legal institutions, and educators, enabling users to compose documents and convert them to PDF on-the-fly online, complete with multimedia (.jpeg, .avi files) attachments. Powered by webProlog (www.webprolog.com), a Prolog-based AI language, the application also allows sharing files within work groups, and online feedback by colleagues. You'll need to contact the people at Tangent to be certain that you remain within licensing guidelines.

Sowedoo Easy PDF Converter

Vendor: Sowedoo

Platform: Windows

URL: www.sowedoo.com

Demo file size: 3.7MB

Full version: 3.7MB

Cost: 99 EUR = $86 US (approximate)

Description: Sowedoo manufactures a variety of low-cost Acrobat plug-ins, which includes the Easy PDF Converter. This plug-in enables you to convert MS Office files, HTML, RTF, and text documents to PDF. You can select multiple document types and drag and drop the files to the Easy PDF Converter window. You have option choices for image downsampling, and Acrobat Distiller Job Options can be selected. For other PDF solutions, visit the Sowedoo Web site.

Editing PDF documents

The following tools are third-party solutions that extend Acrobat's editing capabilities. If you need to modify the content of a PDF and Acrobat won't do the job, look at some of the examples in this section.

ARTS Link Tool

Vendor: ARTS–A Round Table Solution (formerly marketed by Dionis Software)

Platform: Windows/Mac OS

URL: www.aroundtablesolution.com

Demo file size: 166K

Full version: 166K

Cost: $295.00

Description: ARTS manufactures and distributes several Acrobat plug-ins that were formerly marketed by Dionis software, which include ARTS Link Tool. The Link Tool is what you wish Acrobat had provided you for managing links. With this plug-in, you can copy links, paste links, select multiple links, select all links, and delete multiple links. If PDF forms have been created with links to invoke JavaScript actions and you need to manage links, this tool is for you. It's particularly helpful when you work with PDFs that are exported from programs that deliver link actions instead of form field actions and you need to manage the links in the resultant PDF document.

ARTS PDF Tools

Vendor: ARTS–A Round Table Solution

Platform: Windows

URL: www.aroundtablesolution.com

Demo file size: 1.1MB

Full version: 1.1MB

Cost: $149.00

Description: There are more than 70 tools in ARTS PDF Tools nestled together in a floating toolbox, some of which are shown in Figure 14-13. Many of the tools are derived from commands in the Acrobat menu bar with a few that aren't available in Acrobat. ARTS offers you some nice editing features like counting all words in a document, flattening pages, optimizing files through eliminating unnecessary elements predefined by a user, and an almost inexhaustible collection of tools that can be added or removed from the toolbox. The flexibility for customizing the tools and adding your own tool options from menu commands keeps all frequently accessed Acrobat functions at hand in the tool box. Share your tool set with other ARTS PDF Tools users and you can add much more efficiency to your workflow. As a bonus item, click on a tool in the toolbox and the ePublish Store Web page appears in your Web browser where any of the plug-ins listed in this chapter can be purchased.

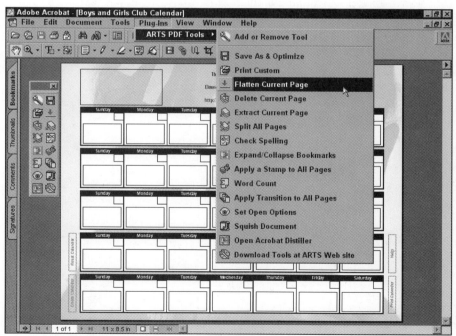

Figure 14-13: ARTS PDF Tools offers one of the best collections of tools and immediate access to user-defined menu options. For PDF editing, the ARTS PDF Tools should be right behind the purchase of Enfocus PitStop.

Enfocus PitStop Professional

Vendor: Enfocus Software

Platform: Windows/Mac OS

URL: www.enfocus.com

Demo file size: 6MB Windows, 7.4MB Mac OS

Full version: 6MB Windows, 7.4MB Mac OS

Cost: $549.00

Description: Enfocus PitStop is the premiere Acrobat plug-in and one of the most comprehensive for PDF editing and management. PitStop is a favorite among prepress professionals for controlling color, certifying PDFs, preflighting files, editing text paragraphs for embedded type, adding trim marks, and similar tasks not offered by Acrobat. For the forms designer, PitStop provides you with the editing tools needed for text editing, copy and paste features for text and graphics, guidelines, and a host of other design features. The PitStop tools are extensive and appear in the Acrobat Command Bar as well as multiple dialog boxes where many attribute choices can be made, as shown in Figure 14-14. Above all, Enfocus PitStop is the first Acrobat plug-in you may wish to acquire.

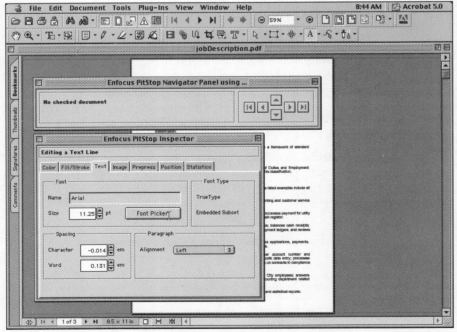

Figure 14-14: Enfocus PitStop is the premiere choice for Acrobat PDF editing tools. After installation, a variety of tools are accessible in the Acrobat Command Bar and additional attribute choices appear in dialog boxes.

Impress Stamper/Impress Stamper Pro

Vendor: MapSoft Computer Services

Platform: Windows

URL: www.mapsoft.com

Demo file size: 740K (Impress Stamper), 1.1K (Impress Stamper Pro)

Full version: 739K (Impress Stamper), 1.0K (Impress Stamper Pro)

Cost: $99.00 (Impress Stamper), $199.00 (Impress Stamper Pro)

Description: Impress is an Acrobat plug-in that enables you to add text to a page or range of pages in an Acrobat PDF file. With an easy-to-use dialog box, you can specify text content and the pages where the new text is to be added. Watermarks can be created on designated layers that may appear behind existing text, form fields, and images, or above them as a user defined option. Impress Pro enables you to batch process multiple files and create multiple impressions. The trial version offers complete access to all features; however, it stamps "Impress tryout" on all the pages in the documents that you process. When you purchase the licensed version, the page stamping is eliminated. The primary distinction between the Impress Stamper and the Impress Stamper Pro is the batch processing is limited to the Pro version.

Pagelet

Vendor: CreoScitex

Platform: Windows

URL: www.creo.com

Demo file size: 2MB

Full version: 2MB

Cost: $249.00

Description: Pagelet is an assembly tool providing support for integration of page elements from several different files into a single PDF. Pagelet offers grids and guides, rulers, snap-to features, and transformations of independent objects. Pagelet is like a mini-layout application, which can help you design a document directly in Acrobat.

Exporting PDF structure

There may be situations when you need to export the PDF content back to an authoring application or to a different format for repurposing the document. If Acrobat doesn't meet your export needs, take a look at some of the examples in this category.

BCL Drake™

> **Vendor:** BCL Technologies
>
> **Platform:** Windows
>
> **URL:** www.bcltechnologies.com
>
> **Demo file size:** 1.1MB
>
> **Full version:** 1.1MB
>
> **Cost:** US $199.00
>
> **Description:** BCL Technologies (formerly BCL Computers) manufactures several plug-ins, some of which are covered in this chapter. If getting your PDF files back to Microsoft Word has been a challenge, BCL Drake™ can help you. The Export to RTF format automatically extracts all the contents of your document while preserving the structure from the PDF file in the RTF file. You can export images and rules along with text while maintaining complete document integrity.

BCL Jade™

> **Vendor:** BCL Technologies
>
> **Platform:** Windows
>
> **URL:** www.bcltechnologies.com
>
> **Demo file size:** 1.3MB
>
> **Full version:** 1.4MB
>
> **Cost:** $199.00
>
> **Description:** If exporting tables with columns and rows is your task, then BCL Jade™ is your solution. Many of the methods for exporting to RTF from untagged Acrobat PDFs won't preserve the document integrity for table data, however BCL Jade™ handles these exports much more reliably. You can use one of the plug-ins noted for flattening PDFs where the data are stamped down on a page (see ARTS PDF Tools above) and the fields are eliminated. Then use BCL Jade™ to extract the table to Microsoft Excel, and you have your data converted to a spreadsheet for editing or other purposes.

BCL Magellan 5.0™

Vendor: BCL Technologies

Platform: Windows

URL: www.bcltechnologies.com

Demo file size: 1.4MB

Full version: 1.3MB

Cost: $199.00

Description: If you want your PDF forms converted to HTML documents for Web publishing, BCL Magellan™ is the plug-in solution. BCL Magellan™ converts the PDF structure to HTML and extracts both vector and raster images. The extracted images are all converted to JPEG with references in the HTML to display them accurately. All hyperlinks that include movie and sound files are mapped in the HTML and function similar to the way they are handled in the PDF file. The demonstration file is completely functional for a 30-day trial period.

Gemini

Vendor: Iceni Technology

Platform: Windows

URL: www.iceni.com

Demo file size: 3MB

Full version: 3MB

Cost: $169.00

Gemini Solo is a standalone application program that supports the export of PDF content. The list of formats that can be exported is comprehensive. Export options include the following:

- Intelligent reflow and dehyphenation even on non-structured PDF documents
- Convert tables into HTML, SYLK, RTF, or Tabbed Text
- Convert images into JPEG, TIFF, PNG, or BMP
- Generation of HTML, eBook, RTF, or ASCII
- Manual overrides for explicitly marking up text, images, and tables
- Preserve reading order in and across pages using Article Threads
- Automatic creation of bookmarks even when the original document has none

Follow the easy-to-use steps in the Gemini dialog boxes and you will quickly master exporting PDF content to the file formats that are supported by Gemini. The Gemini Export Pages dialog box opens when you select Page . . . from the Export menu after installation, as shown in Figure 14-15.

Figure 14-15: The Gemini Export Pages dialog box offers easy access to the attribute choices for file exports when you click on the Options button.

Click on the Options button and the Gemini Options dialog box opens, as shown in Figure 14-16. In this dialog box, the export options are intuitive and, for the most part, self-explanatory. Make the options choices and the PDF file is exported. For a cost-effective plug-in needed for exporting PDF forms, Gemini Solo is one of the best price/performance solutions available from third-party manufacturers.

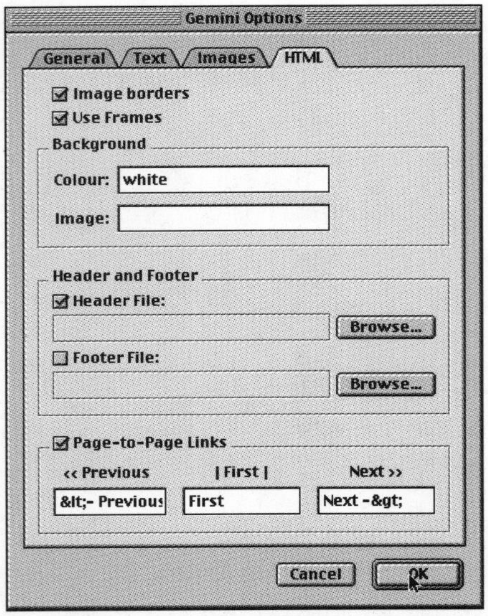

Figure 14-16: The Gemini Options dialog box offers simple, easy-to-understand attribute options for the exported PDF file.

Managing data

Data management in regard to handling form fill-in processes can be simplified and extended through the use of solutions that are listed in this category. For more automated data handling, look over some of the plug-ins and standalone applications mentioned here.

activePDF Toolkit

Vendor: activePDF

Platform: Windows

URL: http://activepdf.com

Demo file size: 3MB

Full version: 3MB

Cost: $249.00

Description: activePDF Toolkit is a "Swiss army knife" of tools that simplify many PDF editing tasks and form field fill-ins. Among the many features, the tools include:

- **Append & Extract Pages.** Any number of pages in a PDF or collection of PDF documents can be appended or extracted both to and from different PDF files. Bookmarks are preserved and transported between files.

- **Stamp Text & Images.** Document stamping and watermarks can be made from text and/or images. Test support is available for any font installed on a server, with color options choices and rotations. Image formats include more than 40 supported file formats.

- **Form Filling.** With activePDF Toolkit, Acrobat Reader users can save form field data when completing Acrobat forms. A *flattening* feature enables you to eliminate the field boxes and stamp the data contained within fields on the PDF page. Form fields add much more memory to a PDF file. By flattening the fields, forms can be optimized for electronic transfers.

- **Stitching.** If you aren't up to speed with pdfmark annotations and using some PostScript files available on the Acrobat installer CD for concatenating PDF files, the stitching feature is an easy way to combine individual PDFs into a single document. For workflow environments, this feature can save you time over using Acrobat's Insert Pages command.

- **Encryption & Decryption.** The server-based encryption feature enables you to encrypt files at either 40-bit or 128-bit encryption.

activePDF manufactures a number of products for supporting the Portable Document Format. Only a few are mentioned in this chapter. For more solutions from the people at activePDF, visit their Web site.

Form Pilot Office

Vendor: Invention Pilot, Inc.

Platform: Windows 95/98/ME/2000/XP

URL: www.colorpilot.com

Demo file size: 2MB

Full version: 2MB

Cost: $245.00

Description: Form Pilot Office is designed for filling out electronic forms. It supports not only PDF, but also DOC, XLS, TXT, and many other document types. The program is especially helpful when Acrobat forms have been created as static forms without form fields, such as many of the Web-hosted forms you can find on the Internet. The program converts any electronic form into a raster image. Once in a raster format, you can modify it or introduce any text or graphics on it.

PDForMail

Vendor: Gordonkent.com, Inc.

Platform: Windows

URL: www.gordonkent.com

Demo file size: 4.3MB

Full version: 4.3MB

Cost: $199.00 for the hosted application; $399.00 for the server application

Description: PDForMail is an ideal solution for providers who wish to have users complete either a PDF or HTML form with the Acrobat Reader software and have the completed form routed back to the user as a populated PDF. The end user need only use the Reader software. The file returned is a PDF with all the data preserved, which can then be distributed to other users. Setting up a file for a round-trip e-mail is easily handled with the addition of a single form field. PDForMail uses a simple tag-like language structure so no complex server-side coding is required to return PDF documents to users. Demonstrations of the product can be seen online or by downloading a trial version. Two versions are available: the hosted application has a $199.00 license fee and the server application (Microsoft IIS servers) costs $399.00. In addition to the PDForMail product, Gordon Kent hosts a Web site for sharing information on PDF forms, XML, HTML, and related topics. Log on to his site and take a look at some of the online publications he offers.

Variform PDF™

Vendor: Lantana

Platform: Windows/Mac OS

URL: www.lantanarips.com

Demo file size: 2.1MB

Full version: 2.1MB

Cost: $199.00

Description: Lantana's Variform PDF provides a set of tools for managing and printing data from external files to PDF form documents. Data files can be created from any application or database capable of exporting records to a delimited file. Variform PDF supports tab, comma, semicolon, or space-delimited formats. Any Acrobat form document using form fields and appropriate security settings can be used as a merge document. Merged data can be printed to any PostScript printer or to a PostScript file. New, merged PDF documents can be created by printing directly to the Acrobat Distiller printer or by printing to a PostScript file and then using Acrobat Distiller. Subsequently, these merged PDF documents may be printed on any PCL or PostScript printer.

Using server-side applications

Server-side applications offer you tools for enterprise-wide PDF and data management. For overcoming limitations with the Acrobat Reader software, server-side tools provide support for data that are submitted by Reader users as well as managing data that are routed to databases.

ExperForms

Vendor: Web Base, Inc.

Platform: Windows

URL: www.experforms.com

Demo file size: 6MB

Full version: 6MB

Cost: $4,995.00

Description: Server-side applications that provide PDF form solutions continue to grow in popularity. Offering super fast implementation and versatile information management, ExperForms is the most robust, comprehensive, and economical of these applications. It's a great application for organizations that need powerful form management capabilities.

ExperForms automates form and data management using Acrobat Reader—submitted data "warehoused" in ODBC databases, and provides features for customizing work flow: PDF hosting, submission, searches, form and data routing, the ability to update collected data, e-mail to user defined destinations, XML-formatted data constructs for integration with other applications, and more.

To top it off, the overall cost of using ExperForms is significantly less than many comparable form management products.

FDFMerge

Vendor: Appligent

Platform: Windows, Solaris, Linux, AIX, HP-UX, Mac OS X, and IBM OS/390

URL: www.appligent.com

Demo file size: n/a

Full version: 1.3MB

Cost: $2,995.00

Description: Appligent's FDF Merge is a server-side command-line application that reliably populates PDF files from FDF data. The complete PDF with associated data is saved on the server and can be returned to the user as a populated form, thereby making it accessible to Acrobat Reader users. A form-flattening feature enables the PDF form to use any system font in form fields and embed those fonts in the PDF so the user can print the form like any other PDF document. Additionally, form flattening along with securing PDF files eliminates any possibility for changing data when a user downloads the PDF. In addition to a command line executable, FDFMerge is also available as a Java linkable library and a Web Service.

Summary

✦ You can purchase many low-cost design programs that enable you to create forms based on templates, which you can use for business and personal needs. All the form design programs allow you to convert the documents to PDF via Acrobat Distiller.

✦ OmniForm is a powerful tool that is designed to scan paper forms and convert them to electronic forms. OmniForm supports the capability of saving directly to PDF.

✦ Many third-party plug-ins are available for adding more functionality to form authoring in Acrobat. You can find all third-party plug-ins at the Planet PDF Web site at www.planetpdf.com.

✦   ✦   ✦

Understanding the Real-World Forms Market

Who uses PDF forms? Where are the most promising markets? The answer to these questions are of interest to people in the marketplace where growth of PDF forms may experience acceleration from the user point of view, and perhaps some of you who may wish to consult and offer services to industries experiencing growth. On the user end, you may be working with forms generated from organizations in these industries and have a need to either author forms or fill in forms. On the consultant end, you may wish to stay abreast of current PDF developments and understand the rising markets. This chapter takes a brief look at some of the current directions for Adobe Systems to promote more PDF usage, where key industries are found, and some specifics on creating and using forms for these markets.

Understanding the Growth of PDF Forms

Providers usually hold in confidence the number of installed users for any given application. Public disclosure on the exact number of Acrobat users or Acrobat Approval users is something you won't find advertised by Adobe Systems. With regard to Acrobat Reader, Adobe has a hard time keeping track of the number of installed users. Estimates run over 300 million people who may be using the Acrobat Reader software as of this writing. However, the number of downloads don't necessarily indicate the number of individual users. Many people upgrade the software or install it on multiple machines, making it difficult to tabulate the total number of individuals who use the Acrobat Reader software.

What we do know is that the number of Acrobat Reader software installations is phenomenal and certainly among one of the most-used computer software applications today. We also know that Adobe has experienced growth relative to products they sell. In the Acrobat market, Acrobat sales rose 45 percent year after year between 1999 and 2000. The next year sales rose over 40 percent year after year resulting in doubling the installed users of the Adobe Acrobat software over the past two years.

The importance of Acrobat PDF forms to Adobe Systems was expressed by Adobe's CEO Bruce Chizen in a 2001 fourth-quarter analyst report as saying, "...Chizen explained that Adobe has recently begun shifting some 60 percent of its sales force to Acrobat, primarily targeting enterprise-wide sales (seats/licenses) in the corporate and government markets. Forms use is in that thick of those intentions, you can be sure." PlanetPDF conducted an interview with Chizen in mid-2001 in which it was reported, "Chizen cites the use of forms as a critical part of every business, and it follows that Adobe hopes to convert many of those core applications to Acrobat 5.0-based PDF Forms."

The fact that Adobe is diverting 60 percent of its worldwide sales force to Acrobat is indeed significant and you can be certain that there are markets of opportunity that Adobe Systems apparently sees as worthwhile and lucrative.

Adobe marketing directions

With the rise in Acrobat sales, where is the market growth and who's buying Acrobat? Certainly sales in the marketing channel have improved the installed user base of the Acrobat software. The number of consumers and individuals who buy in the channel are growing; the result is more people across industries use Acrobat and Acrobat eForms. However, Adobe Systems is not likely to focus 60 percent of its sales force on consumer consumption. For such a dramatic shift in marketing, you can be certain that the targets are large organizations and industries representing huge numbers of users. In regard to potential growth, market directions are now being focused at three groups:

✦ **Government.** The U.S. federal government represents one of the largest bodies of installed Acrobat users. One can verify this claim by visiting the IRS Web site at www.irs.gov and taking a look at Adobe's Web site on April 14 when U.S. citizens are frantically retrieving income tax forms. Adobe's Web site is bombarded with user downloads of Acrobat Reader and the IRS Web site is equally bombarded for downloads of tax forms, all available in PDF. Add to the IRS department, the Department of Defense, HEW, U.S. Treasury, and almost any other arm of the U.S. federal government, all the PDF-hosted forms and documents, and the market is indeed huge. With the addition of Accessibility in Acrobat PDFs, this market is expected to continually expand, especially when you realize there are more than 2.5 million government workers in the United States.

✦ **Legal Profession.** There are more than 1.4 million lawyers in the United States. Sounds incredible when you realize that the number of lawyers represent over 50 percent of all government workers. Adobe sees the legal profession as one of the next large markets for Acrobat and Acrobat eForms.

✦ **Enterprise.** Solutions providers and enterprise markets represent the third target. These entities can include solutions providers such as companies like Cardiff Systems and activePDF, where products are sold to large companies for solutions in working with Acrobat eForms on Web servers, ePaper Solutions(tm), and networks servicing multiple users. The volume of analog documents needing electronic conversion remains a behemoth task, and these solutions providers are offering products to automate the process. With partnership programs and collaboration, Adobe sees the enterprise market as an extension of its own marketing efforts to attract new users to the Acrobat family of products. Add to the solutions providers the core Acrobat features for connectivity with relational databases, and you find business enterprises embracing PDF forms in quantum growths.

These three markets are a major part of the emphasis you can expect to see in forthcoming years to increase Acrobat usage and use for Acrobat forms. If you are not part of the market, you may at some point interact with one or all these industries. As a PDF forms author, you may be called upon to serve any one of the markets. As an author in a different market, you can gain insight and ideas by watching the markets and observing how forms are used and the growth experienced. Furthermore, as an end user, it may be helpful to understand the construction and application of PDF forms in the event you need to use forms within the industries or tap into the various solutions available.

Working with standards

The PDF format has become a standard in many industries. In the area of digital prepress and printing, many service bureaus, print shops, and publishers have developed workflows and standardized on PDF. A good example is the newspaper industry where major publishing chains accept only PDF files for display advertising in their publications. Other industries using manuals, technical guides, help documents, and the like have also standardized on PDF. In regard to forms, there is a standardization attempt by Adobe Systems you should become familiar with. As yet, not too many forms authors have adopted the effort, but it exists and you may see some growth when more industries accept PDF as their own standard for distributing forms.

On the Acrobat installer CD-ROM, you'll find a folder entitled `Forms`. Inside this folder is another folder called `PFN`. The `pfnform.pdf` file inside this folder is a PDF form designed to be used as a standard when creating fields used for personal identifying information. The idea is to use common field names in forms you distribute so an end user can import field data related to his/her personal information without a need for re-keying the same information every time a form is completed. The form contains fields for almost any information related to your personal or business data that may be used in your own business forms. The PFN sample form on the Acrobat installer CD-ROM is shown in Figure 15-1.

When you create a form, you place the PFN icon (shown in Figure 15-2) on your form so other users know the form fields are consistent with the profile they create. A user fills in the form fields on the PFN form and exports the data as an FDF file. The data can then be imported to any form using the same field names as the PFN standard.

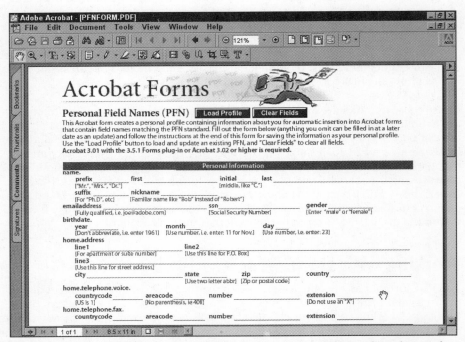

Figure 15-1: The PFN form is provided on the Acrobat CD-ROM and can be used to standardize personal profile information for all forms you create and send to other users.

As I mentioned earlier, the efforts to standardize PFN have not been embraced by many form designers. However, standards exist and they can be used effectively when creating forms. If you create forms and frequently change field names, the ability to import data from exported FDF files will be a continual problem, especially if you haven't adopted any standards in your company and there are several PDF forms authors creating forms. If you're new to Acrobat forms or you need to revisit forms and revise them, you'll be wise to look at the PFN standard and use it if you have no other consistent form field naming conventions adopted.

Figure 15-2: When the PFN icon is placed on a form, it identifies for the end user that the form uses the PFN standard. This icon is also found in the PFN folder inside the Forms folder on the Acrobat installer CD-ROM.

The PFN standard is not widely used by PDF authors. Adobe does offer you a starting point if you don't have a standard in place in your company when you begin to create PDF forms. In many organizations, you'll be wise to set up a custom standard to accommodate your individual forms needs. If you're at a loss for creating a new schema, the PFN files are available to you; however, there may be solutions you can implement that will better suit your needs.

Designing a PFN-compatible form can be handled in one of two ways. If your authoring program supports the import of EPS (Encapsulated PostScript) files, you can import the individual files for form fields. In an authoring program, you can import individual files for each field. Open the folder named EPS that resides in the PFN folder on the Acrobat installer CD-ROM and you find a number of EPS files. Each file corresponds to the field names on the `pfnform.pdf` document. The files are named with the first character of the field names and the first character after each period. For example, a field name like `business.telephone.voice.number` is named `btvn.eps` for the corresponding EPS file.

When you import one of the EPS files in your authoring application, the field may appear invisible when deselected, depending on the authoring program you use.

In some programs, no border is defined for the field appearance. Therefore, you need to use guidelines in such authoring applications and select an imported field to see the selection handles in order to position the fields on your form. An example of designing a form in Adobe PageMaker appears in Figure 15-3.

If you design a form using the PFN standard, be certain to import the PFN logo. The logo is available in the PFN folder in both PDF and EPS formats. The design in Figure 15-3 uses several EPS files for individual fields and the PFN logo imported from the EPS file in the PFN folder.

When the file is exported to PDF, either through a direct export or by printing PostScript and then distilling the file in Acrobat Distiller, the fields are created along with the PDF conversion. When you open the form in Acrobat and select the Form tool, you can see the fields as they were positioned in the original design, as shown in Figure 15-4.

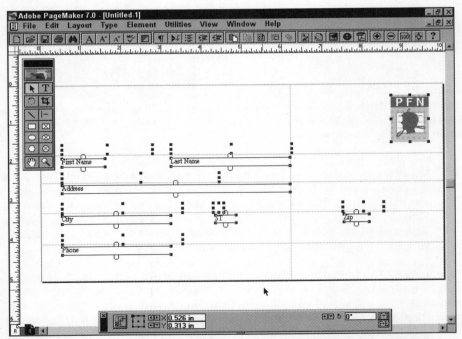

Figure 15-3: In a program such as Adobe PageMaker, the EPS files are invisible unless they are selected. When selected, handles appear around each field displaying the size and position of the field.

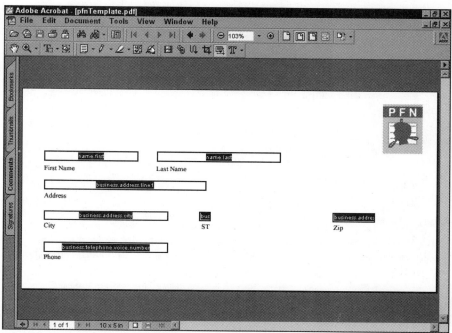

Figure 15-4: After exporting to PDF and opening the file in Acrobat, the form fields are created along with the PDF conversion.

What makes all this work are the EPS file imports and the code associated with the individual EPS files. Each of the EPS files can be opened in a text editor in which you can examine the code, as shown in Figure 15-5. The files contain pdfmark annotations written in the PostScript language. A pdfmark annotation can append data and design elements to a PDF file when an authoring document is converted to PDF or distilled with Acrobat Distiller. If you wish to add your own edits to the files, you can edit the code, however, you'll need to be familiar with the PostScript language. A reference manual is available in your Acrobat Help folder when Acrobat is installed on your computer. To see the Pdfmark Reference manual, choose File ⇨ Open in Adobe Acrobat. Find the Help folder on your hard drive inside the Acrobat folder and open it. Inside this folder is another folder named ENU. Open this folder and select `pdfmark.pdf` and click on the Open button in the Open dialog box. The Pdfmark Reference manual opens. The reference manual provides instructions for writing pdfmark annotations.

A second method for using the PFN standard and naming fields with the same names as the PFNFORM.PDF file is to copy the form fields from the PFNFORM.PDF file and paste them into your form in Acrobat. The form field names remain consistent between the original copied fields and the pasted fields. This method may be easier because you can see the form field rectangles and won't need to work with fields that are invisible until selected.

```
BAC.EPS - WordPad                                              _ □ ✕
File   Edit   View   Insert   Format   Help

 %!PS-Adobe-3.0 EPSF-3.0
 %%BoundingBox: 0 0 216 18

 systemdict /pdfmark known not {userdict /pdfmark systemdict /cleartomark get put } if

 [      /T (business.address.city)
        /Subtype /Widget
        /FT /Tx
        /Rect [ 0 0 216 18]
        /F 4
        /BS << /S /S /W 1 >>
        /MK <<
              /BC [ 1 0 0 ]
              /BG [ 1 1 1 ]
            >>
 /ANN pdfmark

 %EOF

For Help, press F1                                                  NUM
```

Figure 15-5: The EPS files inside the PFN folder use PostScript code in the form of pdfmark annotations to create the form fields when a file is converted to PDF.

Cross-Reference For more on copying and pasting fields between PDF documents, see Chapter 5, "Creating Form Fields."

Tip The `pfnform.pdf` file contains an extensive number of different fields. You may find that you only use a small number of fields in your own designs. You can create your own template using the fields that match your designs and copy and paste these fields in new designs. Create a button field and import the PDF version of the PFN logo on your template, and you can copy/paste this field along with the data fields.

Working with Government Forms

There exists perhaps no greater collection of PDF forms than what has been developed by the U.S. federal government agencies. Add to these forms all state, county, and city government forms in the United States and the numbers rise to extraordinary proportions. In addition, many countries outside the United States are using PDF forms in their government offices. Government and PDF are joined together with a tight knot.

As an end user who works outside government employment, you will eventually find a need to complete a form and submit it to a government office. As an employee of the government, you may be called upon to create a form for the constituency and make the form accessible via a government Web site. This section addresses the needs of users to complete government forms, why government PDF forms are increasing, and some considerations for designs related to forms you commonly see in government.

Reducing and eliminating paper in government

The popularity of PDF forms in U.S. federal government may be due in part to legislation the U.S. Legislature has enacted over the past few years. The U.S. federal government put into law the Paperwork Reduction Act of 1995, which was designed to change various methods of information collection by the U.S. federal government. The law essentially specified provisions for information collection by government agencies. For documents that were solicited from a body of ten or more people, the government is required to make available alternative choices for collection of information among which include electronic transmission of information. These efforts were designed to reduce the amount of paper collected by federal agencies.

In October 1998, the U.S. Legislature passed into law the Government Paper Elimination Act (GPEA). The GPEA amended the earlier Paper Reduction Act to require the Director of Office and Management and Budget (OMB) to promote the use of alternative technologies for collecting information as a substitute for paper submissions. The impact of the legislation extends to individuals, small businesses, educational and nonprofit institutions, federal contractors, state, local, and tribal governments, and other persons where collection of information is made by or for the U.S. federal government.

Compliance with the law is anyone's guess. You may or may not have been impacted by the legislation in your work. What's important to understand is that the U.S. Legislature has been keenly aware of a need to find alternative methods that seriously reduce the millions of pounds of paper collected by government agencies annually in the United Sates, and I suspect you'll see standards developed at the federal level that will filter down to state and local government offices. If your work is related to U.S. federal government contracting, you can expect to see a growing interest in adhering to compliance with the new laws.

For PDF forms authors, there now exists many opportunities to work with agencies that need to comply with existing legislation and legislation you can expect to see to further reduce government use of paper. As the government plans their methods for implementing the law, those of you who offer consulting services may find new opportunities with the vast number of organizations impacted by federal law.

Filling in government forms

The thing I find most astonishing with government forms is that most forms you find from the U.S. federal, state, and local government offices are often no more than authored documents converted to PDF. The forms themselves carry no fields or methods for completing the form in an Acrobat viewer. What's more astonishing is many local government offices host these kinds of forms on Web sites and require you to complete the form on a typewriter. Has anyone seen a typewriter recently?

As a constituent, you may upon occasion need to complete a form from a government office and fill in the fields on your computer. For Acrobat forms that have no form fields, you have three options. You can add text with the TouchUp Text tool and move the text to fit a field box with the TouchUp Object tool. You can add your own field boxes and enter text in the fields you create. Finally, you can import a form into another program better suited for adding text to a document. Of these three options, you'll find importing a PDF in a program like Adobe PageMaker a much easier solution for completing forms when no data fields exist. In Figure 15-6, a form is imported into Adobe PageMaker where text is created with PageMaker's Text tool.

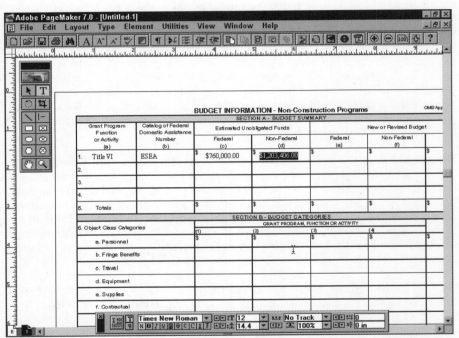

Figure 15-6: You can import PDF forms into other programs to fill in fields that were not included in the original PDF form.

Although a bit awkward, importing PDF forms into other programs to fill out the data fields will often be a much easier task than trying to find a typewriter and adjusting a form to fit the typewriter carriage. When government forms require typewritten responses, you can implement this work-around in layout and illustration programs supporting PDF imports. If you work with the same form many times over, then a better solution would be to take the time to add form fields in Acrobat.

Working with Comb forms

Government and educational institutions sometimes use Comb forms, although they are not necessarily exclusive to these organizations. A Comb form contains Comb fields with individual boxes designed to hold a single character representing a field along a row. Each character in and of itself is a separate field, but is intended to be a part of a larger field, for example, a name field broken up into individual characters. These forms were popularized in earlier data processing days where punch machines and data entry operators transposed data to electronic systems. They still exist and you can find many different forms, especially government tax forms, designed in this fashion. As an example, look at Figure 15-7.

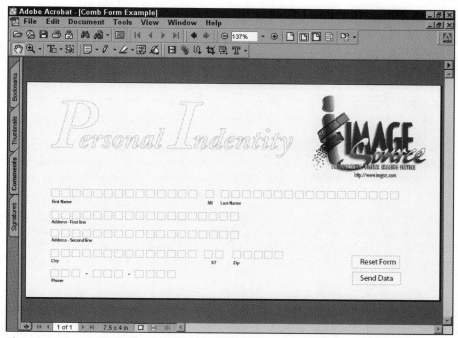

Figure 15-7: Comb forms have individual field boxes designed to hold single characters to collectively represent larger data fields.

Frequently you'll find a few fields on a form that have a similar design, such as the form shown in Figure 15-8. If you design forms with such fields, you'll want the end user to easily complete the form without having to manually tab through each field box. Additionally, you may want the data extracted from the form to be represented as a single string of data instead of separate data fields.

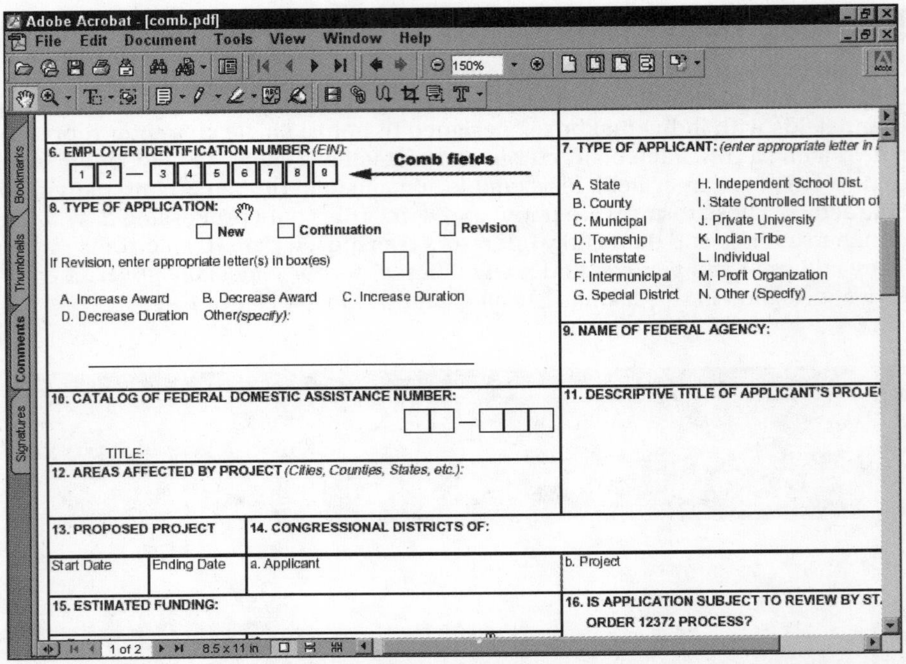

Figure 15-8: Some forms, especially those used in government, use individual field boxes to hold single characters, commonly called "Combs" or "Comb fields."

If you design forms with Comb fields, you have a choice for how to script the fields to make it easy on the end user to fill in your form. Rather than have a user tab through each field individually, you can let a JavaScript do the tabbing for the user. There are two ways to approach the way you script forms like the ones shown in Figures 15-7 and 15-8.

Scripting a single field

If your form contains only a few fields that require individual field boxes to represent a given response on a form like the one shown in Figure 15-8, you can add a single script to the Format properties for each field that auto tabs to the next field after a user enters a value in a field box. To create a sequence for auto tabbing through field boxes, follow these steps:

1. Create a text field for the first field box. In the Options properties, set the Alignment to Center and the character limit to 1, as shown in Figure 15-9.

2. Click on the Format tab.

3. Click Custom and click Edit adjacent to Custom Keystroke Script to open the JavaScript Edit dialog box.

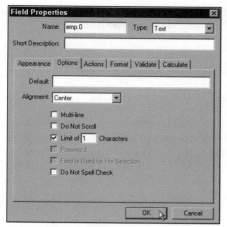

Figure 15-9: Select Center for Alignment and 1 for Limit of [X] Characters.

4. Enter the following code in the JavaScript Edit dialog box:

```
this.getField('nextFieldName').setFocus();
```

The item denoted as `nextFieldName` is the name of the next field to which the cursor jumps. In the example, the field name is `emp.1`. Thus, the code appears as shown in the Custom Keystroke Script in Figure 15-10.

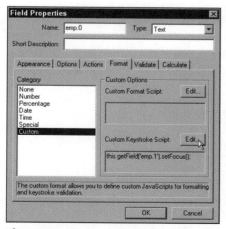

Figure 15-10: Open the Field Properties dialog box and select Custom. Click on Edit and enter the JavaScript code to jump to the next field. Click OK in the JavaScript Edit dialog box and the code appears when you return to the Field Properties dialog box.

5. Repeat the same steps for all fields represented with individual boxes. In each script, be certain to identify the field name for the next field.

6. When you arrive at the last field in the row, be certain to set the field name for the next logical field in your tab order. In this example, the next field is named type.0. Therefore, the code for the last field is:

```
this.getField('type.0').setFocus();
```

When the user enters the first field and types a character, the cursor moves to the next field automatically. When the user enters a character in the last field in the row, the cursor jumps to the next field in the next row.

Scripting multiple fields

If you have a form like the one that was shown previously in Figure 15-7, in which the entire form uses Comb fields, you may wish to use another approach. In the following example, you can use a Document Level JavaScript and use the JavaScript function in the code that is written in the Format properties:

1. Open the file personalIdentity.pdf from the Chapter 15 folder on the book's CD-ROM.

On the CD-ROM   You'll find the personalIdentity.pdf file in the Chapter 15 folder on the book's CD-ROM.

2. Add a document level JavaScript by choosing Tools ⇨ JavaScript ⇨ Document JavaScripts.

3. Enter **nextField** for the script name (or a name of personal choice) and click on the Add button.

4. In the JavaScript edit dialog box, enter

```
function nextField() {

try{
var fieldName = event.target.name.split(".");
var counter = fieldName[1];
var next = fieldName[0] + "." + ++counter;
var nextField = this.getField(next);
if (nextField != undefined)
 return nextField;
else
 return this.getField(fieldName[0] + "." + 1);
 }
catch(e) { app.alert(e); }
}
```

This script loops through all individual fields for each set of fields with a common parent name on the form. In the example, firstname.N is used for the first name fields. N is the child value for the fields and used in this example as firstName.1, firstName.2, and so on. The first line of code splits the parent/child name and is followed by the loop that loops through all the child values to the end of the row. If the field contents are not defined (! = undefined), the next field is returned (jump to next field). The try/catch statements are used to catch exceptions.

5. Create a text form field for the first field and set the Options properties like the example earlier for the character alignment, and limit for the number of characters.

6. Click on the Format tab and click Custom. Click Edit and enter the following code in the JavaScript Edit dialog box.

```
nextField().setFocus();
```

7. Notice the code uses the JavaScript function (nextField). All fields on the form use the same code in the Format Properties dialog box.

8. Duplicate the field by clicking the field and pressing Ctrl (Windows) or Option (Mac OS). Add the Shift key to constrain the movement and drag to the right.

9. The field is duplicated. Press the + (plus) key on your keyboard to increment the field name. In this example, the field name changes from firstName.1 to firstName.2. Continue duplicating fields and changing the name for each field in the group.

Tip   Because the same script is used in the format properties for all fields, you do not need to return to the Field Properties dialog box each time a field is duplicated. You can either manually duplicate fields or create a table array to populate all the individual fields that represent a larger field. By using the JavaScript function, you can quickly create a Comb form.

10. Create the first field in the next group and add the same script for the Format properties. Be certain to use parent/child names and add a script, as described in the previous exercise, to jump to the next group for each field at the end of a given group.

Converting individual field data to strings

You may have a need to collect all the data from individual fields and assemble the data into single strings. Figure 15-11 shows the personal identity form that is populated with data in individual fields.

If you want to take some of the fields and populate a new form and transpose data into single fields, you need to add a new JavaScript. The script needs to loop through all the fields for a given parent name and assemble the data into single string values, as shown in Figure 15-12.

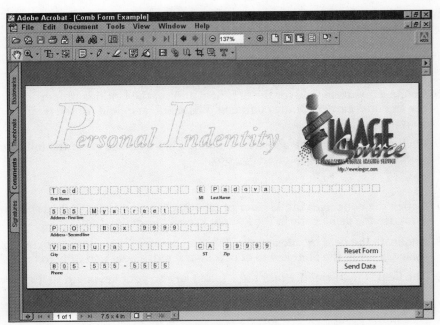

Figure 15-11: After creating the fields, the data was entered on the form.

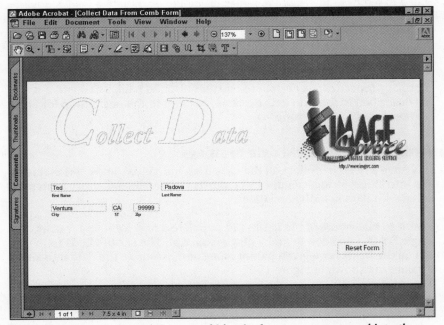

Figure 15-12: Data from the personal identity form was transposed into the data collection form. The data from individual fields are assembled into strings.

On the personal identity form, a button is created to open the `collectData.pdf` form that you'll find in the Chapter 15 folder on the book's CD-ROM. When the button is selected, the second form opens and the data strings are assembled. To create a button to produce this effect, follow these steps:

On the CD-ROM

You'll find the `collectData.pdf` form in the Chapter 15 folder on the book's CD-ROM.

1. Create a button field and open the JavaScript Edit dialog box.

2. Add the following code in the JavaScript Edit dialog box:

```
if (app.viewerVersion < 5)
app.alert("Version 5.0 required. Some features will not
work.");
else {
 this.slave = app.openDoc("collectIdentity.pdf", this);
 slave.bringToFront();
}
{
for (var i = 1,
 newFirstName = "firstName." + i,
 str = ""; i <= 14; i++, newFirstName = "firstName." + i)
str += this.getField(newFirstName).value;
this.slave.getField("first.name").value = str;
}
{
for (var i = 1,
 newLastName = "lastName." + i,
 str = " "; i <= 17; i++, newLastName = "lastName." + i)
str += this.getField(newLastName).value;
this.slave.getField("last.name").value = str;
}
{
for (var i = 1,
 newCity = "city." + i,
 str = ""; i <= 14; i++, newCity = "city." + i)
str += this.getField(newCity).value;
this.slave.getField("city").value = str;
}
{
for (var i = 1,
 newState = "state." + i,
 str = ""; i <= 2; i++, newState = "state." + i)
str += this.getField(newState).value;
this.slave.getField("state").value = str;
}
{
for (var i = 1,
 newZip = "zip." + i,
 str = ""; i <= 5; i++, newZip = "zip." + i)
str += this.getField(newZip).value;
this.slave.getField("zip").value = str;
}
```

3. The script runs a series of loops to loop through each of the fields being assembled. The first loop to assemble the first name gets the parent name for the first name fields. The last two lines of code beginning with `str +=` assemble the string and place the value in the slave document field for the first name field (`this.slave.getField("first.name").value = str;`).The subsequent loops create the strings for the remaining fields on the collect data form.

Working with Legal Forms

A close runner-up to government in terms of paper accumulation is the legal industry. The use of PDF files in law practices should be obvious when you think of the research and need for finding information relative to a legal issue. Using Acrobat Catalog and creating indexes can be a tremendous help in law when precise information are searched and the results need to be returned fast.

With regard to forms in the legal industry, there are almost as many different kinds of legal forms available as you find in government. Whether you're a legal professional or a consumer in need of a legal form that you intend to initiate yourself, you can find forms for almost any legal action readily available on the Internet or through purchase of low-cost software.

Forms for legal professionals

Legal professionals can find forms usually in either PDF or Microsoft Word formats on the Internet. There are non-profit organizations, law firms, universities, courts and government, and special interest sites hosting forms for just about any court action or legal dispute. The PDF forms you download from the Internet are often much like those found on government sites. These forms don't contain data fields; therefore, completing a form needs to be handled much like the government forms mentioned earlier.

Legal forms are easily found on the Internet by invoking a search using keywords such as "legal forms, PDF and legal forms, legal forms Wisconsin, legal forms Alabama," and so on. The number of hits from your search in a Web browser will satisfy your need for just about any kind of form you desire.

When downloading a PDF form to be completed electronically, there is one precaution with which you need be concerned. Be certain the form you download is not secure so you can either add data fields or import a form in an application to add the necessary text to complete the form. If a PDF file is protected with Acrobat Security, you won't be able to import the form in another program.

If you view PDFs in a Web browser with online viewing so the PDF appears inside the browser window, you can check the security before saving the file to your hard drive. Click on the right pointing arrow in the browser window to open the fly-out palette shown in Figure 15-13. From the menu options, select Document Security.

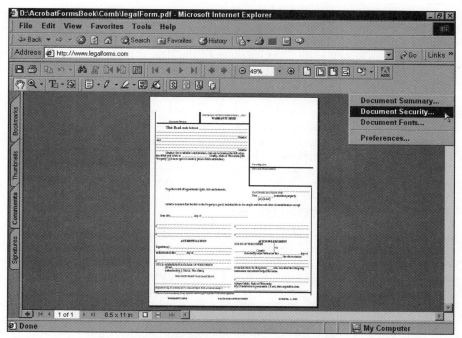

Figure 15-13: Click on the right pointing arrow to open the fly-out menu and select Document Security from the menu options.

A dialog box opens on top of the Document Pane in the Web browser window. From the security settings you can see if the document is secure. In Figure 15-14, the Security Method is None, indicating the PDF file is not secure.

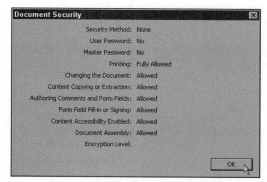

Figure 15-14: A dialog box opens, displaying the current security settings that have been applied to the document.

You can also view the status bar in the Acrobat window inside the Web browser in order to determine if security is used. If you see a *key* displayed in the status bar, you'll know the document is secure. However, the key alone won't tell you the level of encryption or specifically what security settings have been applied. Click on the key to open the Document Security dialog box, then click on Display Settings to see the same dialog box shown previously in Figure 15-14.

When you find a form and wish to download it for later use, click on the Save button in the Acrobat toolbar inside the Web browser window. The icon appearing as a floppy disk in the top left corner of the Acrobat toolbar is the Save as Copy button that appears identical in all Acrobat viewers. If using the Acrobat Reader software, you can save a copy to disk of the file viewed in the Web browser.

Legal forms for consumers

There may be situations in which you need a "boilerplate" form for a business transaction or personal legal issue. Be advised that you may wish to consult with your attorney if you have the slightest doubt about the legality of forms you use and whether they properly address the issue at hand.

In some circumstances, you may just need a little help with the word use and design for a form that you need to employ for a given situation. You can find many forms on the Internet to suit your own personal and business needs for these purposes and you can also find low-cost software packages for less than $20 at computer stores. Most of the software used for legal forms is in Microsoft Word format.

If you find a software CD-ROM loaded with personal and business forms that you wish to convert to PDF, open the file in Microsoft Word and use the Convert to Adobe PDF tool from Word's menu bar, as shown in Figure 15-15.

The PDFMaker Macro installed with Acrobat, which was discussed in Chapter 2, "Using Authoring Applications," converts the document from Microsoft Office applications to PDF such as the form that appears in Figure 15-16. Once in PDF form, you can add fields and use the form like any other PDF document you use for forms. Obviously, the advantage of creating a form with fields in Acrobat may be for those kinds of forms you frequently use such as board actions for small corporations, notices, lease agreements, credit inquires, and so on.

Working with Enterprise Markets

The eForms solutions provided by Adobe Systems in part offer you Acrobat core technology that has been the subject of this book. Acrobat and the Acrobat related products are tools supporting many of your creation and distribution needs. New directions for Adobe Systems that are likely to impact you as a forms designer are extending core Acrobat solutions to enterprise markets where forms design, connecting forms to databases, and routing forms between users embrace additional tools and solutions.

Recognizing the pivotal importance of database access in business applications, Adobe decided to incorporate database connectivity into Acrobat with the release of version 5.0. Thanks to Acrobat JavaScript's new ADBC (Acrobat DataBase Connectivity) plug-in, it's now possible (in Windows only) to create JavaScript-powered PDF forms that present a user-friendly "front end" to relational database systems. Extremely powerful PDF database applications are possible because of the *SQL binding* built into ADBC. (SQL stands for Structured Query Language, the lingua franca of data retrieval.) It's safe to say that ADBC gives an enormous boost to PDF at the enterprise level, because of the critical importance of database access in business.

Unfortunately, database connectivity is an unavoidably elaborate subject, and a comprehensive discussion of how ADBC works would fill a book by itself. In the pages that follow, I don't have room to present anything more than an abbreviated overview of ADBC concepts.

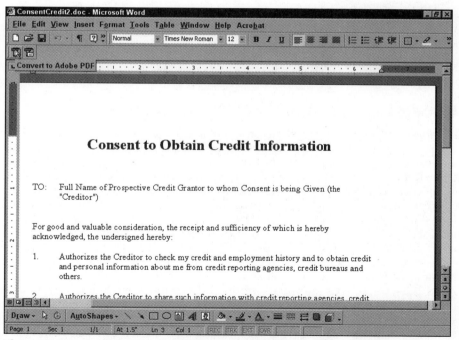

Figure 15-15: For form templates in Microsoft Word format, use the Convert to Adobe PDF tool in Microsoft Word to convert the document to a PDF file.

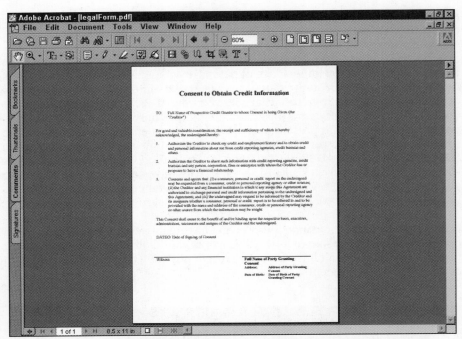

Figure 15-16: Once converted to PDF, the form is opened in an Acrobat viewer where the form fields are added.

Understanding ADBC basic architecture

It's important to get an overall understanding of how database access via ADBC works. ADBC, which requires Acrobat as well as the ADBC.api plug-in (installed automatically with the Acrobat Installer), works in a manner similar to Microsoft's Open DataBase Connectivity (ODBC) model. Under the ODBC model, databases created in diverse software environments can be manipulated via a standard, platform-independent application programming interface (API), using *drivers* (software utilities with no user interface) whose purpose is to handle proprietary interactions behind the scenes so that the database user doesn't have to worry about anything but ODBC-defined behaviors. Almost all database software vendors offer ODBC drivers for their databases, so that any given database can be "reached" by multiple users on multiple platforms, using multiple (diverse) host programs. ADBC likewise isolates the end user from the ugly low-level details of dealing with many types of relational databases, exposing only a common set of features via a common interface. With ADBC (as with ODBC), you can "reach into" a relational database using ordinary SQL queries. As long as you know Structured Query Language, and as long as your database is accessible via a suitable ODBC driver, it doesn't matter whose software created the database, or on what machine. Typically, the drivers are installed when you install an application under Windows.

Acrobat JavaScript defines several objects that play an essential role in database connectivity:

✦ **ADBC Object.** This object has two methods, called `getDataSourceList()` and `newConnection()`. The former returns an array containing a `DataSourceInfo` object (see below) for every available database in the system. The `newConnection()` method allows you to obtain a Connection object that defines session behavior.

✦ **DataSourceInfo Object.** This object, returned by the ADBC object's `getDataSourceList()` method, has just two properties, `name` and `description`. These properties contain strings describing a given DSN (Data Source Name), or database.

✦ **Connection Object.** The Connection object encapsulates session behavior. It provides methods for creating Statement objects (see below), enumerating tables, and enumerating column lists within tables.

✦ **Statement Object.** The Statement object allows you to execute SQL queries against a database and get column and row information of various sorts, plus inspect `columnCount` and `rowCount` status values generated by SQL calls.

✦ **Column Object.** The Column object, which is returned by the `getColumn()` method of the Statement object, encapsulates data associated with a particular column in a given row in a table. The `name` and `value` properties of this object are useful in identifying data of interest.

✦ **ColumnInfo Object.** This object holds basic information (such as name, description, data type, and so on) about a particular column in a table. The `getColumnList()` method of the Connection object returns an array of ColumnInfo objects.

✦ **Row Object.** The Row object is returned by the `getRow()` method of the Statement object. It has one property, the `columnArray` property, which points to an array of Column objects.

✦ **TableInfo Object.** This object is returned by the `getTableList()` method of the Connection object. It holds general information about a table within a database, such as the name of the table and a short description (if available).

At first view, this may seem like a rather complicated list, but in fact each object is just a wrapper for some very basic database-related features, and the relationships between objects are actually quite natural and intuitive.

Bear in mind that the whole point of connecting to a database via ADBC is to be able to make queries via SQL. Everything you do will ultimately be aimed at this goal. Through SQL, you can do just about any kind of database manipulation that you may need to do, whether it involves reading *or* writing data. Obviously, a detailed discussion of SQL basics is beyond the scope of this book and you should consult a good SQL text if you need to know more about that subject.

Understanding DSNs

In order for a database to be visible to ADBC, it must be available under a Data Source Name (DSN) on your system. The DSN is simply an arbitrary string that associates a given database file (which could be a file created by Microsoft Access, Microsoft Excel, say, or Sybase Adaptive Server Anywhere, and so on) with a given ODBC driver. The DSN may be a User DSN (in which case it will be "visible" only to you, on your machine) or a System DSN (in which case all users of your system can see the database, even across networks). Either one works for ADBC.

On Windows machines, you can assign DSNs to database files using the ODBC Data Source utility in the Control Panels folder. On the Mac OS, current implementation of ODBC is not yet available.

Examining a quick code example

Just so you can take a peek at the whole process of using ADBC, let's run through a quick code example that gets information from a known data source. We will assume that a DSN by the name of "MyTestDB" exists on the local machine. In addition, we'll assume that you want to inspect the first available table in MyTestDB so as to develop a list of all the column names in that table. The goal will be to display all column names in an alert dialog box. You can do all this in about eight lines of JavaScript (if we sacrifice error-checking code in the name of clarity):

```
var myConnection =
 ADBC.newConnection("MyTestDB");// open a connection
var myTables = myConnection.getTableList(); // get table info
var theTableName = myTables[0].name; // get name of first table
              // now obtain column info for that table:
var myColumnList = myConnection.getColumnList(theTableName);
// prepare a list of names of columns
var theNames = "";
for (var i = 0; i < myColumnList.length; i++)
theNames += myColumnList[i].name + "\r";
app.alert(theNames); // display the names
```

The easiest way to test this code is to type it into the JavaScript Console window, select all the text, then hit the Enter key on the numeric keypad. Assuming you have a database on your system that's registered under the DSN "MyTestDB," you should see an alert window (perhaps similar to Figure 15-17) pop up, which contains the column headings for all columns in the first table of that database. Each column name will be on a separate line.

Let's look at what was accomplished. First, you opened a connection to the database with `ADBC.newConnection()`. Then you called the connection's `getTableList()` method, which simply returns a JavaScript array containing `TableInfo` Objects corresponding to all the tables in "MyTestDB." Since we're only interested in the first table, you inspect the `zeroth` item of the array, specifically the `name` property of that item. You need the table name as an argument to the `Connection` object's `getColumnList()` method. Once you've called the `getColumnList()` method, you have an array of `ColumnInfo` objects stored in a local variable, `myColumnList`. What we're interested in is the `name` property of each `ColumnInfo` object. To get those names, you must iterate through all members of the `ColumnInfo` array; hence the `"for i"` loop, which concatenates names (and carriage returns) into a single string. Finally, you display the string in an alert dialog box.

Figure 15-17: The result of the "Quick Code Example" displays all column names of the first table in MyTestDB.

Obtaining data via an SQL query

The previous code example is a good one if you don't know the name of the first table in your database nor the names of the columns in that table. But in reality, you probably *will* know the name of the table (and the names of the columns) if you are going to execute SQL queries of the type:

```
SELECT Name, Address, City, State FROM "Customers"
```

In this query, for example, we're interested in obtaining data from the columns named "Name," "Address," "City," and "State" in the table called "Customers." It's a little awkward (though by no means impossible) to construct a statement like this programmatically, in JavaScript, using table and column names looked up at runtime. Real-world SQL statements tend to use hard-coded values for things like column and table names.

So let's pose a slightly different problem. Suppose you want to execute the above SQL query against the Customers table of MyTestDB (which may or may not be the first table in that database). How can you do that in JavaScript? You start, as before, by opening a connection to the database:

```
var myConnection =
  ADBC.newConnection("MyTestDB");// open a connection
```

Next, you have to create a Statement object:

```
var myStatement =
  myConnection.newStatement();// create Statement object
```

For convenience, you'll store the SQL query as a JavaScript string. Notice that you escape the quotation marks around the table name using backslashes:

```
var mySQL = "SELECT Name, Address, City, State FROM
\"Customers\"";
```

Finally, you execute the query:

```
myStatement.execute(mySQL);
```

What does this statement actually do? It tells the JavaScript interpreter to go ask the ODBC driver to query the database and obtain a *result set*, which in this case consists of the requested columns from all rows in the table. The returned data set becomes part of the Statement object. How do you get at each row of data? This is where it gets a bit tricky. You have to ask for each row of data in the following way:

```
var success = myStatement.nextRow(); // returns a Boolean
if (success)
  var myRowObject = myStatement.getRow();
```

The Statement object's nextRow() method must *always* be called before processing any row of data (even the first row). But the return value from nextRow() is just a Boolean value indicating whether the next row could be obtained. (Maybe it doesn't exist.) If the next row does exist and is obtainable, you must then call getRow() to obtain it as a Row object. In the above case, you store the returned Row object in the local variable myRowObject. To loop through all available Row objects in the result set, you could set up a while loop that looks something like:

```
while(myStatement.nextRow() == true) {
myRowObject = myStatement.getRow();
// ... do something with the data
}// end of loop
```

Working with row objects

At this point you may be wondering how to get at the column data obtained via an SQL query. If you're guessing that this data may be reachable via the Row object, you're right. The Row object, as the name implies, contains all the information in a single row of data (consistent with any constraints you may have imposed in your SQL statement). Every Row object has a columnArray property, which is just a JavaScript array filled with Column objects (see Table 15-1).

Table 15-1 Column Object Properties		
Property	**Access**	**Description**
ColumnNum	R	The number that identifies the column's place in the Statement from which the Column was obtained.
Name	R	The name of the column.
Type	R	The SQL Type (data type) of the data. This can be one of 19 predefined types (documented in AcroJS.pdf).
TypeName	R	A database-dependent string that represents the data type. This property may give useful information about user-defined data types.
Value	R/W	The value of the data in the column in whatever format in which the data was originally received.

To iterate through the column values contained in one row of table data, you can do something like the following. Remember that because the columnArray is just an ordinary JavaScript array, it has a length property.

```
var theColumns = myRowData.columnArray; // get column array
for (var i = 0; i < theColumns.length; i++) // loop over length
{
if (theColumns[i].name == "Name")
// do something with theColumns[i].value
if (theColumns[i].name == "Address")
// do something with theColumns[i].value
// etc.
}
```

In many cases, of course, it will be simpler (if you know the column names) just to grab values directly from columns by name. It turns out that although the Row object begins life with just one property, the columnArray, it has additional properties after a result set has been returned to a Statement object. The additional properties are Column objects that have names corresponding to the headings of the columns you requested. So, in the above example, you can alternatively do:

```
var customerAddress = myRowData.Address.value;
// ... do something with customerAddress
var customerCity = myRowData.City.value;
// ... do something with customerCity
// etc.
```

To summarize: The SQL statement generated Row objects, which you must access using `nextRow()` and `getRow()`. Each Row object has multiple Column objects attached as properties, and those properties have names like "Name," "Address," "City," and so on. Because each property refers to a Column object, you must use the `value` property to find the object's data value. (Simple, right?)

Don't worry too much right now if this all seems confusing. It will begin to crystallize for you as you begin working with live code. If all this still sounds beyond your reach, try to employ services of programmers familiar with SQL and ODBC. A little individualized tutorial training will greatly help advance your skills.

Of course, in the space available here we've only been able to scrape a small handful of frost off a very large iceberg. As you know if you've developed database applications before, crafting well-behaved, reliable, user-friendly database management forms is a difficult challenge (particularly in an HTTP environment, in which session state is difficult to track). A great deal of thought and effort need to be devoted to things like user interface design, data validation, error checking, security administration, state management, transaction management (via SQL "commit" and "rollback" verbs), and so on. What PDF brings to this picture is an opportunity for the database application designer to take advantage of exceptional graphic appeal, security, application stability, cross-platform interoperability, and programming power (via Acrobat JavaScript) in database forms that may otherwise be far too unwieldy to implement in HTML, far too sluggish-performing in Java, or far too platform-dependent in a 4GL (fourth-generation language) application. With Acrobat 5.0, it can truly be said that new opportunities await the JavaScript forms developer.

For novice users where access to databases is within much smaller proportions and smaller data files, you can use an alternative and much easier solution. Acrobat 5 also enables you to import delimited data with much less complex coding. The disadvantage of using text files for data management becomes more than apparent when the number of records exceeds a few hundred. Acrobat slows down significantly with larger database files imported via the Import Data command. However, for smaller files, where managing a few hundred records is concerned, you can write effective routines with much greater ease.

Cross-Reference To see examples of JavaScript routines in which data are imported into forms from database files, refer to Chapter 16, "Creating Forms for Real-World Uses."

In terms of enterprise solutions, much development is in progress both within Adobe Systems and from third-party developers to offer products facilitating Acrobat core technology tied to existing databases in corporate environments. If your background is not extensive in programming expertise, your first task is to understand that you can indeed tie Acrobat forms to databases through ADBC connectivity. Once understood, you can solicit help from knowledgeable programmers to assist you with individual solutions. Above all, don't become frustrated by all the technical talk mentioned above. What you don't understand can be overcome by obtaining help from knowledgeable programmers.

Summary

✦ Acrobat-related products are among the fastest growing solutions that are provided by Adobe Systems. A substantial part of the Acrobat market and Adobe Systems' focus is related to PDF forms.

✦ One of the largest markets for PDF forms is the U.S. federal government. With recent enacted legislation, the government is making a strong effort to reduce paper in favor of electronic document routing.

✦ The U.S. legal market is a potential target for introducing more PDF forms usage. Legal forms are prolific on the Internet, and dedicated software packages offer solutions for creating personal and small business legal forms.

✦ ADBC (Acrobat Database Connectivity) opens up new vistas for form designers in enterprise environments by allowing easy, cross-platform access to relational databases. Using JavaScript, you can design sophisticated PDF forms that execute SQL queries against databases—a truly exciting and powerful capability.

✦   ✦   ✦

Creating Forms for Real-World Uses

If you've read through all the preceding pages and understood most of what has been covered, you should be able to tackle almost any kind of Acrobat form job. Creating PDF forms for personal, business, or enterprise use requires some knowledge about the technical mechanics on how to use Acrobat for authoring a form; however, more than the technical skill, you need an imagination. In this chapter, I'll try to summarize much of what has been covered in all earlier chapters and attempt to offer a little imagination for creating forms to suit different purposes. Whether you use a form discussed in this chapter is not as important as freeing up your imagination and perhaps gaining ideas for similar kinds of forms you may use for your own purposes.

Creating Personal Management Forms

In the category of personal management forms, I examine forms that can be used for some personal needs. Managing documents and files, and organizing personal information, and so on is what is discussed in this chapter. There are no doubt thousands of different kinds of forms you can create to manage some information in your home or office. Try to think about the hassles you experience and what solutions may be needed to minimize those hassles. In the following three examples, I offer a few suggestions for overcoming some aggravations I have personally experienced, and I explain how Acrobat forms provided solutions. Let's have a little fun adding some flair to the form designs for PDF documents you can use for personal needs.

All sample forms for this chapter are nested in subfolders inside the Chapter 16 folder on the book's CD-ROM. To easily find the forms addressed in each section, open the folder corresponding to the section name. For example, the first section of this chapter is Creating Personal Management Forms. Find the corresponding sample forms in the Personal Management folder inside the Chapter 16 folder.

Password security form

One major hassle for me is trying to keep track of all the passwords I use for work and leisure activity. Log on to a Web site just to poke around a source for purchasing products, and the Web service wants you to submit a password just to browse their Web pages. So I enter a six-character password, move to another site, and it requires seven characters; the next site requires six alpha characters and a number. Some sites send me a password in an e-mail. I log on to beta test sites and they send me my own personal logon and password. When all is said and done, I have more logon names and passwords than I can ever hope to remember. Because I use three computers for office, home, and on the road, I can't keep all my passwords in any one location.

My solution—create an Acrobat form that I protect with Acrobat Standard Security, and I only need one password to access a catalog of all the passwords I use. I can store my PDF file on my Web site and on all three computers. When I add a new password, I upload it to my Web site and always download the most recent version to any one of my three computers. In this example, I create a page template and use the short JavaScript routine to spawn a page from a template that I discussed in Chapter 9.

Refer to Chapter 9, "Creating Templates and Spawning Pages," for more information.

In this example, we start off with a rather simple form to help organize passwords and serial numbers for software programs. Figure 16-1 shows the opening page when the `passwords.pdf` file from the Personal Management folder inside the Chapter 16 folder on the book's CD-ROM is opened. On the cover page, I have two buttons appearing on the right side of the document page. The top button is used to create a new page from a template and the bottom-right button opens the Find dialog box to search for existing passwords or serial numbers.

You'll find the `passwords.pdf` file in the Chapter 16 Personal Management folder on the book's CD-ROM.

The file contains two pages. When you navigate to page 2, the page appears, as shown in Figure 16-2. This page already has a Web site identified and a password needed to access the site. Beginning at the top of the page, the URL text is a link. When the link is selected, the default Web browser is launched and the site opens in the Web browser. Because the password is accessed easily from the PDF file, you can copy and paste the password or keep the password in view and key it in on the Web site.

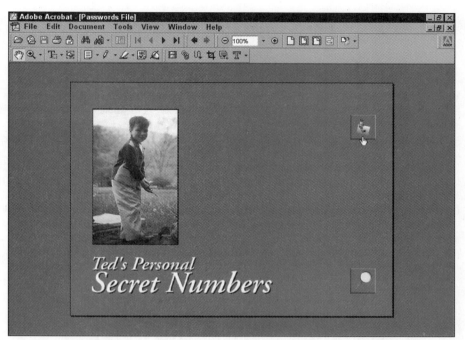

Figure 16-1: The opening page on the passwords.pdf file contains two buttons used for creating new pages and opening the Find dialog box.

Note To open Web links in your Web browser, open the Web Capture Preferences dialog box by choosing Edit ➪ Preferences ➪ Web Capture. In the Web Capture Preferences dialog box, select In Web Browser from the Open Weblinks pull-down menu. If the preference setting is not set to open files in your Web browser, Acrobat converts Web pages to PDFs.

The check boxes on the page are used to easily distinguish a password from a serial number. If the page contains a password, then the Serial Number field can be used to supply a logon name. To create a new page and add a new password or serial number, click on the button in the top-right corner. The JavaScript for this button is coded as follows:

```
this.spawnPageFromTemplate("template");
this.pageNum = this.numPages-1;
var r = [222, 46, 290, 60];
var i = this.pageNum++
var f = this.addField(String(this.pageNum),"text",i,r);
    f.textSize = 14;
    f.alignment = "right";
    f.textColor = color.black;
```

```
f.fillColor = color.transparent;
f.textfont = font.HelvB;
f.borderStyle = border.s;
f.strokeColor = color.transparent;
f.value = util.printd("mm/dd/yy", new Date());
```

We begin with the line of code to spawn a page from a template, as was covered in Chapter 9, "Creating Templates and Spawning Pages." The first two lines of code should be familiar to you if you read Chapter 9. What follows in this example is another section of code used to create a field and add the current date from the computer's clock. Obviously, if your time is not correctly set on your computer, the time entered on the new page reflects a bogus time. The lines of code from the third line to the second-to-last line set the specifications for the field to be added on the spawned page. The last line of code places the current time in the field box after it has been created. The reason this method is used is, if you only use the last line of code, every time the page is opened it reflects a new time. By adding the field and placing the time from the button that spawns the page, the field is time stamped and it won't change each time you open the page.

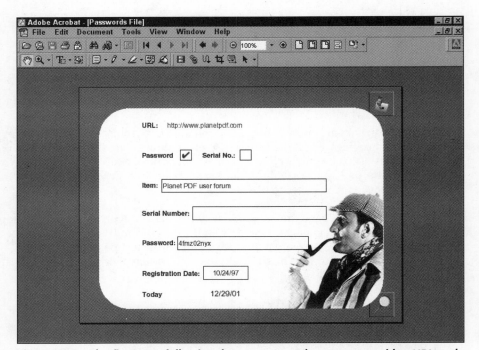

Figure 16-2: The first page following the cover page shows a page with a URL and password to access the Web site. The URL text is a link in the PDF document that launches the default Web browser and takes you to the Web site associated with the link.

The URL on the page is created from the text supplied in the first field on the page. In earlier versions of Acrobat, you had to add raw text to the page with the TouchUp Text tool. If you use an earlier version of Acrobat, create a URL with the TouchUp Text tool and add the complete URL address. After the text has been added in either a field box or with the TouchUp Text tool, choose Tools ⇨ Locate Web Addresses ⇨ Create Web Links from URLs in Text. The Create Web Links dialog box opens, prompting you for the page range where the Web links will be created.

For this kind of form, you'll most likely create a link on the new page added to the file as opposed to creating Web links on all pages. In the Create Web Links dialog box, enter the page number where the link is to be created. Acrobat automatically creates a link rectangle around the text with a hypertext reference to the Web URL specified in the text.

Tip   Acrobat 5.05 supports creating Web links form URLs in text on all text field types, button fields (when text is used for the button face), and Combo boxes. Combo boxes can have only one item in the list used for creating the URL link.

In using a form like this to archive all your passwords and software serial numbers, you can protect the document with Acrobat Standard Security, which was covered in Chapter 11, "Using Acrobat Security". After securing the document, the only way to open the file is to supply the right password. You can leave the file on any computer in your office and be assured your passwords are secure. Furthermore, the only password you need to commit to memory is the password to open the PDF file.

Cross-Reference   Refer to Chapter 11, "Using Acrobat Security," for a discussion of Acrobat Standard Security.

Note   This example can only be used in Acrobat. Creating new pages from template pages is not available to Acrobat Reader or Acrobat Approval users.

File organizer

This example also uses a script to add a field on spawned pages. In this example, we'll add a value to a field on the first spawned page and increment the value for each new field created from spawning additional pages. The form is designed to provide an alternative to a traditional filing system. Rather than using an alpha organization, this method uses numeric values to organize files. If, for example, you have a collection of journal articles that need to be stored in a file cabinet, it can sometimes be a challenge to remember the name of the article containing the information you want at any given time. By using Acrobat, you can search through a digital file cabinet for content information and find the article you want within seconds.

Rather than alphabetizing the documents in your file cabinet, attach a label to a manila envelope and write the number on the label, the folder flap, or even the article cover page. File the papers numerically in a file cabinet. When you want to retrieve a specific article, open the Acrobat file and search for the article.

When you open the pdfFileCabinet.pdf file from the Chapter 16 Personal Management folder on the book's CD-ROM, the cover page shown in Figure 16-3 appears. The arrow in the lower-right corner links to the second page in the file shown in Figure 16-4.

On the CD-ROM   You'll find the pdfFileCabinet.pdf file in the Chapter 16 Personal Management folder on the book's CD-ROM.

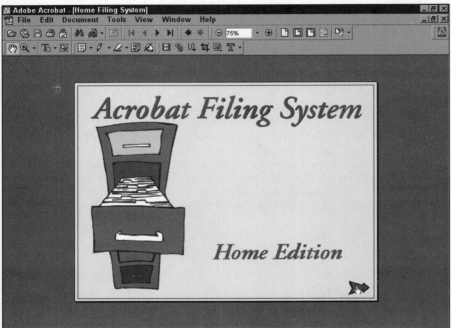

Figure 16-3: The pdfFileCabinet.pdf document has a cover page with a link to the second page in the document. Click on the link and the page in Figure 16-4 opens.

In my example, I use a document acquired from the Internet as the first item in the file cabinet. Note the Location in the top-right corner references file cabinet 1 and the first drawer so I know exactly where my document is located. The Short Description field is used to identify the item, while the Detail field can contain words to help you find the item being searched. All the text in all text fields can be searched with the Find command. In addition to the hard copy, I also have the document as a PDF file stored on a CD-ROM. If I want to retrieve the article, the description tells me what CD contains the document. Furthermore, a Web address provides a URL link in the event I want to return to the Web site and search for additional documents related to the same content or explore the Web site for any updates that may have been uploaded since my last visit.

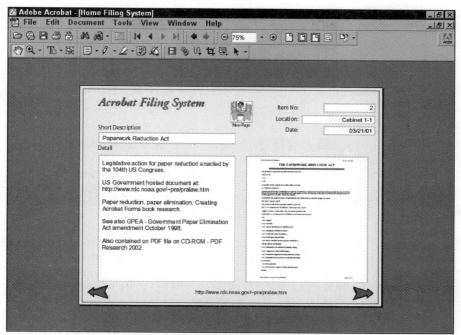

Figure 16-4: The second page in the file pdfFileCabinet.pdf is the first page containing data for the filing system. To add additional pages, click on the New Page icon appearing in the top center of the page.

The image on the right side of the page is a scanned image with a button import as I explained in Chapter 8. If scanning the cover page of an article is too much trouble, you can eliminate the scan and just supply text in the description field.

Cross-Reference Refer to Chapter 8, "Writing JavaScript Routines," for more information.

The most important field is the Item No. field appearing in the top-right corner. The item number is number 2. This is the number written on the manila folder containing my hard copy of the document. When I open the file cabinet and look inside the number 2 folder, the document is safely stored inside the folder. The new page icon at the top center of the page contains the JavaScript to spawn a page from a template and add a new field in the top-right corner. The field contents are automatically supplied from the JavaScript that searches through the pages, finds the last number contained on the last page, and increments it by one to add a new unique number. The script for this action is as follows:

```
this.spawnPageFromTemplate ("newPage") //create a new page
this.pageNum = this.numPages - 1; //move to the new page
var r = [597, 483, 700, 499];
var i = this.pageNum++
```

```
var f = this.addField(String(this.pageNum),"text",i,r);
  f.textSize = 14;
  f.alignment = "right";
  f.textColor = color.blue;
  f.fillColor = color.transparent;
  f.textfont = font.HelvB;
  f.borderStyle = border.s;
  f.strokeColor = color.transparent;
  f.value = String(i+1);
```

The code that distinguishes this routine from the one that was mentioned for the password file is the line of code `var f = this.addField (String (this.pageNum), "text",i,r);`. A field is added to the new page, but the contents include `(String (this.pageNum)` and so on. The variable *f* identifies the field and the last line of code determines the field value. In this example, the value is the loop counter i incremented by one (i + 1).

If you copy and paste this script to another form and you want to add text as the field contents, you can edit the above script and change the last line of code to reflect the text to be added. For example, if you want to add the word *HELP* to the field, you would code the last line `f.value = "HELP";`. By editing the script, you can modify it to fit your needs.

Note   This example can only be used in Acrobat. Like the previous example, creating new pages from templates is not available to Acrobat Reader or Acrobat Approval users.

Recipe shopper

This example is a form that is both fun to work with and a big help in organizing personal information where you accumulate data in one document and summarize it in another document. In this exercise, I use a recipe book for food recipes and take my recipe ingredients and transpose them to a shopping list. In practical terms, you can search for a recipe that you want to use, click on a button, and your shopping list is automatically created. The shopping list is populated with the ingredients for the recipe in question and additional fields on the shopping list offer you space to add other items before visiting the supermarket. You can apply the same kind of design to documents that need to have data summarized in secondary files such as financial information, catalog purchase sales, order forms, or any kind of file that needs to summarize data in a secondary form.

The nice attraction to this kind of form is it works in part in all Acrobat viewers. The actual creation of PDF documents, however, can only be performed in Acrobat. Therefore, the use of the form begins with a prepared form, such as the `recipeManager.pdf` document that is located in the Personal Management folder inside the Chapter 16 folder on the book's CD-ROM.

You'll find the `recipeManager.pdf` and `shoppingCart.pdf` files in the Chapter 16 Personal Management folder on the book's CD-ROM.

There are three parts to using the forms in this exercise. You can use existing documents you may have for recipes stored on your computer or you can find source files on the Internet and download the pages. When the files are converted to PDF, you can use the Insert Pages command to add a recipe in the `recipeManager.pdf` file. If you get ambitious, you can create a new form using the scripts mentioned in this exercise. The third part of the exercise is to key in the recipe items on the last page of the `recipeManager.pdf` file. On this page, you'll find a button that automatically copies the data to the `shoppingCart.pdf` file. The `shoppingCart.pdf` file is the one you print and carry off to the supermarket. To understand how all this works, let's look at each of the three phases.

Collecting the source data

As an example, let's assume you want to find a recipe on the Internet. A good source for food recipes can be found at `www.foodtv.com`. When you arrive at a recipe to use, copy the URL from the Location bar in your Web browser. Open Acrobat and click on the Open Web Page tool. Paste the URL in the Open Web Page dialog box.

A status dialog box displays the progress. Be certain to leave the default levels at 1 if you are converting a single recipe to PDF. If the number is increased, it can take some time to finish the download and you'll no doubt download more pages than you need.

When the download is complete, the pages appear in Acrobat and can be saved to disk as a PDF file. Unfortunately, this feature is not available to the Acrobat Reader or Acrobat Approval user. Users of Acrobat Reader and Acrobat Approval need to start with a file already prepared as a PDF document.

Populating the data fields

For the Acrobat user, our next step is to take the pages from the new download and insert the pages in the `recipeManager.pdf` file. It's easiest to start with a file that clearly separates the ingredients of a recipe from the narrative description for preparing the dish. Insert pages at the end of the document containing a recipe with a description and a list of ingredients.

Tip If you have a PDF file that needs to be inserted in a master file, you can use the Thumbnails palette and duplicate pages between two open documents. Open both documents and choose Window ➪ Tile Vertically. Click on the Thumbnails tab in the Navigation Pane for both documents. Select the thumbnails in the file where the pages are to be copied and drag them to the destination document. You can scroll thumbnails in the destination document to find the location where the pages are to be inserted. Drag the thumbnails to the page position desired and release the mouse button. The pages are copied and pasted in the destination file.

Use the Text Select tool and select the text for the ingredients, as shown in Figure 16-5. You can use the Column Select tool for copying a column of text if the text appears in a column. The important thing to do is copy the ingredients and not the recipe preparation description.

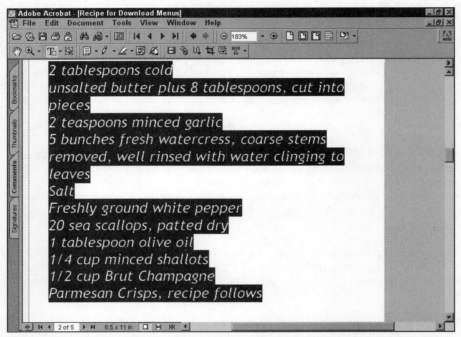

Figure 16-5: Use the Text Select tool or the Column Select tool and marquee the text to be copied. Choose Edit ➪ Copy, or select Copy from a context menu.

Choose Edit ➪ Copy or open a context menu and select Copy from the menu commands. When the text is copied to the Clipboard, click on the Last Page tool to open the last page in the document. Click on the New Page button to spawn a page from a template. The new page contains a field box for adding the description. Click on the Hand tool then click in the large Description field located on the lower-right side of the page and paste the text by choosing Edit ➪ Paste or open a context menu and select Paste. The pasted text appears in the Description field, as shown in Figure 16-6.

The design of this form is intended to prevent you from having to scroll back and forth between the original page where the ingredients were copied, and add them to the fields on the left side of the form. When the text is available on a single page, it makes the data entries much easier. However, you still need to populate the data fields on the left side of the form in order to create the shopping list. This task is the most cumbersome because there is no way to easily code the fields to extract the data from the description field and add the respective items to the data fields within the columns on the left side of the form. In this regard, you need to individually add the quantity, measurement, and item description for each ingredient. When the fields are populated, they should appear as shown in Figure 16-6.

Create a shopping cart

At this point you're ready for Acrobat to help simplify the last step. The button at the lower-right side of the page contains the JavaScript that takes all the populated field data from the current form and adds the data to like fields on a separate document. The shoppingCart.pdf file, located on the book's CD-ROM in the Personal Management folder inside the Chapter 16 folder, needs to be in the same directory as the recipeManager.pdf file. Click on the button and the shopping cart page opens, as shown in Figure 16-7.

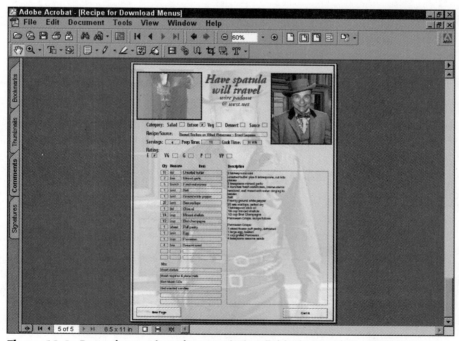

Figure 16-6: Paste the text into the Description field. Then add the individual ingredients in the field boxes on the left side of the form.

On the CD-ROM

You'll find the shoppingCart.pdf and recipeManager.pdf files in the Personal Management folder in the Chapter 16 folder on the book's CD-ROM.

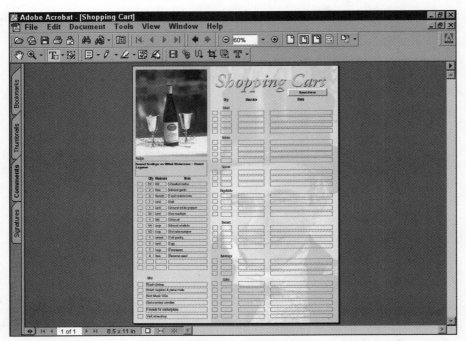

Figure 16-7: The Cart It button on the original file contains a JavaScript that opens a secondary file and adds the data from the first file to like fields in the second file.

The code used for the button that opens a second file and copies the data is described as follows:

```
this.slave = app.openDoc("shoppingCart.pdf",this);
   this.bringToFront();
var j = this.pageNum;
j.value = j+1;

var recipeName =
this.getField("P"+j+(".ingredients.recipeTitle"));
    var result = this.slave.getField("recipe.0");
  result.value = recipeName.value;

for (var i = 0; i < 15;i++) {
var quantity = this.getField("P"+j+(".ingredients.qty."+i));
    var result = this.slave.getField("qty."+i);
  result.value = quantity.value;
var measure = this.getField("P"+j+(".ingredients.measure."+i));
    var result = this.slave.getField("measure."+i);
  result.value = measure.value;
var item = this.getField("P"+j+(".ingredients.item."+i));
```

```
      var result = this.slave.getField("item."+i);
   result.value = item.value;
}

for (var i = 0; i < 6;i++) {
var misc = this.getField("P"+j+(".ingredients.misi."+i));
     var result = this.slave.getField("misi."+i);
   result.value = misc.value;
}
slave.bringToFront();
```

The beginning of this routine starts by opening the shopping cart form and bringing the shopping cart to the front view. The next section gets the title field and takes the contents from the title field in the recipe manager file and adds the value to the title field in the destination document.

You then move to the loop that loops through 15 fields and grabs the quantity, measure, and item data. For each item and each progression through the loop, the *result* statements place the data in the respective fields (+ i) in the slave document. The last loop takes the miscellaneous data for the six remaining fields and places the contents in the resultant document. You'll note the field names begin with ("P"+j+. . . . The form has a button where new pages are spawned and Acrobat renames new fields. Since all the new pages contain unique field names, you need to determine the field names from any page and use them in the formula to transpose the data from the viewed page to the resultant document. The code used above retrieves field names from the page in view. For an amplified description regarding the naming convention for fields spawned from template pages, see the description for the Equipment Inventory (equipmentInventory.pdf) and Equipment Valuation Summary Report (equipValueSummary.pdf) in the Creating Accounting Management Forms section, later in this chapter.

Note   The slave document opened with a JavaScript from the master document needs to have one line of code added as a Document Level JavaScript. Choose Tools ➭ JavaScript ➭ Document JavaScripts. In the JavaScript Functions dialog box, add a name such as *initialize*. Click on the Add button, and enter:

```
this.disclosed=true;
```

This code is necessary to ensure documents can be opened from scripts in one document when using the app.openDoc(); statement.

For each row of data in the shopping cart form, a check box appears. Select a check box if the item is not needed when you visit the supermarket. The remaining fields on the shopping cart form are used for other shopping items that are added manually. If the design does not suit your needs, you can create a new form and copy all the fields and paste them to your new design. Save the new design with the same filename or change the first line of code in the above routine to the filename you wish to use.

Note   This example can be used in Acrobat, Acrobat Reader, and Acrobat Approval for the step where the data are transposed between documents. Inserting pages requires Acrobat. Saving new data in the recipe manager requires Acrobat or Approval.

Creating Printing Templates

Printing templates can be a time saver when printing forms for documents with frequent data changes. Business cards, letterhead for various satellite offices, personalized documents, and so on may need to be revised based on employee changes, relocation of offices, printing a new supply of forms, or other similar needs. As a solution, you can create PDF forms designed for printing and digital prepress and change the data in the form fields when additional forms need to be printed.

As another solution, you can use Acrobat as a means for printing variable data. When each data field changes, you may wish to use a different image on a document. Forms like these can be used to print to copiers and office equipment without the need to purchase additional software designed specifically for variable data printing.

In the category of printing templates, I have three examples for using a template where the data can be changed either through importing text from ASCII text files or changing images. Let's start with a simple example for creating a PDF document as a template and work our way to a more complex form designed for variable data printing.

Business cards

This example is a simple solution for generating new business cards or printing a new supply of business cards for an employee. There are no JavaScripts used in the form for data handling. The form is a template used for importing text containing all the necessary data for printing business cards for a given employee.

Suppose you have an office where the art department prepares the corporate identity and collateral documents. The art department uses high-end imaging software to create the designs. Rather than purchase more copies of the imaging software for personnel who need to make periodic changes, the art department creates a template in Acrobat, and personnel in various departments use the templates to make changes as needed. In regard to an example like business cards, the only data that changes are the name, title, e-mail address, and perhaps a phone number or office extension number.

We start this form with the background design and add the form fields, as shown in Figure 16-8. The form contains fields for the name, title, e-mail address, and a cell phone number. The name field at the top contains two name fields because the text for the name uses a drop shadow. The foreground name field is reversed out (white text) and the background name field is offset right and bottom with black text. When creating a drop shadow like this example, create a name field and set the text color attributes. Create a second field and give it the same field name. Change the appearance attributes on the second name field to reflect either the foreground or the shadow color. You can then align the fields left and top. With the top field selected, press the arrow keys on the keyboard to offset the top field.

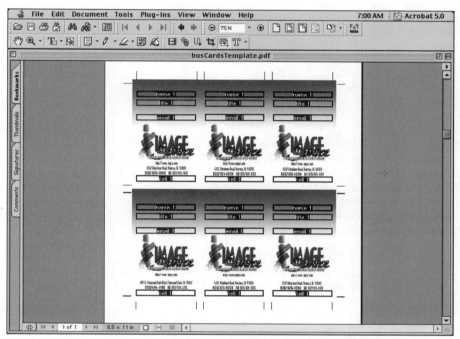

Figure 16-8: The business card template uses the original design that was developed by the art department and then converted to a PDF. Individual fields are created for all data that are changed for each individual employee.

After creating the fields for the first business card, select them and press the Ctrl key (Windows) or Option key (Mac OS) and click+drag to the next card. Duplicate all the fields and leave the field names the same for each card. When data are imported, the field contents are duplicated for each field since the field names are identical for all business cards.

The data to be imported in the template are created in Microsoft Excel or a database manager capable of exporting delimited text. The advantage of using a database file is the text will always be consistent when you print new cards for any given employee. Rather than recreate a business card from a template in a layout or illustration program and risk a chance of misspelling a name or transposing phone numbers, the data file will always be the same if left undisturbed. When the original data file is created or appended, you only need to review the data for correct spelling and accuracy once. After that, each import assures you of using the correct data.

After the template and data files have been created, open the template in Acrobat and choose File ➪ Import ➪ Form Data. Select Text Files (*.txt) for the data type, as I explained in Chapter 13. When the Import Data From Delimited Text File dialog box opens, select the name of the employee to import, as shown in Figure 16-9.

Figure 16-9: Import the text data by choosing File ➪ Import ➪ Form Data and choose Text Files (*.txt) from the Objects of Type pull-down menu. The Import Data From Delimited Text File dialog box opens in which the data record to be imported is selected.

Click OK in the Import Data From Delimited Text File dialog box and the data are imported in the fields with matching names from the header in the text file.

Cross-Reference

To set up the data file, refer back to Chapter 13, "Submitting and Distributing Forms."

Tip

When creating a template for prepress similar to this example, you can use any font loaded in your system. The same font is needed by the imaging center when they print your file. If the service center doesn't have the font used in your design, you can use a plug-in described in Chapter 15, "Understanding the Real-World Forms Market," to stamp down the field contents and embed the font. After embedding the font, send the PDF to the service center and it will be ready to print color separations. In Acrobat 5.05, single-byte fonts are embedded in the PDF file. However, if you experience any problems with problematic fonts, use the plug-in described here.

Note

The above example can be used with Adobe Acrobat and Acrobat Approval. FDF data can be imported with Acrobat or Acrobat Approval. Reader does not support any kind of data imports.

Greeting cards

Another kind of template that works well with Acrobat is one used for printing greeting cards, thank you notes, personalized occasion cards, and similar designs. This kind of example may be used by a Kinko's copy shop, quick printer, or service center that offers personalized greeting cards for customers. Rather than use a fixed design like the example above, this example uses button imports to change the graphic design.

As you know from the exercises in Chapter 8, "Writing JavaScript Routines," you can set up a simple JavaScript to import an image in a PDF file. The foregoing example uses a button import, but I complicate the design by adding two images, one of which contains a clipping path. Figure 16-10 shows an example of where two button images are used to create the design. The head of the Santa image overlaps the background. If you create the design with the Santa figure as part of the background, the field containing the image of the children would knock out Santa's head. In order for the design to appear as shown in Figure 16-10, you need to layer two fields. One field is used to import the family and the other image is a portion of the Santa figure with a mask.

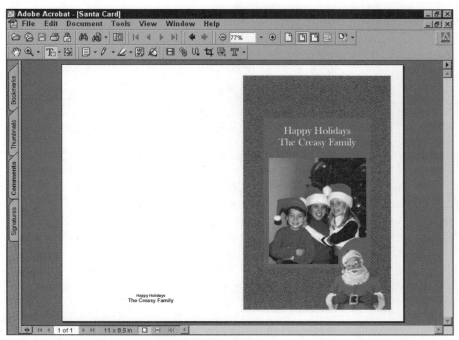

Figure 16-10: Part of one image overlaps the image imported from a button icon. In order to layer the images, you need two button icons.

The challenge for creating this design is not so much what you do in Acrobat, but the work you need to perform in an image editor to prepare the mask on the Santa head. To create the background design, the artwork is prepared in Adobe Photoshop.

While in Photoshop, crop the image to the area to be used as the overlapping element. In this example, the head of Santa is cropped. The path for the mask is the area that includes the image data remaining visible while the area outside the mask remains transparent. In Figure 16-11, the half moon shape is selected while the area outside the selection is transparent.

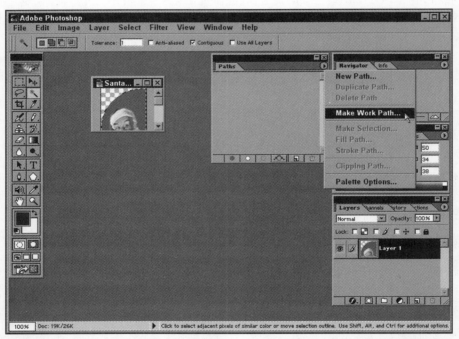

Figure 16-11: The figure is cropped and a selection is made in which the figure is masked. By making a new layer from the selection, the area outside the selection appears transparent.

From the Paths palette, select Make Work Path to convert the selection to a path. The Work Path is created and appears in the Paths palette. Select Save Path from the palette fly-away menu. The Save Path dialog box opens. Type a name for the path and click OK. In this example, I use Santa as the name for my path.

To create a mask, you need to return to the fly-away palette and select Clipping Path from the menu choices. The Clipping Path dialog box opens. From the pull-down menu choices, select the name of the path created earlier. In this example, I choose Santa from the menu choices.

After the clipping path has been created, save the file. Choose File ➪ Save As to open the Save As dialog box. For the file format, select Photoshop PDF. The PDF format preserves the clipping path created in Photoshop.

> **Note** The integration of Adobe imaging software and Acrobat PDF has evolved to help designers create a seamless workflow when exchanging files between applications. All Adobe imaging software supports PDF file formats, and attributes of images such as transparency, masks, type, color, and more are preserved in the resultant PDF files. If your forms require sophisticated designs, you will be best served by acquiring other Adobe products to complement your work in Acrobat.

The hard part of this example is complete. In Acrobat, add the form fields. For this greeting card I add a field with a button import JavaScript similar to the one explained in Chapter 8, "Writing JavaScript Routines," and call the field `import`. A second button field is added and the icon is imported from the Field Properties dialog box, as described in Chapter 3, "Understanding Field Types." I check Read Only in the Appearance settings for this field so the end user would not inadvertently import another image that would disturb the design. A few text fields are added where the text appears in the design. The field positions are shown in Figure 16-12.

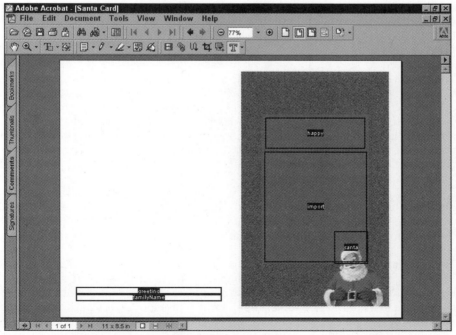

Figure 16-12: Two button fields and three text fields complete the design template.

The only thing remaining to finish the design and make it usable is to move the Santa button precisely in position. To position the button in the right place just takes some time and trial and error. Select the field and press an arrow key to move the field box. Preview the results and return to the edit mode by selecting the Form tool. Move the field again and preview. Continue moving and previewing until the image is in position.

When the template is complete, scan a new image and save as a PDF file or any file format compatible with the Open As Adobe PDF command. Click on the background button and import the image. Add the necessary text to the form fields and print the file.

Tip   When you import the background image, Acrobat may not refresh your screen and the image may appear in the foreground hiding the smaller button import. You can view the final document as it will print and refresh the screen by zooming in or out. If you print the file without refreshing the screen, the file will print properly with the buttons layered appropriately.

Golf tournament invitation

The previous templates are simple designs with little coding for data handling. In this example, we'll look at a more complex template and use some JavaScript to create a file you may use for variable data printing. This example may be used in lieu of a Quark XTension or PageMaker Addition you can purchase to handle variable data printing.

The notion of variable data printing was introduced when on-demand printing machines began to proliferate. The idea is based on creating a marketing piece that advertises to an audience of one. Each piece of paper running through an on-demand press renders a document design with different text and images that are personalized for the recipient. To create files for variable data printing, there are software utilities that can be added to layout programs offering data management control much like a mail merge behaves in a word processor.

If you don't use a layout application or you don't have the extra software utilities designed for variable data printing, you can create a similar kind of result with Adobe Acrobat. In this example, we'll use a data file imported into a PDF template and code the fields to automatically update text and images for variable data printing.

The template created for this exercise is the `golfTournamentCard.pdf` file in the Printing Templates folder inside the Chapter 16 folder. The template shown in Figure 16-13 is used to import data from a database file for creating an invitation to participate in a charity golf tournament. From a previous year's participation, each golf team of four people was photographed and their names and addresses were added to a database file. This year, invitations will be sent to the participants on an invitation card containing a member's name, address, and the photo of the recipient.

You'll find the `golfTournamentCard.pdf` file in the Printing Templates folder in the Chapter 16 folder on the book's CD-ROM.

When the fields are shown in the template, you can see the data fields where data are imported, as shown in Figure 16-13. The template is designed to be copied at a copy shop and trimmed at the edges. The text appearing at the top of the card is rotated 180° so it reads properly when folded on the fold lines shown on the left and right side of the card.

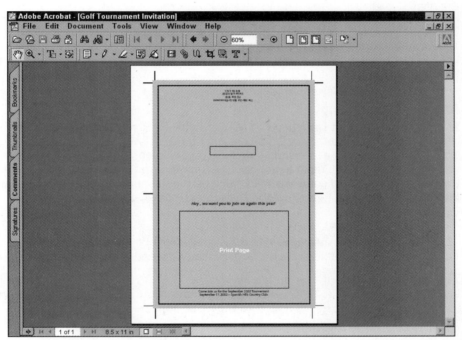

Figure 16-13: The blank template file is used to import data from a database file, which will include the name, address, and photograph of the recipient. The fields at the top of the form are rotated 180° so the text reads correctly when the card is folded.

To create a similar design, there are three stages. You first need to create the template and fields on the card. Some fields are then scripted to automate creating individual cards for each recipient. Finally, the data are imported from the database file. Let's examine each step to see how such an example is put to use.

Creating the template

The original design can be created in any one of the authoring programs described in Chapter 2, "Using Authoring Applications." An illustration program or page layout program will work best for this task. After converting the design to PDF, you need to add the fields in Acrobat. The identifying information fields at the top of the design are text fields; each field is rotated individually 180° in the Appearance Properties dialog box .

The field `imageText` is a temporary holding field that does not print. It is used to store the filename for the image file to be used. The filename is part of the database file and gets imported with the identifying information. When this field is created, the pull-down menu for Form Field Is: is opened and the menu option for Visible But Doesn't Print is selected.

The field `headlineText` contains a message and we'll also add a script to this field that adds the first name from the first name field and includes it in the message. Below the message text are two fields. The background field is where the image appears. The foreground field titled `printPage` contains JavaScripts to import the image associated with the recipient and print the page when the user clicks on the button field.

Adding the JavaScript

The first field to script is the `headlineText` field. The default text in the field reads: "Hey " ", we want you to join us again this year!" As each name is imported in the template, we want the text to include the recipient name to personalize the message. Therefore we need to get the text from the first name field and add it to the message string. To code this field, click on the Calculate properties and select Edit. In the JavaScript Edit dialog box, enter the following code:

```
var f = this.getField("first.name");
event.value = "Hey " + f.value + ", we want you to join us
again this year!";
```

The code should be self descriptive. We get the `"first.name"` field and assign it to variable f. The `f.value` represents the first name of the recipient. Note in the code above, the space after `Hey` is added so the name appears with a space between "Hey" and the recipient name.

When the data are imported, the text is displayed, as shown in Figure 16-14. Notice the rotated text and the field box with the keyline border. The text inside the keyline is only visible on-screen and won't print as we assigned it to not print when the fields were created above. The text value of this field is used to identify the image to be imported.

The next JavaScript is written as an Action for a Mouse Enter mouse behavior and a second script is added for a Mouse Up mouse behavior. When the cursor enters the field, we want to grab the text from the field box containing the filename of the image to be imported and instruct Acrobat to go out to the hard drive, find the image, and import it into the button field behind the print button. The Mouse Up action opens the Print dialog box when the user clicks the button and hides the field where the text appears as `Print Page`.

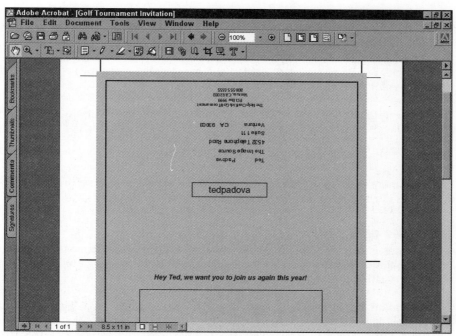

Figure 16-14: When the text is imported, the top of the template displays the rotated text and the field with the keyline displays on-screen text that won't be printed.

For the Mouse Enter mouse behavior, enter the following code:

```
var g = this.getField("imageText");
g.hidden = true;

var f = this.getField("import");
var filename = g.value;
f.value = (f.buttonImportIcon("/D/AcrobatFormsBook/"+filename+"
.pdf"));
```

The first thing the script does is import the imageText field and hide it. This action is not necessary to print the form, but offers the user a view of what the template looks like when printed without any disturbing text.

Next, the *import* field is assigned to variable f (this field is the button where the final image appears). We then assign variable filename to the value of g, which is the name of the image to import. The final statement imports the image according to the filename. Notice the directory path is specified and the filename needs to be placed in the designated folder following the same path. Also, the filenames contain the PDF extension, but the database only uses the filename without the extension. Therefore, the extension is added in the JavaScript.

Note

To use the files on your hard drive, be certain to change the directory path to match the location for where you copy the files. Mac OS users should use a path like: *"MacintoshHD/Creating Acrobat PDF Forms/Chapter 16/"+filename+".pdf"* or similar syntax describing the name of your hard drive and folders containing the sample files. Windows users need to edit the sample script above and change the names for drive designation and folder names.

The last script is added to the Mouse Up mouse behavior. Select Mouse Up and open the JavaScript Edit dialog box and enter the following code:

```
this.print (true, this.pageNum,this.pageNum);
```

This statement opens the Print dialog box. If you want the user to print the file without the Print dialog box opening, change `true` to `false`.

Import the data

After the design is complete and the scripts have been added, save the template as a Read Only file (Windows) or Lock the file in the Get Info dialog box (Mac OS) to avoid overwriting the template.

Cross-Reference

For more on locked and read only files, see Chapter 13, "Submitting and Distributing Forms."

Choose File ➪ Import ➪ Form Data. This of course assumes you have a database file created with the necessary data and a header matching the field names on the form. The Import Data From Delimited Text File dialog box opens, as shown in Figure 16-15.

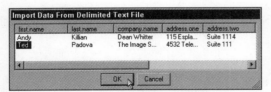

Figure 16-15: Import the data from a text file by choosing File ➪ Import ➪ Form Data.

Select the record to be imported and click OK. The data fields are populated, but in order to see the image, you need to move the cursor over the button used to print the file. If the name of your PDF document matches the name supplied in the `imageText` field, the button displays the imported image, as shown in Figure 16-16.

You can further automate this example by spawning pages from a template and modifying the code to progress through a loop to import text and images. The PDF can be created for all the recipients, printed, and trimmed at the copy shop and the invitations mailed to all the parties.

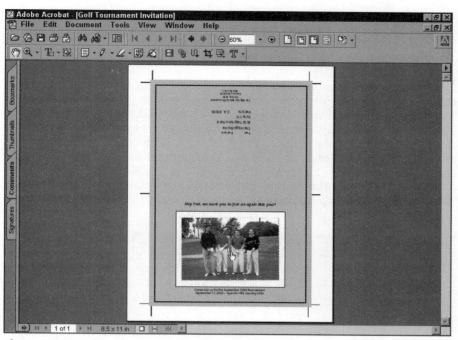

Figure 16-16: When the mouse cursor enters the print field button, the image from the *imageText* field name is imported into the button field behind the print button.

Creating Customer Service Forms

For commercial enterprises selling products or services, you can help your client base obtain prices on your products and submit order forms from Web-hosted PDF documents. This process makes your sales delivery accessible to anyone in your service area and, hopefully, helps you increase sales. When creating forms used for pricing items and filling in order forms, you'll want to use Acrobat features that are equally functional in all Acrobat viewers. You may wish to host some additional documents on your Web site to walk users through the process of completing an Acrobat PDF form and post a link to Adobe's Web site where the Acrobat Reader software can be downloaded. You may also wish to inform your clients about some of the benefits of using the low-cost Acrobat Approval software if they make frequent purchases from you.

As an example of a real-world form, I'll use some forms that are hosted on my own company's Web site to serve my customer base. The products sold are digital printing, prepress, and commercial photo finishing. With almost all the products in this industry, there are many different sizes for output and products sold. Pricing usually requires an elaborate calculation for determining material, size, device, and finishing. Therefore, customers typically want a quote on a job before they fill out an order form. As a result, I have a form designed as a quote calculator that my customers can download from the company Web site, and an order form to order a given product. As a benefit, I make the forms interactive where the quote amount is automatically placed on the order form when the user clicks a button.

I start my customers off with an order form, as shown in Figure 16-17. This example is an order form used for large format display prints, mounting, and lamination. The devices used are capable of printing a number of different sizes ranging from standard letter size up to 59 inches wide by 108 inches long. For each increase in size, there is an increase in price. The finishing for lamination and mounting is also available in varying sizes and materials. In addition, there are a number of different substrates used for the kind of output desired. As an example, if a customer wants 6 Duratrans prints printed on backlit material and laminated on one side, the total cost includes the prints and lamination.

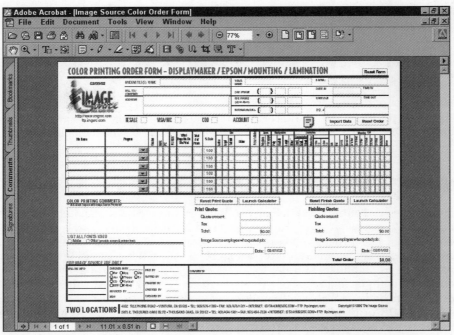

Figure 16-17: The order form contains the necessary fields to place the order, but no pricing information is available on the order form.

To obtain a price quote, a button on the form launches the quote calculator, shown in Figure 16-18. The range of fixed sizes appears on the left of the form and columns individually identify device and substrate. The price for each row is tabulated in the column on the right side of the form. As the quantity is supplied and the columns checked for size and material, the subtotal field in the top-right corner automatically sums the total of the price fields. There are check boxes for determining taxable sales or resale sales, a discount field for customers who have been provided quoted discounts, and a grand total field that calculates the total less any applied discounts and the addition of applicable taxes. When the customer obtains a quote for a job, s/he can then click another button to finish obtaining any added finishing costs. The results of both quotes are then transferred back to the order form by clicking buttons on the respective quote forms.

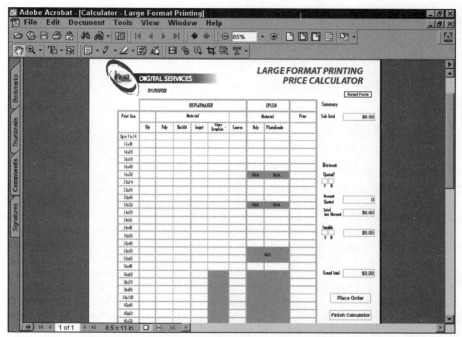

Figure 16-18: When a button is clicked on the order form, the quote calculator form opens in Acrobat. After the quote has been calculated and a button clicked, the quote information is transferred to the order form.

To understand how these forms interrelate and what scripts are needed to create the calculations and transfer data between the documents, we'll start with the initial order form and continue later to the quote calculators.

Creating an order form

The order form is designed as the central navigation point to place an order for large format color printing and finishing work. The customer can also begin by opening either quote calculator because the forms are linked via buttons with the `app.openDoc()` statement contained in JavaScripts on all forms. Therefore, it's not necessary to begin an order process with the order form, but we'll start here to simulate the workflow as it was intended.

In this example, use the `order_color.pdf` file contained in the Chapter 16 folder inside the Customer Service folder. The order form has two calculator buttons, as shown earlier in Figure 16-18. One button launches the quote calculator for the color print costs and the other button launches the quote calculator for the finishing costs. For each of these buttons, a simple JavaScript is created for a button field to open the respective file. The script to open the `displayMakerCalculator.pdf` file, also contained on the book's CD-ROM in the same folder, is displayed below:

On the CD-ROM

You'll find both the `order_color.pdf` file and the `displayMakerCalculator.pdf` file in the Customer Service folder in the Chapter 16 folder on the book's CD-ROM.

```
if (app.viewerVersion < 5)
    app.alert("Version 5.0 required. Some features will not
work.");

else {
    this.slave = app.openDoc("displayMakerCalculator.pdf",this);
    slave.bringToFront();
}
```

The script begins above with determining the version of the Acrobat viewer. Although the button action works in all viewers, the viewer version needs to be version 5 or greater. You can also add a line informing the user to visit your Web site URL where a link button opens the Web page on Adobe's Web site where the most recent version of Acrobat Reader can be downloaded.

The second part of the script uses the `app.openDoc()` statement to open the quote calculator file and bring it to the front of the Document Pane. For each of the two buttons shown in Figure 16-18, the same routine is written with the only change being the filename. With the exception of the two total fields that sum the amount and tax fields, there are no other scripts for fields in this document.

Creating a quote calculator

The more complex routines are contained in the quote calculator files. These forms can easily use a formula to calculate a price based on square footage, however, my clients have requested price lists broken down into fixed sizes associated with prices. To keep consistent with the price forms also hosted on the company Web site, the calculator uses the same format. In this example, the complexity of each script is quite extensive because the size needs a new formula to calculate the price for each material and each device.

When creating the fields, what's important is to use the same field name for each check box for the material fields for a given row. I have a field beginning in the top-left corner called `qty.0`. The remaining fields across the first row are check boxes used to determine what material is used. For the first row, all the fields are titled `material.0`. The price field in the last column is named `price.0`.

In order to distinguish one column selection from another in the `material.0` check box fields, a different export value needs to be supplied in the Field Properties dialog box when the price changes for a different material. Figure 16-19 shows the Options tab. Note the `material.0` field has an export value of 1.

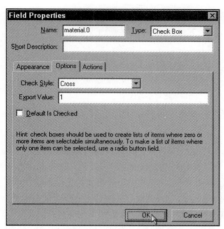

Figure 16-19: The export value for the first *material.0* field is 1. Each subsequent field in the row has a different export value when prices are unique to the material ordered.

When you script the code to perform calculations, you instruct Acrobat to examine the export value. If the number is 1, you supply a formula to calculate the price. If the number is 2, you supply a different formula to calculate a different price, and so on. In this example, there are seven different columns for a user to select a different material or a different device used to create the print. To complicate the matter more, a price break is offered for different quantities. A single item is priced at one value. If fewer than 10 copies are ordered, the price breaks after the first print price. If more than 9 and less than 50 units are ordered, a different price is applied to the order plus the first print price. More than 50 prints yields yet another price plus the first print price. Two of the fields across each row are identical; therefore, the same export value is used with fields that calculate identical prices. The complete routine that is applied to the Calculate tab in the Field Properties for the `price.0` field is

```
var f = this.getField("qty.0");
var m = this.getField("material.0");


// up to 11x14
{
// poly
```

```
if (m.value == 1)
if (f.value == 1 )
   event.value = 12.50;
else
if (f.value >1 &&  (f.value <= 9))
   event.value = (((f.value -1) * 8.00) + 12.50);
else
if (f.value >= 10 && (f.value <= 49))
   event.value = (((f.value -1) * 7.00) + 12.50);
else
if (f.value >= 50)
   event.value = (((f.value -1) * 5.00) + 12.50);

//backlit/canvas
if (m.value == 2)
if (f.value == 2)
   event.value = 12.50 * 1.4;
else
if (f.value >1 &&  (f.value <= 9))
   event.value = ((((f.value -1) * 8) + 12.50)*1.4);
else
if (f.value >= 10 && (f.value <= 49))
   event.value = ((((f.value -1) * 7) + 12.50)* 1.4);
else
if (f.value >= 50)
   event.value = ((((f.value -1) * 5) + 12.50)* 1.4);

//lexjet
if (m.value == 3)
if (f.value == 2)
   event.value = 12.50 * 1.8;
else
if(f.value >1 &&  (f.value <= 9))
   event.value = ((((f.value -1) * 8) + 12.50)*1.8);
else
if (f.value >= 10 && (f.value <= 49))
   event.value = ((((f.value -1) * 7) + 12.50)* 1.8);
else
if (f.value >= 50)
   event.value = ((((f.value -1) * 5) + 12.50)* 1.8);

// floor graphics
if (m.value == 4)
if (f.value == 1)
   event.value = 12.50 + 26.00;
else
if (f.value >1 &&  (f.value <= 9))
   event.value = ((f.value -1) * 8) + (12.50) + (26 * f.value);
else
if (f.value >= 10 && (f.value <= 49))
   event.value = ((f.value -1) * 7) + (12.50) + (26 * f.value);
else
if (f.value >= 50)
```

```
    event.value = ((f.value -1) * 5) + (12.50) + (26 * f.value);

//epson
if (m.value == 5)
if (f.value == 1)
    event.value = 13.75;
else
if (f.value >1 &&  (f.value <= 9))
    event.value = (((f.value -1) * 8.80) + 13.75);
else
if (f.value >= 10 && (f.value <= 49))
    event.value = (((f.value -1) * 7.70) + 13.75);
else
if (f.value >= 50)
    event.value = (((f.value -1) * 5.5) + 13.75);
}
```

You start by assigning two variables. Variable f gets the quantity value. Variable m gets the export value from all the material.0 fields. We then move to the first condition and check if variable m is equal to 1 (the export value determined in the Options properties), then we progress to the calculations. However, we need to accommodate the quantity discounts. If a customer orders 1 print, a single price is calculated. If the customer orders more than one print, but less than 10 prints, the first print price is added to duplicate prints at a lower price. If the customer orders 10 or more prints and fewer than 50 prints, the duplicate price changes. If 50 or more prints are ordered, then the duplicate price print changes again. The first print price is always added to the duplicate print prices because it takes a technician time to prepare and print the first print. The first print price is intended to cover these labor costs.

When you examine the formula for the first export value, the code starts with

```
// up to 11x14
{
// poly
if (m.value == 1)
if (f.value ==1 )
    event.value = 12.50;
else
if (f.value >1 &&  (f.value <= 9))
    event.value = (((f.value -1) * 8.00) + 12.50);
else
if (f.value >= 10 && (f.value <= 49))
    event.value = (((f.value -1) * 7.00) + 12.50);
else
if (f.value >= 50)
    event.value = (((f.value -1) * 5.00) + 12.50);
```

The comment line tells you that the price is being calculated for prints up to 11x14 inches and the second comment tells me the material used is poly-coated stock. You start the calculation with finding the value of f and m. If they are both equal to 1, then you calculate a price for 1 print at $12.50. This value is placed in the price.0 field by the event.value statement. You have already determined the value of f for the quantity. If the quantity is greater than 1 &&, the quantity is less than or equal to (<=) 9, then the price for copies 2 through 9 is $8.00. To be certain you calculate duplicate prints, you take the f.value and subtract 1 from it to calculate only the duplicates. Then you multiply it times the duplicate price of $8.00 and add the first print price of $12.50. This calculation is performed in the statement:

```
event.value = (((f.value -1) * 8.00) + 12.50);
```

The next statement following the above code is used for prints equal to or more than 10, but equal to or less than 49. The last part of the routine deals with more than 50 prints.

For the next field in the same row, the JavaScript is identical with the exception of the export value and fixed price amounts. In the next script, you would use if (m.value == 2). The remaining lines of code only change the fixed price costs. In this example, the cost for backlit material is greater than the cost for poly coated stock. Therefore, the fixed price values reflect the increased costs. The formulas, however, remain the same.

Tip

If you have many fields with common lines of code that need minor changes, you can duplicate fields with the same code, then open the JavaScript Edit dialog box by choosing Tools ⇨ JavaScript ⇨ Edit All JavaScripts. The JavaScript Edit dialog box opens with all scripts in the document appearing in the editor window. You can copy/paste lines of code and make changes without opening each Field Properties dialog box. If the code is extensive, you may need to use an external editor (Windows) that you can assign in the General Preferences dialog box. If you prefer to open the Field Properties dialog box and edit the JavaScripts, select the Form tool and press the Tab key to move to the next field. Press Enter on the Num Pad keypad to open the Field Properties dialog box. Use Tab/Enter to quickly move through the Field Properties dialog boxes.

As the price fields are scripted, it is best to check the calculations as you create each new total, especially with a form like the example used here. When the prices are calculated correctly, summary fields on the right side of the form contain scripts and calculations to summarize data. Taxable sales are determined from user responses and a special set of fields exists for any quoted discounts. These calculations are relatively simple and only contain a few lines of code to create the data summaries.

Cross-Reference

For formulas that are used for creating sales tax, see Chapter 8, "Writing JavaScript Routines."

The more complex script is contained in the two fields at the bottom of the right side of the form. The first field titled Finish Calculator is a button field used to open the quote calculator for the finishing work. When the user clicks on this button, the button action performs two steps. The summarized data from the print quote calculator is placed on the order form and the quote calculator for the finishing work opens. If the user selects the last button titled Place Order, the data are transposed to the order form and the order form opens in the front view. Essentially, the two fields perform the same calculations, but a different form is opened depending on which button is selected.

The script to perform the data integration with the order form, and subsequently open the Finish Calculator is

```
if (app.viewerVersion < 5)
  app.alert("Version 5.0 required. Some features will not
work.");

else {
    this.slave = app.openDoc("order_color.pdf",this);
}

var q = this.getField("quoted");
var sub = this.getField("subtotal");
var a = this.getField("discountAmount");
var resultAmount = this.slave.getField("amount");

    {
    if (q.value ==1){
    resultAmount.value = a.value }
  else {
    resultAmount.value = sub.value }
    }
var tax = this.getField("tax");
var resultTax = this.slave.getField("tax");

   resultTax.value = tax.value


var emp = this.getField("employee");
var resultEmployee = this.slave.getField("employee");

resultEmployee.value = emp.value;

this.newSlave = app.openDoc("mountFinish.pdf",this);
newSlave.bringToFront();

this.closeDoc();
```

Once again, you check for the viewer version in the first few lines of code. If the version is 5.0 or greater, the order form is opened. Four variables are assigned at the beginning of the routine. If the job has been quoted (q.value == 1), then the discountAmount is used for the resultAmount. If the job has not been quoted and no discount is applied, the resultAmount is taken from the subtotal field. The tax values are assessed and sent to the slave document. If the job was quoted, the name of the employee who quoted the job is also sent to the slave document. At the end of the routine, the Finish Calculator is opened. Inasmuch as the order form now contains the data from the quote calculator, it remains in the background when the Finish Calculator is opened and brought to the front view. The print quote calculator, however, is closed after the data are transposed (`this.closeDoc();`).

The last button on the print calculator has the same script with the line of code opening the finishing calculator eliminated. The order form is brought to the front at the beginning of the script and remains there while the data are transposed from the quote calculator to the order form.

As part of the final script that is added to both calculator files, you need to add a Document Level function to ensure the file opens properly. The note described earlier in this chapter set forth the steps to open the JavaScript Functions dialog box and add the line of code:

```
this.disclosed=true;
```

Be certain to add this line of code as a Document Level JavaScript for all forms that are opened with the `app.openDoc()` statement.

Both calculator forms open an alert dialog box when the file is opened prompting a user to clear the form. If a user saves old data, then the form should be reset before performing another quote. However, if the user saves the form and wants to reopen it, then you need to inform the user the form will be reset upon opening the file. The following code is applied to a Page Open action:

```
var n = app.alert("Do you want to clear the form?", 2,2);
    if (n == 4)
this.resetForm();

var msg = this.getField("discountText");
msg.value = "Image Source employee who quoted job";
```

In the above script, the `this.resetForm();` statement is used to clear all data on the form. One field, however, is a message box. When the form is cleared, all the message text is wiped out of the message field. The last two lines of code add the message text back into the message field after the form is reset.

Note   A better choice for preserving a message would be to use the text in the Default for the Field Properties. The above may be a bit awkward, however it's used as an example here to show you that if fields are reset, the message text clears. If you don't use a Default in the Field Properties dialog box, you can overcome clearing the text data with a short script.

In this example, when a customer places an order where a discount has been used on the order form, the customer service representative checks with the employee who quoted the discount or retrieves a file where quotes are stored. If no name is associated with the quote, the customer service representative inquires with the customer as to who provided the quote.

You can explore the remaining scripts by opening the files in the Customer Service folder inside the Chapter 16 folder on the book's CD-ROM. The finish calculator is included on the CD so you can follow the process and examine the scripts used to produce the final results. Additionally, an instruction form is also included, which walks a user through the process. Open the `instructions.pdf` file and follow the steps to understand the order process.

On the CD-ROM   You'll find the `instructions.pdf` file in the Customer Service folder in the Chapter 16 folder on the book's CD-ROM.

By providing forms on a Web site where customers can initially quote their own jobs, the amount of employee time is reduced and the amount of paperwork flowing between a vendor and a customer is reduced. In this example, all the order process can be handled electronically.

User guides

Many readers of my *Acrobat PDF Bible* have asked me the question, "How can I open a secondary document, then return a user to the same page in a master document?" If a user clicks on a button in one document to open a second file, a user may wish to return to the same page from which the button was selected. In essence, you want to return to somewhere in the middle of the host document. If you use a Page Open action and the Open File action Type, by default, Acrobat opens a file on the first page or the page determined to be the default open view in the Open Options dialog box.

Returning to the last page viewed in a file after opening a secondary file may be something you wish to apply in user manuals, employee manuals, customer order catalogs, or description files that use a secondary file to illustrate a point or display an example. In a logical flow, a user may read through some description and click on a button to see a sample form. After reviewing a form, the user may wish to close the form and return to the same page where s/he left off in the description document. You could create some links to destinations that navigate to fixed pages in documents or you can use JavaScript to accomplish the task. From what you learned in the earlier examples, you can add just a little bit of code to the `app.openDoc()` statement described earlier.

Figure 16-20 shows an example of the instructions document referred to in the last exercise. The page displayed in Figure 16-20 provides instructions for filling out the print quote and finish calculators discussed earlier. If a user wants to see a price sheet, the quote calculator doesn't offer all the prices at a glance. A price list, however, can be helpful to users who want a price review rather than a price for a given size and material. To accommodate the user, I have a button on the page that opens the price list for color printing. After a user views the printing price list, the user is returned to the same page in the instructions file. Notice in Figure 16-20 that the page is page 2 in the document.

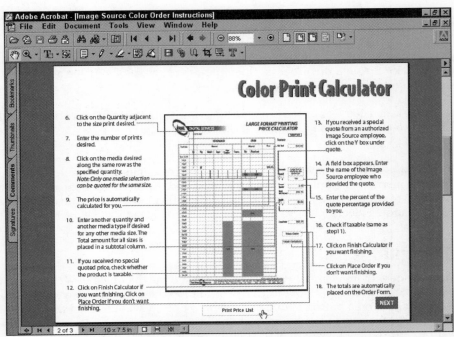

Figure 16-20: The description file has a button on page 2 that opens a secondary document. When the user closes the secondary document, we want the user to return to page two in the instructions file.

To open the price list, use a JavaScript with the following code:

```
if (app.viewerVersion < 5)
   app.alert("Version 5.0 required. Some features will not
work.");

else {
   this.slave = app.openDoc("printPrice.pdf",this);
}

this.closeDoc();
```

The first part of the routine warns users that Acrobat 5 or greater viewers may be needed to view the files. The app.openDoc() statement is used to open a secondary file (printPrice.pdf) and the last line of code closes the instructions document.

Tip   You may wonder why the closeDoc() statement is used in the routine described above. If you don't force the file to close, the file may close for some users and remain open for other users. Whether the file remains open or closes is determined in the General Preferences dialog box for the Options settings when the Open Cross-Document Links in Same Window check box is either selected or deselected.

Because user preferences can create some inconsistencies, you can force the original file to close regardless of what preference a user chooses. In this manner, you can keep all file management consistent and prevent any unexpected results due to differences among user preferences.

When the user clicks on the Print Price List button in the instructions file, the price list opens. The price list occupies most of a standard letter page. When the view in a Fit in Window view opens on a small monitor, the detail may be too difficult to see by many users. If you want to zoom in to the document and override the Open Options settings, you can ask JavaScript to set the zoom level. To zoom in to the document, add the following line of code just before the last line of code noted above.

```
this.slave.zoom = 150;
```

The page zoom opens at 150% when this line of code is added to the routine, as shown in Figure 16-21.

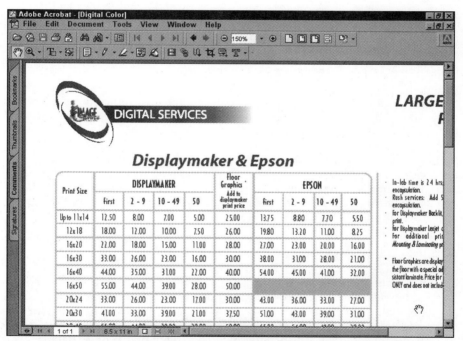

Figure 16-21: When the Print Price List button in the instructions file is selected, the secondary file opens at a 150% zoom level.

To return to the instructions document, you can add a button to the page or use a Page Action. In this example, use a Page Action. If you prefer a button, you can add a JavaScript to the button using the same code. For a Page Action, use the Close Page action Type and add a JavaScript with the following code:

```
if (app.viewerVersion < 5)
   app.alert("Version 5.0 required. Some features will not
work.");

else {
   this.slave = app.openDoc("instructions.pdf",this);
}

this.slave.pageNum=1;

this.closeDoc();
```

Most of the code above should be familiar to you from previous examples. The one line that takes the user back to the original view in the instructions file is `this.slave.pageNum=1;`. Because JavaScript is zero based, page 1 is the second page in the document. In this example, it is the point of origin when the button was clicked. By default, the page view in the instructions file returns the user to the same view; therefore, you don't need to assign a zoom when returning to the file.

Creating Accounting Management Forms

Many different forms can be used for accounting management. Summaries of financial reports extracted from databases, balance sheets, operating statements, cash flow summaries, and the like can all be routed electronically as PDF files. With these kinds of routine documents, not much imagination is needed to develop the forms that a company can use to cut down the paper flow.

In this category, I use two examples to illustrate how PDF forms can be helpful in accounting and finance departments. The first example is a simple form designed to save time when making purchase orders. The second example is more elaborate and demonstrates how a little creative thought can be used to create forms for useful accounting management purposes.

Purchase order form

If your work involves interacting with an accounting department with various forms for creating purchase requisitions, purchase orders, and the like, then you are likely to complete forms where you supply the accounting department with information to process your forms. Ultimately, a various assortment of vendors may be used in your everyday activities. The accounting department may require data, such as vendor addresses, contacts, shipping information, and so on, before it can process your request. This responsibility lies on your shoulders and you are the individual who must keep the vendor list updated to successfully complete forms routed to other departments.

If you spend much time searching through phone books, rolodex cards, invoices, and other records to find a vendor contact and address each time you make a purchase request, then the time used for searching information can become an aggravation. An easy way to alleviate the problem is to keep a vendor list or other similar lists for contacts updated in a spreadsheet application or another PDF form. Each time you complete a requisition, you access the database and find the vendor to be used in completing the form.

The poApproval.pdf form is similar to forms that are used in exercises in Chapters 8 and 11. The date field in the top left portion of the form (as shown in Figure 16-22) is calculated automatically when the Reset button is selected on the form.

 You'll find the poApproval.pdf form in the Accounting Management folder in the Chapter 16 folder on the book's CD-ROM.

 Refer to Chapter 8, "Writing JavaScript Routines," and Chapter 11, "Using Acrobat Security," for more information.

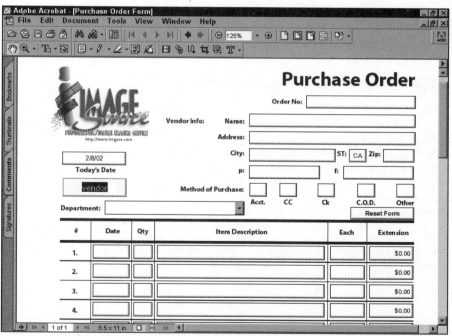

Figure 16-22: The date is calculated automatically each time the Reset button is selected.

To calculate the date on a form, open the Calculate properties and add a Custom JavaScript with the following code:

```
event.value = util.printd("mm/dd/yy", new Date());
```

This script revises the date each time the form is reset. If you want the date fixed after it has been added to the form, you can create a Page Action or button field and use the `add.field()` statement covered earlier in this chapter when we reviewed the `passwords.pdf` file.

Use of the form is much like other forms discussed earlier in this chapter where field data are imported from a text file. In this example, we'll go a few steps further and create a button that automatically opens the data file and adds a vendor based on a vendor name you add to a vendor name field. Using a similar example, you won't need to remember the data filename each time you use the form and you won't need to address any menu commands to import data.

Below the date field that appears in Figure 16-22 is a text field with a JavaScript action to import data on an On Blur mouse behavior. When a vendor name is added to the field and the user tabs out of the field Enter key, the JavaScript action is invoked.

Data are contained in a spreadsheet file saved as text from Microsoft Excel. Figure 16-23 shows a data file with three records. If you type one of the names in the vName column in the vendor field and tab out of the field, the data for the record matching the name you enter are imported in matching fields on the form.

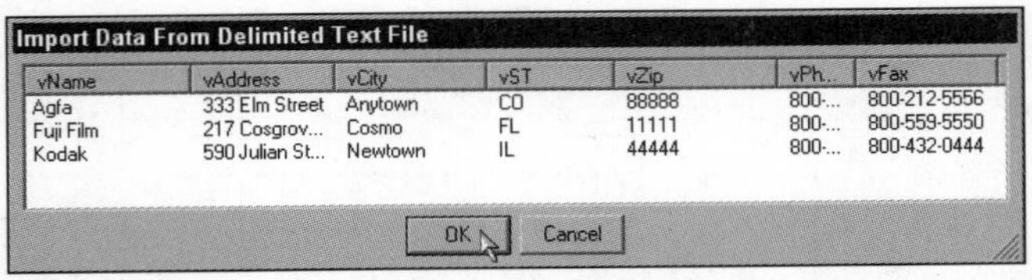

vName	vAddress	vCity	vST	vZip	vPh...	vFax
Agfa	333 Elm Street	Anytown	CO	88888	800-...	800-212-5556
Fuji Film	217 Cosgrov...	Cosmo	FL	11111	800-...	800-559-5550
Kodak	590 Julian St...	Newtown	IL	44444	800-...	800-432-0444

Import Data From Delimited Text File

OK   Cancel

Figure 16-23: A data file contains vendor information. After a name is entered on the form in the vendor field, the data are imported from the matching record into matching fields without having to address a menu command to import data.

Open the Field Properties dialog box and click on Action. Add a JavaScript action type and enter the following code in the JavaScript Edit dialog box.

```
records = 0;

// loop thru all records:
do {

this.importTextData("/d/AcrobatFormsBook/vendors.txt",records);
    if (getField('vName').value == getField("vendor").value)
    {
        getField('vName').value = getField("vendor").value;
    break;
    }
} while (records++ <4)
```

```
var f = this.getField("vendor");
f.hidden = true;
```

The do loop begins by accessing the data file. (Note: The directory path is fixed. Change the path to match the path used on your computer.) The field where we enter the vendor name is called vendor. We look for vName in the data file beginning with the first record and search until we find the name that matches the vendor typed into the vendor field. After the vendor name is matched and the data imported, we hide the field. If the form is electronically routed, the appearance is a little neater by hiding redundant fields used for temporary items to complete the form.

Note   Using this example requires Acrobat or Acrobat Approval. Acrobat Reader doesn't support importing data from text files.

Equipment inventory and valuation summary

The next example illustrates how an Acrobat form can be more advantageous than many different kinds of database forms. With the ability to store images as well as data fields, you can add more functionality to your forms. In this example, I use a form to catalog equipment inventory. The form can be copied to a CD-ROM and provided to an insurance carrier and various finance vendors who may be interested in assessing some value to your company according to the asset value. If you file an insurance claim or wish to calculate a current value on assets, all the parties having a copy of your form can easily make judgments by reviewing the form. A photo appears on each page of the form making it easy to communicate what claim you are filing or what specifically is involved in calculating assets.

The equipmentInventory.pdf file in the Accounting Management folder inside the Chapter 16 folder on the book's CD-ROM contains a cover page, as shown in Figure 16-24. To make it easy for others to navigate to a specific piece of equipment, an application pop-up menu is used to send the user to a destination where the respective item is found.

Cross-Reference   For JavaScripts that are used to create application pop-up menus, see Chapter 10, "Creating Advanced Form Designs."

The pop-up menu is linked to destination pages in the open document.

On the CD-ROM   You'll find the equipmentInventory.pdf file in the Accounting Management folder in the Chapter 16 folder on the book's CD-ROM.

The form design

The form contains data that are used among several departments in a company. Figure 16-25 shows a page following the cover page where the data are supplied. Beginning with the top field, the department using the equipment is identified. In this example there are six different departments using different equipment assets. The second field at the top of the form is used to specify the piece of equipment related to the data on the page and a digital camera photo is imported under the Item description.

The remaining fields contain data for the vendor information, the equipment specification, the finance company used to purchase the equipment, the insurance company covering the piece of equipment, and a comments field for miscellaneous information. The accounting department can use the form for inventory and asset accumulation, the production departments can use the form for contacting technical support help, the insurance carrier can use the form to assist with claims processing, and the bank can use the form for assessing value based on the company's assets.

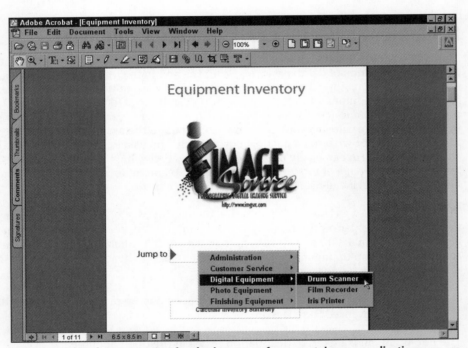

Figure 16-24: The cover page for the inventory form contains an application pop-up menu with the menu options linked to destinations in the file.

The form contains a page template that can be spawned from the New Page button on the top-right corner of each page spawned from the template. The script for spawning the page template is the same one that was mentioned in Chapter 9, "Creating Templates and Spawning Pages," in which spawning pages from templates was discussed.

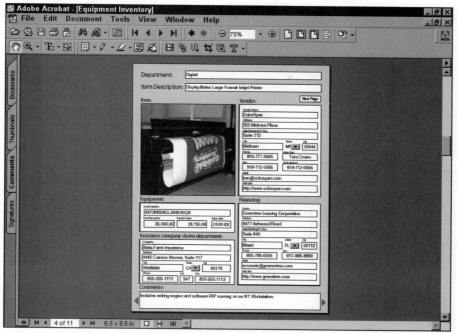

Figure 16-25: The pages following the cover page contain the data describing each individual item on separate pages in the PDF document.

Returning back to the cover page, a button exists below the pop-up menu for calculating a valuation summary. When the button is selected, the equipValueSummary.pdf file in the Accounting Management folder inside the Chapter 16 folder on the book's CD-ROM opens. The summary adds all the purchase value fields according to department and all the current value fields according to department, as shown in Figure 16-26.

On the CD-ROM You'll find the equipValueSummary.pdf file in the Accounting Management folder in the Chapter 16 folder on the book's CD-ROM.

Calculating the summary

Setting up the fields on a template page, spawning pages from a template, and creating application pop-up menus have all been covered in earlier chapters. The field used to summarize the data contains a more complex script that loops through all pages and first looks at the Department field. Each department is assigned two variables to collect the purchase value and the current value, and sum the values specific to the department. The amount sums are then placed in the summary document according to department. As pages are appended to the equipment value document, clicking on the Calculate Inventory Summary button on the title page creates a new summary including the values from the appended pages.

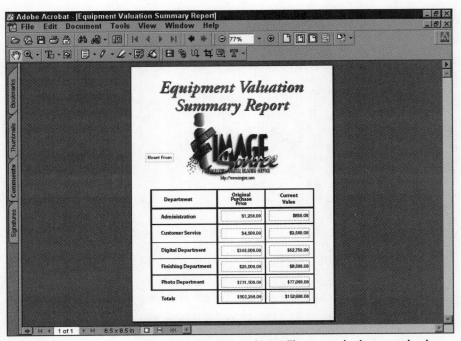

Figure 16-26: The summary report is a second PDF file opened where total values are placed according to department.

The following script was added to the Create Valuation Summary button in order to perform the calculations and place the results in the summary document:

```
//determine the viewer version
if (app.viewerVersion < 5)
   app.alert("Version 5.0 required. Some features will not
work.");

//open the summary document
else {
   this.slave = app.openDoc("equipValueSummary.pdf",this);
   slave.bringToFront();
}

//zero out the summary fields
var sumAd = 0;
var adPrice = 0;

var sumService = 0;
var servicePrice = 0;

var sumDigital = 0;
```

```
var digitalPrice = 0;

var sumFinish = 0;
var finishPrice = 0;

var sumPhoto = 0;
var photoPrice = 0;

// loop through all fields to summarize data
for (i = 1; i < this.numPages; i++) {
    var getCurrent = this.getField("P" + i +
(".addPage.item.currentValue"));
    var getPrice = this.getField("P" + i +
(".addPage.item.price"));
    var department = this.getField("P" + i +
(".addPage.department"));

    if (department.value == "Administration") {
        sumAd = getCurrent.value + sumAd;
        adPrice = getPrice.value + adPrice; }
else
    if (department.value == "Customer Service") {
        sumService = getCurrent.value + sumService;
        servicePrice = getPrice.value + servicePrice; }
else
    if (department.value == "Digital") {
        sumDigital = getCurrent.value + sumDigital;
        digitalPrice = getPrice.value + digitalPrice; }
else
    if (department.value == "Photo") {
        sumPhoto= getCurrent.value + sumPhoto;
        photoPrice = getPrice.value + photoPrice; }
else
   if (department.value == "Finishing") {
        sumFinish = getCurrent.value + sumFinish;
        finishPrice = getPrice.value + finishPrice; }

//put the summarized data in the slave doc
var currentAd = this.slave.getField("adminCurrent");
var priceAd = this.slave.getField("adminOriginal");
currentAd.value = sumAd;
priceAd.value = adPrice;

var currentDigital = this.slave.getField("digitalCurrent");
var priceDigital = this.slave.getField("digitalOriginal");
currentDigital.value = sumDigital;
priceDigital.value = digitalPrice;

var currentService = this.slave.getField("csCurrent");
var priceService = this.slave.getField("csOriginal");
currentService.value = sumService;
priceService.value = servicePrice;

var currentFinish = this.slave.getField("finishCurrent");
```

```
var priceFinish = this.slave.getField("finishOriginal");
currentFinish.value = sumFinish;
priceFinish.value = finishPrice;

var currentPhoto = this.slave.getField("photoCurrent");
var pricePhoto = this.slave.getField("photoOriginal");
currentPhoto.value = sumPhoto;
pricePhoto.value = photoPrice;
}
```

The script begins with assessing the viewer version as described earlier in this chapter. The summary document is then opened and brought to the front of the Document Pane. Fields are then assigned variables and zeroed out. The ten variables initially at the beginning of the routine hold the sums for each department and the values associated with the purchase and current price data.

The loop examines each field on each page and gets the purchase value, the current value, and the department. Notice that the field names being retrieved are expressed as `this.getField("P" + i + (".addPage.item.currentValue"))`. When fields are spawned from pages, Acrobat adds P and a page number to the field name plus `addPage` plus `item`. Thus, a field may be named `P1.addPage.item.currentValue`. Therefore, to retrieve the current value on the first page, we take `"P"` and add it to the `i.value` (in this case the first time through the loop which would be 1), and add that to `addPage.item.currentValue`. The `currentValue` string is the name of the field on the page template.

The conditions then look at each department value. If `department ==` `Administration`, the variables associated with Administration are added together to create the revolving total. The last segment of the routine takes all the totals and places the values in the respective fields in the slave document (`equipValueSummary.pdf`).

This form is designed for use in a business environment where asset accumulation may be important in-house or with different vendors. You can easily adapt the same concept for a personal form where you may wish to organize all your personal assets for a homeowner's or renter's insurance policy. Provide a CD to your carrier and when a claim needs to be filed, your carrier can begin the claim preparation from the document you send them.

Animating Presentations

Form fields in Acrobat can be used for animation sequences like the examples that are discussed in Chapter 10, "Creating Advanced Form Designs." You can use animation effects on Acrobat forms for helping users understand your forms and assist them in filling in a form. You can also use fields for animation effects when preparing PDF files for presentations that you may use to deliver seminars and talks at meetings and conferences.

Obviously, there are some programs more suited for presentations, like Microsoft PowerPoint, where animating text and images can be handled without complex JavaScripts. On the other hand, if your discussions are confined to talking about PDF documents, then you may find more advantage in taking the time to add animation to PDF files, especially if you move back and forth between PDFs and your presentation slide show.

The following examples may not be a frequent feature you'll use with your forms or presentations, but the capability does exist and it's offered here in the event you wish to add more animation than was discussed in Chapter 10. In this section, we'll look at creating a ticker-tape type of display and animating motion effects with images.

Ticker tape displays

A ticker-tape motion is similar to revolving text you might see on electric signs or billboard advertising. You may have use for such a display on a PDF form where a special product, service, your Web site address, or any other text you want the user to see when either a form is opened or a specific page in a document is opened.

In Figure 16-27, I use a ticker-tape display to begin a motion when the file is opened. (See the `tickerTape.pdf` file in the Presentations folder inside the Chapter 16 folder.) This example is used when I give presentations on Acrobat and add a little fun to a discussion involving PDF forms. The arrow in the figure points to the text that scrolls across the text field.

You'll find the `tickerTape.pdf` file in the Presentations folder in the Chapter 16 folder on the book's CD-ROM.

To begin, I start by creating a document level JavaScript as a function used to start the ticker tape. The start begins with a Page Open command and the stop is assigned to the Page Close command.

The document level function is scripted as

```
//document level JS
function Motion(msg,n)
{
var f = new String(msg);
return f.substr(n)+f.substr(0,n);
}
```

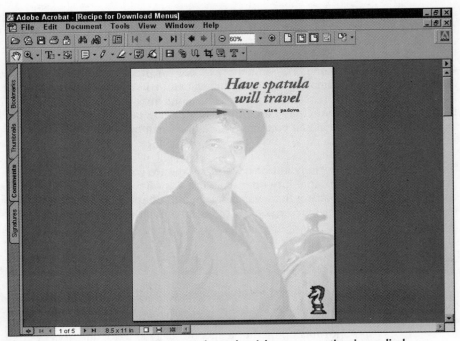

Figure 16-27: The arrow points to where the ticker-tape motion is applied.

The Page Open script begins the ticker-tape motion, and the following script is used for the page action:

```
// on page open, begin interval
var f = this.getField("textLine");

var code = new String("this.getField('textLine').value =
\Motion(this.getField('textLine').value,3);\");

global.ttIsRunning = 1;

global.run = app.setInterval(code,150);
```

When creating an animation effect, you should always instruct Acrobat when to stop the motion, otherwise the loop runs in the background continually until you quit Acrobat. When the page is closed, the motion effect is halted with the following script:

```
//on page close, stop interval
var f = this.getField("textLine");

if (global.ttIsRunning == 1)
{app.clearInterval(global.run);
global.ttIsRunning = 0;
}
```

The document level script identifies a string and a number. The string is the message (msg) to rotate and the number (n) is the amount of characters to rotate. The substr() is a core JavaScript function that implements the rotation.

The Page Open action gets the text field containing text in the Default field box specified in the Options properties when the Field Properties dialog box is opened. The function Motion is called from the document level script and the value, 3 item determines the number of characters being rotated at a time. Changing this value will have an effect on the speed of the text scrolling across the screen. As you lower the value, the text scroll appears slower. Raising the number speeds up the motion. The last line of code determines the interval, which also has an effect on the speed of the text scrolling. The value set in the example is 150, which represents 150 milliseconds. Adjust this value to suit your needs. As the value is increased, the speed of the scrolling text slows down.

The last routine for the Page Close action stops the interval. The routine begins with examining whether the ticker tape is running (ttIsRunning == 1). If it is, the interval is stopped (ttIsRunning == 0).

Tip When you create animation effects that are applied to Page Open and Page Close actions, you need to save the document and reopen it to test any edits in your code. To make your initial coding and debugging easier, create a start and stop button with the JavaScript coded for the start action and stop action on separate button fields. After you know the routine runs as you wish, copy the code to Page Open and Page Close actions and delete the buttons.

Note The ticker-tape motion appears the same in all Acrobat viewers.

Animation graphics

Image animation can be used with presentations or on forms where you wish to make the form interactive for a user to complete fields, select options, or illustrate help. In this example, I use a slide that might be used with a presentation to discuss the flow of forms electronically.

When the animationExample.pdf form from the Presentations folder inside the Chapter 16 folder on the book's CD-ROM opens, an image appears on the left side of the slide. Click the image and an arrow moves across the screen, as shown in Figure 16-28. The motion illustrates the electronic flow of a form from the image on the left side of the page to a destination on the right side of the page.

On the CD-ROM You'll find the animationExample.pdf form in the Presentations folder in the Chapter 16 folder on the book's CD-ROM.

When the arrow arrives at its destination, a message and another image are displayed on the slide. Click on this image and another arrow moves left across the screen, as shown in Figure 16-29.

Figure 16-28: When the mouse button is clicked on the image, an arrow moves across the screen toward the right.

As the arrow moving left arrives at its destination, the message is hidden and a third image is displayed on the screen.

This example uses four different functions at the document level. One function is used to create the motion of the arrow moving to the right, another for the motion to the left, another function to show the frames, and a final function for hiding the frames.

The two functions for showing and hiding the frames are coded as

```
// hide all the frames
function hideall () {
    for (var i = 0; i < 13;i++) {
    (frame+i).display = display.hidden;
    }
}
//show all the frames
function showall () {
    for (var i = 0; i < 13;i++) {
    (frame+i).display = display.visible;
    }
}
```

Figure 16-29: When the mouse button is clicked on the image at right, another arrow moves left across the slide.

These routines loop through the fields for the arrow icons and hide the fields or show the fields, respectively.

The other two functions create the motion effects and are coded as

```
//moov function
function moov () {
var show = eval ("frame" + i);
show.display = display.visible;
if (i == 1) {
  frame12.display = display.hidden;
  }
else {
  var hide = eval ("frame" + (i-1))
  hide.display = display.hidden
  }
i++
if (i == 13) {
  app.clearInterval (y); //stop
  woman.display = display.visible; //show image
  instr.display = display.visible; //show message
  frame12.display = display.hidden;
```

```
      }
    }


  //moov2 function
  function moov2 () {
  var show = eval ("frame" + i);
  show.display = display.visible;
  if (i == 1) {
    frame12.display = display.hidden
    }
  else {
    var hide = eval ("frame" + (i-1))
    hide.display = display.hidden
    }
  i++
  if (i == 13) {
    app.clearInterval (y); //stop
    man.display = display.visible;
    instr.display = display.hidden; //show message
    frame12.display = display.hidden;
    disc.display = display.visible
    }
```

These two routines loop through the fields and individually show and hide the respective fields to simulate a motion effect. The distinction between the two functions is the image that is displayed at the end of the interval. In the moov function, the woman.display is true. In the moov2 function, the disc.display is true. The images are displayed after the animation effects complete the cycles.

The button on the first image contains the script to start the motion. The JavaScript is coded as

```
  var woman = this.getField("s8.2");
  var instr = this.getField("instructor");
  var frame1 = this.getField ("arrow.1");
  var frame2 = this.getField ("arrow.2");
  var frame3 = this.getField ("arrow.3");
  var frame4 = this.getField ("arrow.4");
  var frame5 = this.getField ("arrow.5");
  var frame6 = this.getField ("arrow.6");
  var frame7 = this.getField ("arrow.7");
  var frame8 = this.getField ("arrow.8");
  var frame9 = this.getField ("arrow.9");
  var frame10 = this.getField ("arrow.10");
  var frame11 = this.getField ("arrow.11");
  var frame12 = this.getField ("arrow.12");
  i=1;

  y = app.setInterval ("moov ()", 125);
```

You start by assigning two variable names to the fields that are displayed when the loop finishes. The display of the two fields is determined in the `moov` function discussed earlier. There are 12 fields and each field is assigned the `frameN` name. The frames are then made visible or hidden from the functions created earlier. The last line of code calls the `moov` function and sets the interval to 125. Increasing or decreasing 125 slows down or speeds up the motion, respectively. The JavaScript for the second image is identical to the previous one , but the field values correspond to the field names for the arrows moving left. Additionally, the final image to be displayed is assigned a variable name used in the `moov2` function.

As a final edit, a Page Close action hides the fields that were opened with the button actions. You can choose to script the fields to be hidden or use the Show/Hide field action type when adding the action in the Page Actions dialog box.

Note The animation is visible in all Acrobat viewers.

Creating Forms for Non-Profits

I singled out non-profits to illustrate some creativity when creating Acrobat forms and how a little imagination can help with concerns related to these organizations. Similar designs, however, can be applied to for-profit enterprises or any other kind of entity.

Non-profits are commonly involved in fundraising activity to generate revenues for sustaining operations and improving their services. The forms discussed in this section are intended to help market an organization and offer a little more presence on the Web by attracting visitors. In the first example, I use a form that can be easily updated by an employee to reflect a fundraising venture. The amount of collected revenue is diagrammed along a path toward an eventual goal. In the second example, a perpetual calendar is designed for Web hosting where visitors can download the file and use it for personal use. As an advertising gimmick, the organization keeps information specific to their organization in front of end users whenever the calendar is opened.

Fundraising barometer

The `fundBarometer.pdf` file in the NonProfits folder inside the Chapter 16 folder on the book's CD-ROM is used as an example for reporting current contributions toward a goal for a building project. As the amount of received funds increases, the barometer reports a graphic representation of the amount of money collected, as shown in Figure 16-30.

On the CD-ROM You'll find the `fundBarometer.pdf` file in the NonProfits folder in the Chapter 16 folder on the book's CD-ROM.

Figure 16-30: The barometer graphs the amount of funds displayed in the text field at the bottom of the form.

The design of this form is intended to make it easy for an authorized individual to change the amount of funds in the text field and have the graph updated to reflect the new values. A quick change on the form and a quick upload to the Web server eliminates any need for recoding an HTML form. In order to ensure that only authorized individuals make the updates, the field for the data entry is password-protected. When the form is saved with Acrobat Standard Security, as was covered in Chapter 11, the password in the JavaScript routine remains protected.

Cross-Reference   Refer to Chapter 11, "Using Acrobat Security," for information about Acrobat Standard Security.

You can create the graph that appears on this form by displaying fields with a common background color. The bubble at the top of the barometer uses clipping paths to properly display the circular icons as I described earlier in this chapter when we looked at printing templates. When the form is viewed with the Form tool selected, the fields appear, as shown in Figure 16-31.

To edit the contributions amount, place the cursor inside the contributions amount field and click the cursor. An application response dialog box opens and prompts you for a password, as shown in Figure 16-32. The password to access the field is *roadrunner*.

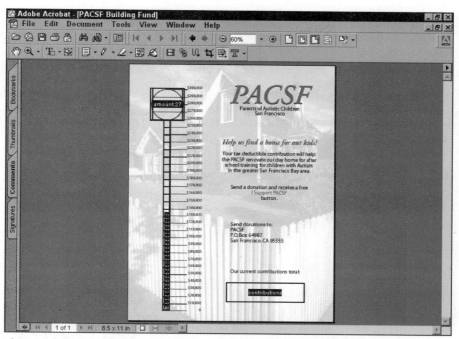

Figure 16-31: The graph is created by displaying fields according to the amount that is entered in the text field at the bottom right side of the form.

If you enter the wrong password, an alert dialog box opens. The message in the alert dialog box indicates the wrong password was supplied. Additionally, the message informs the user to reopen the file and try again. In the script, the field is immediately set to Read Only and the field is locked. Without locking the field, the user would be able to enter data in the field even if the wrong password was used.

There are three scripts used with this form. The first script is used to create the application response dialog box and ask for the password. The mouse behavior where the JavaScript action is assigned is set to On Focus. If the user tabs to the field or clicks on the field, the following script is executed:

```
// ask for the password
var f = this.getField("contributions");
f.readonly = true;

var cResponse = app.response({
cQuestion: "A password is required to change the contributions
total. Please enter the access password",
cTitle: "Password to change fund contributions"});

        if (cResponse == "roadrunner") {
        f.readonly = false;
```

```
        }
    else {
                app.alert("You entered the wrong password! Reopen
        the file and try again.");
            }
```

The first two lines of code get the contribution field and set it to `readonly`. If the password is incorrect, the field remains locked. If the password is correct, the `readonly` is false (unlocks the field) and the cursor is active in the field where the user can add data.

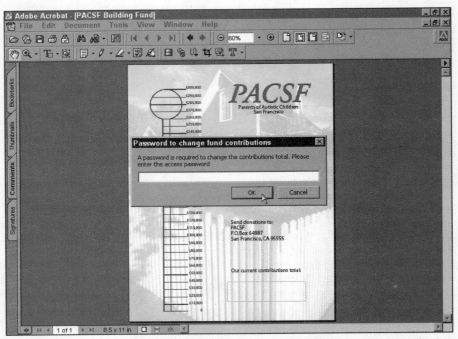

Figure 16-32: When the cursor is clicked in the text field to change the contribution amount, an application response dialog box opens asking for a password. The password used in the JavaScript is *roadrunner*.

For a correct password, the user edits the field. When finished editing and the user tabs out of the field or clicks the cursor outside the field, a JavaScript assigned to the On Blur mouse action is executed. The routine to display the field associated with the contribution value is as follows:

```
// loop through all fields and hide them
var numberOfFields = 31;

for (var i = 1; i < numberOfFields; i++){
    var f = this.getField("amount."+ i);
```

```
        f.hidden = true;
}

//get contribution amount and show field
{
    if (event.value < 100) {
        var show = this.getField("amount.1")
        show.hidden = true }
else
if (event.value < 10001) {
        var show = this.getField("amount.1")
        show.hidden = false }
    else
        if (event.value < 20001) {
            var show = this.getField("amount.2")
            show.hidden = false }
    else
        if (event.value < 30001) {
            var show = this.getField("amount.3")
            show.hidden = false }
    else
        if (event.value < 40001) {
            var show = this.getField("amount.4")
            show.hidden = false }
    else
        if (event.value < 50001) {
            var show = this.getField("amount.5")
            show.hidden = false }
    else
        if (event.value < 60001) {
            var show = this.getField("amount.6")
            show.hidden = false }
    else
        if (event.value < 70001) {
            var show = this.getField("amount.7")
            show.hidden = false }
    else
        if (event.value < 80001) {
            var show = this.getField("amount.8")
            show.hidden = false }
    else
        if (event.value < 90001) {
            var show = this.getField("amount.9")
            show.hidden = false }
    else
        if (event.value < 100001) {
            var show = this.getField("amount.10")
            show.hidden = false }
    else
        if (event.value < 110001) {
            var show = this.getField("amount.11")
            show.hidden = false }
    else
        if (event.value < 120001) {
```

```
                var show = this.getField("amount.12")
                show.hidden = false }
        else ·
           if (event.value < 130001) {
                var show = this.getField("amount.13")
                show.hidden = false }
        else
           if (event.value < 140001) {
                var show = this.getField("amount.14")
                show.hidden = false }
        else
           if (event.value < 150001) {
                var show = this.getField("amount.15")
                show.hidden = false }
        else
           if (event.value < 160001) {
                var show = this.getField("amount.16")
                show.hidden = false }
        else
           if (event.value < 170001) {
                var show = this.getField("amount.17")
                show.hidden = false }
        else
           if (event.value < 180001) {
                var show = this.getField("amount.18")
                show.hidden = false }
        else
           if (event.value < 190001) {
                var show = this.getField("amount.19")
                show.hidden = false }
        else
           if (event.value < 200001) {
                var show = this.getField("amount.20")
                show.hidden = false }
        else
           if (event.value < 210001) {
                var show = this.getField("amount.21")
                show.hidden = false }
        else
           if (event.value < 220001) {
                var show = this.getField("amount.22")
                show.hidden = false }
        else
           if (event.value < 230001) {
                var show = this.getField("amount.23")
                show.hidden = false }
        else
           if (event.value < 240001) {
                var show = this.getField("amount.24")
                show.hidden = false }
        else
           if (event.value < 250001) {
                var show = this.getField("amount.25")
                show.hidden = false }
```

```
else
    if (event.value < 260001) {
        var show = this.getField("amount.26")
        show.hidden = false }
else
    if (event.value < 270001) {
        var show = this.getField("amount.27")
        var xtra = this.getField("amount.26")
        show.hidden = false
        xtra.hidden = false }
else
    if (event.value < 280001) {
        var show = this.getField("amount.28")
        var xtra = this.getField("amount.26")
        show.hidden = false
        xtra.hidden = false }
else
    if (event.value < 290001) {
        var show = this.getField("amount.29")
        var xtra = this.getField("amount.26")
        show.hidden = false
        xtra.hidden = false }
else
    if (event.value < 300001) {
        var show = this.getField("amount.30")
        var xtra = this.getField("amount.26")
        show.hidden = false
        xtra.hidden = false }
}
```

Depending on the amount entered in the contribution field, the corresponding field is visible (show.hidden = false). The last four values display the field up to the bubble in the barometer and the respective field for the segment of the bubble. Therefore, two fields are shown when the amount is over 260,000.

If a user enters the wrong password and saves the file, then there is no way to regain access to the contribution field when it is locked. Therefore, a Page Open action is created to make the field accessible each time the file is opened. The script below sets the read only value to false:

```
var f = this.getField("contributions");
f.readonly = false;
```

When Acrobat Standard Security is used to prevent changes to form fields, the end user won't be able to access the contribution field. Because this field contains the password to execute the script above, there is no way to edit the form without knowing the password in advance.

Note   The chart can be created in all Acrobat viewers. To save the chart and upload the file to a Web server with new data, Acrobat or Acrobat Approval is needed.

Calendar maker

The `calendarMaker.pdf` file in the NonProfits folder inside the Chapter 16 folder on the book's CD-ROM is designed for a user to create a perpetual calendar. The form can create reliable calendars over the next decade. Additional years would need more scripting to account for leap years.

On the CD-ROM

You'll find the `calendarMaker.pdf` file in the NonProfits folder in the Chapter 16 folder on the book's CD-ROM.

The idea behind this example is that users can download a calendar from a Web site and create their own calendars for any given month within the decade. When a calendar is created, images of an organization's events and days of annual events are displayed for a given month. Much like a company that prints a calendar for advertising a business, this form is intended to be a paperless form suiting a similar purpose.

The form design

Buttons exist for creating a calendar for a given month, clearing the form, printing the form, and opening a help file to determine what day a month starts over the next decade. The form doesn't use a formula to create a perpetual calendar for an infinite number of years or use dates to plot the month. For this form, the user needs to know what day each month starts with during a given year. A calendar created for April 2002 appears in Figure 16-33.

The help button on the right side of the form opens a help file (`calendarDays.pdf` is located in the Chapter 16 Non Profits folder) in which a user can determine what day a month starts between the years 2002 and 2011, as shown in Figure 16-34. The months of the year appear in the left-most column and the years appear across the top of the first row. At a glance, a user can pick a month and year and read the day the month starts for that particular year.

The day of the month is important because it is used in the script to create a calendar. To create a new calendar, a user clicks on the Create Calendar button on the lower-left side of the calendar maker. When the Create Calendar button is selected, an application response dialog box opens, as shown in Figure 16-35.

The first question posed to the user is for what year the calendar will be created. Enter a year in the application response dialog box and click OK. Another dialog box opens and is similar to the dialog box that was shown in Figure 16-35.

The next question to answer is for what month the calendar will be created. Each of the response dialog boxes shows the format for year and month to be entered. Type a month name using the format described in the dialog box and click OK. A third response dialog box opens and is also similar to the dialog box that appears in Figure 16-35.

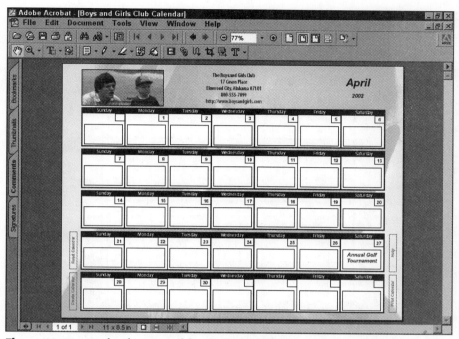

Figure 16-33: A calendar created for April 2002 displays an image that is associated with the month and a day that is marked in which an annual fundraising event occurs.

The response dialog box for month demonstrates the need for knowing what day the first day falls on when creating a new calendar—hence, the help file. When the day is entered in the response dialog box and the OK button is clicked, a JavaScript routine plots the calendar beginning with the day when the month starts and numbers each day up to the total days of a given month including leap years.

Buttons exist for clearing the form and printing the form. These two buttons, in addition to the buttons for creating the calendar and opening the help file, are not visible on the printed form. These button fields were assigned properties to not print in the Appearance properties. As a precaution against preventing old data remaining on new calendars, when the Create Calendar button is selected, the JavaScript also clears the form. The Reset Calendar button also clears the form, although it is not necessary to click on this button when creating a new calendar.

Plotting the calendar

The button to create the calendar contains all the JavaScript to open the response dialog boxes and plot the days of the month according to the responses supplied in the dialog boxes. One thing the form doesn't do is check for misspellings, which you can do by adding more to the routine.

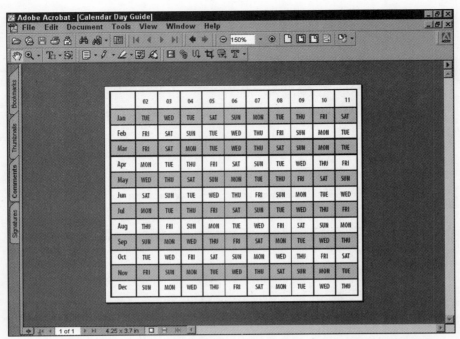

Figure 16-34: The help file contains the months and years that are plotted with the day a given month starts in a given year over the next decade.

Figure 16-35: To create a calendar, click on the Create Calendar button and a dialog box opens prompting you for the year the calendar will be created.

There are several subroutines to achieve the end result. The script is long, so let's examine it in parts beginning with the following:

```
//reset the form
this.resetForm();
```

The script begins by clearing the form of all data.

```
// hide all the images
for (var i = 1; i < 13; i++){
    var hide = this.getField("image."+ i);
    hide.hidden = true; }
```

When a user creates a calendar for a given month, a photo appears in the top-left corner of the form. The photo changes for each month. Therefore, the preceding subroutine loops through all the button fields and clears the fields:

```
//start with getting the year to plot
var j = this.getField("year"); // the target field
var cResponse = app.response({
cQuestion: "What calendar year (i.e. 2002, 2003, etc.)?",
cTitle: "Enter the Year"});
{
    if ( cResponse == null){ // if Cancel is selected
        cResponse = "error"; }
else
    j.value = cResponse; // places the data from the dialog to
the target field

    if (cResponse == "2000") {
    var leap = 29; }
else
    if ( cResponse == "2004") {
     var leap = 29; }
else
    if ( cResponse == "2008") {
    var leap = 29; }
else
    var leap = 28;

var leapYear = leap;
}
```

This part of the script starts with the application response dialog box requesting the year. The years 2000, 2004, and 2008 are leap years. Therefore, the month of February needs to be treated differently during these years. The variable leap holds the value for the total days for February. We determine if the year is a leap year and store the value in variable leapYear. The j.value is the year for all other months. We'll pick up both these variables later in the routine. Notice also that if the user clicks cancel in the application response dialog box, the word *error* is reported for the month. If a user sees an error, it will be obvious that the calendar needs to be replotted:

```
//get the month
var f = this.getField("month"); // the target field
var cResponse = app.response({
cQuestion: "What calendar month (i.e. January, February,
etc.)?",
cTitle: "Enter the Month"});
    {
```

```
if ( cResponse == null){ // if Cancel is selected
    cResponse = "error";
}
f.value = cResponse; // places the data from the dialog to
the target field
```

The preceding subroutine asks for the month to be created. The response from the dialog box is transferred to the field *month*:

```
var totalDays = this.getField("days");

if (cResponse == "February") {
totalDays.value = leapYear;
var show = this.getField("image.2");
show.hidden = false; }
else
if (cResponse == "September") {
        totalDays.value = 30;
        var show = this.getField("image.9");
        show.hidden = false;}
else
    if (cResponse == "April") {
        totalDays.value = 30;
        var show = this.getField("image.4");
        show.hidden = false; }
else
        if (cResponse == "June") {
        totalDays.value = 30;
        var show = this.getField("image.6");
        show.hidden = false; }
else
        if (cResponse == "November") {
        totalDays.value = 30;
        var show = this.getField("image.11");
        show.hidden = false; }
else
        totalDays.value   = 31
```

The variable `totalDays` stores the number of days in a given month. The beginning of the routine sorts out the month of February by taking the `leapYear` value and storing it in the `totalDays` variable if the month variable was February. The remaining months are either 30 or 31 days and all the 30 day months are individually assigned in the `totalDays.value`. If none of these months are retrieved from the response, the `totalDays.value` is 31:

```
if (cResponse == "January") {
        var show = this.getField("image.1");
        show.hidden = false; }
if (cResponse == "March") {
        var show = this.getField("image.3");
        show.hidden = false; }
if (cResponse == "May") {
```

```
            var show = this.getField("image.5");
            show.hidden = false; }
if (cResponse == "July") {
        var show = this.getField("image.7");
        show.hidden = false; }
if (cResponse == "August") {
        var show = this.getField("image.8");
        show.hidden = false; }
if (cResponse == "October") {
        var show = this.getField("image.10");
        show.hidden = false; }
if (cResponse == "December") {
        var show = this.getField("image.12");
        show.hidden = false; }
if (cResponse == "April")  {
            var a = this. getField("dayText.27");
            a.value = "Annual Golf Tournament";
    }
```

The above subroutine displays an image according to the response. The last line of code adds text to a field to advertise an annual fundraising event. This line of code is specifically placed here in the event you wish to take the form, modify just a few lines of code, and add your own events to appear in any of the text fields on the calendar:

Note These fields are named dayText.*n*, in which n is equal to the day of the month. Just append more lines after any month where you want a message displayed on the calendar for a given dayText field.

```
// dump the total days in the month to a blind field
var t = this.getField("days");
t.value = totalDays.value;
}
```

This short subroutine takes the totalDays.value and stores it in the field days. The days field appears on the form, but remains hidden from view. It's used to temporarily store the value for the total days to be plotted:

```
// get the day of the month where the data begins
{
var cResponse = app.response( {
cQuestion: "Day Month Starts (i.e. Monday, Tuesday, etc.)?",
cTitle: "Enter the Day" });
{
if ( cResponse == null){ // if Cancel is selected
    this.resetForm();
    var start = 0; }

    if (cResponse == "Sunday") {
    var start = this.getField("day.0");
```

```
var s = 0;  }

if (cResponse == "Monday") {
var start = this.getField("day.1");
var s = 1;  }

if (cResponse == "Tuesday") {
var start = this.getField("day.2");
var s = 2; }

if (cResponse == "Wednesday") {
var start = this.getField("day.3");
var s = 3; }

if (cResponse == "Thursday") {
var start = this.getField("day.4");
var s = 4; }

if (cResponse == "Friday") {
var start = this.getField("day.5");
var s = 5; }

if (cResponse == "Saturday") {
var start = this.getField("day.6");
var s = 6; }
start.value = 1;
}
}

// get the total days and add the data from day 1 to total days
{
    var numberOfFields = totalDays.value+s;
    var j = 1;
    for (var i = s; i < numberOfFields; i++){
    var newDays = this.getField("day."+ i);
    newDays.value = j++; }
}
```

The last part of the routine plots the days of the month. The first section deals with an error catch in the event a user selects Cancel. If Cancel is selected, the form is reset and the user needs to begin again. The remaining statements indicate what field occupies the `start.value`. In the last subroutine, the loop plots the days in the `day.n` fields up to and including the `totalDays.value`.

You can modify the above form or other forms discussed in this chapter to suit your individual needs. Look over all the forms in the Chapter 16 folder and examine the scripts. You can copy and paste fields and then modify them for your own forms. By reworking some Acrobat PDF forms, you can employ scripts and advanced Acrobat features even if you have no programming background.

My sincere wishes for much success with all your PDF form designs!

Summary

✦ You can use an Acrobat PDF for securing personal and business passwords and software serial numbers. Protect the PDF with Acrobat Standard Security and all your passwords are stored safely with immediate access.

✦ You can make a PDF form to organize files and articles, thus providing faster document retrieval than analog filing systems.

✦ PDF forms can be used as printing templates in which data can be imported from text files and sent to service centers for output to digital prepress.

✦ Printing templates can offer a solution as an alternative to variable data printing without the need to acquire additional software.

✦ Customer service forms can be used as quote calculators for providing customers with opportunities to quote their own jobs.

✦ Data can be imported automatically in PDF forms from text files, based on field entry conditions.

✦ Data can be collected and calculated from data fields on one form and then transposed to another form.

✦ JavaScript can be used to animate PDF forms with ticker-tape displays and motion graphics.

✦ Non-profit organizations can make effective use of Acrobat forms for Web hosting documents that are used as fundraising charts, and perpetual calendars that are used for marketing services.

✦ ✦ ✦

What's on the CD-ROM?

This appendix provides you with information on the contents of the CD-ROM that accompanies this book. For the latest and greatest information, please refer to the ReadMe file located at the root of the CD. Here is what you will find:

✦ System Requirements

✦ Using the CD with Windows

✦ Using the CD with the Mac OS

✦ What's on the CD

✦ Troubleshooting

System Requirements

Make sure that your computer meets the minimum system requirements listed in this section. If your computer doesn't match up to most of these requirements, you may have a problem using the contents of the CD-ROM.

For Windows 9x, Windows 2000, Windows NT4 (with SP 4 or later), Windows Me, or Windows XP:

✦ PC with a Pentium processor running at 100 mHz or faster

✦ At least 32MB of total RAM installed on your computer; for best performance, we recommend at least 64MB

✦ A CD-ROM drive

For Mac OS:

✦ Mac OS computer with a 68040 or faster processor running OS 7.6 or later

✦ At least 32MB of total RAM installed on your computer; for best performance, we recommend at least 64MB

Using the CD with Windows

To install the items from the CD-ROM to your hard drive, follow these steps:

1. Insert the CD into your computer's CD-ROM drive.

2. A window appears with the following options: Install, Explore, eBook, Links, Author, and Exit:

   - **Install.** Gives you the option to install the supplied software and/or the author-created samples on the CD-ROM.

   - **Explore.** Allows you to view the contents of the CD-ROM in its directory structure.

   - **eBook.** Allows you to view an electronic version of the book (in PDF format).

   - **Links.** Opens a hyperlinked page of Web sites.

   - **Author.** Opens a PDF document in which you can navigate to pages describing the Acrobat PDF forms that are contained on the CD-ROM. Also describes the forms that are used in the exercises in chapters.

   - **Exit.** Closes the autorun window.

If you do not have autorun enabled or if the autorun window does not appear, follow the steps below to access the CD-ROM:

1. Choose Start ➪ Run.

2. In the dialog box that appears, type ***d*:\setup.exe**, where *d* is the letter of your CD-ROM drive. This will display the autorun window that is described previously.

3. Choose the Install, Explore, eBook, Links, Author, or Exit option from the menu. (See Step 2 in the preceding list for a description of these options.)

4. The folder titled Author contains subfolders for chapters in which forms are used in exercises respective to each chapter. Copy the entire folder with the subfolders to your hard drive or copy any chapter subfolder when working on a respective chapter.

Note   This step can bypass the Install step if you want individual folders copied to your hard drive.

5. Manually copy the tutorial.pdx file and the tutorial folder to your hard drive. This file and folder, respectively, contain a search index for all the author material.

Note Follow directions in bonus Chapter 17, "Organizing Real-World Workflows," for loading the index file in any Acrobat viewer. (You'll find the bonus chapter on the book's CD-ROM.) The index can be searched for all the author-created PDFs that are contained on the CD-ROM.

Using the CD with the Mac OS

To install the items from the CD-ROM to your hard drive, follow these steps:

1. Insert the CD into your CD-ROM drive.

2. Double-click the icon for the CD after it appears on the desktop.

   Most programs come with installers; for those, simply open the program's folder on the CD and double-click the Install or Installer icon. If an installer decompresses a demo plug-in file, and the Acrobat plug-in is not installed in your Acrobat folder, copy the plug-in folder to the Adobe Acrobat Folder: Plug-ins folder.

3. Follow the same steps noted previously for step 4 on Windows.

4. Follow the same steps noted earlier for step 5 on Windows.

What's on the CD-ROM

The following sections provide a summary of the software and other materials you'll find on the CD-ROM.

Author-created materials

All author-created material from the book, including code listings and samples, are on the CD-ROM in the Author folder. Within this folder are separate folders for each chapter with PDF forms that are related to the steps described in each chapter. Copy the forms contained in this folder according to the installation instructions above.

Applications

The following Acrobat plug-ins and standalone applications are from Adobe Systems and third-party manufacturers. You'll find them in the Applications folder:

All the applications that are mentioned here are described in Chapter 14, "Using Form Design Assistants." For detailed descriptions of these applications, refer to the chapter.

Adobe plug-ins

The following plug-ins are available as free downloads from Adobe's Web site. They are also included on the CD-ROM. An authorized and licensed copy of Adobe Acrobat is required to use the plug-ins.

SaveAsXML (Windows/Mac OS)

Vendor: Adobe Systems (www.adobe.com). Platforms: Windows/Mac OS. Free download for registered users of Acrobat.

Paper Capture (Windows)

Vendor: Adobe Systems (www.adobe.com). Platform: Windows. Free download for registered users of Acrobat.

MakeAccessible (Windows)

Vendor: Adobe Systems (www.adobe.com). Platform: Windows. Free download for registered users of Acrobat.

Third-party plug-ins

The CD-ROM includes the following third-party plug-ins. You can also visit the manufacturers' Web sites for more information.

ActivePDF Portfolio

Vendor: activePDF (www.activepdf.com). Platform: Windows. Demo software. The Portfolio setup allows you to install six activePDF applications. You can install Server, Printer, DocConverter, WebGrabber, Toolkit, or Spooler.

ARTS PDF Tools

Vendor: ARTS – A Round Table Solution (www.aroundtablesolution.com). Platform: Windows. Demo software.

BCL Drake

Vendor: BCL Computers (www.bclcomputers.com). Platform: Windows. Demo software.

BCL Jade

Vendor: BCL Computers (www.bclcomputers.com). Platform: Windows. Demo software.

BCL Magellan 5.0

Vendor: BCL Computers (www.bclcomputers.com). Platform: Windows. Demo software.

Compose

Vendor: InfoData (www.infodata.com). Platform: Windows. Demo software. Trial downloads are obtained by first calling InfoData at: 1-800-336-4939. Platform: Windows. Demo software.

EnFocus PitStop Professional

Vendor: EnFocus Software (www.enfocus.com). Platforms: Windows/Mac OS. Demo software.

FormBar

Vendor: Actino Software (www.actino.com). Platform: Windows. Demo software.

Gemini

Vendor: Iceni Technology (www.iceni.com). Platforms: Windows/Mac OS. Demo software.

Impress Stamper/Impress Stamper Pro

Vendor: MapSoft Computer Services (www.mapsoft.com). Platform: Windows. Demo software.

ISIToolbox

Vendor: Image Solutions (www.imagesolutions.com). Platform: Windows. Demo software.

PageForm

Vendor: MapSoft Computer Services (www.mapsoft.com). Windows demo version works with PageMaker 6.52 on Windows.

PDFForMail

Vendor: gordonkent.com, inc. (www.gordonkent.com). Platform: Windows. Demo software.

Sowedoo Easy PDF Converter

Vendor: Sowedoo (www.sowedoo.com). Platform: Windows. Demo software.

Veriform PDF

Vendor: Lantana Research (www.lantanarips.com). Platforms: Windows/Mac OS. Demo software.

Note about shareware, freeware, and evaluation versions of software

Shareware programs are fully functional, trial versions of copyrighted programs. If you like particular programs, register with their authors for a nominal fee and receive licenses, enhanced versions, and technical support. *Freeware programs* are copyrighted games, applications, and utilities that are free for personal use. Unlike shareware, these programs do not require a fee nor do they provide technical support. *GNU software* is governed by its own license, which is included inside the folder of the GNU product. See the GNU license for more details.

Trial, demo, or evaluation versions are usually limited either by time or functionality (such as being unable to save projects). Some trial versions are very sensitive to system date changes. If you alter your computer's date, the programs will "time out" and will no longer be functional.

eVersion of Creating Adobe Acrobat Forms

The complete text of this book is on the CD-ROM in Adobe's Portable Document Format (PDF). You can read and search through the file with the Adobe Acrobat Reader (also included on the CD). If you wish to perform the exercises and use the forms that are contained in the *Author* folder, you'll need the complete Acrobat software.

Bonus chapter

The CD-ROM includes bonus Chapter 17, "Organizing Real-World Workflows." This chapter includes useful information and suggestions for organizing and storing forms and other PDF documents. The chapter also discusses creating a PDF workflow, and how to search files to minimize the time for locating PDF forms.

Troubleshooting

If you have difficulty installing or using any of the materials on the companion CD-ROM, try the following solutions:

- ✦ **Turn off any antivirus software that you may have running.** Installers sometimes mimic virus activity, and can make your computer believe incorrectly that a virus is infecting it. (Be sure to turn the anti-virus software back on later.)

- ✦ **Close all running programs.** The more programs that you're running, the less memory that is available to other programs. Installers also typically update files and programs; if you keep other programs running, installation may not work properly.

- ✦ **Reference the ReadMe file.** Please refer to the ReadMe file that's located at the root of the CD-ROM for the latest product information at the time of publication.

If you still have trouble with the CD, please call the Customer Carezphone number: (800) 762-2974. Outside the United States, please call 1 (317) 572-3994. You can also contact Customer Service by e-mail at techsupdum@wiley.com. Wiley Publishing will provide technical support only for installation and other general quality control items; for technical support on the applications themselves, consult the program's vendor.

If all else fails, send me an email at ted@west.net.

✦   ✦   ✦

Index

Continued

Continued

Continued

Continued

Continued

Continued

Continued

Wiley Publishing, Inc.
End-User License Agreement

READ THIS. You should carefully read these terms and conditions before opening the software packet(s) included with this book "Book". This is a license agreement "Agreement" between you and Wiley Publishing, Inc. "WPI". By opening the accompanying software packet(s), you acknowledge that you have read and accept the following terms and conditions. If you do not agree and do not want to be bound by such terms and conditions, promptly return the Book and the unopened software packet(s) to the place you obtained them for a full refund.

1. **License Grant.** WPI grants to you (either an individual or entity) a nonexclusive license to use one copy of the enclosed software program(s) (collectively, the "Software" solely for your own personal or business purposes on a single computer (whether a standard computer or a workstation component of a multi-user network). The Software is in use on a computer when it is loaded into temporary memory (RAM) or installed into permanent memory (hard disk, CD-ROM, or other storage device). WPI reserves all rights not expressly granted herein.

2. **Ownership.** WPI is the owner of all right, title, and interest, including copyright, in and to the compilation of the Software recorded on the disk(s) or CD-ROM "Software Media". Copyright to the individual programs recorded on the Software Media is owned by the author or other authorized copyright owner of each program. Ownership of the Software and all proprietary rights relating thereto remain with WPI and its licensers.

3. **Restrictions On Use and Transfer.**

   (a) You may only (i) make one copy of the Software for backup or archival purposes, or (ii) transfer the Software to a single hard disk, provided that you keep the original for backup or archival purposes. You may not (i) rent or lease the Software, (ii) copy or reproduce the Software through a LAN or other network system or through any computer subscriber system or bulletin- board system, or (iii) modify, adapt, or create derivative works based on the Software.

   (b) You may not reverse engineer, decompile, or disassemble the Software. You may transfer the Software and user documentation on a permanent basis, provided that the transferee agrees to accept the terms and conditions of this Agreement and you retain no copies. If the Software is an update or has been updated, any transfer must include the most recent update and all prior versions.

4. **Restrictions on Use of Individual Programs.** You must follow the individual requirements and restrictions detailed for each individual program in the "What's on the CD-ROM" of this Book. These limitations are also contained in the individual license agreements recorded on the Software Media. These limitations may include a requirement that after using the program for a specified period of time, the user must pay a registration fee or discontinue use. By opening the Software packet(s), you will be agreeing to abide by the licenses and restrictions for these individual programs that are detailed in the "What's on the CD-ROM" and on the Software Media. None of the material on this Software Media or listed in this Book may ever be redistributed, in original or modified form, for commercial purposes.

5. **Limited Warranty.**

   (a) WPI warrants that the Software and Software Media are free from defects in materials and workmanship under normal use for a period of sixty (60) days from the date of purchase of this Book. If WPI receives notification within the warranty period of defects in materials or workmanship, WPI will replace the defective Software Media.

   (b) WPI AND THE AUTHOR OF THE BOOK DISCLAIM ALL OTHER WARRANTIES, EXPRESS OR IMPLIED, INCLUDING WITHOUT LIMITATION IMPLIED WARRANTIES OF MERCHANTABILITY AND FITNESS FOR A PARTICULAR PURPOSE, WITH RESPECT TO THE SOFTWARE, THE PROGRAMS, THE SOURCE CODE CONTAINED THEREIN, AND/OR THE TECHNIQUES DESCRIBED IN THIS BOOK. WPI DOES NOT WARRANT THAT THE FUNCTIONS CONTAINED IN THE SOFTWARE WILL MEET YOUR REQUIREMENTS OR THAT THE OPERATION OF THE SOFTWARE WILL BE ERROR FREE.

   (c) This limited warranty gives you specific legal rights, and you may have other rights that vary from jurisdiction to jurisdiction.

6. **Remedies.**

   (a) WPI's entire liability and your exclusive remedy for defects in materials and workmanship shall be limited to replacement of the Software Media, which may be returned to WPI with a copy of your receipt at the following address: Software Media Fulfillment Department, Attn.: *Creating Adobe Acrobat Forms,* Wiley Publishing, Inc., 10475 Crosspoint Blvd., Indianapolis, IN 46256, or call 1-800-762-2974. Please allow four to six weeks for delivery. This Limited Warranty is void if failure of the Software Media has resulted from accident, abuse, or misapplication. Any replacement Software Media will be warranted for the remainder of the original warranty period or thirty (30) days, whichever is longer.

   (b) In no event shall WPI or the author be liable for any damages whatsoever (including without limitation damages for loss of business profits, business interruption, loss of business information, or any other pecuniary loss) arising from the use of or inability to use the Book or the Software, even if WPI has been advised of the possibility of such damages.

   (c) Because some jurisdictions do not allow the exclusion or limitation of liability for consequential or incidental damages, the above limitation or exclusion may not apply to you.

7. **U.S. Government Restricted Rights.** Use, duplication, or disclosure of the Software for or on behalf of the United States of America, its agencies and/or instrumentalities "U.S. Government" is subject to restrictions as stated in paragraph (c)(1)(ii) of the Rights in Technical Data and Computer Software clause of DFARS 252.227-7013, or subparagraphs (c)(1) and (2) of the Commercial Computer Software - Restricted Rights clause at FAR 52.227-19, and in similar clauses in the NASA FAR supplement, as applicable.

8. **General.** This Agreement constitutes the entire understanding of the parties and revokes and supersedes all prior agreements, oral or written, between them and may not be modified or amended except in a writing signed by both parties hereto that specifically refers to this Agreement. This Agreement shall take precedence over any other documents that may be in conflict herewith. If any one or more provisions contained in this Agreement are held by any court or tribunal to be invalid, illegal, or otherwise unenforceable, each and every other provision shall remain in full force and effect.

CD-ROM Installation Instructions

The exercises throughout this book help you learn to use Adobe Acrobat for designing PDF forms. All the author-created material from the book, including code listings and samples, are included on the CD-ROM in the `Author` folder. Within this folder, you'll find separate folders for each chapter with PDF forms that are related to the steps described in each chapter. Copy the forms contained in this folder according to the installation instructions in the appendix.

In addition to these files, you'll find Acrobat plug-ins and standalone applications from Adobe Systems and third-party manufacturers. You'll find them in the `Applications` folder.

Please read the "What's on the CD-ROM?" appendix for more information about using and installing the contents of the CD-ROM.